Foucault,
Cultural Studies,
and Governmentality

Foucault, Cultural Studies, and Governmentality

Edited by
Jack Z. Bratich
Jeremy Packer
Cameron McCarthy

State University of New York Press

Published by
State University of New York Press, Albany

For information, address the State University of New York Press,
90 State Street, Suite 700, Albany, NY 12207

Production by Michael Haggett
Marketing by Patrick Durocher

Library of Congress Cataloging-in-Publication Data

Foucault, cultural studies, and governmentality / edited by Jack Z. Bratich, Jeremy
Packer, Cameron McCarthy.
    p. cm.
    Includes bibliographical references and index.
    ISBN 0-7914-5663-3 (alk. paper) — ISBN 0-7914-5664-1 (pbk. : alk. paper)
    1. Power (Social sciences) 2. State, The. 3. Culture—Study and teaching.
4. Foucault, Michel. I. Bratich, Jack Z., 1969– II. Packer, Jeremy, 1970–
III. McCarthy, Cameron.

JC330.F63 2003
306.2—dc21   2002036484
10 9 8 7 6 5 4 3 2 1

Contents

Acknowledgments

Foucault, Cultural Studies, and Governmentality emerged out of intense conversations among the members of the student/faculty Cultural Studies and Foucault Reading Group that has been meeting at the University of Illinois at Urbana-Champaign since the autumn of 1997. The group consists of the following members: Steve Bailey, Ted Bailey, Jack Bratich, Heidi Brush, Andy Cantrell, Kevin Carollo, Mary Coffey, Greg Dimitriadis, Michael Elavsky, Richard Freeman, Kelly Gates, James Hay, Lisa King, Sammi King, Marie Leger, Cameron McCarthy, Tim McDonough, Shawn Miklaucic, Mark Nimkoff, Jeremy Packer, Carrie Rentschler, Craig Robertson, Paula Saukko, Rob Sloane, Beth Starr, and Jonathan Sterne. Participants come from a wide range of disciplines: anthropology, art history, communications, educational policy studies, English, kinesiology, law, medicine, philosophy, and speech communication. Some of these members have moved on to other institutions to begin their tenures as professional academics but still maintain active correspondence with and participation in the group. So, the group is both cross-disciplinary and cross-institutional.

As a collective, our interdisciplinary group has engaged in critical and supportive debate both around Foucault's writings and the individual research projects of each member. This collective focused on the later works of Foucault, paying particular attention to the last two volumes of the *History of Sexuality* and his writings and lectures on governmentality. The group took up work in and out of cultural studies that dealt with this later thought, including Toby Miller, Nikolas Rose, Tony Bennett, Andrew Barry, Thomas Osborne, Judith Butler, and Wendy Brown. Thus, this collection benefits from the multiplicity of perspectives inherent in an interdisciplinary group, yet coheres through its status as a collaborative project on the thought of Michel Foucault and its powerful implications for cultural studies.

As editors, we would like to express our sincerest appreciation to group members for their intense commitment to *Foucault, Cultural Studies, and Governmentality*. We would like to express our profound appreciation to Dale Cotton, Ron Helfrich, Jane Bunker and Michael Haggett at SUNY Press. A special thank you is also due to our editor Laura Marks without whose scrupulous appraisals our book would not have been completed in its present form. Thanks also to Milla Rosenberg for her helpful comments on the introduction. Larry Grossberg, Toby Miller, and Tony Bennett have been keen supporters of this book project all along. We thank them for their encouragement, participation, and genuine assistance in helping us to both conceptualize this volume and to bring it to fruition. We also express our gratitude to Clifford G. Christians and Paula Treichler, who, as directors of the Institute of Communications Research, provided generous financial support for this project. Finally, our research assistants, Kelly Gates, Michael Giardina, Susan Harewood, Marie Leger, Jin Park, and Craig Robertson provided us with invaluable and keen editorial support throughout the entire period of preparation of our manuscript. Thank you especially to Craig for his ceaseless efforts to keep us abreast of recent publications on governmentality, as well as his persistence in keeping the contributors on track for final deadlines. We would like to express our profound gratitude to all of them for their inexhaustible involvement in the production of *Foucault, Cultural Studies, and Governmentality*.

Introduction

Chapter 1

Governing the Present

Jack Z. Bratich, Jeremy Packer, and Cameron McCarthy

It is almost impossible to discuss contemporary Foucauldian scholarship or cultural studies research without recognizing the mutual effect the two fields have had on each other. The arrival of Foucauldian thought to cultural studies reshaped the way cultural studies defined its problematic around culture and power, challenging the very assumptions that informed a Gramscian framework for almost two decades now.[1] Conversely, cultural studies as an interdiscipline became a conduit for the deployment of Foucault into a variety of disciplines. Any work which attempts to situate itself within cultural studies and within a Foucauldian framework must take into account a sometimes messy array of texts on Foucault across various disciplines by scholars who consider themselves cultural studies practitioners and some who do not.

Furthermore, there have been very explicit attempts within cultural studies that have demanded a paradigm shift—one that overturns many of the historically significant terms of cultural studies' theoretical arsenal. *Foucault, Cultural Studies, and Governmentality* is not a call to arms to radically overturn or redirect cultural studies. It does however take into account many of the debates over Foucault's position in cultural studies; for the most part, the work in this collection builds upon the premise that cultural studies has benefited tremendously from the influx of Foucauldian theory. Furthermore, the arrival of Foucault into cultural studies altered its problematic in such a way that proponents or critics of cultural studies have to address this Foucauldian influence.

But the intersection of Foucauldian work and cultural studies has never been a uniform or singular project. Partially this is the case because there are both many "Foucaults" and many versions of cultural studies. Cultural studies has been marked by a persistent questioning of its fundamental assumptions, political imaginaries, and interdisciplinary boundaries. This self-problematization was evident when cultural studies encountered Foucault's work (see the interview with Lawrence Grossberg and Toby Miller in this volume for a history and contemporary analysis of this contested terrain). As Meaghan Morris and John Frow (2000) have argued, Foucault's influences have been multiple. His conceptualization of power/knowledge, for one, has assisted cultural studies in analyzing the links between meaning and social relations (p. 328). In addition, Foucault's work on the materiality of discourse (in *Archaeology of Knowledge*) allowed cultural studies to depart from more text-centered concepts of discourse (p. 331). Finally, Foucault's *History of Sexuality* not only challenged the ways identity and sexuality were historically fused, but also began to provide a new mapping of power (the microphysical analysis [p. 331]). This new analytics has provoked a full-scale problematization of neo-Marxist understandings of the nature and limits of the role of culture in political action itself.

We would also add that Foucault's work on disciplinarity primarily has been highly influential in cultural studies. Cultural analyses of the "disciplinary society" or "surveillance society" have cited this research extensively.[2] But while this cultural work has produced innumerable insightful accounts of recent trends, it has often remained squarely within the neo-Gramscian framework of cultural studies. In other words, this current brand of scholarship has instrumentalized Foucault within the traditional paradigm of cultural studies while leaving that fundamental framework intact, extending the shelf life of neo-Gramscian notions of hegemony, resistance, and the State.

The articles in this collection are situated in this heterogeneous tradition where Foucault and cultural studies have a restless relationship. Along with the threads discussed above, the pieces in this collection draw from a recently emerging strain of Foucauldian work that could be described as "governmentality studies." Arising from his germinal essay titled "Governmentality" and a series of lectures and course summaries (some of which have only recently been translated into English), this field of inquiry emerged in the 1990s as a powerful new approach to rethinking politics, the social, and power. It made explicit a different relationship between governance and the subject as a way of drawing together the micro and macro analyses of power (Gordon, 2000).

In simplest terms, governmentality refers to the arts and rationalities of governing, where the conduct of conduct is the key activity. It is an attempt to reformulate the governor-governed relationship, one that does not make the relation dependent upon administrative machines, juridical institutions, or other apparatuses that usually get grouped under the rubric of the State. Rather, as this collection demonstrates, the conduct of conduct takes place at innumerable sites, through an array of techniques and programs that are usually defined as cultural.

Governmentality addresses a formation of power that differs from disciplinarity and sovereignty (Foucault, 1991, p. 102). This formation is derived from the recognition that the strength of the state is dependent upon the proper disposition of humans and things.[3] But, this recognition is not the state's alone. It is not so much that the state's reach is all-consuming; instead, the techniques of governmentality emanate from numerous sources and without them the state would not be what it is (p. 103). Governmentality is an analytic perspective that defines the state's role as one of coordination, one that gathers together disparate technologies of governing inhabiting many sites. The *importance* of this coordinating function (its relative strength and effectivity and its centripetal force) is historically variable.

Perhaps the most prominent statement on this Foucauldian framework is *The Foucault Effect: Studies in Governmentality* (1991), which not only reprinted Foucault's essay, but published a series of projects informed by a study of the "arts of governing" (some of which emerged from his courses). Throughout the 1990s, this work was carried on in other collections (e.g., *Foucault and Political Reason* [1996], *Foucault: The Legacy* [1997], and *Governing Australia: Studies of Contemporary Rationalities of Government* [1998]), in the pages of the journal *Economy and Society*, and in book-length treatments by Nikolas Rose (1998, 1999), Mitchell Dean (1991, 1994, 1999), Tony Bennett (1995, 1998), Barbara Cruikshank (1999), and Ian Hunter (1988, 1994).

These studies in governmentality constitute a growing body of work, though one that should not be characterized as unitary. This field of inquiry does not seek to simply apply the concept to political and social phenomena, but questions the very limits of and characteristics of governmentality (especially its neoliberal form). We can see this debate at work in Colin Gordon's (1999) review of the *Governing Australia* collection, where he sharply distinguishes his approach to governmentality from others working in the area. We can also see it in this volume's interview with Grossberg and Miller, who often disagree with each other on the form and effects of liberalism, even while distinguishing themselves from Rose, Dean, and others. All of this is to say that, while an emergent body of work, governmentality studies has already matured to the point where clear differences in position are beginning to be drawn.

But governmentality studies has not been a field of inquiry isolated from cultural studies. At the groundbreaking cultural studies conference at the University of Illinois in 1990, Tony Bennett (1992) presented a paper titled "Putting Policy into Cultural Studies" which put the issues of culture and governing on the table. In his influential piece, cultural studies as a field was challenged for its reliance on defining culture as a set of signifying practices, and for its exclusive adherence to a political practice of forming counter-hegemonic subjects through those signifying practices. Bennett's primary critique of Gramscian cultural studies relied upon the incorporation of Foucault's notion of "police" into the underexplored dimension of Raymond Williams' conceptualization of culture as the "generalized process of intellectual, spiritual, and aesthetic development" (p. 25). Here Bennett pointed out, quite insightfully, that cultural studies had depended, perhaps, too completely, on Williams' much more often cited definitions of culture as a "particular way of life and the artistic deeds of men and women" (p. 25). According to Bennett, what William's less popularized definition of culture (the "general process of intellectual, spiritual, and aesthetic development") makes historically evident is that "culture" has often been both the object and the instrument of governmental policy that regulates social life. Provocatively integrating Foucault and Williams, Bennett conceptualized culture as

> a historically specific set of institutionally embedded relations of government in which the forms of thought and conduct of extended populations are targeted for transformation—in part via the extension through the social body of the forms, techniques, and regiments of aesthetic and intellectual culture. (1992, p. 26)

Bennett's configuration also called upon Foucault's notion of police as a distinctly modern form of power which intervenes in citizens day-to-day lives in a noncoercive fashion in order to simultaneously nourish the life of the individual and the State. Culture, as defined by Bennett, is thereby an integral part of the policing process. His work on the history of the modern museum articulated the specific "museological" techniques for managing the conduct of conduct (1995). Bennett continues this reformulation of culture in his contribution to this collection, where he challenges us to re-examine the relations between culture and the social via the mediation of governmentality.

At the same conference, Ian Hunter (1992) brought culture and governing together in his problematization of cultural studies' critique of aesthetics. Hunter proposed a study of aesthetics as an ethic, one whose practical activity of the self on the self became technologized into a governmental sphere primarily through the rise of public education. Hunter called for a genealogy of this ethic, one that pays close attention to how forms of denunciation of the governmental sphere themselves have been governmentalized. Hunter then found in Foucault's work on sexuality a different set of concerns than those mentioned by Frow and Morris cited above. In this conception, it is not just the ethical basis of sexuality as self-reflection that is problematized, but self-reflection itself and its cultural and social deployments that Hunter argues must be addressed. Hunter specifically examined how literature, as a pedagogical formation, not an ideological practice, operated as a means for altering ethical conduct.

Since that conference at the beginning of the 1990s, the relation between governmentality and cultural studies has primarily revolved around issues of cultural policy and policy studies. Housed mainly in Australia, the cultural policy studies field has included works by Bennett, Hunter, Tom O'Regan, and a whole host of others who occupy positions in the academy and/or policy sectors. As a field of study (examining the genealogical ties between culture and policy) and a public intellectual practice, policy studies has come to fuse Foucauldian governmentality and cultural studies in a specifically Australian context. Yet one dislocated Australian, Toby Miller, has started thinking about how governmentality operates in America, or at least the level of the American-dominated global culture industry. Miller's unique take on governmentality, in this media context, foregrounds the issue of "truth" and more specifically "popular truth." He argues that genre, the demographic construct audience/nation, and specific cultural formations of modernity and postmodernity have all been utilized in forming a productive and consuming citizenry (1998, pp. 14–36).

NEW DIRECTIONS/NEW ENGAGEMENTS

In *Foucault, Cultural Studies, and Governmentality*, we critically interrogate these new lines of thought while attempting to extend and deepen this trend of thinking at the limits of cultural studies. Through a variety of methods and empirical studies, this collection foregrounds new and unique approaches that attempt to: (a) bridge the gap between cultural analysis and governmentality studies in the United States, (b) open up new lines of inquiry into cultural practices, and (c) offer fresh perspectives on Foucault's writings and their implications for cultural studies.

Much of cultural studies, we contend, has focused on the discipline pole of Foucault's triangle "discipline-sovereignty-governmentality" (1991, p. 102). Here, we seek to supplement that work by accentuating the governmentality pole (though the other poles are represented here as well). We take on board this concept not merely to apply it to the same objects of study, but to problematize the relationship between culture and power altogether. Although not all our contributors agree with each other on the usefulness of the "governmentality" literature, all operate within the provocative and highly productive zone where culture and governing meet, and where the very possibility of a Foucauldian cultural studies is interrogated and put to empirical test. Ultimately, this collection seeks to extend the relation between culture and governing in three major ways.

First, this collection seeks to broaden the theater of intellectual debates over "culture and governing" studies from their current locales in Australia and Great Britain to the United States.[4] At the risk of sounding parochial, these studies begin to ask how neo-liberal strategies of governing operate in their specificity in the United States. As has been noted elsewhere, the greater state sponsorship of culture in Australia and the United Kingdom continues to impact cultural policy debates and arguments about the role of cultural studies (Morris & Frow, 2000; Bennett, 1997).

We seek to assess cultural practices in the United States, where the State is not as central a player in organizing the relationship between "culture and governing." Instead, culture is more deeply inscribed in a privatized, corporate set of conditions. The issues of State cultural policy, then, are not the only, or even the primary, way of thinking about culture and governing in the U.S. context. As such, the authors examine numerous State, quasi-State, and private institutions, practices, and policies that work to elaborate core state interests, but, at other times, operate in conflict with the State.[5] Insurance companies, volunteer organizations, pharmaceutical companies, architectural designers, private security companies, universities, education, talk shows, political science discourse, community museums, urban planners, and computer games are all examined as a part of this process.

This brings us to our second major extension of the culture and governing field. For whereas in cultural studies the primary way of thinking about governmentality has been through policy, we seek here to push the "culture and governing" debates into practices not typically understood as policy. Bennett, for instance, wants to consider the culture and governing relation through Foucault's conception of the "police" (that is, a form of governance Foucault defines around total administration of the social field through knowledge of the tiniest detail). This allows for a stronger focus on the state policy sector (which again has a particular historical and geographical location). If we are to begin situating culture in the liberal and neoliberal art of governing "at a distance," then policy (whether State-derived or not) becomes only one component of this governance—the codified, instrumentalized and institutionalized sort.

In accordance with this move of studying culture in its relation to governing at a distance, we take culture to be a set of reflections, techniques, and practices that seek to regulate conduct. In other words, instead of examining culture as primarily a policy issue, we look to culture as the intersection of policy and ethos (the practices of the self on the self and the technologies of subjectification). These ethical technologies are autonomous yet enrolled to perform tasks in a rationale of governing at a distance.[6] That is, culture finds itself caught up in the processes of government without a necessary reliance on the codified, institutionalized forms of governing culture. And, when policy *is* a primary concern, it is often non-State institutions that are concerned with managing conduct. At the end of his "Governmentality" essay, Foucault makes this very point and, in fact, elsewhere warns against placing too much emphasis on the State (1991, p. 103).

With the expansion of neoliberal forms of governing, it is not only in institutional life that we recognize how we are both governed and govern ourselves. For one thing, culture is embroiled in modes of political subjectification. Liberal political rationality, according to Mitchell Dean (1994), is defined by the organizing of the relation between self-governing citizens and members of a governed flock, between the liberty of the governed and the need for properly loyal subjects (p. 185). This self-governance is secured through a deployment of a series of ethical techniques of self-fashioning, ones that can have a strong cultural component.

The intersection of the production of truth and processes of subjectification *with* these institutions must also be taken into account. Throughout, we argue that in everyday life, knowledge is formed across multiple discourses organized by noninstitution-specific regimes of truth. These truths play an increasingly larger role in processes of subjectification pertaining to the ways we form our identities and subjectivities through an attachment to the games of truth about ourselves and the world. We use this understanding as a springboard to delve into areas of governance not typically addressed by cultural studies. In this book, the various analyses of museums, technologies of safety and security, new media practices, education practices, styles of thought, volunteerism, community and domesticity all have policy components, but in each case the institutional/codified components do not tell the primary story.

The third significant way that the work in this book breaks with previous work at the crossroads of policy and governmentality is that it does not clearly call for policy advocacy. The debate over the political efficacy of cultural studies policy practitioners has been fierce and still seems to rage a decade after the debate began.[7] We would argue that as important as this debate is, it has clouded the importance of the critical genealogical work that has actually been done by those working in policy studies. Rather than simply dismissing the work or thinking in terms of its applicability, we choose to appreciate the work for what it has contributed to our understanding of how institutional rationalities are formulated, how it has expanded and articulated the relationships between culture, power, and subjectivity, and what new methods of analysis are now more clearly available.

The intellectual's role in policy decisions was also an issue that was hotly debated by members of our Foucault reading group collective. It was from these debates that the essays in this volume emanated. In fact, we would argue that there is no necessary correspondence between the study of policy or governmentality and a political prescription for the role of the intellectual. It would be unfair to characterize all contributors as sympathetic to the policy studies position, particularly in regards to the role of the policy practitioner. It would however, be accurate to state that the geneological work done in the field has compelled many of the authors to rethink and reorient their own research regardless of policy applicability.

CONSTRUCTING OBJECTS

Foucault, Cultural Studies, and Governmentality foregrounds 12 essays and an interview that engage directly with efforts to problematize cultural studies by drawing on Foucauldian frameworks of analysis. Writing from embattled oppositional spaces within a cross section of disciplines—communications, educational policy studies, art history, kinesiology, philosophy, and literature—contributors examine Foucault's work as an analytics of culture or a style of analysis. Our guiding objective here is to translate Foucault's analytics of the arts of governing into the field of cultural studies, integrating these analytics into the very conceptualization of the objects of study pursued in this volume. Rather than just a series of case studies of Foucault-in-action, this collection contributes to studying contemporary "rationalities" of governing in a manner that alters the very conception of what an object of cultural studies is.

Even Foucauldian cultural studies scholarship has most often entailed piecemeal uses and applications of particular strands of Foucault's thought (especially concepts such as discourse, discipline, and panopticism). Although these approaches have been crucial in providing new tools for understanding particular social and cultural phenomena, they have not concerned themselves with rethinking the type of research objects that have been brought on stream in cultural studies itself.

This reconceptualization opens up new objects of study for cultural analysis. For instance, at one level, one could read this collection as taking up the cultural phenomena of automotive driving, museums, urban design, computer games, conspiracy theories, education policy, architecture, even the subject. However, once these phenomena are considered governmentalized, we could view this collection as studies of the technologies of governing through subjectification (be it through volunteerism, safety, security, pedagogy, moderated thought, community, automobility, or gaming-logics). That is, it is not just a matter of simply altering the objects of analysis in an attempt to either validate a new object of study (low culture or the popular) or expand the scope of the discipline's reach. Rather, this collection seeks to alter the very forms of analysis, the frameworks that would allow new objects to become intelligible. Lastly, there is always the demand to think in terms of the field itself, to think in terms of cultural studies as defined by a problematization of its own limits as a field, and the limits of culture (its object). As Tony Bennett argues in his contribution to this volume, the very definition of culture (once governmentality is put into the analytic mix) moves from a general mechanism (i.e., language-based) to a set of particular, technical practices rooted in particular historical moments. Cultural studies as a field and Foucault himself have both continually called for this type of theoretical and intellectual self-reflection and alteration.

We hope that this volume provides, instead, examples for locating and investigating new cultural formations, not for their novelty, but because of their role as a means of governing conduct. This is not to say that all cultural studies work should be focused upon this specific formulation, nor is it to say that all cultural formations are part of governmentality or neoliberalism. It is to say that some cultural formations which were outside the purview of cultural studies were "made visible" due to this perspective.

We can turn to Foucault's notion of "problematization" to elaborate[8]. For Foucault, analysis itself often produces its own object. This is because one does not study objects, so much as investigates how a given phenomenon came to be thought of in terms of a problem—how it was problematized. This approach often entails answering such questions as:

- How did a particular form of conduct come under scrutiny?
- Who was enabled to make such determinations?
- What programs of rehabilitation or alteration were set in motion?
- How did these programs affect other domains of governance?
- What forms of knowledge were created for, directed at, and affected by this conduct?
- Under what regime of self-reflection and self-identification were the offending parties and persons supposed to adhere?
- By what schema was the conduct to be measured?
- According to what rationalities was governance put into play?
- What conduct is made intelligible for reflection and guidance?

Any question that directs attention to the particular relationships between knowledge, power, and subjectification helps orient researchers toward an understanding of something akin to a Foucauldian method.

Besides providing new objects for analysis (by placing culture into the domain of governing), the investigations of our contributors open up new theoretical and methodological issues not previously brought to light in the work that has merged cultural studies and Foucault. To date, the unique methodological demands of bringing together truth, power, and subjectification through discursive analysis, with an emphasis on governmental practices, have not been adequately elaborated. We hope these essays will further thinking in this direction, just as the work cited throughout this introduction has influenced our own thinking about Foucault and cultural studies.

THE CHAPTERS

Following the introductory section, *Foucault, Cultural Studies, and Governmentality* is divided into three parts that loosely adhere to investigations of knowledge, power, and subjectification. In the Preface to *The History of Sexuality, Volume 2*, Michel Foucault (1997b) outlines a programmatic explanation of his life's works. Foucault claimed that each of his major studies could be thought of as having dealt with a particular form of experience, be it sexuality, madness, or criminality. Each "locus of experiences" was the correlation of three axes, unequally apportioned in the various cases. Foucault provides multiple terms to describe the three axes, but in the simplest sense they deal with knowledge, power, and subjectivity. For instance, in the experience of madness there needed to be a type of understanding that described insanity through the disciplines of medicine and later psychiatry; a knowledge of mental illness was formed. Second, an apparatus was produced that managed the experience of madness through normative practices of internment and treatment; power relations manifested themselves. Third, a relationship be-tween oneself and others as possible subjects of madness was specified; a "mad" subjectivity was produced. This "Preface" can be seen as an attempt on Foucault's part to resituate the corpus of his work within a systematization that did not exist up until his latest work on sexuality, and he goes as far as saying so. However, this does not necessarily weaken his formulation, instead it provides a new articulation for his work and more importantly it provides something of a working schema, if not a methodology, for critical research. By using this same schematic, we recognize that as with the work of Foucault, these three axes only exist in relationship to each other.

Chapter one, "Governing the Present," elaborates the intersections of Foucault and cultural studies, with particular attention to the Foucaultian strand known as "governmentality studies." Following the introduction, Lawrence Grossberg and Toby Miller (in an interview with Jeremy Packer) provide historical depth and critical perspective on the often uneasy relation-ship between Foucault and cultural studies. This history elaborates the con-textual contingency of Foucault's application to cultural studies. It also provides a much-needed explanation of what forces, political, theoretical, and aca-demic, moved cultural studies practitioners to Foucault at various moments and in various places. They also discuss in some detail their own philosophical negotiations of Foucauldian thought and its wider relevance and application to contemporary cultural politics. Although they agree that Foucault's work should continue to inform cultural studies, the specific nature of that role is debated. Most significantly, they disagree on the very character of governmentality and on its current applicability to contemporary formations of power and governance.

Tony Bennett's chapter, "Culture and Governmentality," speaks from the long view of developments in cultural studies over the last decade since the publication of his influential Foucaultian essay, "Putting Policy Into Cultural Studies" (1992). Bennett compares Stuart Hall's reading of Foucault's notion of discourse with Nikolas Rose's interpretation, and finds in their divergence a new way of theorizing culture. Governmentality, according to Bennett, is not simply added to the mix of theories about culture and society—it funda-mentally changes the definition of culture from a general mechanism (akin to language) to "a distinctive set of knowledges, expertise, techniques and apparatuses." Culture becomes technical, and this notion of a "culture complex" alters the history of relations between culture and the social.

Knowledge, Rationality, and Expertise

The first section is comprised of essays that deal most explicitly with issues of knowledge, rationality, and expertise. Jack Z. Bratich ("Making Politics Reasonable: Conspiracism, Subjectification, and Governing Through Styles of Thought") and Jonathan Sterne ("Bureaumentality") begin this section with chapters that directly engage key oppositions that have informed cultural studies and other forms of radical neo-Marxist scholarship for some time but are now thoroughly unsettled by the philosophical interventions of Michel Foucault. Bratich explores the pivotal opposition in cultural studies between thought and materialism, in which the former is often conceived as an epiphenomenon of the latter. Drawing on Foucault's writings on thought as an ethos, Bratich insists that thought has had a dynamic role in modern politics since its concrete incorporation into nineteenth century liberalism as a form of active political rationality. He argues, with illustration, that political experts have problematized "conspiracy theories" to form a style of thought that mobilizes technologies of truth in an ethos of self-reflection. Thought, then, instead of being inert or inactive, is now at the seismic center of contemporary political calculation and political action.

Following Bratich, Sterne casts critical attention to another type of opposition that has been a longstanding organizing principle separating structuralism and poststructuralism from Marxist forms of culturalism: the opposition between humanism and antihumanism (see e.g., Stuart Hall's [1980] pivotal essay, "Cultural Studies: Two Paradigms"). Unlike some forms of cultural studies formulations, this opposition between humanism and antihumanism is not, Sterne argues, as clear-cut in the writings of Foucault bearing upon topics such as governmentality. Quite provocatively, Sterne insists that Foucauldian thought betrays an ambivalence in its very silence on the political agency of the masses. In his very silence on human agency, Sterne argues Foucault's work reveals a hidden investment in mass insurgency or a "black populism" to use the language of Carlo Ginzburg (1980). Sterne further maintains that this issue is not particularly well resolved by Tony Bennett and other exponents of the Australian policy studies approach to cultural studies. He takes on the latter's attempts to counterpose a putative outmoded humanism of Antonio Gramsci and its foregrounding of a heroic status for "the people/the popular" to the presumably more pragmatic and efficacious contemporary site of institutional policy and politics. Unlike Bratich, Sterne comes out on the other side of poststructuralist thinking as illustrated in the antihumanist reading of Foucault to be found in the cultural policy studies movement. Sterne ultimately raises a very difficult question for this genre of Foucauldian merger with cultural studies: What happens to representational politics, social justice and a mass-based sense of the good life when you banish humanism?

Jeremy Packer ("Disciplining Mobility: Governing and Safety") looks at techniques of governing at a distance through mobility and freedom and the related production of safety regulations and safety discourses in post-War United States. Deploying a Deleuzean strategy of analysis, he unpacks the discourse of safety and its naturalization as a global set of rules and goals of state trusteeship of modern populations. Packer ultimately demonstrates the ways in which safety exceeds a concern for the well being of the "public" and contributes instead to techniques in which modern individuals and populations organize, rationalize, and inhabit their world.

These chapters primarily concern themselves with the technologies of truth, the expansion of expertise, and rationalities of governing. Recognizing that culture is often the domain of knowledge-production, these pieces begin to shift the definition of culture away from signifying practices and towards one that encompasses truth-telling practices and the discursive mechanisms of governance.

Policy, Power, and Governing Practices

In this section, the authors analyze a number of cultural practices, institutions, and discourses from a Foucauldian cultural perspective. They approach these research objects as a set of cases of the application of government and discipline. Here, the technologies of governing themselves are foregrounded in order to explain the concrete workings of power.

James Hay ("Unaided Virtues: The (Neo)Liberalization of the Domestic Sphere and the New Architecture of Community") takes up the central question of the meaningful limits of neoliberalism and its broader imbrication in the elaboration of mass communications technologies and the normalization of cultural practices since the latter part of the twentieth century. A fascinating feature of this chapter is Hay's deft treatment of the theoretical connections between Foucault's concept of governmentality and Raymond Williams' deployment of the term "mobile privatization." Hay merges Foucault's and Williams' theories concerning the pivotal role of culture in the emergence of modern practices and environments of governing in order to better understand the impact of communication technologies, specifically television, within contemporary social formations. He ends by examining the relations between New Urbanism, cultural technologies, and community as a way of understanding recent strategies of "governing at a distance."

   The deployment of community within the terms of neoliberal political rationality is also analyzed in the chapter authored by Mary K. Coffey ("From Nation to Community: Museums and the Reconfiguration of Mexican Society Under Neoliberalism"). This contribution explores the relevance of governmentality to the workings of culture and the renarration of the state/civil society couplet in the Mexican national context. Coffey is concerned with the discursive and practical entailments of the policy initiatives of the benevolent modern state and its impositions on modern populations. Unlike Sterne, though, Coffey draws empathetically on Bennett's deployment of a theory of governmentality to understand the policy work of the contemporary museum as a cultural institution in late twentieth century Mexico. Her focus here is on the critical role of community-based museology in the elaboration of the neoliberal cultural policy initiatives of the postrevolutionary Mexican state as it strove to mold a new democratic order.

   The chapters by Carrie A. Rentschler ("Designing Fear: How Environmental Security Protects Property at the Expense of People") and Greg Dimitriadis and Cameron McCarthy ("Creating a New Panopticon: Columbine, Cultural Studies, and the Uses of Foucault") address the rather alarming contemporary pattern of intensification of surveillance and regulation of social space within the education setting. In Rentschler's chapter, she calls attention to the changing dynamics within the university that foreground the use of a totally planned environment to regulate the movement of bodies on the University of Illinois' campus. The university's environmental planning goal here is to anticipate and to eliminate all crimes based on the principle of excluding the unwanted stranger from the campus environs. Rentschler argues, persuasively, since sexual assault against women is predominantly an acquaintance phenomenon, that this fact of familiarity complicates the private/public split so central to the university's crime prevention philosophy. The university's attempt to regulate public spaces privileges the idea of the protection of private property and consequently marginalizes the security needs of women on campus in an effort to deploy power spatially.

   Greg Dimitriadis and Cameron McCarthy call attention to the intensification of surveillance technologies in American schools in the aftermath of the Columbine School massacre at Littleton, Colorado in April of 1999. They argue that current cultural studies in education approaches to these developments are inadequate in that they continue to rely on neo-Marxist, Frankfurt School, psychoanalytic and neo-Gramscian models of analysis that reduce youth violence to models of "resistance." Drawing on Foucauldian concepts of discipline, surveillance, and panopticism they argue that the modern school has become a site in which the contemporary school curriculum has been displaced by models of cultural style and the regulation of conduct produced in popular culture. They maintain that in a striking manner, too, the school is being transformed by the world of commodified popular culture in which violence and its antithesis of technological fantasies of security are all-pervasive themes. These latter two essays focus on the environmental changes in education and the deepening patterns of commodification and surveillance associated with the greater infusion of commercialized cultural initiatives into the university and school settings.

Technologies of the Self

The chapters in Part III address technologies of the self more explicitly. The first chapter in this section, by Samantha J. King ("Doing Good By Running Well: Breast Cancer, the Race for the Cure, and New Technologies of Ethical Citizenship") examines the powerful nexus of sport, volunteerism, and the elaboration of neoliberal forms of self-management and privatization of social problems. As a powerful example of these dynamics, King explores in some detail the way in which the Komen Foundation's annual fundraiser for breast cancer, "Race for the Cure," a 5K run held in Washington D.C., links a "fit and healthy body" to the task of neoliberal governance and the privatization of social causes concerning the national welfare. King foregrounds these economic and cultural practices as ethical practices, where consumption, health, and citizenship converge in a relation of self to self, and by extension to others.

Shawn Miklaucic ("God Games and Governmentality: *Civilization II* and Hypermediated Knowledge") looks at the productive epistemologies of popular simulation in computer games, linking this new technology with technologies of subjectification. For Miklaucic, computer games are not simply articulated to questions of surveillance in a practical sense; they, in fact, function more powerfully as conceptual and interpretive tools of self-problematization and system organization. Computer games such as Civilization II simulate reflexive models that valorize hierarchical, state-centered forms of political rationality. Drawing on Tony Bennett's work on museums, J. David Bolter and Richard Grusin's work on hypermediation, and Frederic Jameson's concept of metacommentary, Miklaucic makes the case for greater attention within cultural studies to computer games as sites of the production of contemporary political rationalities. In turn, he offers the outlines of a new methodological approach to these sites of political simulation that involves modes of reflexive textual analysis that read narrative content against the formal qualities of interface and game play.

While authors of the previous chapters tend to foreground macrological concerns with the subjectivization of populations, Lisa King ("Subjectivity as Identity: Gender Through the Lens of Foucault") concludes this section with an intensive micrological exploration of the implications of Foucault's problematization of the self for a reconsideration of the nature and experience of gender identity in modern life. Drawing on the first volume of Foucault's *The History of Sexuality*, King calls attention to "the modern compulsion to tell the truth about ourselves." She uses a single case—the case of David Reimer, the boy who lost his penis to a botched circumcision, was raised as a girl and then through sex reassignment as a teenager, became a boy—to draw normative lessons about the politics of identity. King argues that political action based on essentialized identities that presume an a priori coherence unmodulated by social forms of problematization reside on very shallow and unstable ground indeed. Instead, King calls for a practice and technology of the self enacted through an aesthetico-political lens.

GOVERNMENTALITY AND WAR

In the post-9/11/2001 world, we can see how these analytic frameworks have even stronger purchase on contemporary events. From one perspective, these governmental rationalities under scrutiny are "peacetime" rationalities, counterposed to a "wartime" scenario (that we were under as this book went to print). However, if we take Foucault's claim seriously that "politics is war pursued by other means" (1980, p. 93), then the peace/war distinction no longer holds regarding governmentality. Thus we take a different perspective, one that argues that recent events are an *intensification, acceleration,* and *integration* of governing strategies under a state of emergency, or permanent war.

We can just take some of the more obvious examples from this volume to make our point. Samantha King's analysis of the enrollment of volunteerism and consumption as a governing strategy has a newfound resonance with the recruitment of nationalist citizen-subjects through donations, patriotic shopping, and community service. The production of subjects through discourses of safety (see Packer's chapter) and apparatuses of security (see Rentschler) has taken on heightened visibility with life-and-death stakes. Bratich's discussion of the governance of thought as a self-reflective ethos has acquired new valences, as George W. Bush declares a National Day of Reflection and the White House calls for a "re-examination of culture" while citizens are warned to watch what they say and think. The imaging of wars through popular culture has become problematized, and Miklaucic's analysis of *which* kinds of violence count in computer games becomes even more relevant, as the gaming industry regulates itself regarding the kinds of terrorism allowable in future games. McCarthy and Dimitriadis' assessment of critical pedagogy's possibilities takes on a more urgent tenor, as schools become the sites for nationally coordinated pledges of allegiance as well as sites for contestation over the meaning of national symbols like the flag.

What these examples demonstrate is that the strategies of governmentality, rather than being displaced by older forms of war-sovereignty, are indeed

crucial to composing this "new war." Governmentalizing culture through
processes of power, knowledge-production, and subjectification does not take
a back seat to a reemergence of State-power. Instead, following Hardt and
Negri (2000), the techniques of govermentality analyzed in this volume are
remarkable for being "immanent' strategies of governing, deployed in a
biopolitical context (pp. 24–28, 329–332).

Seeing as the formation of power relations which governmentality describes takes populations and citizens as not only the object toward which
power is directed, but its means as well, then given the current "domestic
readiness," the current form of war is necessarily undertaken via the American
citizen. We are all then (and not just to the degree that we are loyal and
supportive of state military action, but in our daily lives) at war; either "against
terrorism," as citizen/surveillors and self-monitors, or "for terrorism" if we
speak out or fail to remain vigilant and afraid. We have the freedom to
respond, but the popular truth-value of that action has been severely circumscribed. Wartime rule is not simply legitimated by sovereign and consenting
subjects, but exercised through their mundane habits and communal interactions in the name of their "own" defense.

Just as culture has been made amenable to technical concerns for over a
century (see Bennett's chapter), now that same governmentalized culture can
be enlisted and redirected under the state of war (e.g., the centralizing and
coordinating function of the Office of Homeland Security). The techniques
of governing, already immanent to the productive process of life itself, have
been articulated together in a wartime-mobilization that has *made war itself
immanent to everyday life.* While the relation between the specificities of the
current state of war and governmentality need further conceptual elaboration,
suffice it to say that "new war" depends upon a domain of everyday life
already saturated with governmental techniques.

CONCLUSION

In our uses and application of Foucault, we aim to provide direction for future
cultural studies work which still carries on the traditional commitments while
addressing the unique circumstances facing cultural studies scholars in the
historical moment in which we live. These unique circumstances include the
following: an increasing globalization of culture, the emergence and extension
of neoliberal governance, in addition to the growing importance of electronic
mediation, migration and diaspora formation in the production of notions of
popular memory, history, subjectivity (specifically citizenship and community), and truth. The book does not claim to address all of the characteristics
of this historical moment. Rather, the emphasis here is on recent rationalities
of governing (especially the link between practices of governing and practices

of the self). These circumstances demand a reconceptualization of the relationships between truth and ideology, the State and power, as well as identity and subjectification. In sum, they require a redefinition of culture itself, one that does not simply reduce it to the site of ideological reproduction or to the location of resistance.

Rather than diagnose a current "conjuncture" (called neoliberalism), we wish to perform what Foucault calls an "ontology of the present." Our primary concern in this volume is to provide critical frameworks to analyze cultural practices and strategies of governing as ways of better answering the contemporary conjunctural questions—What are we? How do we navigate the expressions of meaning and power in everyday life and the institutional logics that bear down upon us as modern subjects living in a new millennium? In performing an ontology of the present, we seek a better understanding of the contingent yet sedimented strategies of neoliberal governing that compose everyday life. By making these techniques and tactics intelligible, we can begin to make them amenable to strategies of contestation.

NOTES

1. Lawrence Grossberg for instance, in his 1984 essay "Formations of Cultural Studies" attempts to steer cultural studies in a Foucauldian direction, primarily through the concept of the apparatus which creates "an interested mapping of the lines of concrete effects" (1997, p. 228). Barry Smart argues that Foucauldian conceptions of power should replace Gramscian theorizations in his book, *Foucault, Marxism and Critique* (1983).

2. Perhaps the most widely recognized and cited instance of this kind of work is Mike Davis' *City of Quartz* (1990).

3. Foucault summarizes the art of dispositions in this way. "The things with which in this sense government is to be concerned are in fact men, but men in their relations, their links, their imbrication with those other things which are wealth, resources, means of subsistence, the territory with its specific qualities, climate, irrigation, fertility, etc.; men in their relation to that other kind of things, customs, habits, ways of acting and thinking, etc.; lastly, men in their relation to that other kind of things, accidents and misfortunes such as famine, epidemic, death, etc." (1991, p. 93).

4. The exception, Mary K. Coffey's piece on Mexican community museums, remains in North America.

5. But even "resisting the State" does not guarantee that governmentality, the conduct of conduct, is not present. Indeed, liberal forms of governance, as Foucault (1997a) argues, have as their regulative principle that "one always governs too much, or, at any rate, one always must suspect that one governs too much. Governmentality should not be exercised without a 'critique'" (p. 74). Liberalism is "a tool for criticizing reality," and "a form of critical reflection on governmental practice" (pp. 75, 77).

6. Similarly, as Foucault examines in *Discipline and Punish* (1977), disciplinarity is a technology of power, though it had specific conditions of emergence in the panopticon, used in various social situations to achieve the same ends.

7. Tony Bennett provides an excellent account of both the debate and its historical precedents in *Culture: A Reformer's Science (1997)*. Jim McGuigan (2001), on the other hand, critiques the policy studies approached based on its misapplication of political engagement. To avoid this quagmire he suggests returning to a definition of culture comprised only of signifying practices.

8. See especially Foucault (1988, 1997b).

REFERENCES

Barry, A., Osborne, T., & Rose, N. (Eds.), (1996). *Foucault and political reason*. Chicago: University of Chicago Press.

Bennett, T. (1992). Putting policy into cultural studies. In L. Grossberg, C. Nelson, & P. Treichler (Eds.), *Cultural studies* (pp. 23–37). New York: Routledge.

Bennett, T. (1995). *The birth of the museum: History, theory, politics*. New York: Routledge.

Bennett, T. (1997). *Culture: A reformer's science*. Thousand Oaks, CA: Sage.

Burchell, G., Gordon, C., & Miller, P. (Eds). (1991). *The Foucault effect: Studies in governmentality*. Chicago: University of Chicago Press.

Cruikshank, B. (1999). *The will to empower: Democratic citizens and other subjects*. Ithaca, NY: Cornell University Press.

Davis, M. (1990). *City of quartz: Excavating the future in Los Angeles*. New York: Verso.

Dean, M. (1991). *The constitution of poverty: Toward a genealogy of liberal governance*. New York: Routledge.

Dean, M. (1994). *Critical and effective histories: Foucault's methods and historical sociology*. New York: Routledge.

Dean, M. (1999). *Governmentality*. London: Sage.

Dean, M. & Hindess, B. (Eds.) (1998). *Governing Australia: Studies of contemporary rationalities of government*. New York: Cambridge University Press.

Foucault, M. (1972). *Archaeology of knowledge* (A. M. Sheridan Smith, Trans.). New York: Pantheon.

Foucault, M. (1977). *Discipline and punish* (Alan Sheridan, Trans.). New York: Pantheon.

Foucault, M. (1980). *The history of sexuality, Vol. 1: An introduction* (R. Hurley, Trans.). New York: Vintage.

Foucault, M. (1988). The Concern for truth. In L. D. Kritzman (Ed.), *Foucault, Politics, Philosophy, Culture* (pp. 255–267). New York: Routledge.

Foucault, M. (1991). Governmentality. In G. Burchell, C. Gordon, & P. Miller. *The Foucault effect: Studies in governmentality* (pp. 119–150). Chicago: University of Chicago Press.

Foucault, M. (1997a). The birth of biopolitics. In P. Rabinow (Ed.), *Foucault, ethics: Subjectivity and truth* (pp. 73–79). New York: New Press.

Foucault, M. (1997b). Preface to the *History of sexuality*, Vol. 2. In P. Rabinow (Ed.), *Foucault, ethics: Subjectivity and truth.* (pp. 199–206). New York: New Press.

Ginzburg, C. (1980). *The cheese and the worms: The cosmos of a sixteenth-century miller* (J. & A. Tedeschi, Trans.). Baltimore: Johns Hopkins University Press.

Gordon, C. (1999). Under the beach (review article). *The UTS Review: Cultural Studies and New Writing*, 5(1): 157–177.

Gordon, C. (2000). Introduction. In J. D. Faubion (Ed.), *Foucault: Power* (pp. xi–xli). New York: New Press.

Grossberg, L. (1997). The formation(s) of cultural studies: An American in Birmingham. In *Bringing it all back home: Essays on cultural studies*. Durham, NC: Duke University Press.

Hall, S. (1980). Cultural studies: Two paradigms. *Media Culture and Society* Vol. 2 Newbury CA: Sage.

Hardt, M., & Negri, A. (2000). *Empire*. Cambridge: Harvard University Press.

Hunter, I. (1988). *Culture and government: The emergence of literary education*. Hampshire, United Kingdom: Macmillan Press.

Hunter, I. (1992). Aesthetics and cultural studies. In L. Grossberg, C. Nelson, & P. Treichler (Eds.), *Cultural studies*. New York: Routledge.

Hunter, I. (1994). *Rethinking the school: Subjectivity, bureaucracy, criticism*. New York: St. Martin's Press.

Miller, T. (1998). *Technologies of truth: Cultural citizenship and the popular media*. Minneapolis, MN: University of Minnesota Press.

McGuigan, J. (2001). Problems of cultural analysis and policy in the information age. *Cultural Studies <—> Critical Methodologies*, 1(2).

Morris, M., & Frow, J. (2000). Cultural studies. In N. K. Denzin, & Y. S. Lincoln (Eds.), *Handbook of qualitative research (2nd ed.)* (pp. 315–346). Thousand Oaks, CA: Sage.

O'Farrell, C. (Ed.). (1997). *Foucault: The legacy*. Brisbane, Australia: Queensland University of Technology.

Rose, N. (1998). *Inventing ourselves: Psychology, power, and personhood*. New York: Cambridge University Press.

Rose, N. (1999). *Powers of freedom: Reframing political thought*. New York: Cambridge University Press.

Smart, B. (1983). *Foucault, Marxism and critique*. London: Routledge.

Chapter 2

Mapping the Intersections of Foucault and Cultural Studies

An Interview with Lawrence Grossberg and Toby Miller, October 2000

Jeremy Packer

Packer: As you know, this interview is going to appear in a book that is partially concerned with Foucault's impact on cultural studies. What I'm hoping we can accomplish in this interview is to provide some historical and theoretical background for our readers and possibly suggest some future possibilities. To this end, I want to begin by posing a few very general questions that can open up a space for a discussion of these issues. How and why has the work of Michel Foucault infiltrated cultural studies over the last 20 years? What are the most important theoretical concepts of Foucault's which have been useful in furthering cultural studies, and who has been responsible for bringing Foucault and cultural studies together?

Grossberg: I think it varies a lot in terms of national formations. For the most part I can only speak about parts of the English speaking world—England, the United States, and Australia. In England, if you go back to the '70s, there were groups that were strongly influenced by Foucault that were not central to cultural studies (for example, there was a debate between Stuart Hall and *Ideology and Consciousness*, a journal that was trying to bring Foucault and Lacan together). For the most part the Birmingham Center was not very open to Foucault because of their sense of what Foucault was. In my opinion this was not actually Foucault but the English use of Foucault—a focus on micropolitics—largely through people like Barry Hindess and Paul Hirst and journals like *Ideology and Consciousness*. Although there were people at Birmingham more interested and sympathetic to Foucault, the critique at Birmingham was that there was no way to talk about larger macrostructures of power in Foucault. But then there were other people who were using Foucault, especially in the '80s, through the notions of discourse. Obviously Ernesto Laclau and Chantel Mouffe were using Foucault to some extent and James Donald's work on education and Frank Mort on consumption comes out of Foucault's work. Foucault's work was around a lot but it was not until the mid to late 1980s that Foucault comes in more prominently.

Miller: In addition to *I & C*, a couple of other journals are important. One is *Economy and Society*, which is what your are referring to when you mention Hindess and Hirst, and the other is *m/f.* So with *Economy and Society* and the work of Hindess and Hirst, these were the bad boys, enfants terribles, of British sociological Marxists, and I think that it's fair to say that they took Althusserian ideas of nonnecessary correspondence and necessary non-correspondence, etcetera, to the point where it was hard for many people to see what their relationship in fact was to class politics or to Marxism or to whatever. But I think that they were very important in that they brought a British uptake of Foucault through Althusser in a way that I think was less true, to a certain extent, in the U.S. And so this is a distinctly antihumanist, posthumanist Foucault, and one that is less, therefore, connected to identity politics at one level, and perhaps also less connected in certain ways to philosophy, as Larry suggested. And *Economy and Society* has continued to be an important place for those kinds of people to publish.

Grossberg: And it's now become a center for the British governmentality work.

Miller: Right, which is also a link to *I & C*, which is where Jacques Donzelot and Nikolas Rose were being read in the late 70s in Britain. The other journal, *m/f,* has been interpreted in numerous ways: marx/freud, marxism/feminism, male/female, michel/foucault. And they even wrote about those things! This is a journal that only lasted about 10 issues or so, but was in fact a very interesting place for on the one hand the spread of various kinds of psychoanalytic film theory but also for really questioning the idea of originary subjects in a Foucauldian frame.

We're talking about a period when for many people cultural studies was regarded as something quite small, off to one side, and somehow separate from feminism and separate from film theory in a way that just doesn't seem apparent to us when we look back anachronistically and assume that there are connections. But there was definitely, I think it's fair to say, more of a class politics presence that significantly stakes out cultural studies from film theory in the late 1970s and the early 1980s. And as I said before, in sociology there was definitely a notion of trying to react against class politics, but not in a textualist way, rather down what we now might think of as the governmentality path.

Grossberg: Now if you look at Australia, and Toby knows this better than I do, largely out of Sydney a very different Foucault was being offered—a much more philosophical Foucault. Through people like Paul Patton and Meagan Morris and all of these small presses and journals that were coming out, it was a Foucault that was more in line with Gilles Deleuze and postmodernist philosophy. I don't think that these people knew cultural studies, and insofar as they knew what cultural studies was, it was probably more in line with John Fiske's work. I don't know that there were a lot of relations between early mainstream Australian cultural studies and this group, although I certainly think that the Sydney group was doing cultural studies from a different perspective. And their work had quite an influence on me.

Miller: It's much less institutionalized academically in Australia. As Larry mentioned, there were small presses that published translations of Foucault. It's always complicated when you speak for others, but I don't think that people like Paul Patton and Meagan Morris were trying to build academic careers. I think that they were probably interested in reviving a new or different kind of leftism, one that had connections to libertarianism, probably, a left libertarianism certainly, and one that looked at what Larry was mentioning—micropolitics, and microtechnologies of everyday life and the formation of the subject and so on. It was not so much about building journals or building departments or institutionalizing anything.

Then you get people who are more within universities (not that Paul was outside them) like Noel King and Ian Hunter who are clearly associated with ongoing university projects in specific locations and who are interested in trying to understand the relationship of the disciplines they've come out of, and a future for interdisciplinarity. This is partly because there are new universities being developed in the late 70's and early 80's that are meant to be completely interdisciplinary. So this becomes part of the project and then that relates in turn to a more institutionalist take on the use of Foucault to explain, for instance, the pastoral power of literature, and to try to adduce connections between that original pastoral power, the displacement by it of religion at the center of the curriculum, and then to extrapolate further towards textual analytic appreciation forms in the contemporary educational mode as forms of governing subjects, so I think that's part of that trajectory.

Grossberg: Well I think that you could say that there are a number of ways at looking at how Foucault appears and they're different in different countries. If you were actually going to write this history, the dominant one in America is through disciplines. Because the US is such a strongly institutionalized academic culture. *Semiotext(e)* was the major equivalent to what was going on in Australia, the nonacademic highly intellectualized journal. *Semiotext(e)* was crucial in bringing a philosophical postmodernist Foucault into debate. I don't know if they were doing cultural studies or not, but it was certainly being read. There were others like *SubStance* which were more academic. You also had people like Hayden White and other historians bringing Foucault in as a kind of Nietzschean critique of historiography, which is where I first learnt of Foucault. And then of course there is the way that Foucault got taken up in literature and other disciplines.

But I don't think this that interesting a story. The other more interesting way is to say it seems to me that Foucault has been taken up in two dimensions. One is, who do you link him with. So in some cases like *I & C*, it was with Lacan so it was a kind of psychoanalyzed Foucault. In the case of Hindess and Hirst in *Economy and Society* it was an Althusserian Foucault. In Australia with people like Paul and Meagan and others it was a kind of Deleuzian Foucault being read. So you get Foucault read with other people, and that makes for different Foucaults.

In all of these it seems to me, you could also try to identify and compare broad ways of using Foucault. You could use Foucault on a model of a historian. It seems to me that you get a lot of work out of queer theory and out of literature, which takes Foucault's various ways of doing history, and Foucault's rereadings of the history of modernity, and brings it to bear on other issues, or work that expands Foucault's readings on the emergence of sexuality, etcetera. Another is Foucault as a theory of power, and micropolitics in particular, which is what Hindess and Hirst emphasize, and what I would argue governmentality as a variant of this way continues, as it combines in a way with the first. And a third major way is the notion of discourse, and how that plays out in someone like Laclau, or Foucault on power-knowledge, and how it plays out in Stuart Hall. And the fourth way is as a philosopher, where you have that Australian group that we talked about a moment ago. Micropolitics was part of this but their work was in many ways a broad philosophical challenge to the way that cultural studies operated. This was not just a specific critique about issues of cultural studies and the micro-political but it meant you had to deal with cultural studies on difference and on discourse and on micropolitics and on a whole range of different issues. Recently you have the emergence in Australia and England of two different paradigms of governmentality. Although there are similarities, these two versions of governmentality have very different relations to both Foucault and cultural studies.

Miller: I'd like to add one quick thing—to take us back a paragraph or two. I think that Foucault as a model of intellectual is important, too. And that's because one of the things that he theorized was the idea of the specific vs. the general intellectual, but in fact he is the general intellectual par excellence. His books are either principally theoretical, like *The Archeology of Knowledge* or they're histories of thought, like *The Order of Things*, or they're histories of events or processes like *Birth of the Clinic* or *Discipline and Punish*—an exemplary work of political economy, by the way.

However most of the interviews are clearly either defenses of the self, or they're interventions into contemporary politics. That linkage to contemporary politics is significant for a lot of the followers. People are prepared to read about topics from thousands or hundreds of years ago, from countries that they've never visited, that are closely empirical whether accurate or not, depending upon whom you read as a critic because they believe that they can draw from those forms of everyday life and everyday politics. Some of that is articulated through the existence of all these interviews. It is in the interviews that you see embodied the possibility of picking up on these histories and theories and deploying them to talk about sexuality, incarceration, insanity, and all forms of normalization. It is really easy to blend this historical and philosophical figure through the possibility of what is really a very generalized intellectual critique and intellectual intervention that claims itself to be something quite other. And that's one of the reasons there are so many Foucaults and they are so available to different projects.

Packer: Does that help to legitimate Foucault's uptake within cultural studies—his ability to connect these general studies to specific politics?

Miller: Well one of the things that helps in cultural studies is the quixotry of it all. That this is a person who surprises you when you turn the page. And one of the things that I think is fetishized in cultural studies is surprise. You are meant to make interventions, you are meant to annoy people, you are meant to grandstand, you are meant to be hysterical. And the fact is that when you turn the page in Foucault you are told something that you didn't expect to be told. I don't think that this is a trivial point—it's actually what I like so much about him. In other words his projects are sometimes summed up as trying to make one imagine how it might have been otherwise. Or to make people think otherwise, and that trying to make people think otherwise is ongoing. The notion of autocritique as a means of thinking otherwise is central to cultural studies, and I think that's one of the reasons why there has been such uptake of him.

Grossberg: I don't know that Foucault's commitment as a political intellectual and what Toby describes as a sense of surprise legitimated the take-up so much as it made connections somewhat easier. Cultural studies does purport to have a commitment to a kind of political intellectual. It does have a commitment to surprise, to learn something that you didn't know, to say things that aren't quite so predictable and expected. And so the fact that Foucault fit that model made it easier for the people to eventually see Foucault as someone who fit into the broad paradigm of cultural studies. Of course there is a lot of Foucauldian work that hasn't anything to do with cultural studies, but has a lot to do with critical work. But I'm talking about when Foucault gets taken up in very particular ways, when Foucault begins to speak more directly into a kind of cultural studies discourse, or the people who use it begin to speak into that discourse.

Another way in which Foucault's work has been taken up—and these overlap—is a tendency to take a concept from Foucault, to take one of Foucault's surprising rereadings of that concept and how it plays out in modernity, and go with it. And so you get lots of books that discover the disciplinarity of X, or they take up some other moment, like the confessional. That is perfectly consistent with Foucault's self description as a kind of toolbox. But that is a different way of using Foucault.

Miller: A classic example of that for me would be the way in which "discourse" gets picked up as something that is allegedly nonmaterial, anti-Marxist, not about empirical reality. And this either becomes Foucault as a kind of whipping boy, or alternatively, a means of trumping Marxism for the umpteenth time. Whereas another way of doing it would be to say that the discourse model is a form of specifying—as is the whole micro-politics shtick—the materiality of politics within discrete sites in a way that is, in my opinion, completely compatible with Marxism, except for the notion that all forms of life should reference a teleological form of economic determinism. Instead, this is to say, all sites, forms of knowledge, discourse, and so on will have their own political technology, their own material aspects. It doesn't mean it's immaterial, it doesn't mean that it isn't real, it just means that it can't be read off against a prevailing mode of production.

I guess that within cultural studies one hopes that there is something about power and subjectivity and connectedness to social-movement politics that maps out the enterprise, at least rhetorically. Those are concepts that compel Foucault, that are there throughout genealogy, archeology, discourse, any of these other concepts that get applied to answer how is the world constituted through power relations, how are persons made up, and how is space occupied. These things are meant to be fairly constant concerns that are integral to much of what goes on under the sign of cultural studies. Not that this can be summed up in a sentence, but I want to put that on the table.

Packer: I want to go back to the point that Larry was making regarding governmentality and the two uptakes of it. I was wondering if you could talk about the differences between the two and what's significant about each.

Grossberg: Well, that's difficult. I'm trying to write my own take on governmentality vis-à-vis my own Foucauldian commitments. So this is all very tentative. But I would say that the impact of Ian Hunter on the Australian notion of governmentality is absolutely crucial. The centrality of Hunter's reading of the relationship of aesthetics and the pastoral and the constitution of what Toby called the well-tempered subject, the well-tempered citizen, is, it seems to me a much more powerful and dominant theme in the writings of Australians than it is in the English writings of Nikolas Rose, etcetera. I need to develop that and ask why and see how it plays out in Tony Bennett and others writing on policy issues. Secondly, it seems to me that for the Australians there are two meanings of policy. One of them Toby called the provenance of culture—the production, distribution, and access to culture itself. This is always a central concern with the Australians whereas it's not a very central concern with the British. In fact if you take Nikolas Rose as the obvious leading figure there, I don't know that he's all that concerned with culture as a particular domain of human practice and enterprise. I can't see Nikolas Rose going out and doing the kind of Bordieuian study that Bennett, Frow, and Emmison did in *Accounting for Taste*. It doesn't seem relevant to the kind of governmentality that Rose does. And the third difference I'd point out is that, obviously, the British are much more concerned with transformations of state government. Rose's last book, *Powers of Freedom*, is about the transformation from the liberal to the neoliberal state. One of the odd things about the Australian moment, I don't know if people are still doing it, is a lack of serious grappling with the transformations of liberalism into something else, involved with the new forms of globalization and governmentality. Obviously their interests are different, which leads me to another point. What you read in Rose and others in England is a new practice of micropolitics. Rose's book isn't particularly concerned with the subjectivity of the well-tempered citizen. He's concerned with describing the micro-strategies of controlling people's conduct and how that reorganizes the nature of power and social relationships. Of course there is a micropolitical theory in the Australian approach but it isn't the dominant analytic strategy in their work whereas it's the overpowering strategy in Rose's work. So that the kind of critique Stuart Hall and others made of micropolitics in the late 1970s and early 1980s seems to me an ongoing debate in England. The Gramscian (cultural studies) critique of governmentality is that it's all micro; there's a leap to a unity called neoliberalism but without any demonstration of how the micro-strategies get articulated into larger structures of power. Whatever the failures of Tony Bennett and Stuart Cunningham that's not where one would focus a critique. The rhetoric of the Australian version of governmentality, with its focus on policy, was presented in a way that defined it against the Gramscian; Tony Bennett's presentation of his paradigm is certainly Foucault against Gramsci. The British version seems not to have bothered with that. I don't know what Rose or Dean or any of these people would say about it, but they haven't taken up that rhetorical strategy.

Miller: I think there's a huge amount of renunciation going on in the Australian model that you are talking about. There's a strong sense that people are renouncing former selves—misplaced, misguided selves. Either their own or those that are close to them. I think that with Rose the work can be tied to Donzelot, and the emergence of the policing of families and that logic of the construction of the social in the late 1970s. So a lot of it connects to a sociological critique of psychology, and that's probably why it isn't so concerned with the pastoral as a form of humanities education. Whereas, even though Bennett is a professor of sociology, I think people like him and Hunter are trying to renounce literary studies, and specifically the figure of Raymond Williams, and are trying to deal with issues of totality that are inbred to left-leaning literature theorists.

Another part of this is something conjunctural. It fascinates me that the moment that it's clear that Thatcherism is there to stay, which is the early 80s, there is a certain exodus from Britain. People who know that they are not going to get jobs, like Paul Smith and Andrew Ross, come to the States, and people who are not certain what life will be like for whatever reason, like Tony Bennett, John Tulloch (who was perhaps already there), John Hartley, and John Fiske come to Australia for all kinds of diverse reasons. But one of the things that I think is transformative for some of those people is moving from a political economy that is clearly inimical to the left, and clearly inimical to leftist forms of reasoning within the academy at a national level, to a place where a social-democratic, feminist-inflected national government has just been elected, and it's comparatively benign, and it's something that you can be affiliated with.

I remember Larry coming to Australia in the late '80s and seeming to be astonished by this faith in the state, saying respectfully and heard as such, "well after 8 years of Reaganism, I'm not saying you're wrong but I can not believe that people feel able to say this." There's something conjunctural in turning away from an idea of hegemony and towards an idea of governmentality that is about seeing the left-liberal state as comparatively benign and is also a part of the renunciation protocols that those people in Australia put themselves through. Now of course when a more conservative government is elected in Australia, they all run back to the UK, where a social democratic government has just been elected and where there are opportunities of this sort again. By "they all," Hartley did it, Bennett did it, Tulloch did it, Mercer did it, Frow did it. So there are all sorts of reasons that they might give for doing it, whether personal, political, professional, and so on, but nevertheless, it is an interesting Rod Stewart *Atlantic Crossing* move. I think it's partly to do with a certain kind of theorization that fits a particular place at a particular time.

There's one other aspect of governmentality in the U.S. and that's around *Social Text*. Because you can see in that journal a transformation from something that was very clearly committed to Marxism as its imperative, yet was interested in questions of consumption and so on, to something that was partly influenced by George Yúdice to look at relations of consumption and their connection to governmentality, beyond governmentality just being about the state, but being just as much about corporations, unions, and non-governmental organizations such as foundations.

Grossberg: I think that there is a third spoke to this wheel. One is, if you have the Australian group, and you have the *Economy and Society*/Nikolas Rose group, and there is in this country *Social Text* and *Public Culture*, both of which are interested in bringing issues of political economy and the State back into cultural studies. But I wouldn't describe those two as governmentality. Insofar as governmentality is a particular theoretical paradigm I think that both of them take something out of governmentality but I don't know that I would describe Yúdice's work or Arjun Appadurai and Dilip Ganokar and the people at *Public Culture* as sharing much with the Bennett/Rose take. It seems to me that neither *Social Text* nor *Public Culture* is particularly committed to micropolitics. Neither of them has a microanalytic take, nor do they have a particular focus on subjectivity that for me constitutes governmentality. You're right that *Social Text* and *Public Culture* are trying to come up with an alternative paradigm, to try as you've said before to take both meanings of policy—as making culture available, and as the construction of a polity together. In the English version not only does Rose in the end not have that much to say about culture per se, but I'm not sure that you can even describe this as policy, even in the sense of constructing a polity. He is concerned quite literally with the conduct of conduct, with the action upon action. With Rose you are going to discuss the microtechniques by which people's conducts are being reorganized through strategic responses to local problems. *Social Text* has tried over the years to bring together the different levels of analysis which in some ways if it succeeds is a much more ambitious project. I think that it's interesting that you would call it governmentality.

Miller: Let's look at the signified. If governmentality is an unfolding of the modern republican ideal western state, and its attempt to understand its population and to invest power and capacity in that population, not of accumulating wealth and power in the sovereign, but instead generating certain social norms, generating the conditions of existence for primary and secondary accumulation of capital and also permitting the generation of a flexible and ongoing workforce, then that would suggest a very state-centered view of governmentality. But when you start to think of it as also something to do with a form of social organization that doesn't just reach out from the state, but that touches everything and then everything touches back on the State, then you might want to include within it Taylorism and scientific management the paradigm that is as Leninist as it is Taylorist in the U.S. It is taken up in the Soviet Union just as it is here with the production-line, and criticized by Gramsci. But that is part of governmentality. There is a response to that, a human relations side to scientific management that says that the worker must smile as she's being screwed rather than being unhappy while he's being screwed. That too is about an attempt to invest power in the population—not in an innocent, happy pollyannaish way, but in a way that is quite keen towards certain outcomes. Then these forms of influence in populations get taken up by institutions that are more than relatively autonomous from either the focus of the state or secondary accumulation—universities, foundations, churches of different kinds, etcetera. And so it is the social infesting the state, the state infesting the social, and forms of both corporate and not-for-profit activity increasingly seeing themselves not just as agents of their own constitution, not just out to make money or rule, for example, but agents of corporate citizenship that are responsible beyond the self. And this is why I think that neoliberalism, as a kind of totalizing device for understanding our contemporary moment is somewhat misguided unless it allows for the idea of responsibility and salvation and the social—something that really competent hegemones know all about. They're not just about the entrepreneurial, ratiocinative, calculating, self-actualizing, selfish subject. And that's why I think that governmentality is so significant, because it encompasses those kinds of activities.

Grossberg: But I'm wary, because then governmentality loses all specificity. It becomes a kind of *ur*-concept for a theory of micropolitics. The concept of governmentality served a twofold function in Foucault's career. One was as a response to the charge that he had nothing to say about the state. Now I agree with you, Foucault then wants to very carefully say, but it's not just the state that's implicated in governmentality, it's also nonstate institutions that get involved, but that's part of the nature of the liberal state. And that's the second function of governmentality in Foucault. He wants it to say something about the peculiarity of the liberal government and its transformation of pastoral power into a liberal republican society. The danger is, if it becomes the new model by which one talks about gaining particular forms of knowledge and acting upon the forms of conduct of a population, then it becomes so broad and general that I'm not sure what purchase it gives you as a specific concept. It operates at a level of abstraction, often without any reference to the actual specificity of Foucault, as is often the case with the variety of ways people use discourse.

Miller: It becomes like "society" in sociology.

Grossberg: Right. Part of my problem with governmentality in the narrower sense is the sense that neoliberalism becomes too easy. Neoliberalism becomes too much of an intentionalist project, and too much of a singular model. What is lost is Foucault's particular and peculiar sense of agency which, for me at least, is embedded in the concept of a discursive formation, a discursive apparatus. People do things but the results are not what people intended. People end up creating an apparatus that is not of their own model. As you're saying, moreover, there needs to be a recognition that there are a variety of discursive apparatuses competing across the terrain of politics, economics, society, and culture, and that which we are calling neoliberalism is the difficult articulation of a fractured set of discursive apparatuses, none of which actually embodies the particular intentions of any single group to begin with, and those apparatuses are now struggling with and against each other. There is a conservative faction that's opposed to neoliberalism, but there is also that conservative faction that while saying that they are opposed to neoliberalism, is working with neoliberalism. And because it operates only at the microlevel in Rose's work, it loses that sense of agency and struggle and articulation. So you get in Rose the sense that there is either this kind of neoliberal transformation of the society on the ground as a totality, or that there are so many particular local strategies, things going on that don't add up to anything, except that he wants to call it neoliberalism in the end.

Miller: Well, this is one of the problems that I think you can get with Foucault in general. And that is on the one hand an extraordinary totalization, and on the other hand a total specification. So there are moments when a Foucauldian making an argument will move towards very generalized accounts of the world. This is the prevailing epistemology of the time that appears to infiltrate absolutely everything. This is the discourse. This is the epistêmê, whatever it is. This is how linguistics works, these kinds of gigantic statements. And then the minute that any remark is made to the effect that "wouldn't that then suggest a nonreductive politics that would be connected to generalized trends in the mode of production political economy approach" the reply comes "no I'm not saying that, you have to be much more specific than that," and fetishized microexamples are brought in against ideas of a foundational problem to do with the division of labor. So there is a two-step happening between totalization of an extraordinary kind and reductionism of an extraordinary kind that is the clever Foucauldian move, and that's what I think is going on in what you're describing, and that is a problem. It's fast and loose and complex. And that's the flip side to the "turn the page and be astonished" and it happens again and again. I don't think that Foucault quite ever makes that mistake, but I think that many of the followers do. I think that there is an incredible reductionism to a lot of this material. And an antieconomism, that frustrates me intensely, that won't attempt to correlate any of the events to the developments that are being described in the areas of culture or of personhood. Not just to correlate with the ideology of the time, but actually with shifts in the distribution of wealth, because there is a desire to allow such relative autonomy between the spheres. Particularly not to allow a material base to appear to reflect anything else. And that's my concern with what you are describing.

Grossberg: I want to say two things to what Toby said. The one is that yes, I agree that a lot of people who use Foucault make the mistake of leaping from the micro to the macro. And the importance of Foucault's interviews on theory and the essay on discourse and others, is that he then fills in what he has taken for granted. Like when people say that Foucault isn't a Marxist, he says well, I cite Marx all the time, but I just don't put quotation marks around it. And if you don't recognize it, then you had better go back and read Marx before you accuse me of not being a Marxist. He takes an enormous amount of work for granted in each of his books that is filling in the kind of mediating levels of what I would call the discursive apparatuses that he's hinting at and that some people leave out.

The second thing that I want to say, and I'm still thinking through this, is that if we take Foucault seriously that governmentality is a practice of the liberal state under conditions of republicanism, then it seems to me that we need to ask what happens to that theory, governmentality, under conditions when that liberal state is under attack. Which isn't to say that the liberal state has disappeared. It's to say that the liberal state is under attack in a variety of ways from a variety of sources, and is being reformed in a number of ways both in the first world and in the third world. So that which is being put into place in the third world as the liberal state doesn't quite look like . . .

Miller: . . . the governmentality model. Because it's in countries where 80% of people don't have access to a telephone, where there is no serious effort to invest capacities and powers in them whatsoever. There are efforts to provide telecommunications infrastructure, but it's known that you can only do that through corporations, or you'll lose your IMF or World Bank money. And the idea that this then leads to a generalized educational project or even the quieting of the working class, as per Britain in the late nineteenth century or the U.S., is laughable. No one is interested in these people as consumers, no one is interested in them as citizens.

Grossberg: But then I have the problem—if it was a historically specific formation for Foucault, then simply describing it as Rose does as conduct upon conduct isn't sufficient. And then I want to know what has changed. What doesn't work about Foucault's description of governmentality into the present? In the introduction to the Australian cultural studies reader Meagan Morris and John Frow say that something has changed, and one of their metonyms for that change is Murdoch's response to the question "How do we solve the Australian economy?" And his answer is "Change the culture." Well how's that response different from Foucault's description of governmentality? There's something different, but I don't know if we've come to terms with it because Murdoch is saying, conduct upon conduct. You change people's everyday conduct in order to change the economy. But there's something different that Murdoch has in mind from what the liberal state had in mind. And I don't think that Rose has adequately historicized that theory. And perhaps because of the conjunctural conditions, what looked like the return of a good liberal state in Australia, that Tony Bennett and Ian Hunter were working under, they didn't think that they needed to raise that question. But I think this is the crucial question. And the answer that it's neoliberal—that doesn't hold water, it's too simple.

Miller: There's also a foundational question here for me. Think about the attempts in the 1970s and 1980s to restore the state to the center of Marxism, or to complete the job that people felt that Marx and Engels hadn't finished; to derive a theory of the state where the state isn't just about making life secure or being in control and in authority—a Weberian/symbolic interactionist account—but where the state is principally a mechanism for securing the conditions of the possibility of accumulation. How does that rank alongside governmentality? Isn't this the core question for the left to sort out at some level? You can get rid of capitalist accumulation, you can put in patriarchy or rationalization, any number of the big-ticket items that are about forms of social division that might have their creative sides, that might have their empowering sides, but are designated and designed as forms of structuring inequality into domination. Race, class, gender, sexuality. So you don't have to make the economy at the heart of it (although of course I would) you could make race, gender, whatever you like at the heart of it. Where then, if you pose that kind of antimony, does governmentality stand? Is that something that just gets incorporated into it?

Grossberg: Well that's why the total microanalysis of someone like Rose is problematic. It doesn't articulate to issues of economics, for example, or accumulation, the unequal distribution of wealth. It does not articulate to structures of colonialism and neocolonialism. It doesn't articulate to the reformulation of structures of racism in various parts of the world. I was thinking about another metonym of this change to think about—if you look at what's happening to the state in the United States in regards to the state's function of accumulating knowledge of the population. Since Reagan, the state has been systematically giving up that function. And it's interesting if you look at the debates on the census. The census is precisely the archetypal mode, in Foucault's governmentality, to maximize the information that we have. Look at the debates on the census where basically neoconservatives are saying "we don't want the information." We don't want to get the best information that we have.

Miller: That's for political reasons. I mean the reason for doing that is to ensure that districts are drawn so that the Republicans remain in power.

Grossberg: But that's been going on for a hundred years. It goes back to the post-Civil War. When the whole sense of the census was redefined in terms of keeping blacks out of power. But the discourse here is different. It's not that we aren't collecting data, of course but we're collecting different forms of data and different people are collecting it.

Miller: Do you know the Melissa Nobles book *Shades of Citizenship* which compares the U.S. and Brazilian census? She uses governmentality but she shows how successive regimes have always claimed complete objectivity. And what's interesting to back up your point, against me in a sense, is that this is one of those moments in time when every person who does statistics favors the Democrats' line against the Republicans.' The Republicans want to count real bodies and persons. The Democrats want extrapolations. They want normal samples from which you can extrapolate, which work, basically, as everyone knows. And they are going to be more accurate than the impossibility of counting real people.

Grossberg: So many of the histories of statistics are now Foucauldian.

Miller: But by the same token, if you go back 100 years, racial science is the animating logic, supposedly completely objective, to the census. No need to go back 100 years, perhaps 50 or 60. But certainly things are changing. There's no doubt about that. But one of the ways that they are changing is the role of social movements in the census in the U.S. in pushing for transformations. And I think that this is where governmentality comes through in its multifaceted, more politically interesting way. Which is to say that here are these nasty categories that have been generated through racial science. That are invidious, insidious, and so on. But after a while, and Stuart Hall talks about this with reference to the reclamation of the term "black," these terms get inside you. You are queer. Which is a "bad" word, but then it's redesignated, resignified. It's taken on board as a part of you, and you want to own it in a way that forgets its linkage to the state or its lineage in racial science or in psychological science, or whatever it might be. That term then gets resignified and is used in a more positive way. So some of these groups that didn't like racial science pick up the very terms of racial science, redesignate them as their own, in order to make sure that they still get specified in the census, so that they then can claim that there are this many of us, we require this kind of treatment, we have this kind of income profile, we want data. We want to be numericized.

Grossberg: I don't claim to understand this transformation. All that I want to say is that my understanding of governmentality from Foucault is that it is a particular set of strategies on a level of abstraction equivilent to discipline, that is specific to a particular conjunctural formation. And that as those transformations occur, then those categories need to be called into question. And I certainly have argued in the past that it's not clear to me we are living in an age in this country in which discipline is still the dominant formation or modality of power, as we increasingly go back to a kind of pure penality and forms of corporeal punishment, etcetera. So it's just that transformation. I don't think this is a critique of *Social Text* or *Public Culture*, but I do think that it's a problem in the narrower sense of governmentality as a paradigm, such as with Rose, Dean, Valentine, and Minson for example.

Miller: There's still another "G" word that we haven't used, and this is the "globalization" word. This is particularly interesting in an era in which the state is supposedly decaying, dying, and so on, though I guess Paul Hirst and Graham Thompson have done interesting work contra that. But it raises the issue of a more global governmentality. The idea of global government was written off by realists in international relations theory as impossibly utopic, something related to an entire moral universe or to a leftist workerist fantasy. Now, global government, not necessarily through the UN but through a number of institutions that certainly we could all name, seems really much more practical in the sense of the complexity of the promise of state representativeness being continued. If you think about what happens after the Depression in the West and after colonialism in the South, certain promises are made. Promises are made at the end of the Depression that we will now genuinely look after you. The UN convention on full employment that all of these countries signed—Keynesianism, but not only Keynesianism, anything that's required. We'll actually make sure that you don't all starve. This is a guarantee. This is why you can have renewed faith in the state. And if you think about things like the GI bill it's also about acknowledging the sacrifices in the Second World War, laying down their lives for themselves, for others, for ideals and so on. And the fetishization of that recently by every TV newscaster and the networks is itself fascinating. But that greatest generation ethos in the U.S., which could be applied to many other countries as well, is about a renewal of faith in the state through the promise of genuine pastoral care.

For those peoples in national liberation struggles in the 1930s, 1940s, and 1950s that bear fruit in that 20-year-period between Ghana in 1957 and Timor and Angola in 1975, the promise of the emergent states is that a) you will get genuine representation from people who are like you, but b) again,

there will be the oportuninty for economic sovereignty. So there's economic
sovereignty and care, both in the case of the post-Depression first world
states and the postcolonial third world states. It mixes with the sovereign
representative promise, which has been around for a long time in the West,
gradually expanding its providence, and suddenly is around in the third world.

Nowadays, the possibility of each of those is problematized. The possibility of powers and capacities and welfarisms being extended into the community by the State is diminished because of changes by the international
capitalist ruling class and its notion of redistribution, because of changes in
intellectual fashion, because of economic problems, because of the power of
different international organizations and the idea of representativeness is
problematized. Whom do you go to represent your interests, when your interests at the moment may be determined by various international organizations, both public and private, that have no clear affinity to a democratic
representative structure of the kind that you live within or allegedly live
within? And that's a big problem for thinking about governmentality today—
the other "G" word. On the other hand, one could say that the World Trade
Organization, the IMF, the WHO, the International Telecommunications
Union, these institutions—some of them long-standing, some of them new—
are crucial sites for playing out this question. Where national governments are
still the crucibles, and negotiations with multinational corporations are still
conducted in this international frame. On the other hand, one could say, it
seems as though the state is now essentially powerless to represent, and it
really is just there as an assistance to the accumulation. And that kind of
gutter-Marxist vulgar attitude to the state is increasingly appealing to many
of us. Not to say that the State is all-powerful, but to say that it really is there
in the service of accumulation. And not just in the last instance.

Packer: Something that I'm still unclear about has to do with the question
of accumulating knowledge of the population and the rise in advertising
demographics that you write about in *Technologies of Truth*. There is an intense corporate investment in knowing the population. Is that a form of
governmentality? It is working on the conduct of conduct as far as purchasing
habits go. But, I think that Larry is saying that these attempts to control
conduct is outside of governmentality because it is not state initiated, and
you, Toby, are suggesting that it is. I'm also wondering if that links
governmentality to cultural issues traditionally dealt with in cultural studies
that have to do with media, representation, communications, ideology, and
consumption? I'm not talking about State-organized forms of culture, like
Tony Bennett's work on the museum, but rather commercial culture.

Miller: Well, take an example like drug testing and pharmaceutical companies, where in the last decade there is a transformation from a principally

publicly funded form of university research to a principally privately funded form of university research. A governmentality analysis that is interested in the state at its center would have said ten years ago here's a classic example of a desire to know and understand and reform a population that is undertaken *tout court*. Ten years on, who is to say that that is not part of governmentality because it is not done by the state?

Grossberg: Well, maybe. I think that we need to define what we mean by the term. Which we still haven't done, and I think that it's very difficult to do. It's often raised as a question by people who say what's the difference between governmentality and disciplinarity, and when Foucault says that we move from a society of sovereign power, to a society of disciplinary power, and then he says that liberalism has moved into a society of governmentality. So there are all these terms, but what are the relations amongst them?

For me, I want to take governmentality to be a historical conjunction and articulation of a variety of practices, some of which overlap with disciplinarity and other categories. But its an articulation of a variety of modalities and techniques and technologies of power, in a particular formation, in a particular conjuncture of the liberal State, which involves more than the State. For example, one of the crucial apparatuses or technologies of power is that you have specific and broad knowledge of the population. Does that mean that any form of power which is built on the need for specific and broad knowledge of the State is governmentality. My answer would be no. It's an empirical question because, for me, governmentality is the articulation of that to other apparatuses, to other technologies. I mean, yes, governmentality is conduct on conduct, but my reading of Foucault is that all power is conduct on conduct. Now we add something. It's conduct on free conduct. Governmentality assumes and constitutes the freedom of the actor in itself. That's an intersection. But is all conduct on conduct governmentality, no. Is all conduct on free conduct, well I don't know. Is that what's going on now, because it seems to me that you could make a case that increasingly forms of power are operating on a division of the population whereby a certain part of the population is constituted as free, and we act on that part of the population as conduct on free conduct, and another part of the population is increasingly constituted as not free, and we act on the conduct of that population as conduct on conduct, but not free conduct. We're not reconstituting their freedom at all, we're reconstituting their radical subjugation, so it seems to me that identifying governmentality with any single technology of power is a problem. Maybe the best way to read Foucault then is to say that this is a diagram that brings together a variety of technologies and apparatuses, and if you disarticulate them, which is a better way of thinking about neoliberalism, it's not about a new conjuncion, it's not a new diagram, as Rose says, but it is the struggle to disarticulate some of the technologies in the liberal diagram, and to begin to try to rearticulate them in new ways.

And so, when you ask is the question of gathering knowledge on the population governmentality, it is for me an empirical question. If you say, what happens when it's not the State gathering the information but commercial enterprise, through monitoring consumption, for example, or through network computer systems sharing data, my answer is, well, I don't know. I can imagine a situation in which that transformation would not be significant enough to say this isn't a governmental situation, and I can imagine a situation in which you could say, well, look, it's articulated to a whole variety of other rearticulations and transformations. So there are some grounds for saying if governmentality describes, in its purest form, nineteenth century republican societies, then we are at least witnessing the deconstruction of governmentality, and perhaps something in its place, but we don't know what it is yet. Neoliberalism is much too vague and homogeneous of a term.

Miller: Well would it have something to do with endowing the known population with new politics? In other words it's knowing the population not just for its own sake, as an object of knowledge, and not just in order to sell it things, but actually to transform it. Maybe that would be part of it. And one way in which the free-subject idea would be helpful is to get back to your penal concerns. Take the case of the U.S. where in some states people are placed in the ultimate disciplinary sanction in which they become *civiliter mortuus*, literally civilly dead. They are not citizens any longer, they are imprisoned, and in some cases face capital punishment. That is where discipline really hits. That is where discipline is, and not where governmentality is.

Governmentality is not just about accumulation, because it is about the notion of a quasi-unselfinterested dispersement of power into others. And that's why the American educational system is so interesting a form of governmentality. When you look at the public money in this country that is expended on education, particularly higher education, and you compare it to the welfare systems of first world countries as opposed to their educational systems, you see that we actually spend proportionately just as much on welfare as anybody else does, but we put it into places like the universities of North Carolina and Illinois. And that follows onto Gary Becker's book *Accounting for Tastes*—the same title as Bennett, Frow, and Emmison's book. Becker's model of human capital is par excellence an account of American higher education it seems to me, and very good for this notion of governmentality. If we specify governmentality as trying to transform the population through acting upon it such that the population in consideration gains and develops in ways that are not just about some form of accumulation benefit to the agent that has made that transformation.

Grossberg: I think that's a very good way of putting it, and thinking through what that was. The liberal republican state was a model of empowering the citizen, of really distributing power. And of course at the same time, there was a model continually committed to the accumulation of wealth, and the unequal distribution of value of all sorts, not just of economic capital. The leap, the gap between those two models, is precisely what creates the space for the centrality of ideology. It now becomes incumbent upon capitalism to convince the population, to create a consensus that what's good for General Motors is good for the country. So the rise of advertising, the rise of ideological politics, the rise of consensus, is all about empowering people, and then having to struggle to convince them to let you stay in power. And they do it very successfully. The two are intertwined. So you empower people precisely by constructing the consensus.

I would argue that that system has collapsed. Whatever we have today it's not looking to empower the entire population, and it doesn't care much about consensus, and it doesn't care much about ideological commitment in a way. However it is organizing and distributing power, but it's doing it in a very different kind of way. This is what someone like Bill Readings wants to argue or what Michael Hardt and Antonio Negri want to argue in *Empire*— that in a sense ideology and the construction of the well-tempered subject, the well-tempered citizen is no longer how the game is being played. And if they're right, then it seems to me, that governmentality in the strict Foucaldian sense, is not the useful phrase, but what becomes useful is to say that what Foucault was trying to do in that notion is to describe the articulations between the state, the distributions of power, the formations and modalities of power, and implicitly political economy in this republican formation. It is now incumbent upon us to ask: What are those articulations in the contemporary world? How is this being transformed? What about the republican system is still there? We have a system in which someone is elected president with 15% of the popular vote—this significantly transforms the very meaning of representation.

Miller: Yes, I have no question about that. But I think that the neoliberal mythos of the ratiocinative calculating Western utilitarian subject, is still very, very, very powerful as an analog and an animator of policy; of educational policy in this country for those who are in college; and of policies in other countries that are made by international institutions. For example, the neoliberal wave of deregulation that hits India even though the idea of the rational consumer as applied to millions upon millions of people in dreadful penury unable to consume anything is the animating logic for a lot of that policy. Policy by individual states, policy by federal states, policy by international organizations. There's no need to have an Africa-wide State-based attempt to generate an internet system. Leave it up to private corporations, or public corporations from other countries that come in and make like they are private there, like the French do, for example, because this will liberate local entrepreneurial energies, that no longer have to pay inflated taxes to support inefficient industries, and then there will be general wealth. However much of an ideological slight of hand one might think that to be, that logic of investment in human capital and faith in the rational consumer, and in the rational subject, not just in the consuming position but in other positions too, it seems to me that it is still very powerful. That is the dominant trope.

Grossberg: It is still a very powerful trope in the discourses of economics which feeds into policy debates. But it seems to me that part of what is happening in neoliberal economic theory is the substitution of the rationality of the market for the rationality of the subject. Now of course in neoclassical economics, theoretically those are the same thing. But I think that what is happening is that these are no longer the same thing. That in fact we assume an irrational subject who needs to be controlled and who acts more and more affectively. But the market itself is rational! So whatever people do, the market will lead to the best system. No matter how irrational the people are, and we don't have to worry about constructing rational subjects, and we don't have to worry about giving them information, we just have to worry about letting the market play itself out. I think that that's one of the breaks that's taking place in a subtle transformation of neoclassical economics—the assumption that the rationality of the market and the rationality of economic subjects. There is now the assumption the latter is going to become unnecessary.

Miller: Well, the market has always been an umpire between selfishnesses. Competing subject positions where people have different interests at heart, both of which are solipsistic, as it were, and the market is an umpire. Nevertheless, it seems to me that for what you're saying to be true, wouldn't there need to be a massive disinvestment worldwide in education? And isn't it that education is again and again lifted up as a panacea? And that public expenditure on education internationally is regarded as legitimate in the way that public expenditure on health, retirement and industry is increasingly problematized? Because of the mythology of the United States as the human capital center of the globe that manages to base its successful economic resurgences on an investment in higher education.

Grossberg: Interesting. But I think that it's more contradictory than that. I think that the radical reinvestment in education is very mixed. For example, in the U.S. there is a kind of disinvestment in education despite the rhetoric, in terms of people's willingness to support education, in terms of amount of money when adjusted for inflation invested per student. Moreover, education, though it's the topic, has become rationalized. This is the second contradiction. Yes, it is education, but look at the ways in which education is being redefined in this process. The meaning and value of education is less in creating the rational subject or the good citizen, but it is preparing people with the skills necessary to compete in the marketplace, and those skills can now be measured quantitatively by examinations. The whole reinvestment in education entails a redefinition of what education is going to be in the twenty-first century, which is entirely different than the discourse of education in the nineteenth and twentieth century.

Miller: Right. But if you think about a general education or a liberal education in the American ideal as being about a prep for good citizenship, that's still the case of the liberal arts colleges that are trying to reproduce the ruling class through personal instruction. It's probably not the case for the vast majority of students in American universities, who are not in fact between 18 and 22, but are mature-aged students doing night-time learning or distance learning. At the same time, there's something about some aspects of the liberal general education, and Jeremy was telling me about transformations in the destinations of speech communication graduate students from his university that could back this up, that suggest that what used to be quasi-nonvocational general education that teaches you how to be a nice person, how to fit in, how to listen and so on, is for all kinds of complicated reasons that we don't necessarily understand, now taken as some kind of preparation for corporate levels, quite senior levels, in a way that it wasn't before.

So yes, there might be a sense of a focusing and a concentration on outcome-based education that's not about generalized civics knowledge but that is about preparation not for being a reserve army of labor but for being a manager, that is still drawing on a very generalized nonspecific model of learning. The claims about lifelong learning and skill formation and so on, are that the problem with having highly specified knowledge in area P, is that area P is the old economy in 6 months time, and you need to be ready for area Q. Hence these statements about learning how to learn, and being flexible, and that lifelong learning is lifelong employment. Not staying with one corporation. Yadah yadah. We all know the rhetoric. These claims are very much about a governmentality model of the investment of generalized skills and abilities in a population that are outside the absolute fitting or control of the investment.

Grossberg: Well, again, you are pointing to the contradiction between the residual formation of the university where we have deep investment in liberal education and the pressure from government to reconstitute this. A contradiction which you can see much better at the public schools than you can at universities. So we get rid of the arts, everything that isn't about becoming a good corporate citizen. The liberal education was always, yes, good corporate citizen, but also good political citizen, good cultural citizen. It was all three. But increasingly the cultural and the political are defined vis-à-vis their relation to the corporate citizen. So, yes you should know something about culture if you are in that 20% of the population which is more likely to go to a private liberal arts university rather than a state university, that is going into the upper echelons. But if you're in the majority of students who are not going to a Research One University, or to an elite private liberal arts college, we can't afford that. We can only afford things that are going to define the corporate job market or partnerships with corporations. I don't want to say it's all accomplished, I want to say it's in struggle. That's why I say that we are seeing the deconstruction of governmentality and its rearticulation into something else which has some of the same strategies of governmentality, some of them slightly altered, like corporations are going to get the knowledge of the population rather than the state, but some fairly radically new structures. Like we just don't care about creating good citizens. We just don't care about that model. Now is it done? Well of course not. It's just one of the tendencies.

Packer: Is this then a new definition of what a good citizen is?

Grossberg: If it is a new definition of the citizen, then that's a fairly radical transformation from liberal society. If a citizen is no longer the articulation of cultural, political, and economic citizenship, which is what the republican ideal was, then we are witnessing a significant transformation. If the citizen is no longer, at least for 80% of the population, about constructing a certain kind of subjectivity, then we're witnessing a significant transformation. That's always what history is about. History is never about giving up entirely on one thing and moving to another. It's about transforming the terms and technologies.

Miller: I guess that my anxiety about this is that I'm a faithful reader of the only two class-conscious English language publications that I know, the *Wall Street Journal* and *The Economist*. And the *Wall Street Journal* is forever immensely concerned about deficits in social capital, forever worried about gnomic, purely utilitarian subjects, and the lack of a sense of community service and giving. That long-standing tradition in the U.S. that everything that you got you owe to someone else, that in a sense you must pay back. It's almost like a Jewish notion of hand-in-hand. Very, very powerful. Of course it's facilitated by taxation structures and so on, but very powerful. And the welcoming that's been given to the belated establishment of philanthropic activity by the so-called new economic czars, for example, is an instance of anxiety about that loss of social capital and the requirement to give back and precisely what gets lost when everything is utilitarian.

The Economist, more clearly antiracist, prodemocracy, antihomophobia than the *Wall Street Journal*, but brutally neoliberal, is also something that always wants to know about questions of social capital. And so it seems to me that whilst the brutality of gubernatorial educational policies and congressional educational debates and the brutality of their relationships to colleges is no doubt how you describe it, there are a hell of a lot of people in the corporate sector, who really believe in corporate citizenship, who are really not so keen on this kind of model. Why? Because they know that part of maintaining a relatively stable population that isn't going to engage in any kind of revolutionary activity through thick and thin, through economic cycles up and down, is to have people with an investment in something beyond themselves, and an investment in community or society or whatever it might be. That's what the third way is tapping into.

Grossberg: It is certainly true that the economic sector is saying, look we need well educated people. We need kids who know how to write, and how to read, and how to make an argument, and how to imagine. We can teach them the skills. On the other hand, those same corporations are not funding the programs in writing and in all of those things, nor are they backing programs and politicians consistent with this rhetoric. I don't know what to make of that contradiction. Nor are they pushing the government to say, stop funding this pragmatic view of education, we want people who can read and write creatively, you know? And I don't know what to make of that contradiction. But I have to say that this is why Foucault, for me, is so crucial. Because even if I assume that it's true that major forces in the economic sector are struggling over the production of social and meaning capital, what reality ends up being isn't the expression or the intention of any one sector. The apparatus of education isn't formed by any one group's intentionality. So what we get out is the result of the contradictions among the various fights within the economic sector, and then between the economic and other sectors, and the enactment of the battle between the conservative and liberal views of education, all of these things enter in, each with their own problems, problematics, solutions, etc. But the result is a kind of apparatus of education, which seems to me not to favor human capital, the production of the very kind of social capital that everyone is saying the new economy is going to need. We talk to the people in Hollywood and say what do you want our kids in media studies to learn? And they say we don't care at all if they know how to work a camera. But what we need them to know is how to write and read, how to view a movie, how to think critically. We need to have them understand something about institutional dynamics. All of the technical stuff they can learn in 6 months. But you turn it around, and where's the funding, it's always on the technical skills. Oh yeah, well, teaching them about media criticism isn't going to get them a job. It's how the contradictions in those projects get played out. And we're seeing them most clearly at the public school level.

Chapter 3

Culture and Governmentality

Tony Bennett

In assessing how Foucault's perspective of governmentality has influenced the concerns of the social and political sciences, Mitchell Dean suggests that its main effect has been to substitute what he calls an analytics of government for a theory of the state. What he means by this is clarified in the definition he gives for the expanded concept of government that the perspective of governmentality entails:

> Government is any more or less calculated and rational activity, undertaken by a multiplicity of authorities and agencies, employing a variety of techniques and forms of knowledge, that seeks to shape conduct by working through our desires, aspirations, interests and beliefs, for definite but shifting ends and with a diverse set of relatively unpredictable consequences, effects and outcomes. (Dean, 1999, p. 11)

As such, he suggests, and in contradistinction to the typical focal concerns of theories of the state (the sources of state power, who possesses it, the role of ideology in the legitimation of power), an analytics of government is more concerned with the mechanisms of government, with its routines and operations, paying particular regard to four sets of questions:

1. characteristic forms of visibility, ways of seeing and perceiving
2. distinctive ways of thinking and questioning, relying on definite vocabularies and procedures for the production of truth (e.g., those derived from the social, human and behavioural sciences)
3. specific ways of acting, intervening and directing, made up of particular types of practical rationality ("expertise" and "know-how"), and relying upon definite mechanisms, techniques and technologies
4. characteristic ways of forming subjects, selves, persons, actors or agents. (p. 23)

What is striking here is the extent to which formulations which, in other contexts, would be treated as a part of culture are included in this definition of government (to the extent that it works through "our desires, aspirations, interests and beliefs") and in the checklist of the mechanisms through which government is said to operate ("ways of seeing and perceiving," "ways of thinking," "characteristic ways of forming subjects, selves, persons, actors or agents"). Two points follow from this: first, that, questions concerning the analysis of culture are accorded a more significant role within an analytics of government than they are within theories of the state; and second, that the place they occupy within such an analytics is a radically different one in being conceived as central to the mechanics—the operations and procedures— through which governmental forms of power work rather than, as in typical constructions of the state-ideology relation, legitimating power in ways that are not immanently tangled up in its exercise. Dean notes as much himself when, in discussing the forms of rule associated with neoliberalism, he notes the extent to which these center on "the task of cultural reformation" (p. 172).

This is, however, an argument in which what might be meant by "culture" is taken pretty much for granted; however central cultural mechanisms might be to the mechanisms of government in general, and to those of neoliberalism in particular, Dean does not offer any extended consideration of the concept of culture or of how its role within an analytics of government might best be theorised. The same is true of Nikolas Rose who, indeed, writes disparagingly of what he refers to as the "amorphous domain of culture" (Rose, 1998, p. 24) as a concept whose use has now become so generalized and diffuse as to seriously weaken any analytical value it might once have had, or have again.

Somewhat contrary to what might have been expected, then, the concept of culture has not been effectively knitted into the concerns of those who have most consistently, and most influentially, elaborated the perspective of governmentality. While the relevance of cultural questions is clearly acknowledged, there has been no systematic attempt to think through what the perspective of governmentality might mean for earlier understandings of the concept of culture or how these might need to be revised in order to find a place within, and contribute to the development of, an analytics of government. I imply no criticism of either Dean or Rose here, for their main interests clearly lie elsewhere. The problem is rather that the passage—still uncertain and faltering—of the perspective of governmentality into the concerns of cultural studies has not occasioned any major revision of the concept of culture on the part of those working at the interfaces of questions of culture and government. Nor has it yet occasioned an adequate review of the legacy of earlier theories of culture of a kind that might then be imported back into the broader concerns of an analytics of government.

This is not to deny the value of the work that has been done through the application of the perspective of governmentality to particular cultural processes or in the analysis of particular cultural technologies. To the contrary, the insights generated by the other chapters in this collection is sufficient testimony of the extent to which the perspective of governmentality is provoking both new questions and new answers within cultural studies. Yet the passage of that perspective will always be to some degree an obstructed one unless, rather than being approached as a perspective that has simply to be added and stirred to the already somewhat overvolatile theoretical brew that cultural studies has become, it is seen as one that entails a significantly different approach to our understanding of the relations between culture, society, and the social.

This is not, let me say immediately, a question that is likely to prove susceptible to a quick fix. To the contrary, it will require a sustained reexamination of the ways in which this relationship has been posed as a problem within post-Enlightenment social and cultural theory. While this cannot be attempted here, some pointers as to the direction such an inquiry might take can be offered by looking a little more closely at the respects in which the theoretical vocabularies of culture and governmentality are most obviously at odds with one another and at the reasons for this. I shall do so by considering the different ways in which Stuart Hall and Nikolas Rose draw on the Foucauldian concept of discourse. For it is in their contrasting uses of the Foucauldian lineage that we can see the effects of gratingly incompatible ways of replacing earlier questions concerning the relations between culture and society with ones centred on the relations between culture and the social.

THE "CULTURAL TURN" AND THE
LINGUISTIC CONSTRUCTION OF THE SOCIAL

First, though, a little background is in order if we are to place both bodies of work in the context of broader transformations in recent approaches to the relations between culture, society, and the social. These have been registered principally in the form of a series of departures from, or adaptations of, Marxist constructions of culture/society relations as ones of dependency and determination. For Raymond Williams, from *Culture and Society* (1958) through to *Marxism and Literature* (1977), the central task was to insist, against idealist conceptions, that culture was both dependent on and determined by the social relationships of class arising from the organization of economic production while also—in retaining a Romantic stress on the role of creativity—setting limits to such relations of dependency. Similarly, the insistence, in Althusserian parlance, on the "relative autonomy" of culture and ideology countered, without overcoming, the stress that had previously been placed on economic, social and political relationships as having a more primary force and influence in determining the makeup and developmental trajectory of a social formation.[1] Within both formulations, however, the concepts of society and social formation (while differing significantly in other respects) referred to a totality that was definable in terms of relatively fixed and knowable properties, and one that might be called on to account for the cultural forms it generated.

The direction of more recent debates, by contrast, has tended to dispute the value of an analytical topography that lays out the relations between culture and society for examination in these terms. This has reflected the tendency, commonly referred to as the "cultural turn," to accord an increasingly formative role to culture by imbuing it with the capacity to actively shape and organize—to constitute from within—a whole range of economic, social, and political relationships and practices. For Hall, the "cultural turn" thus constitutes "a paradigm shift in the humanities and social sciences" and, as such, consists in the contention that culture is "a constitutive condition of existence of social life, rather than a dependent variable" (Hall, 1997, p. 220). Its constitutive role in this regard derives from the fact that—in this account—culture functions like a language. It is, essentially, a meaning-making mechanism whose operations, while working at a higher level of signification, replicate the diacritical structure of language associated with the findings of post-Saussurean linguistics. Meaning is lodged not in things themselves but in the varying constructions of the relations between them that arise from different languages or systems of classification:

> The "cultural turn" is closely related to this new attitude towards language. For culture is nothing but the sum of the different classificatory systems and discursive formations, on which language draws in order to give meaning to things. The very term "discourse" refers to a group of statements in any domain which provides a language for talking about a topic and a way of producing a particular kind of knowledge about that topic. The term refers both to the production of knowledge through language and representation and the way that language is institutionalised, shaping social practices and setting new practices into play . . .

> The "cultural turn" expands this insight about language to social life in general. It argues that because economic and social processes themselves *depend* on meaning and have consequences for our ways of life, for who we are—our identities—and for "how we live now," they too must be understood as cultural and discursive practices. (p. 222)

Having thus given culture "a determinate and constitutive role in under-standing and analysing all social relations and institutions" (p. 223), Hall goes on to qualify this argument by setting limits to culture's sway over the social. Clearly aware of the risk that extending culture's role in this way can result in an analytical stew in which "everything is 'culture'" and "'culture' is every-thing" (p. 225), Hall argues that culture supplies only one of the constitutive conditions for other spheres of practice. Economic, political, and social prac-tices all have their own distinctive conditions and effects, but they are also constituted in and by the culturally organized relations of meaning and iden-tity through which social agents come to take up particular subject positions and to act accordingly.

The question is: does this qualification do the trick? Does it, as Hall would want, allow him to respect the autonomy of economic, social, and political practices and relations while also insisting on their cultural consti-tution? At one level, yes: Hall has no difficulty, on the basis of this qualification, in arguing that each of these practices interacts with and conditions the others while also, of course, influencing the conduct of cultural practices. At another level, no: there is an asymmetry in the relations between culture and other regions of practice to the degree that the former exercises less a role of determination in the last instance (the role reserved for the economy in Marxist formulations) than one of constitution in the first instance. Culture, that is to say, is always there, and there first, immanent within economic, social, and political practices, organizing them from within, while it can itself be affected by such practices only to the extent that they supply external conditions for the operation of cultural practices which—since they too are language-like in their organization—are themselves, of course, also always culturally structured from within.

What this means becomes clearer in Hall's more theoretically developed discussions of the relations between cultural and ideological practices and the organisation of the social.[2] Two aspects of these discussions are relevant to my concerns here. The first consists in Hall's displacement of the concepts of society or social formation in favor of a conception of the social as a set of relations between the discursively constructed positions of meaning and iden-tity which individuals—through mechanisms that are both semiotic and psy-choanalytic—come to occupy. The second concerns the respects in which, in accordance with the requirements of poststructuralist conceptions of lan-guage, the relations between these positions are understood as ones of differ-ence and deferral—or, in Derrida's sense, of *différance*. They are, that is to say, positions that are defined in relation to each other as specific forms of raced, classed, gendered, sexed, regional, or national identities which, in their com-plex interactions, define the plane on which social relations are organized—but never in permanently fixed forms. The relations between different discursive positions are articulated in different ways at different historical moments depending on how cultural and ideological struggles align them to, or disconnect them from, one another.

I do not want to question here the value of the work that has been made possible by bringing these formulations to bear on questions of race and ethnicity or, for that matter, of class and gender. To the contrary: Hall's contribution to the debates through which questions of difference and identity have been deessentialized has been of inestimable importance, especially in the critiques of identity politics that it has made possible. The construction of the relations between culture and the social that emerges from these formulations does, however, generate a number of difficulties, less because it dissolves social relations into cultural relations of meaning than because it leaves the realm of culture peculiarly empty of any definite content of its own. It is not, that is to say, the application of the linguistic model to social relations that matters so much as its prior application to culture. For it is this, the linguistic paradigm on which the "cultural turn" ultimately rests, that makes it difficult to theorize culture in terms of its own set of distinctive properties except of a most general, transhistorical and anthropological kind. What culture is, and how it works: these questions are answered in advance of their being put in relation to the operation of cultural practices in any specific set of historical relations. Culture, always and everywhere, consists of a set of language-like operations through which specific relations of meaning and identity are organized. Culture, to recall Hall's formulation, is "nothing but the sum of the different classificatory systems and discursive formations, on which language draws in order to give meaning to things" (Hall, 1997, p. 222). And it works, always and everywhere, through the mechanisms of language and representation to shape social relations by organizing the frameworks of meaning which govern the conduct of social agents.

There is little scope here for any definition of, or attention to, culture that would specify its operations in terms of distinctive institutional or technical relations and processes. There is, similarly, little scope for any variable conception of the nature of the social. For the organization of this, too, is given in advance of the analysis of any specific set of circumstances by the assumption that culture acts on the social through its role in endowing social agents—whether as individuals or as groups—with the means of making their experience meaningful and intelligible. It is through this double move—the first through the notion of the linguistic construction of the social, and the second through the poststructuralist destabilization of the relations of meaning through which the social is thus constructed—that earlier conceptions of society and social formation are called into question. And what takes their place is a concept of the social as the product of a mobile set of relations of signification whose "fixings" of the social through the relations between the different discursive positionalities that they effect is always provisional, incomplete, and on the way to being unfixed again. The social, in this view, is similar to sociological accounts of the plane of social interaction; but it is also, in registering the effects of deconstruction, unlike such accounts in the inherent slipperiness that it builds into the sociosemiotic relations through which social interrelation is said to take place.

GOVERNMENTALITY AND THE TECHNICAL CONSTRUCTION OF THE SOCIAL

It is, I think, this aspect of Hall's position—or ones like it—that Nikolas Rose has in mind when he argues that "*the relations* that human beings have established with themselves," while "constructed and historical," are "not to be understood by locating them in some amorphous domain of culture" (Rose, 1998, p. 24). For Rose, an adequate account of subjectification—that is, after Foucault, of our relations to ourselves—is not available via a generalized mechanism in which, for example, the self is formed as an identity that is diacritically structured in relations of difference. Rather, what is needed, Rose argues, is an examination of the role played by historically specific techniques in organizing particular kinds of person and, equally important, shaping commensurately particular configurations of the social. Here is how he puts the matter:

> Subjectification is not to be understood by locating it in a universe of meaning or an interactional context of narratives, but in a complex of apparatuses, practices, machinations, and assemblages within which human being has been fabricated, and which presuppose and enjoin particular relations with ourselves. (Rose, 1998, p. 10)

The perspective informing these concerns derives from a different reading of Foucault's work. As we have seen, for Hall, the epistemological claims of the cultural turn are buttressed by aligning a Foucauldian concept of discourse with the role that language plays, in both structuralist and poststructuralist thought, in rerouting the constitution of the social through the systems of meaning that inform social actors' perceptions of themselves and of their relations to others. Rose, by contrast, interprets the Foucauldian concept of discourse in the light of the role it plays in Foucault's account of governmentality where it refers to the distinctive apparatuses and programs of governing which, working through particular regimes or games of truth, aim to involve us actively in the government, management, and development of our selves. Discursive practices, as Foucault puts it, do not simply generate discourses as representations:

They take shape in technical ensembles, in institutions, in behavioural schemes, in types of transmission and dissemination, in pedagogical forms that both impose and maintain them. (Foucault, 1997, p. 12)

Expertise plays a crucial role in this definition of discursive practices and, in contrast to pastoral power which had aimed to conduct individuals throughout their lives by placing them under the authority of a guide responsible for what they do and for what happens to them" (Foucault, 1997, p. 67), their relations to contemporary forms of government power. It is centrally involved in the mechanisms through which the truth claims of particular discourses are organized and connected to particular apparatuses and programs of government. As Rose puts the matter in connection with the role of expertise in psychology:

By expertise is meant the capacity of psychology to provide a corps of trained and credentialed persons claiming special competence in the administration of persons and interpersonal relations, and a body of techniques and procedures claiming to make possible the rational and human management of human resources in industry, the military, and social life more generally. (Rose, 1998, p. 11)

It is through the deployment of particular forms of expertise in particular relations of government that particular ways of speaking the truth and making it practical are connected to particular ways of acting on persons—and of inducing them to act upon themselves—which, in their turn, form particular ways of acting on the social. Persons, in this approach, are just as much constructed or made-up entities as they are in Hall's. There are, however, significant differences in the manner and form of their composition. These derive from Rose's contention that discourse, to become effective, must pass through the mediation of the technical. Eschewing the temptation of a general account of the ways in which experience is made meaningful—such as that of the role accorded discourse-as-language in the "cultural turn"—Rose opts instead for a more differentiating and particularising history of the various "devices of 'meaning production'—grids of visualisation, vocabularies, norms, and systems of judgement"—through which experience is produced and organized to yield historically specific forms of relating to others and acting on the self:

These intellectual techniques do not come ready made, but have to be invented, refined, and stabilised, to be disseminated and implanted in different ways in different practices—schools, families, streets, workplaces, courtrooms. If we use the term "subjectification" to designate all those heterogeneous processes and practices by means of which human beings come to relate to themselves and others as subjects of a certain type, then subjectification has its own history. And the history of subjectification is more practical, more technical, and less unified than sociological accounts allow. (p. 25)

What Rose means by "technical" here emerges more clearly when, a little later, he elaborates on Gaston Bachelard's notion of science as a "phenomeno-technology": that is, a means for acting on the objects it constructs through the instruments in which its theories are materialized. Viewed in this light, he argues, the reality of psychology has to be understood as neither cultural, in the sense of comprising a particular system of meanings, nor as discursive if this is understood as a synonym for representation. Its reality, instead, is technological in the sense that it comprises:

an ensemble of arts and skills entailing the linking of thoughts, affects, forces, artifacts, and techniques that do not simply manufacture and manipulate, but which, more fundamentally, order being, frame it, produce it, make it thinkable as a certain mode of existence that must be addressed in a particular way. (p. 54)

In the tradition of work that Rose represents, then, the makeup of the person emerges as what can perhaps best be described as artifactual: that is, as the contingent outcome of an ad hoc assemblage of particular technical forms and devices. It places the stress on the historical description of these forms and devices and the surfaces of their operation rather than on a general account of the role which language plays in forming identities in the midst of a linguistically patterned tissue of social differences. These differences of emphasis are, in turn, related to different conceptions of the social. For Hall, as we have seen, the social is constituted in and by the cultural representations through which relations of meaning and, as a part of these, differentiated social identities are formed. In Rose's approach, by contrast, the social has no such general characteristics but rather takes the form of a set of relations and conducts that have been problematized in particular ways with a view to being acted on with specific governmental aims in view. It is these relations and conducts—arising out of particular games of truth, the social apparatuses in which these are inscribed and the governmental programs to which they are attached—that constitute the surfaces to which particular forms of expertise are to be applied through the diversity of the technical forms they have devised for acting on and shaping conduct. It is thus that the social may mutate from one historical form to another: from its social welfarist forms in which the provision of social insurance and security stave off the threat to social solidarity arising from a conception of the social as immanently conflict-ridden to the communal

structure of the social which, for both Rose and Dean, characterizes contemporary forms of neoliberal government in the importance they accord
programs of cultural management in staving off the social instabilities that
might arise from colliding identities.

The advantage of Rose's formulations, then, is that they allow for a
greater degree of historical variability in their account of the processes of
subjectification and the construction of the social, and of the relations between the two. They also, as I argue later, allow the concepts of the social and
society to be usefully distinguished from one another. The implacability of his
opposition to accounts of the formation of persons that are couched in terms
of the role of culture is, however, somewhat puzzling. For there is no need to
theorize culture in the form, as Rose puts it, of an "amorphous domain." It,
too, can be approached as consisting of a range of particular forms of expertise arising out of distinctive regimes of truth that assume a range of practical
and technical forms through the variety of programs for regulating "the conduct of conduct" that they are, or have been, attached to. The expertise of the
literary critic within literature's distinctive regimes of truth;[3] of the art gallery
and museum curator; of the community arts worker; of broadcasters and
journalists; of censors and media regulators: these are all forms of expertise
subjected to particular forms of validation and translated into particular technical forms through their inscription within particular technical apparatuses.
It is, moreover, important that the realm of culture should be theorized in this
way if questions concerning the relations between culture and governmentality
are not to become—as they tend to do in Dean's formulations—a loose and
general description for governmental programs which work, through whatever means, to bring about a change in norms, beliefs, and values. This is
simply to call on the existing concept of culture and knit it into the perspective of governmentality without asking what differences that perspective might
enjoin for the ways in which the concept of culture and its relations to the
social should be approached. Instead, then, we need to ask: How does the
concept of culture need to be approached if it is to be effectively integrated
into an analytics of government? And what difference does it make to place
governmentality between culture, society, and the social?

CULTURE, GOVERNMENTALITY, SOCIETY, AND THE SOCIAL

I find myself, faced with the prospect of raising general questions of this kind
about the concept of culture, agreeing both with Raymond Williams, when he
said he wished he had never heard of the damned word, and with James
Clifford when he remarked that, although the concept is a deeply compromised
one, we cannot yet do without it.[4] Adam Kuper, in reviewing the recent trials
and tribulations of the term, offers a useful reminder of some of the more

conspicuous difficulties that have attended its extended anthropological usage (culture as a whole way of life) while also cautioning that it would be unwise to pin too much on the prospect of a more circumspect and exact usage. His own preference, he records, would be to "avoid the hyper-referential word altogether, and to talk more precisely of knowledge, or belief, or art, or technology, or tradition, or even ideology" (Kuper, 1999, p. x). While I shall not follow him in this, his discussion does provide a broader setting for considering the currency of the cultural turn by tracing the parallels between its recent formulations in cultural studies and the tradition of post-Parsonian U.S. anthropology represented by writers like Clifford Geertz and Marshall Sahlins. What becomes clear from his account are the respects in which, for all that they purport to overturn deterministic accounts of the relations between culture and society, both traditions are committed to a similar kind of theoretical enterprise to the extent that what both aim for remain general accounts of the culture/society relation that will apply to all cultures and all societies.

Victoria Bonnell and Lynn Hunt touch on my point here when they note that, with the cultural turn, culture and society in effect swapped places with regard to which of these was assigned the role of *explanandum* and which the role of *explanans*. "The social," as they put it, "began to lose its automatic explanatory power" once social categories "were to be imagined not as preceding consciousness or culture or language, but as depending upon them" (Bonnell & Hunt, 1999, p. 8–9). Of course, this reversal of emphasis is neither a trivial nor an inconsequential matter. However, it matters less, from the point of view of my concerns here, that the cultural turn inverts the order of explanatory priority between these two realms, than that what is still at issue is a theoretical procedure—a mode of reasoning—that aims to arrive at some general theoretical intermediation of the relations between culture and society. From this perspective, however much they might differ in other respects, all such accounts can be placed on a spectrum according to the relative degree of precedence they accord to culture or society or the ways in which they account for their coconstitutive intermingling.

One of the casualties of debates couched in these terms has been the implicit merging of the concepts of society and the social. The literature on governmentality has registered a distinction between these in accounting for the emergence of the social as a distinctive field of problematic behaviors that are to be defined, managed, and regulated in certain ways and for the parallel emergence of the object of society within sociological discourse as a means of observing and accounting for regularities of conduct in ways that would help render the social governable.[5] Instead, in passing over from *explanans* to *explanandum*, society, in the cultural turn, usually reappears on the other side in a different guise in being equated with a different sense of the social as the sociosemiotic ground on which the relations between social actors (individual and collective) take place.

How, from the perspective of an analytics of government, can questions concerning the relations between culture and the social be placed on a different footing? Let me advance four arguments which, while far from answering this question satisfactorily, might point out some directions for its further exploration.

The first is to suggest that the problem does not concern the decipherment of any general set of relations between two realms—as if, in the terms of Roger Chartier's formulation, it were a matter of in some way sorting out and reconciling the relations between practices and representations.[6] The issue, rather, concerns the relations between culture and the social within different strategies of rule. This means attending to the ways in which cultural techniques and technologies are expected to act on the social to bring about specific kinds of changes (or stabilities) in conduct where the social is interpreted as a specific constellation of problems—of attitude and behaviour—arising out of distinctive strategies of rule.

The second is to suggest that what is at issue here are historically specific relationships in which neither side of the equation is to be regarded as a constant. This is a necessary adjustment to the degree that the concept of governmentality specifies a historically distinctive form of rule whose development is tied up with the emergence of the notion of population as the object and end of government. There can, then, be no question, if the concepts of culture and governmentality are to be aligned with one another, of treating the former as an anthropological constant that has to be so defined as to allow its relationships to the social to be theorized in an invariant and uniform manner across all historical and contemporary societies. What has rather to be attended to are the ways in which there emerges, alongside the emergence of governmental forms of rule, new constellations of relations between what were hitherto diverse practices so as to allow them to be conceived and operationalised as an integrated ensemble brought under the heading of culture as, precisely, a new effective reality. This is to suggest that the analytical task is to account for what we might call "the cultural" developing, alongside the emergence of "the social," as a particular set of instruments—technologies—for acting on the latter with specific ends in view.

Let me offer two asides to amplify what such a perspective might mean.

First aside: We might think of the cultural in the terms suggested by Foucault's discussion of the relations between technologies of sign systems, technologies of power and technologies of the self. It would belong within, as Foucault characterizes them, those "technologies of sign systems, which permit us to use signs, meanings, symbols, or signification" (Foucault, 1988, p. 18), but it would not be coextensive with this domain. It would not, that is to say, comprise the totality of such technologies, only those which—from the perspective of an analytics of government—it would be intelligible to group together because of their mode of functioning in relation to, as Foucault defines them, specific "technologies of power, which determine the conduct of individuals and submit them to certain ends or domination, an objectivising of the subject" (p. 18) and through which their specific mode of relation to the social would be effected. As such, the cultural would operate through the mechanisms of (to cite Foucault one more time) "technologies of the self, which permit individuals to effect by their own means or with the help of others a certain number of operations on their own bodies and souls, thoughts, conduct, and way of being, so as to transform themselves in order to attain a certain state of happiness, purity, wisdom, perfection, or immortality" (p. 18). Again, the cultural would be no more coextensive with the totality of such technologies of the self than it would be with the totality of technologies of sign systems. Rather, for example, than subsuming the psy-complex into such a redefinition of the cultural, the logic of an analytics of government would require the identification of a "culture complex" operating alongside the psy-complex but by different means, deploying different forms of expertise, translating these into technical forms in different ways, bringing about specific ways of relating to the self whose characteristics relate to the specific kinds of self-management and development that are prompted by specific forms of governmental alignment of the relations between the culture complex and the social.

Second aside: A different historical perspective would be required to account for the emergence and development of the cultural and the culture complex in the senses sketched above. Different, but not entirely new: we already know, from a number of accounts, how the historical emergence of the concept of culture in the third of Williams's three senses ("the independent and abstract noun which describes the works and practices of intellectual and especially artistic activity") (Williams, 1976, p. 80) was made possible by the reassembly, in new institutional and discursive spaces, of practices which had hitherto been dissociated from each other and—as something which had also previously been lacking—by their conscription for governmental purposes in the reformatory tasks they were assigned in relation to the newly constructed field of "the social."[7] We also know that it was also over roughly the same period that the second of Williams's three senses of culture ("a particular way of life, whether of a people, a period, or a group") (p. 80) began to emerge, albeit that its full development was to await the twentieth century. It is customary to account for the emergence of this sense of culture as a democratic extension of its earlier restricted definition as, in essence, the elite arts. From the perspective of an analytics of government, however, this development presents itself in a different light: that is, as a result of the incorporation of ways of life within the orbit of government and, thereby, the production of a working interface between culture and the social. Roger Chartier, in considering how to think historically about cultural forms and practices, suggests that it is always necessary to specify the relations between two senses of the term 'culture':

> The first designates the works and the acts that, in a given society, concern aesthetic or intellectual judgement; the second aims at the ordinary practices—the ones "with no qualities"—that weave the fabric of daily relations and express the way a community lives and reflects its relations with the world and with the past. (Chartier, 1997, p. 21)

It is in relation to the first of these two senses of culture that, in the late eighteenth and nineteenth centuries, particular forms of expertise and regimes of truth were constituted and translated—to recall Rose's earlier formulation—into varied "devices of 'meaning production'—grids of visualization, vocabularies, norms, and systems of judgement" through which culture, in the second sense, was to be acted upon in accordance with varied aims and programs. And it was through the way in which culture in this second sense—the field of everyday conduct and behavior—was conceptualized that culture, in the first sense, was able to be brought into a productive connection with the social which, hitherto, it had lacked entirely. But, of course, when looked at in this way, these two different senses of culture and their relations to the social are not locked into unchanging relationships with each other. Rather, given that the ways in which they are aligned in relation to each other depend on their how they are inscribed within historically mutable governmental programs, then so changes in the latter are likely to reorder the relations between them. It is clear, for example, that the division between the two senses of culture that Chartier posits above has become progressively blurred as the relations between commercially produced forms of mass culture and ways of life have, from a governmental perspective, displaced the significance of aesthetically-grounded nineteenth-century programs of cultural reform.

But I must leave this aside aside! My point is that to place governmentality between culture and the social means that we have to think the history of relations between them in new terms. But this leads nicely into my third argument, for it is clear that, if we are to do this, it is necessary to subsume the concept of culture within that of discourse rather than, as the move which sustains the cultural turn, the other way round. For what I have suggested above, in following Rose's specification of the concept of discourse, is a way of treating culture as discourse which, rather than tending to merge the relations between culture and the social by construing the former as constitutive of the latter, retains a distinction between them. It does so by representing culture as a distinctive set of knowledges, expertise, techniques, and apparatuses which—through the roles they play as technologies of sign systems connected to technologies of power and working through the mechanisms of technologies of the self—act on, and are aligned in relation to, the social in distinctive ways.

And this brings me to my final argument—or, more accurately, counter-argument—which is to anticipate at least some of the objections that might be raised in relation to the line of reasoning briefly sketched above. For there is, admittedly, something awkward and unwieldy about the vocabulary of governmentality which—with all its references to expertise, the technical, apparatuses, and the like—sits ill at ease with the vocabularies of culture as these have been developed within the varied, but intersecting histories, of sociology, literary studies, anthropology and cultural studies. This often results in shadow debates which arise from translation difficulties more than anything else—as when, for example, post-Foucauldian uses of the notions of expertise and the technical are misaligned with the role that these play in Habermas's account of the relations between system and lifeworld.[8] The question I want to address here, however, is a more directly political one. For doesn't speaking of the relations between culture, government, and the social in the ways I have suggested rule out the prospect of a critical politics by making it impossible to offer any account of resistance and agency?

I have to say: no, I don't think so, not if we take the care to remember that, for Foucault, the concept of government is not to be confused with that of the state but refers to the much broader sphere of practices in which claims to particular forms of knowledge and authority are invoked in the context of attempts to direct "the conduct of conduct." And if we remember also to disentangle the questions of resistance and agency. Rose is especially helpful here. For if by resistance, he argues, "one means opposition to a particular regime for the conduct of one's conduct" (Rose, 1998, p. 35), this requires no general theory of agency of the kind that seeks to locate in individuals or particular social groups inherent capacities to strive for emancipation that exist "prior to and are in conflict with the demands of civilization and discipline" (p. 35). Why not? Simply because those demands do not have a unified and coherent form emanating from some single organizing center of power. We live our lives, Rose argues, in constant movement across different practices that seek to mould and form us in different ways, and it is the contradictory effects that this generates that give rise to specific forms of agency—not agency in general—as we take issue with, say, an economic system that generates inequalities in the light of those practices (humanistic or religious) which endow us with a sense of the equal worth and dignity of all human beings. Or, as an example more pertinent to my theme, it is surely clear that if the promotion of cultural diversity now stands as one of the most pressing challenges for contemporary cultural policies, this is because of the extent to which the homogenizing strategies of nationalist cultural policies have been questioned by the representatives of both indigenous and diasporic formations—not because of some general capacity for resistance that indigenous and diasporic peoples have and others do not, but because of the different knowledges, traditions, authorities, technologies, and temporal and spatial coordinates that are involved in the production of indigenous and diasporic identities and persona. If we look at the matter in this way, it just might prove possible to escape from those political topographies that Foucault took issue with, but which have proved so resilient, which polarize the political field between the power of government descending from above and that of resistance emerging from below. We might consider, instead, the more complex intersections between different ways of making up persons and regulating the relations between them which, while unequal in terms of their social weight and influence, operate through mechanisms which are broadly similar.

Notes

1. Yet the Althusserian construction placed on these questions did register a significant advance on earlier Marxist formulations in allowing a greater degree of flexibility and open-endedness regarding the relations that might obtain between economic, social, political, and cultural or ideological practices in any particular moment. The matrix role of determination that was assigned the economy in the context of this structural theory of causation meant that the relative importance attributed to these different forms of practice could be allowed to vary from one set of historical circumstances to another (Althusser & Balibar, 1970). Althusserian formulations also lent a greater degree of specificity to the argument that cultural and ideological practices were characterized by distinctive properties that were peculiar to them.

2. See, for examples, Hall (1986) and Hall (1996).

3. See, for an earlier discussion of this, Chapter 10 of Bennett (1990).

4. See Kuper (1999, pp. 1 and 212).

5. I draw here on the formulations in Dean (1999) and Rose (1999).

6. See Chartier (1988): my reference here is to both the title of the book and the dominant theoretical refrain that runs through it.

7. The influential essay by R. G. Saisselin (1970) is especially suggestive in this respect. I have briefly discussed its implications elsewhere: see Chapter 5 of Bennett (1998).

8. This is a significant flaw in Jim McGuigan's (1996) assessment of the relations between the literature on governmentality and the Habermasian tradition. See, for a more detailed discussion of this, Bennett (2000).

References

Althusser, L., & Balibar, E. (1970). *Reading capital.* London: New Left Books.

Bennett, T. (1990). *Outside literature.* London: Routledge.

Bennett, T. (1998). *Culture: A reformer's science.* Sydney: Allen and Unwin, London: Sage.

Bennett, T. (2000). *Intellectuals, culture, policy: The technical, the practical and the critical.* Pavis Papers in Social and Cultural Research, 2. Milton Keynes, UK: Open University.

Bonnell, V. E., & Hunt, L. (Eds.) (1999). *Beyond the cultural turn: New directions in the study of society and culture.* Berkeley, CA and Los Angeles, CA: University of California Press.

Chartier, R. (1997). *On the edge of the cliff: History, language, and practices.* Baltimore: Johns Hopkins University Press.

Chartier, R. (1988). *Cultural history: Between practices and representations.* Cambridge, UK: Polity Press.

Dean, M. (1999). *Governmentality: Power and rule in modern society.* London: Sage.

Foucault, M. (1997). *Ethics: The essential works, Vol. 1* (Ed. Paul Rabinow). London: Allen Lane.

Foucault, M. (1988). Technologies of the self. In L. H. Martin, H. Gutman, & P. H. Hutton (Eds.), *Technologies of the self: A seminar with Michel Foucault.* London: Tavistock.

Hall, S. (1986). On postmodernism and articulation: An interview with Stuart Hall. *Journal of Communication Inquiry,* 10(2), pp. 45–46.

Hall, S. (1996). Who needs identity? In S. Hall & P. du Gay (Eds.), *Questions of cultural identity.* London: Sage. pp. 1–17.

Hall, S. (1997). The centrality of culture: Notes on the cultural revolutions of our time. In K. Thompson (Ed.) *Media and cultural regulation.* London: Sage.

Kuper, A. (1999). *Culture: The anthropologists' account.* Cambridge, MA: Harvard University Press.

McGuigan, J. (1996). *Culture and the public sphere.* London: Routledge.

Rose, N. (1998). *Inventing ourselves: Psychology, power and personhood.* Cambridge, UK: Cambridge University Press.

Rose, N. (1999). *Powers of freedom: Reframing political thought.* Cambridge, UK: Cambridge University Press.

Saisselin, R. G. (1970). The transformation of art into culture: From Pascal to Diderot. *Studies in Voltaire and the eighteenth century,* vol. LXX.

Williams, R. (1963). *Culture and society, 1780–1950.* London: Chatto and Windus.

Williams, R. (1976). *Keywords: A vocabulary of culture and society.* London: Fontana/ Croom Helm.

Williams, R. (1977) *Marxism and literature.* Oxford, UK: Oxford University Press.

Part I

Knowledge, Theory, Expertise

Chapter 4

Making Politics Reasonable

Conspiracism, Subjectification, and Governing through Styles of Thought

Jack Z. Bratich

We must free ourselves from the sacralization of the social as the only reality and stop regarding as superfluous something so essential in human life and in human relations as thought. Thought exists independently of systems and structures of discourse. It is something that is often hidden, but which animates everyday behavior. There is always a little thought even in the most stupid institutions; there is always thought even in silent habits.

—Michel Foucault, "Practicing Criticism"

As evidenced in this epigraph, assessing how the present is governed entails more than a sociological description of various mechanisms, techniques, and institutions of governance, that is, more than the "actually existing" (Gordon, 1991, p. 8). According to Nikolas Rose (1999), studies of governmentality "entail a work of thought on the present that is itself, inescapably, a work of thought" (p. 58). A scandalous statement for proponents of a kind of materialism that would relegate thought to the thin atmosphere of ideology and phenomenological consciousness, if not idealism. But in order to proceed on the effectivity of these kinds of studies, according to Rose,

> it is necessary to discard the last vestiges of those nineteenth-century philosophical disputes between materialism and idealism . . . they have done much to constrain our ways of understanding the materiality of ideas, and to recognize the embeddedness of thought in the most prosaic aspects of social and economic life." (1999, p. 58).

That is, thought cannot merely be reduced to the diluted and auxiliary domain of ideological representation, or even to discourse. Foucault is delineating a different status for thought-practices, one that has a more productive and active force to it, not just the reactive force almost always accorded to "ideology" given the idealism/materialism binary. As Gilles Deleuze stated it when interviewed about Foucault's work, "thinking's a capacity, a capacity to set forces in play . . . [where forces mean] acting upon actions. . . . That's thought as strategy" (1986, p. 95).

Foucault often described his own work as an "ontology of the present" which includes the "different ways of thinking about who we are" (Dean, 1996, p. 210). According to Mitchell Dean (1996), an ontology of the present "seeks to define the conditions in which we are led to problematize what we are, what we can and should do, and the world in which we find ourselves" (p. 225). It asks, "how is reason exercised?" (Rabinow, 1997, xxiv). In other words, an ontology of the present requires thought on thought.

This conception of thought has very practical, concrete effects for political action, since "as soon as one can no longer think things as one formerly thought them, transformation becomes both very urgent, very difficult, and quite possible" (Foucault, 1988b, p. 155). Or, as Rose (1999) puts it, "showing the role of thought in holding [contingent arrangements] together . . . also show[s] that thought has a part to play in contesting them" (p. 59). More than just being a condition for change, thought is also imperative to prevent a return or doubling of the institutions and practices targeted for transformation. Without "the work of thought upon itself . . . whatever the project of reform, we know that it will be swamped, digested by modes of behavior and institutions that will always be the same" (Foucault, 1988b, p. 156).[1]

Acknowledging the density and importance of thought does not situate it as the only or even primary mechanism of coordination in governmental cultural strategies. Nor is it to erase the crucial role of social, political, and economic determinations in shaping the forms of experience characteristic of this conjuncture (more on this later). And it is certainly not a call (as is so often the case of critical thinkers) for "more thought" as an antidote to the "unthinking" practices of everyday life. This quantification of thought ignores the way liberal governing has predicated itself on this activity. Rather, it is to argue that thought, because it has been made governmental under liberalism, is an important point of contestation.

As we shall see, liberal arts of governing have persisted in large measure due to an ethos of self-critique, to the harnessing and deployment of thought as a political rationality and a strategic process of subjectification. The task, then, is to analyze the ways thought has been governmentalized, as a way of making this rationality contingent, thus opening up a thinking-otherwise (and a becoming-free-otherwise). And, as I will argue later, this contingency is not just due to its historicity; it is located in the ambivalence of the very practice of governance that requires thought in order to persevere.

With this in mind, I will first examine how Foucault defines thought as a methodological issue, in terms of its relation to practice, action, and ideas, in order to give thought its own specificity. Second, I will explore how, following the Enlightenment ethos of self-criticism, thought is taken up by liberal governance. In the third section, I take up Judith Butler's account of the power/subjectification dynamic as a "trope of the turn" in order to complicate the way thought can be turned on itself. Finally, I will use the recent problematizations of conspiracy theories in American political thought as an example of how, in advanced liberalism, thought is still required to be folded as a target of modification. Overall, the goal of this essay is to show the importance of thought in understanding how the present is governed—specifically the liberal styles of thought that organizes consent and dissent.

How are the contemporary problematizations of "conspiracism" attempts to secure consent (to a regime of truth) and modify dissent? How do neoliberal political rationalities attempt to organize styles of thought in the name of freedom? In the case of conspiracy theories (problematized as "the paranoid style," or "conspiracism") different styles of thought are marked, I argue, by the degree of *skepticism* that composes them. The very skepticism that defines liberal political rationality also marks its vulnerability when it comes to "paranoid" styles of thought. This continuing controversy over conspiracy theories foregrounds the implications of a "reasonable politics" in thought and action.

THOUGHT AND PRACTICE: QUESTIONS OF METHOD

When assessing the role of thought in governance, one finds little that is coherently stated in Foucault's writings (mostly because there is very little on governmentality in general).[2] In Foucault's other writings, however, thought as an ethos emerges as a crucial component in assessing conduct in general. The history of thought is

> distinct both from the history of ideas (by which I mean the analysis of systems of representation) and from the history of mentalities (by which I mean the analysis of attitudes and types of action). . . . Thought is not what inhabits a certain conduct and gives it its meaning; rather, it is what allows one to step back from this way of acting or reacting, to present it to oneself as an object of thought and to question it as to its meaning, conditions, and its goals. Thought is freedom in relation to what one does, the motion by which one detaches oneself from it, establishes it as an object, and reflects on it as a problem. (Foucault, 1997b, p. 117)

Reflection, examination, and objectification: these are neither ideas nor "material" activities (in the traditional sense) but practices, movements, techniques, or figures. It is this characteristic of thought, as a turn, a fold, a motion, that I wish to emphasize in this essay.

In the introduction to *The Use of Pleasure*, Foucault (1985) defines a history of thought as "a matter of analyzing, not behaviors or ideas, nor societies and their 'ideologies,' but the *problematizations* through which being offers itself to be, necessarily, thought—and the *practices* on the basis of which these problematizations are formed" (p. 11). Far from being a secondary, auxiliary level of legitimation,

> Thought is understood as the very form of action—as action insofar as it implies the play of true and false, the acceptance or refusal of rules, the relation to oneself and others. The study of forms of experience can thus proceed from an analysis of "practices"—discursive or not—as long as one qualifies that word to mean the different systems of action *insofar* as they are inhabited by thought. (Foucault, 1997c, p. 201)

For practices to *be*, they must pass through thought (as objects of problematization). Thought is necessary, but not in the sense of required maintenance or reproduction. It is a condition of possibility for those experiences.[3]

And what is this relationship between thought and practice? As mentioned above, thought's movement is not one that infuses and resides in practices to give them meaning. Thought is not necessarily coherent or systematic: as a turn (to itself, reflexivity) it introduces a difference, a detachment. It inhabits as interruption, as that which allows a practice to transform itself. It is that carving out which allows the practices to "take place" at all: "a practice of freedom that could have taken (or could take in the future) a different form" (Rabinow, 1997, p. xxxvi). Thought infuses practices as an ethos of self-reflection, a task that in its performance requires a provisional yet persistent dislodging, which is the condition for (and enactment of) freedom and alterity.

As I will discuss later, this opening finds its closure in the technologized form of political rationality, giving liberalism its effective strategy of governing. However, in keeping this closure in mind for later, I would also like to mention Foucault's (1997d) assessment of practices "simultaneously as a technological type of rationality and as strategic games of liberties" (p. 319). This twofold composition will become crucial in examining liberal deployments of thought, as we cannot just emphasize the first component of practices (thought as unity, presence, positivity) but must also take into account the rupture, distance, difference introduced by this ethos.[4]

Before moving to liberal governance's deployment of thought-as-ethos, it is necessary to mention that Foucault examines this concept of thought (as the motion of self-presentation, of a turning upon itself) as an Enlightenment phenomenon. In "What Is Enlightenment?" Foucault (1997d) reads Kant as introducing this "turn" as an ethos, a form of reflective relation in which the present is presented as an object of thought. The Enlightenment is "neither a world era to which one belongs, nor an event whose signs are perceived, nor the dawning of an accomplishment . . . [it is] an 'exit,' a 'way out' " (p. 305). As "a modification of the preexisting relation linking will, authority, and the use of reason," the Enlightenment is "a task and an obligation" (p. 305). This task is a reflection on the present as "difference," a "permanent reactivation of an attitude . . . a permanent critique of our historical era" (pp. 309, 312). That is to say, it is an ethos not constrained to its embeddedness in an age.

Foucault alters the inflection of this ethos; he turns this turn. Rather than a Kantian transcendental critique of the necessary limitations of any given structure, Foucault defines the ethos as "a practical critique that takes the form of a possible crossing-over" (1997d, p. 315). With this redefinition, "Foucault hopes to invent a mode of subjectivation in which this ethos would be a practice of thought formed in direct contact with social and political realities" (Rabinow, 1997, p. xxxi). Making Kant's philosophical musings on the present political would make an ontology of present "at one and the same time the historical analysis of the limits imposed on us and an experiment with the possibility of going beyond them " (Foucault, 1997d, p. 319; Rabinow, 1997, p. xxxii). The notion of "ontology of the present" for Foucault thus contains both impulses.

Making the Enlightenment ethos a political practice is an "experimental" task, in the sense that thought puts itself to the "test of reality . . . both to grasp the points where change is possible and desirable, and to determine the precise form this change should take" (p. 316). With this begins "the undefined work of freedom" (p. 316). The Enlightenment ethos is thus not a general and universal a priori logic; as an experimental task it is contingent, reactivated, and thus incomplete. Foucault defines these projects as "partial and local" tests, but these tasks do not end as particular actions, in "disorder and contingency" (pp. 316-317). The Enlightenment ethos has "its generality, its systematicity, its homogeneity, and its stakes" (p. 317).[5] The Enlightenment turn of thought upon itself is thus necessary to understand the present (as the present is defined by it), but is also the exit from it, the crossing over from it. This practice of thought becomes more focussed in liberal styles of governing, which I assess in the following section.

LIBERAL GOVERNING AND THOUGHT

Foucault defines liberal forms of governing, in some measure, by this Enlightenment ethos. Liberalism is not a theory or an ideology, but "a practice . . .

regulating itself by means of a sustained reflection" (Foucault, 1997a, p. 74). Its principle of reflection is that "one always governs too much, or, at any rate, one always must *suspect* that one governs too much. Governmentality should not be exercised without a 'critique' " (p. 74). Liberalism is "a tool for criticizing reality," and "a form of critical reflection on governmental practice" (pp. 75, 77). As Gordon Burchell (1991) argues, it is a "constant reflection on and criticism of what is. Its internal regulative principle is seen as the need to maintain a suspicious vigilance over government so as to check its permanent tendency to exceed its brief in relation to what determines both its necessity and limits—society" (p. 143).

A mode of governing defined around self-reflection, liberalism takes its own activity and its limits as objects of concern.[6] Why must one govern at all? Unlike the previous *raison d'etat* liberalism begins not with the State (and its principle of self-maximization) but with society (with its own particularity, density, dynamics and laws) which puts governing's limits in question. Liberalism has an ingenious suppleness because of this, as it allows for a self-modification through perpetual self-problematization. This self-reflective criticism and skepticism regarding the limits of governing will be crucial in my later analysis of the problematizations of the paranoid thought-style.

For my purposes here, liberalism's unique art of governing consists in this: it takes this Enlightenment ethos, the turn, into itself as its form of rule. Actions and conduct are not allowed to persist as a given, but are made uncertain and questionable, allowing "one to step back from this way of acting or reacting, to present it to oneself as an object of thought and to question it as to its meaning, conditions, and its goals" (Foucault, 1997b, p. 117). The "conduct of conduct" means problematizing actions incessantly as a technique of governing cautiously, and thus effectively.[7] Liberalism technologizes thought and freedom as a rationality of governing.[8]

Technologizing Freedom: Rationality and Games of Truth

And how does it do so? At least since John Locke, governmentalized freedom has been linked to the "use of Reason" (Hindess, 1996, p. 129). Liberalism is concerned to ensure that people's public and private behavior will be conducted according to appropriate standards of civility, reason, and orderliness, outside of State regulation. In this formulation, developing "appropriate habits of thought and behavior" is crucial to liberalism's "indirect regulation" (pp. 129–130). The liberal political subject would become responsible through reasoning, even through responsible reasoning. And via this self-reflexive subjectification, the political actor locates its source and parameters for freedom. To perform a style of reasoning as a guide to free thought is already an attachment to its authority.[9]

This particular arrangement of freedom and rationality entails a certain relation to the prevailing regime of truth.[10] Modern regimes "for the conduct of conduct that have taken shape in the West, and those strategies that contest them, are ineluctably drawn to rationalize themselves according to a value of truth" (Rose, 1999, p. 24). What are the games of truth by which individuals come to recognize themselves as rational political beings, and seek to regulate the conduct of others and self accordingly? How do games of truth participate in the self-reflection that constitutes the citizen-subject, and organize political possibilities (Miller, 1998)? And this is where the issue of a "general politics of truth" reemerges, as particular courses of action can be taken only through a general regime of truth, through political rationalities that preexist particular programs, through problematizations that render reality thinkable in a certain way.[11]

Conduct is much more than the visible action or movement of bodies and populations. Rather, conduct can only take shape through "the forms and modalities of the relation to self by which the individual constitutes and recognizes himself *qua* subject" and affirms itself as such when it performs that conduct[12] (Foucault, 1985, p. 6). Conducting oneself as a citizen is thus not simply a behavioral matter; it requires an active and persistent self-problematization, one that is operable only through a certain style of thought, a relationship between truth and reason.

Strategies of Freedom: Games of Truth

So far, I have focused on the way liberalism's technologies of freedom and the subject fold thought upon itself in a manner consistent with the general liberal principle of self-reflection as efficient governing. In this regard, the technologized turn links programs, policies, and institutions through a rationality, giving liberalism a consistency and generality across its loose assemblage of instances. However, folding thought upon itself is more than a technology: It is also an ethos, a task, and as such thought cannot be fully fixed into a rational form.

Governmentality, like practices in general described earlier, has two components: "on the one hand, rational forms, technical procedures, instrumentations through which to operate, and, on the other, strategic games that subject the power relations they are supposed to guarantee to instability and reversal" (Foucault, 1997c, p. 203). Although I have so far stressed the former component (the technologization/instrumentalization of thought), both aspects need to be addressed vis-à-vis thought as an ethos.[13]

As a task of permanent criticism, thought is deployed as an injunction to reactivate "a stylized relation to the real" (Foucault, 1997d, p. 309). Thought is not only "already existing" (i.e., as a coherent structure coextensive with governing): it has to be reiterated. As a strategic *task*, then, it cannot be frozen into a "dominant mode of experience" nor codified by policies, institutions, and programs, since the *ethos* of thought works as an exit, a way out, a crossing-over.

Thus it is not enough to describe the positive techniques and rationalities of governing-through-thought, even to make them contingent (the historicist project). To reduce thought to its positive deployment is to give in to liberalism's own fantasy of its overwhelming effectiveness. Thought is folded into positive mechanisms of rule (liberalism's ingenuity), but this is only the first, technical component of governing. Thought is also a necessary aspect of the second component discussed above: a subjectification deployed as *strategy*, necessary for autonomization, for governing-at-a-distance. It is in this sense that I would elaborate Gilles Deleuze's (1986) description of Foucault's later works as "the discovery of thought as a 'process of subjectification'" (p. 95).

Thought's inexhaustibility makes it part of the strategic games of liberty which, I argue, provide the moment of reversibility that allows for the possibility of transforming those conditions. It is caught up in a "relationship between power relations and confrontation strategies" in which "each constitutes for the other a kind of permanent limit, a point of possible reversal" (Foucault, 1982, p. 225). The "strategy of struggle" provides "points of insubordination," the condition for an ungovernable freedom, a freedom otherwise-than-rationality, of the yet-to-come (p. 225).

To summarize: liberal governing requires the ethos of thought. Governing the present means conceiving it (in both senses of the term), as the present does not present itself. Reflection is a necessary condition of practices, of the Enlightenment, of liberalism yet is also the moment of liberty from these. Enfolded into a style of governing, this ethos marks the generalizability of local technologies of subjectification, but it also inscribes their possible unworking. Governing through this technologized, rationalized turn makes objects and subjects of governing intelligible, but it also embodies a strategic deployment of difference, of the moment of exit. It can harness this ethos, but never contain it. Liberal governance is a *persistent* reactivation of a turn at a distance, allowing for a liberal rationality of freedom but also an activation of other turns. With this, we can begin to locate a practical contingency (not just historical, but formal and strategic) in liberalism's style of governance. But to make this claim of contingency or vulnerability even stronger, I would like to shift to Judith Butler's description of the power/subjectification dynamic as a "turn."

Thought as a Turn: Ambivalence and Freedom

In *The Psychic Life of Power: Theories in Subjection*, Judith Butler (1997) argues, following Foucault, that while power at first appears external to the subject, "pressing the subject into subordination," it is indeed the case that the subject's self-constitution is already marked by power turning on *itself* (pp. 3, 6). And it is this "figure of the turn" that Butler demarcates and follows in her text. It is a turn without a subject-who-turns; rather "the turn appears to function as a tropological inauguration of the subject, a founding moment whose ontological status remains permanently uncertain" (pp. 3–4). And since "trope" itself is translated as "turn," what is important is that "the trope of the turn both indicates and exemplifies the tropological status of the gesture" (p. 4). A trope is never fully instantiated or fixed in place. It requires an active reinstigation, which never guarantees that it will perform properly. That is to say, the figure of the turn is itself a turn, and thus can be turned differently. This is the moment of necessary instability, never guaranteed to return as designed.

This is important to Butler's analysis for a number of reasons. For one thing, it allows for a discussion of "passionate attachments" to subjectification, opening up questions of the "psychic form" power and subjectification take (pp. 3, 6–10). How do we understand "not merely the disciplinary production of the subject, but a disciplinary cultivation of *an attachment to subjection?*" (p. 102). Certain attachments and investments precede and condition the formation of subjects.[14]

In addition, the trope of the turn takes subjectification beyond the mechanical version of reproduction or maintenance of an external power. The processes of subjectification are marked by a constitutive ambivalence. On one hand, any act of the subject depends upon the technology of power that produced the subject, as power "*enacts* that subject into being" (p. 13). This is the pessimistic part of the story: "The agency of the subject appears to be an effect of its subordination" (p. 12). But this is not the end of the story, as it would make power external to, and only expanded by, the subject. As Butler argues,

> Assuming power is not a straightforward task of taking power from one place, transferring it intact, and then and there making it one's own; the act of appropriation may involve an alteration of power such that the power assumed or appropriated works against the power that made that assumption possible. (1997, p. 13)

Thus the power *presupposed* (as that which the subject depends upon for its very existence) may not be the same as the power *reinstated*. For power to be effective it must dissimulate itself as the subject's free capacity: "A significant and potentially enabling reversal occurs when power shifts from its status as a condition of agency to the subject's 'own' agency (constituting an appearance of power in which the subject appears as the condition of its 'own' power)" (p. 12). A subject's activity exceeds the power by which it is enabled, as power must split itself in the turn to itself, producing an excessive, and potentially ungovernable, power. This is the ambivalence at the heart of subjectification, which sets up the subject "in a relation of contingency and reversal to the power that makes it possible" (p. 15).

On one hand, this shift in power's character is contingent (in the form it takes), but on the other, its dissimulation is *necessary* for it to persist. "If conditions of power are to persist, they must be reiterated; the subject is precisely the site of such reiteration, a repetition that is never merely mechanical" (p. 16). Power has a need for this repetition, what we might call a moment of power's own dependency and unfreedom. The conditions of the subject's existence have "exigencies of their renewal," marking a "temporally based vulnerability" (p. 12). Power "turns against itself in the course of that reiteration" and "shows these conditions to be, not static structures, but temporalized—active and productive" (pp. 12, 16). From this logical assessment Butler asks the pivotal question, "How might we think resistance within the terms of reiteration?" (p. 12).

I have gone through this exegesis of Butler's insights into the processes of subjectification because I want to argue that this trope or figure of the "turn" is endemic to thought under liberal technologies and strategies of governing. As I have already shown above, liberalism's defining characteristic (perhaps inherited from the Enlightenment ethos) is precisely this turn as permanent self-critique, and a related process of subjectification in which the freedom of the political subject is paramount. That is to say, liberal governing requires a subject-becoming-free-agent in order to govern effectively.

However, given Butler's assessment of the ambivalence and attachment of any subjectification, I want to reemphasize the claim that critique-as-ethos cannot be contained by any technology of subjectification. Taking thought as an ethos into liberal governance is not mere incorporation or instrumentalization of thought (for the ends of better government). Instead, as part of a strategy of games of liberty, thought is deployed as a turn that operates ambivalently. In fact, there are different kind of turns (what I am calling styles of thought) which compose the strategic field of capacities and the processes of subjectification.

For one thing, there is a break in power when it produces the liberal subject (that is to say, in its deployment of technologies of subjectification). This ethos produces conditions of reversibility as it must alter itself in order to become the subject's "own" ethos, its "own" thought, its "own" freedom. Governing occurs as power before subjectification, but also necessarily *through* it, thus producing a different power (self-government). Because power transforms itself into its opposite (freedom) in order to persist, it is not guaranteed to remain as it is. [15]

And it is precisely the fact that it governs through freedom that gives liberalism its peculiar reversibility. Governing through freedom does not and cannot contain freedom; it requires freedom and the capacities of its subjects to perform effectively. It unleashes freedom, but as a formula of rule. Liberal governing works on and through capacities, folding them upon themselves through rational self-regulation. According to Paul Patton (1998), permanent self-criticism "presupposes the existence of possible subjects of such activity" which can then "be led to oppose forms of domination which prevent such activity" (p. 72). In other words, while liberal styles of governing cultivate and harness capacities to act, these capacities can never be fully domesticated by the technologies that require them in governing through freedom. Similarly, styles of thought may be technologized but never fully captured, because liberal political rationality requires styles of thought to operate "autonomously."

The ambivalence in liberalism is located not only in a splitting in the power of governing, but also in liberalism's very need to reiterate itself. Its particular exigencies of renewal include the need to govern without a center, "at a distance." As a persistent self-critique, as an incessant task, as perpetual self-problematization, the liberal art of governing obviously needs to instigate this ethos again and again. This obligation is the hallmark of liberalism's success, but also inscribes its instability. It is indicative of liberalism's flexibility; its "polymorphism and its recurrences" (Foucault, 1997a, p. 75), but also its vulnerability; its persistence, and its possible demise.

This practical vulnerability, especially because it takes the form of subjectified freedom, can produce conditions of reversibility. Paraphrasing Butler (1997), under what conditions does a technology or political rationality monopolize the terms of freedom? Is this a theological fantasy of liberalism (p. 130)? This is also a question of consent as attachment. What kind of being does a particular arrangement of freedom and rationality promise? Which freedom is this, articulated as it is to being-as-identity? As Butler notes, new passionate attachments can form, ones which do not look to the technologies and their authority for freedom (pp. 129–131). Capacities, *acting in their own name* (the freedom enabled by liberal technologies) can be mobilized in new ways, turning even against their own conditions (Patton, 1998, pp. 69–71).

Such new mobilizations would institute a turn away from the lure of "being free" promised by the particular political rationalities composing our time. It would entail turning differently, against the turn that would secure an articulation between freedom, rationality, and identity. It would mean deploying a different set of passionate attachments, even to freedom; for example, one not predicated on an investment in a particular regime of truth and its authority. As Butler argues, reading Giorgio Agamben, it is possible to intensify "the potentiality that remains unexhausted by any particular interpellation" (p. 131).[16]

It is this becoming-otherwise, this futurity announced in the strategic vulnerability of liberal governing, that I wish to explore more concretely in the next section. As we shall see, the scholarly critiques, or problematizations, of conspiracy theories as "styles of thought" promote liberal technologies of subjectification (fusing freedom, truth, and rationality). But in doing so, these problematizations mark a constitutive ambivalence in the liberal art of governing.[17] These reflections instigate a certain excess of turning, in which turning itself cannot be contained in the rationality that seeks to instrumentalize it. In trying to contain certain styles as "paranoid," these official turns/styles unleash a skepticism against dissent that is not guaranteed to remain *liberalism's* skepticism.

CONSPIRACISM, POLITICAL PARANOIA, AND STYLES OF THOUGHT

Problematizations

From the mid-1990s until the present, the United States has seen an explosion of commentaries on the "flourishing" of conspiracy theories in the political landscape.[18] Pundits from a variety of academic disciplines have chimed in to this discussion. While there are many "problematizations" of the conspiracy theory phenomenon, I will focus here on those that have most systematically and doggedly defined conspiracy theories as a political "problem" (in the common sense of being a threat).[19] These texts comprise what Keith Goshorn (2000) calls the recent "anti-conspiracy discourse."

These texts are a series of meditations that link political forces to styles of thought. In these works, we can see an intertwining of two themes or problems: on the one hand, a pathological style of thought (outside the boundaries circumscribed by the regime of truth), and on the other hand, an extremism in political activity (beyond the pale or at the fringes of normal political discourse). Through a transposition of a clinical term to the field of politics, "paranoia" and "extremism" are conceptually fused into a new intelligible object: "the paranoid style," or the more recent terms "political paranoia" and "conspiracism."[20] Once this object is given comprehensibility, pronouncements are made upon the possible effects of this phenomenon, and remedies are prescribed. By providing "commonsense" about political paranoia as a descriptive term, these experts render the political field intelligible "in such a way that it is amenable to political programming" (Rose, 1996, p. 42).[21]

Before delving into the details of how they problematize "the paranoid style," I want to mention briefly that these texts tend to open their meditations with a description of their social contexts and conditions. These reflections appear to respond to conjunctural moments of political destabilization, ones with peculiar emphases on populism and the confusion of political positions.

Beginning with Richard Hofstadter (1967), the paranoid style is intimately linked with populism.[22] This classic essay, a version of which was published soon after the assassination of John F. Kennedy and soon before the resultant Warren Commission Report, accounted for the then-booming popularity of conspiracy theories by tracing them back through American history. Dating at least back to the American Revolution, these irrational thoughts accompanied populist grumblings, even leading to paranoid social behavioral patterns, such as the formation of the Anti-Masonic Party in the early 1800s (pp. 14–19). For Hofstadter, the Cold War 1960s was another moment when the paranoid style was emerging. But he found something peculiar to that historical conjuncture: this is a "new phenomenon; the threat is not foreign, but home-grown" (p. 24). Unlike much of the history of American domestic dissent-management in the twentieth century, or as Michael Rogin (1987) calls them "countersubversive practices against dissent," the paranoid style does not require a "foreign" element which is targeted as the real enemy (p. 4). In the case of the paranoid style, no outside force is culpable; it is domestic and popular.[23] Once the danger is located within the borders of the national political identity, a new framework is required to render this danger intelligible.

The more recent problematizations of the paranoid style also articulate it to populism, but with new inflections. Conspiracism is linked to new motivations (hate speech, resentful backlashes), new targets (globalization) and new kinds of groups (for example, African Americans who believe that AIDS and the crack epidemic are genocidal strategies against them, and militia organizations—usually coded as white and male—who fear a New World Order enough to take up arms in defense). The paranoid style's re-emergence is also notable for its newfound visibility in popular culture (Hollywood films, TV shows, magazines, websites, books) (Pipes, 1997, p. 17; Knight, 2001). But the predominant indicator in these works of political and cultural destabilization tends to be the fact that conspiracy theories permeate both the Left and the Right. Often in the earlier studies (like Hofstadter, 1967; Lipset and Raab, 1970; and Overstreet & Overstreet, 1964), political paranoia is deemed to be primarily a right-wing phenomenon, while the left is merely susceptible to it. However, the more recent analyses of both political paranoia and extremism stress this bipolar tendency (perhaps most famously summed up in Michael Kelly's [1995] term, "Fusion Paranoia," chronicled in George & Wilcox, 1996, and most systematically analyzed by Pipes, 1997, pp. 154–170).[24]

But what I would point out here is that the fundamental binary that organizes these articulations is not left/right, but center/fringes. Though the two terminal points of the political spectrum structure the official texts, the problem is not located in the content of any conspiracy theory's political affiliation. Rather, the concern is over the moment when elements detach from the mainstream and flee to the extreme, and then return to seduce and infiltrate that mainstream. The anxiety is over widespread "popular confusion," the moment when the political spectrum is troubled, and needs to be re-established as a legitimate categorizing system for political possibilities

(Carpenter, 1964, p. 1). In general, this destabilized scenario, with its multi-plicity of political forces and alliances, new technologies of communication (the Web is often cited as a culprit), and new threats to authority can be defined as a moment of disorderly political populism. This unruly force is then met by the problematizers with a reinvigoration of technologies of governing. I want to now proceed to one of these technologies, a mode of subjectification in which a rational style of thought is advocated.

Problematizing a Style of Thought

As described above, political paranoia does not refer to the particular content of the knowledge claims offered up in dissenting knowledges. It is a "paranoid *style*" after all, which, according to Richard Hofstatder (1967), is "not about the truth or falsity of the content" of the knowledge but rather refers to the "manner of belief and expression" of the ideas (p. 5).[25] It is also not just about a belief in a conspiracy theory, but a worldview, "conspiracism" (Pipes, 1997, p. 20). The distinction from ordinary political beliefs is not in "the absence of facts, but the leap of imagination at critical points" (Hofstatder, p. 37). It is a "style of mind, marked by heated *exaggeration*, suspiciousness, and con-spiratorial fantasy" (p. 3). It does not refer to particular beliefs, as "all ideas could potentially be espoused in 'the paranoid style,' it's just that certain ones only appear there" (p. 5f). Thus, the paranoid style is marked as different by its essentially unique form, yet is close enough to commonsensical ideas as to be able to house their contents and deform them.

Hofstatder elaborates on this proximity of the paranoid to the common-sensical. In his defense of using a clinical diagnostic term (paranoia) upon the field of politics, he takes great pains to empty the term of its strictly psycho-logical connotations. These people are "not clinically deranged: it is the very use of the mode by more or less normal people that makes it significant" (p. 4). Following this line of thought, Robins and Post (1997) describe the para-noid as "not having fully departed the world of reality. Rather, the paranoid clings to a part of that world . . . it is a pathological *exaggeration* . . . a *form of adaptation gone wrong*" (p. 19; italics added).

For the Overstreets (1964), extremism's repetition of the mainstream is an "extravagance . . . for we are a nation of moderates" (p. 13). In their view, extremism is an "nth degree exaggeration of traits common among us in gradations" (p. 20). And for Robbins and Post (1997), the political paranoid is "perfectly normal except for delusions of conspiracy and victimization" (p. 4). Hofstatder concurs with this when he defines the "paranoid style" in relation to normally functioning rationality: the paranoid style can be seen as an "imitation of the enemy. . . . It is nothing if not coherent [and] intensely rationalistic" (pp. 32, 36). What emerges again and again in these texts is the theme that political paranoia is a hyperbolic mimic of the mainstream.

Pipes (1997), too, has much to say about this mimicry. In a chapter titled "House of Mirrors" he borrows a definition of conspiracism as a "secret vice of the rational mind" and argues that it is seductive because it comes in the form of "pseudoscholarship" (p. 34). In fact his entire chapter is designed to address how it is "maddeningly difficult to keep [conspiracism] in focus" and the "difficulty in distinguishing the real from the imaginary" (p. 20). Pipes begins to perform a sorting operation upon the problem, crucial because "[r]eader and author alike need markers to distinguish the solid ground of fact from the swamp of fantasy, for it is this insidiousness that permits conspiracism to spread from the extremes to the mainstream" (p. 38). I will return to this call for a "style of thought" that seeks division between the rational and its simulated excess, but for now I will just emphasize that the sorting procedure so crucial to the problematizations of political paranoia does not concern itself with distinguishing true from false. To do so would place conspiracy narratives squarely within the "regime of truth" (in the sense that they *could be* true or false).

Rather, what is at issue is differentiating a style or manner of thought from the very style that *composes* that regime of truth, the rational style that could distinguish true from false. And, most significantly, this differentiation is difficult to do because the paranoid style is not inherently distinct from what we might call "the noid style." It is in seductive proximity to it, a deformation, an excessive mimicry, a phantasmic exaggeration of the ordinary.[26] I now wish to turn to how this insufferable simulacrum (political paranoia) is a peculiarly liberal excess, one that impacts directly on the practices of consent and dissent, and the processes of subjectification.[27]

Liberalism's Exaggeration

Seymour Lipset and Earl Raab (1970) locate a paradox in political extremism: "the same values and moral commitments that have been the constant strength of our democratic life (individualism, antistatism, egalitarianism) . . . provide the substance of extremist threats to that democratic life" (p. 30). According to these researchers, "extremist movements have been powerfully spawned by the same American characteristics that finally reject them" (p. 30). Lipset and Raab are content to leave this shared set of characteristics as a "paradox" and a curious contradiction. Other political paranoia experts, however, explore this doubling in more specific terms.

What is it exactly that gets exaggerated in the paranoid style? According to Robins and Post, the "primary distortion is of the necessary suspiciousness in American politics," an "exaggeration of the tried political style of alert suspicion" (1997, pp. 5, 18). They go on to argue that political paranoia "distorts conventional and useful responses to danger . . . it is a malignant distortion of an otherwise adaptive response, a useful mode of behavior that has misfired, a dangerous and destructive *parody* of prudent coping behavior" (p. 18). Robins and Post argue that what is at stake is the preservation of a particular kind of skepticism. Healthy political suspicion must be saved from its deformers who threaten to take it away to the extremes and into the realm of parody. The authors also warn against the danger of this hyperbolic mimicry returning to the center and *masquerading* itself as legitimate.

For Pipes (1997), this excess reaches its pinnacle in the conspiracist statement "appearances deceive," in which even "the most benign governments in human experience (the British and the American) [are turned] into the most terrible" (p. 48). What emerges from his pages is the sense that skepticism turns into suspicion, a lack of trust in the basic integrity of Western governing.[28] Pipes argues that it is ironically those nations "with a substantial body of opinion that suspects . . . its own government [which are the] most targeted by conspiracism" (p. 174). But this is more than irony, as it returns us to the logic of exaggeration, excess, and simulation.

This political suspicion is a necessary component in liberalism's ethos of permanent self-criticism. Being-free liberally one must employ a vigorous skepticism upon governmental activities, as a way of keeping governing in check. But skepticism, once exaggerated and deformed, can threaten the very political structure that requires it. In other words, Robins and Post's "Save Our Skepticism" campaign is a call for a *moderate* skepticism, one well within the boundaries of a regime of truth. It is this set of acceptable limits for skepticism (and thereby dissent) that I wish to link up to liberal political rationality.

For Lipset and Raab (1970), it is "an American article of faith that because of the ultimate efficacy of human reason, error is legitimate and tolerable. A direct attack on the popular properties of human reason has never been politically possible in America" (p. 6). The problem with extremists is that they refuse to recognize "error," and instead ascribe evil intentions to political actors (pp. 7, 14). Through their hypersuspicion, conspiracy theories are "designed to legitimate the closing down of the ideational market place" (p. 17). The problem is not that extremists do not share a consensual official truth, but that they do not subscribe to the *regime* of political truth, where sorting truth from error is the required procedure in the marketplace of ideas.

This is a tightly drawn articulation of political action with rationality: "extremism" as such is not violent action or conflict with particular values (individualism, freedom, equality). Rather, it is the very refusal to subscribe to a faith in Reason, to the rules and procedures for distinguishing truth from error in opinion, and to the markeplace of ideas, that makes them extremists. The desire to contest the very procedures of contestation removes conspiracists from the field of politics (where freedom is circumscribed by the regime of truth). Thus, reflections on political paranoia and extremism are not about ideas, but the procedures of governing. This is not about a consensus in outcome (agreement, uniformity in opinion) but consent to the rules, procedures, and forms of dissent and difference.

What all of these problematizations of political paranoia agree on is that the self-critique and political self-reflection that define liberalism have gone awry. Political paranoia is not marked by a lack or failure to resemble the model, but rather is an amplification of the ordinary, a parody of convention. As skepticism it has gone too far in its hyperbolic mimicry. The "paranoid style" is outside the lines (of both the political spectrum and rational games of truth); it is extremism *as such* that needs expelling. Conspiracism, because it takes the legitimate liberal *style* of thought out of bounds, is the "intolerable": it subverts faith in the marketplace of ideas, in the link between freedom and rationality, and in the regime of truth itself. Liberal self-problematization has hypertrophied; the turn to the self has exceeded the kind of rationality required to make responsible turnings. Only a reasonable criticism is allowable, only a moderate form of modulation.

Once this excess has been defined as the problem, what responses are proposed? What is interesting in all of these problematizing texts, from Hofstatder to Pipes, is the fact that not only are coercive measures (punishment, detention, repressive measures against speech) not endorsed, they are actively disavowed. What is uniformly agreed upon in these analyses is that repression cannot and should not be carried out upon political paranoia.[29] Two reasons are given to avoid these harsh measures.

The first is tactical, as this kind of subjection "would split society even further, and thereby give extremism further draw" (Overstreet & Overstreet, 1964, p. 21). Targeting, isolating, and suppressing political paranoia would create a scenario where the "paranoid person feels cast out by society, which increases their paranoia" (Robins & Post, 1997, p. 40). If "alienation from normal political processes" is the condition upon which paranoia flourishes, then direct suppression would only inflame the problem (Hofstatder, 1967, p. 39).

The second reservation against repressive techniques is, at first glance, less about strategy than it is about national moral integrity. Brute censorship, according to the Overstreets (1964), only happens "in totalitarian systems . . . there is an obligation to defend extremism's constitutional rights, so we cannot use coercion"; prohibition is "un-American" (p. 21). And for George and Wilcox (1996), there is a "certain danger in the notion that we should be 'intolerant of intolerance'" (p. 10). Strategies of dissent-management must, thereby, be more supple and differentiated than simple negation. In a liberal art of governing, this is not surprising, as "political rationality . . . replaces violence as a mode of governance" (Brown, 1998, p. 43). So, two rational proposals are made:

One tactic advocated is to refold the extremists into the mainstream. "[We are] not trying to ostracize or liquidate extremists—we want to bring them to the center" (Overstreet & Overstreet, 1964, p. 292). That is, through a strengthening of national patriotism, a revitalization of education, and flexibilization of the political structure, extremists can find a space of action within the center, but no longer as extremists. This strategy of incorporation seeks, then, to bring the alienated back into the fold as a way of reinvigorating the center.

There is a more prevailing nonrepressive tactic in these texts, however. Calling for similar techniques (bolstering of education, rejuvenation of citizenship through grassroots activity, and refamiliarization with America's foundational political tracts), this response strengthens the norm by incessantly positioning the dissenter as an alien, as not one of us. Rather than bringing the "outsider" back into the mainstream, this conceptual strategy seeks to turn the domestic dissenter into an outsider, and keep it at bay.

But banishing the irrational dissenter is not done with an imposition of rationality (as reasoned argumentation) onto subjects. A "return to common sense" is more than a pervasive acceptance of dominant ideas, or a consent to authorities. "[S]ound logic and superior leadership do not of their own appear sufficient to make the paranoid style fade away; more profound changes need to take place . . . *a thorough reevaluation of self,* plus fundamental changes in *thinking processes* and social perception" (Pipes, 1997, pp. 184–185; italics added). Rather than being suppressed knowledges, these conspiracy narratives are made useful, as a target of modification, as a renewal of the political subject's relation to reason, even as a fostering of a "democratic personality" (George & Wilcox, 1996, pp. 88–91).[30] This is where I want to argue that these problematizing texts are attempting to fuse reason and politics in a way that promotes a liberal technology of citizen-subjectification.

Problematizing As a Style of Thought

In addition to making thought-style an object of concern, these problematizations of conspiracism also offer their own style of analysis as a model. They do not offer simply a set of knowledge-claims which require agreement, or a consent to their authors' authority. It is not just that these texts promote a certain object (reason) over its deviant (paranoia); they do not consist of an invitation to share a classificatory scheme. Rather, I would argue that these problematizations offer up their own styles of thought, ones which attempt to invigorate liberal technologies of governing through banishing liberalism's excesses.

They display the very style of thought that the readers, as citizens, should employ when they encounter political paranoia. These are "practical" texts, "functional devices that would enable individuals to question their own conduct, to watch over and give shape to it, and to shape themselves as ethical subjects" (Foucault, 1985, pp. 12–13). It just so happens that the prescriptive texts here are taking as their object the very style of thought needed to be a proper citizen. As practical texts they have as their focus the games of truth necessary for political subjectivities, the appropriate modes of thought in relation to modes of political action, the links between rational thought, reasonable politics, and freedom. Prescription through example, presented as scholarly description.

These are turns to thought, where thought works on thought to provide a manual for turning. And these problematizations are presented not just as alternatives to the paranoid style, since the paranoid style's intelligibility only emerges as a result of the noid style. Proper turns are performed at the very moment the paranoid style is rendered an object. In a way, these turns problematize types of problematization: they ask, what are the proper styles of *thinking* politics? What forms of questions, what manners of inquiry, what statements are allowable? *Problematizing style is itself a style of problematization.*

And what is this official style? As noted earlier, this style involves a serious devotion to differentiation, in which false pretenders and excessive mimics can be distinguished from proper moderate reasonings. Pipes (1997), for one, offers "tools . . . to identify conspiracy theories" which include "common sense, a knowledge of history, and the ability to recognize distinct patterns of conspiracism" (p. 38). It is crucial that he defines these as tools, rather than conceptually asserting them as expert truth-claims, as this sorting procedure "is a subjective process" (p. 37). The goal is not a subject's obedience or agreement, but the willing and reasonable choice to take up the noid style as one's own.

In addition to being a subjective process, this sorting operation is not done once and for all in an imposition of a regime of truth upon the field of political knowledges. The paranoid style "manages to insinuate itself in the most alert and intelligent minds, so excluding it amounts to a perpetual struggle, one in which the reader is invited to join" (Pipes, 1997, p. 49). That is to say, the sorting mechanism needs uninterrupted renewal and deployment; the political subject needs continuous modification of itself as a self-turning actor.

Pipes is essentially encouraging, through his own example, a liberal technology of subjectification, one in which permanent self-criticism is necessary for the continuation of governing through freedom. It is one in which subjects turn on themselves properly, with a modicum of rationality that will turn against liberal rationality's excesses. Stylizing a conduct of thought involves an incessant task: sorting, scapegoating, exiling, othering, rooting-out the unjust pretender.

This ethos of moderate skepticism as a perpetual struggle has two effects. On one hand, it seeks a subjectification through a hermeneutics of differentiation in the self (sorting out the simulation of rationality from the authentic and the copy, avoiding the seduction of the simulation). On the other hand, it involves a hermeneutics of suspicion of others. This "administration of fear"

(Virilio, 1990) around conspiracism promotes a mistrust among people, encouraging amateur political psychologists to actively monitor other citizens as way of reaffirming investment in a commonsensical "people."

The cohesion of liberalism's political rationality comes with this injunction: to modulate thought and behavior with an eye towards limits and extremes. This responsible thought entails a modification of thought in accordance with a principle of moderation. The ethos as *modus*: a modulation through moderation, and vice versa.[31] A will-to-moderate in which dissent itself is problematized, where reasonable skepticism and rational critique are both effected and called upon to justify its performance.

The experts problematize conspiracism, but call not just for an affirmation of *their* sorting, but an invitation to readers (as citizens) to perform their "own" differentiations, to produce their "own" knowledges through meditations on political thought itself. Thus, these training manuals present a new set of questions: namely, what is the authority of these prescriptions? These manuals for thought prescribe an object to be problematized, but what calls for an affirmation of this particular turning, as opposed to other kinds (even paranoid ones)? In other words, what makes these positive mechanisms of ethical formation stick? What are the passionate attachments to this authority, this rationality which promises being and freedom?

This returns us to the issues of generality and coordination raised earlier in this essay. Can this authority be "consented" to? Perhaps consent, rather than being a deliberative rational submission, can be defined as an attachment, an affirmation of or sticking to a technology of subjectification. Is this subjective process of sorting out political excesses and simulations a local technology of political subjectivation (i.e., only when presented with "extremist" or dangerous dissent)? Or is it a more general condition of *technologizability* (the ability for a technology to stick)? This is a question of the authority of any technologized freedom, since what runs through these technologies is the regime of truth in which we can identify ourselves as free beings. Consent here would be a coordinating force, a translating or articulating mechanism, one traversing particular policies, institutions, programs, individuals insofar as it refers to the authority of any of them.[32]

Consent is made, on the one hand, to the parameters of dissent, to the distribution of proper political positions and forms (moderation). Consent, as well, must be given to the regime of truth that underpins this distribution. Consent, finally, is rendered to the particular technologies of subjectification that, in their incessant turning upon the self to differentiate and upon others to monitor, produce those parameters and rejuvenate that regime (modulation). This kind of consent is a particular subjectification with general ramifications and stakes. Skepticism is moderately enacted, mistrust is itself mistrusted, and distinguishing Us from the pretenders becomes a citizen's duty. And all of this in the service of "making politics reasonable" again.

No Guarantees: The Recoil of Thought

So far, I have concentrated on the problematizations of the paranoid style as an official turning on styles of thought. But this discussion cannot exhaust the analysis of these problematizations, for it would reduce thought to its technologized form in a liberal political rationality. It would ignore the other component of governmentality: the strategies of games of liberty. To end this essay with the success of these technologies through consent would erase the ambivalence at the heart of governing mentioned above, in which liberal governing, because of its exigencies of renewal, performs both effectively and vulnerably. What I want to point out briefly here at the end is how this ambivalence in the problematization of paranoid styles of thought accesses a possible otherwise.

As it will be recalled, what liberalism finds intolerable is that conspiracism, as simulation, will not contain itself to being a mere copy of rational thought. It will always masquerade, dissimulate, and seduce, producing halls of mirrors, muddy waters, and (con)fusion. In distinguishing the moderate from the extreme, the rational from the paranoid, and the mainstream from the mimic, the problematizations of political paranoia cannot completely fix their object in representation. They continuously find themselves reiterating the sorting process and sending the simulacrum down a scapegoated line of flight.[33] By incessantly requiring subjects to modify and moderate themselves, and to form themselves in the process, these strategies depend upon a modicum of freedom that cannot be completely domesticated. Subjects do not just repeat or reiterate the differentiating process as given; they are let loose to do it as a moment of their "own" activity. This is that fissure in governing, where power dissimulates itself as freedom. The activity of subjectification, organized by a particular configuration of reason and freedom, can indeed turn back upon the technologies themselves.

1) This can be done, for one thing, because of the "making-visible" of conspiracism and the attending spectacle of expulsion. By bringing conspiracy theories to the light, the "problems" can backfire. That is to say, conspiracy theories, no matter how they are technologized and represented, can still seduce the readers.

2) This re-turn can also occur through and excessive carrying-out of the subjectification tasks prescribed by the experts themselves. There is no assurance that harnessing capacities through self-reflection will be moderate (obviously, conspiracy theories are not). This would be a case of "poor" execution: an excessive self-reflection as an intensification of its liberalism's strategies, which are its weakest points. This is done to effectively enhance the feeling of agential power, which turns against the power that produces subjects (Patton, 1998, p. 75).

3) Third, what is the guarantee that this reflection will not turn to the authority of this injunction? Unleashing official modes of turning (modification,

suspicion) can recoil upon the authoritative manuals themselves. The *official* turns can come under scrutiny by these subjects, who, in carrying out their tasks, do it excessively. A chain reaction of critical turns could travel back to accentuate the contingency of the political rationalities themselves.[34] In all three instances, turning in the name of freedom is not guaranteed to perform properly.

It is important to note, however, that these recoils themselves do not guarantee a preferred politics. Excess itself is not to be affirmed or championed as a politics in itself. It merely marks the inexhaustibility that constitutes liberal styles of thought and rationality. To put it another way, it is not about affirming irrationality as it is about assessing rationality.

My argument, then, is not to be confused with what Mark Fenster (1999) calls the attempt "to celebrate the 'pathological' uncritically as necessarily leading to the liberation of social order from the chains of the dominant" (p. 18). The disruptive possibilities of conspiracy narratives are a starting point of analysis, not a final judgment. Not all excessive narratives gathered under the term "paranoid style" are worthy of championing. The question "which one?" would have to be determined through the concrete work of political articulation (Grossberg, 1992; 1997). This difficult work would be done *outside* of the liberal anti-conspiracy discourse, which scapegoats conspiratological dissent in the name of "reasonable politics."

CONCLUSION

These official reflections on conspiracist styles of thought return us to the constitutive role of thought in liberal governance. Bound up with consent, these reflections attempt to promote a thought that acts as an adhesive force, coordinating governmental strategies through games of truth and subjectification. At the same time, this adhesion is an active and persistent task, to be renewed by the subject acting in the name of freedom and reason. This incessant reactivation speaks its vulnerability at the very moment thought-styles are deployed as technologies of subjectification.

There are at least three turns, then, in the relation of thought-styles to governance: 1) the ethos of a liberal art of governing (perpetual self-criticism, problematization, skepticism); 2) the paranoid style of thought (extreme reflections on rule, excessive skepticism, unruly problematizing); and 3) the conspiracism experts (reflections on thought-styles, problematizing conspiracy theories, sorting and rooting out false from true pretenders). The third exists as a folding of the second into the first. It is performed in order to deploy technologies to produce political subjects. In doing so, however, a vulnerability of the liberal ethos itself is also instituted. Here we can see the unruliness of extravagant skepticism: while dependent upon liberal arts of governing, it exceeds these conditions. This vulnerability of the liberal ethos pivots on the necessity of renewal and the fact that the folding is done in the name of freedom.

To preserve the act of freedom in liberalism, freedom is also risked. As governmentalized freedom is a harnessing and deployment of human capacities, there is no necessary articulation between freedom and reason, such that the former will necessarily be directed or authorized by the latter. Since it is enacted as a *strategy* of liberty, rationality's authorization as freedom-giver cannot determine freedom's return to its conditions, especially when those conditions have an unfree component (namely the need to reiterate, to renew its identity). Thus a necessary anxiety over authority, rules, truth, and subjectification, which demands an exiled scapegoat again and again, occurs as a block to freedom, one which could itself become an object of concern. Reiteration is a moment of vulnerability in which freedom, a capacity deployed *as the very name* of the liberal art of governing, can dislodge liberalism itself. This vulnerability instills an anxiety over integrity, evidenced both in the problematizers' allusions to a (con)fused political context and in their textual prescriptions for subjective action.

Liberalism's need for perpetuity is geared to survival. But what if this need marked a certain ephemerality as well? Might it imply a demise not only for the governing rationales and strategies, but the kind of subject who depends on them, and is required by them; a vulnerability in the technologies and strategies of liberalism, as well as the attachments to their authority? It would mean, as Toby Miller (1993) argues, "putting an end to attempts to embrace one's incompleteness in the service of obedience. In order to begin again, we must lose ourselves, and do so in sight of danger" (p. 231). This moment of ephemerality would be the moment of risking being itself, for "without a repetition that risks life—in its current organization—how might we begin to imagine the contingency of that organization, and performatively reconfigure the contours of the conditions of life" (Butler, 1997, p. 29)? This is the moment of freedom, one not liberated from reason's determinations, but turned differently: geared towards enhancing life, developing new capacities, and signalling a futurity, a life and a freedom otherwise-than-being.

NOTES

1. This view of the relation between thought and governance begins to address the question of the generalizability of governing. What links local and specific programs, policies, and institutions into a strategy? What is the coordinating element, or as Barry Smart (1986) calls it, "the forms of social cohesion" (p. 170)? Nikolas Rose (1999) occasionally calls it the "will-to-govern" (pp. 5, 52–53). What is this will? Not a monolithic, uniform force that finds its manifestations in local practices, but perhaps

a generalizing, cohesive, even adhesive force. This will be important later when I discuss consent and authority.

2. There is no mention of it in his "Governmentality" (1991a) lecture, for example. There is only the emphasis on knowledges employed in the arts of governing, which is different from thought, as I will explain later. However, one can get some sense of the importance of thought through some of his other concepts, especially the regime of truth (Foucault, 1980a), the specific intellectual (Foucault, 1988c, p. 265; 1980a, pp. 126–133), problematization (Foucault, 1988c, p. 257; 1985, p. 11), and the practice of criticism (Foucault, 1988b, pp. 154–156).

3. However, this is not an idealistic notion of the world's construction. While the phrase "insofar as" in the passage above can be interpreted as the *necessity* of thought inhabiting practices, it also limits thought's inhabitation. As Paul Rabinow (1997) reads this passage, thought is not "totally co-extensive with the object of analysis," which is the danger of idealism (p. xxxv). Thought is a necessary component of analyzing actions, conduct, and behaviors, but not a sufficient tool of explanation. Singular forms of experience "may well not be independent of the concrete determinations of social existence" (Foucault, 1997c, p. 201). However these determinations cannot "allow for experiences (that is, for understandings of a certain type, for rules of a certain form, for certain modes of consciousness of oneself and others) except through thought" (p. 201). This is the first principle of thought: its *irreducibility*. The second principle is the *singularity* of the history of thought: "thought has a historicity which is proper to it" (1997c, p. 201). Again, it is not that thought is "independent of all the other historical determinations (of an economic, social, or political order) but that it has complex relations with them, which always leave their specificity to the forms, transformations, and events of thought" (p. 201). The third principle is *critical activity*, since "transformations could not take place except by means of a working of thought upon itself" (p. 201). Together, these principles compose "singular forms of thought . . . what constitutes the subject in its relations to the true, to rules, to itself" (p. 202).

4. Another way of describing this two-fold composition is through Hardt and Negri's (2000) analysis of U.S. constitutional sovereignty, in which regulative mechanisms of self-reflection draw from and operate through the immanent field of conflictual counterpowers. These logics of sovereignty have to be renewed and recreated as they expand into new terrains (see especially pp. 164–167).

5. Due to spatial constraints I do not have room to elaborate each of these. Briefly, the stakes of the Enlightenment ethos involve how the growth of capabilities can be disarticulated from the intensification of power relations (how has power harnessed and technologized capacities, and how can they be directed towards projects of liberty?). Homogeneity refers to the consistency of "practical systems," defined earlier has having the dual components of technology/rationality and strategic games. Systematicity involves the three axes of relations that have come to define Foucault's own work: knowledge, power, and ethics (forms of experience, subjectification). Generality refers to the sense that problematizations tend to recur (not as a constant or chronological variation but a persistent array of objects, rules, and modes of self-relation). Foucault's examples here are the relationship between sanity and insanity, and the recurring concern over sexual relations (1997d, pp. 317–318).

6. "Reflexivity" thus is not a general characteristic of a late modern age (a la Giddens) but characterizes "liberal political rationalities from their inception" (Rose, 1996, p. 47; see also Dean, 1996). This turn, following Kant, is precisely constitutive of modernity, but as we shall see later, reflexivity is not merely a self-grounding act of an age. At the same time, self-reflexivity, through the act of departicularization, is not easily defined as the Habermasian means for emancipation.

7. Thought here is thus more than knowledge or technical expertise. Thought is the active effort to distinguish a realm called "society," with its own logics and rules. Thought is that which allows governing itself to be problematized, articulating a "nongovernmental" sphere to be governed at a distance. Only then are knowledge and expertise of that realm possible.

8. While liberalism is often described as an ensemble of techniques, programmes, and strategies, what is often emphasized in studies of governmentality is the multiplicity and dispersion of these positivities. What I want to evaluate here is the way these multiplicities are coordinated and arranged. This is where the concept of "political rationality" is crucial. This "political rationality" is not a monolithic concept, referring to an ideal type or to a universalizing logos: "it's not 'reason in general' that is implemented, but always a very specific type of rationality" (1988a, p. 73). The specific forms of rationality are what Foucault is after, not Rationality as such. Similarly, specific styles of thought need to be evaluated, not thought as such. This specificity (asking "which rationality?") is not, then, a wholesale denunciation of the Enlightenment for its instrumental reason, which could be negated through critical thought.

But while it is not universalized, political rationality does seem to act as a *generalizing* force, or coordinating force. Political rationality, or thought, exists prior to the specific programs and institutions being formulated and implemented, since programs "either articulate or presuppose a *knowledge* of the field of reality upon which it is to intervene and/or which it is calculated to bring into being. . . . Furthermore, the condition that programmatic knowledge must satisfy is that it renders reality in the form of an object which is *programmable*" (Gordon, 1980, p. 248). That is to say, a rationality cannot be located within any particular institution as *its* logic, or in a specific program as *its* means and ends. "Programming depends on forms of rationality much more general than those which they directly implement . . . the generalisation and interconnection of different techniques themselves designed in response to localised requirements . . . this is what gives the resulting apparatus (*dispositif*) its solidity and suppleness" (Foucault, 1991b, pp. 80–81). Critique must target more than any particular institutional practice (prisons, psychiatry): it must ask "how are relations of power rationalized? Asking it is the only way to avoid other institutions, with the same objectives and same effects, from taking their stead" (1988a, p. 84). Political rationality, then, can be seen as the force that co-ordinates particularities to compose a liberal style of governing.

9. This opens up a number of issues around a contested term like "consent." Consent, in this formulation, is not just obedience to a code or a law, nor is it assent to leadership or representation. Rather, it points to a mode of political subjection in which the subject recognizes itself as a rational being, thus guaranteeing its freedom. It is an adherence to the very processess of subjectification, in which one freely

chooses his or her responsibilization, thus allowing one's freedom to begin with. The circle of consent: accepting the rationality of freedom is a responsible and rational act, therefore a free act. And this consent is not about what people think, believe, or value. Consent is not something that can be distinguished from, and compared to, behavior. A consent without ideology: the question is Foucault's (1983), in the Preface to Deleuze & Guattari, *Anti-Oedipus*: how is it that people come to desire their own subjugation? But this is not an issue of falsity. Consent is not against one's own natural interests or will, but directed at a particular will-to-truth. Consent as investment of desire, as passionate attachment to authority.

10. "Each society has its regime of truth, its 'general politics' of truth: that is, the types of discourse which it accepts and makes function as true; the mechanisms and instances which enable one to distinguish true and false statements, the means by which each is sanctioned; the techniques and procedures accorded value in the acquisition of truth; the status of those who are charged with saying what counts as true" (Foucault, 1980a, p. 131).

11. In the United States, this regime of truth could be said to take the metaphorical form of the "marketplace of ideas," which will become important for the problematizers of conspiracy theories later.

12. In his research on the Christian confessional, Foucault discovered a practice called "exomologesis" which speaks to this relation between conduct and an affirmative relation to the self. Exomologesis is "an act meant to reveal both a truth and the subject's adherence to that truth . . . [it is] not merely to affirm what one believes but to affirm the fact of that belief; it is to make the act of affirmation an object of affirmation, and hence to authenticate it either for oneself or with regard to others. Exomologesis is an emphatic affirmation whose emphasis relates above all to the fact that the subject binds himself to that affirmation and accepts the consequences" (1997e, pp. 81–82). Before the verbalization of impulses, before the obligation to confess, there is the binding affirmation that commits a subject to an affirmation. This will bear on how consent is discussed later: consent includes a moment of affirming the very act of consent. A subject binds itself to the authority of consent, to the obliging impulse, to the forms of experience regardless of the content of belief.

13. While governmentality studies does stress thought as an ethos, the writers often do not elaborate what it entails (outside of intellectual work in the occupational sense). For Nikolas Rose (1999) "thought becomes governmental to the extent that it becomes technical, it attaches itself to a technology for its realization" (p. 51). But more than attaching to a technology, thought itself is *technologized*. It is deployed as a rational form or procedure at the expense of its deployment in a game of liberty.

14. In her analysis of Althusser's conception of interpellation, Butler says, with regard to the turn towards the hailer, that there would not "be a turning around without some readiness to turn," without an attachment to the law's authority. This turn is compelling "because it promises identity" (1997, pp. 107–108). Consent, then, could be redefined as this kind of desire (for being). But there are other promises, other becomings (pp. 129–131).

15. For Butler, this is a temporal matter, but especially in advanced liberal governance, it is also a spatial matter. That is, "governing at a distance" is required for liberalism to be effective. It disorganizes itself to make it work as dissimulation. We

could also define this as a moment of deterritorialization (Deleuze & Guattari, 1987). While Deleuze (1977) posits that society is defined "first by its points of deterritorialization," liberalism is singular insofar as it takes its own deterritorialization as its practical regulative principle, and because it reterritorializes its governing onto its subjects (as "free citizens") (p. 135).

16. Or, as Lee Quinby argues in *Freedom, Foucault, and the Subject of America*, the tradition of American ethics as a practice of self includes an "aesthetics of liberty," a practice of freedom "as an activity of artistic creation . . . by which Americans challenge disciplinary power relations" (1991, p. 3). This legacy of subjectification is an "activity made possible by disruptive energies," a "secular sublime" which is a revolutionary force (pp. 11–12). And, as Paul Rabinow (1997) discusses, Foucault himself suggested that processes of subjectification became disarticulated from "care" in favor of "knowledge," and thus could be rearticulated (pp. xxv–xxvii).

17. This notion of problematization resonates with Foucault's call for an insurrection of subjugated knowledges (1980b), which entails not only those phenomena within the regime of truth (dividing the true from the false), but those "Outside the True:" that is to say, those "local and popular forms of knowledge [which] have been steadily discredited, disqualified, or rendered illegitimate by the very institutions and effects of power associated with the prevailing 'regime of truth' within which the modern intellectual operates" (Smart, 1986, p. 165).

18. Throughout the 1990s, books and articles on conspiracy theories multiplied, for both academic and popular audiences. After the Oklahoma City bombing in the spring of 1995, published commentaries rose significantly. A Lexis-Nexis search for the term "conspiracy theory" in the *New York Times* and the *Washington Post* found a combined total of 514 citations in the years 1990–1994. From 1995–1999 this number jumped to 896. A scan of *Time* magazine found no citations in the first half of the decade, but 21 in the second half. In the first 5 years of the 1990s, the *Reader's Guide to Periodical Literature* cites a total of 20 articles on the topic of "conspiracy" or "paranoia," with a total of 88 listings for the years 1995–1999. In 1995 alone this number jumped to 22 articles. With the amount of prominent scrutiny paid to conspiracy theories of late, it is obvious that political paranoia has become a significant object of concern in political discourse.

19. These recent iterations include *Conspiracy! The Paranoid Style and Why It Flourishes* (Pipes, 1997), *Political Paranoia and the Psychopolitics of Hatred* (Robins & Post, 1997), *American Extremists* (George & Wilcox, 1996), and *Limits of Dissent* (Halpern, 1996). The recent problematizations of conspiracy theories have antecedents in earlier tracts, as well. The older texts include the seminal essay by Richard Hofstadter (1967), "The Paranoid Style in American Politics," *The Politics of Unreason: Right-Wing Extremism in America, 1790–1970* (Lipset & Raab, 1970), *The Strange Tactics of Extremism* (Overstreet & Overstreet, 1964), and *Extremism USA* (Carpenter, 1964). For brevity's sake, I will concentrate here on Hofstadter, Lipset and Raab, and the Overstreets as indicative of the earlier research and on Pipes and Robbins/Post as the more recent commentary.

20. It is important here to note that these problematizations tend not to emphasize individual conspiracy narratives, but quickly move to conceptually capturing them into some kind of manageable unity, like "political paranoia" or "conspiracism." However,

belief in any one conspiracy theory can be a gateway to conspiracism (Pipes, 1997, p. 20).

21. The works comprise a set of problems formed and disseminated by "experts." These include academic researchers, watchdog groups (especially the Anti-Defamation League with its Center on Hate and Extremism), and public intellectuals (most notably Chip Berlet of the Progressive Resource Center). Barry, Osborne, and Rose (1996) argue that the role of expertism in the history of liberalism has been to provide "particular conceptions of the objects to be governed" (p. 42). That is, a certain amount of autonomy is granted to scientists and intellectuals who can provide "action at a distance" in such a way as to legitimate the workings of the State on particular arenas of everyday life without recourse to direct forms of State-intervention (pp. 10–11). Empowered with the authority to problematize and reflect on the present state of affairs, these experts link technical know-how with political practices. In the case of "political paranoia" these experts are non-State monitors, citizen watchdog groups, "independent" scholars, and private intelligence gathering organizations—or, as Guy Debord (1998) called them, "professional accusers" (p. 24). Their technical expertise in the fields of political psychology, sociology, political science, history, current affairs, and cultural analysis are not directly tied to the State, but they do eventually get linked with State practices (most notably their appearances in the news media and at Congressional hearings).

22. For an excellent critique and contextualization of Hofstadter's essay as emblematic of liberal consensus approaches to conspiracy theories, see Mark Fenster (1999), especially Chapter 1.

23. This is especially evident in the recent discourse surrounding the proliferation of American militias, and most acute in the articulation of these groups to the Oklahoma City Bombing. As the titles of popular books on Timothy McVeigh (*One of Ours* 1998 and *American Terrorist* 2001) suggests, the concern over the *domestic* nature of political paranoia (in tandem with domestic terrorism) still presides over the experts' problematizations.

24. Pipes, for instance, makes it clear that the left is perhaps even more insidiously promoting conspiracism, because of the overattention to the right, and because the left is more sophisticated, subtle, and convincing (pp. 159–165). I believe there is a more interesting fusion of left and right going on, one at the level of the problematizations themselves. In the mid-90s panics over U.S. militias, this scapegoating of conspiracism produced strange bedfellows, positioning left/liberal commentators with the State in calling for stricter regulations and increased surveillance powers. But this is not that unusual if one recognizes that the "opposition" shares the same form of thought, or problematization.

25. This is not to say the content itself does not matter. As will become apparent later in this chapter, the fact that "political paranoia" takes "governing" as *its* object of concern is of great importance, as political paranoia does what liberal governance requires, but it does it *excessively*.

26. Even the etymology of the term *paranoia* speaks this characteristic. From the Greek *para* and *nous*, paranoia is defined as *beyond* or *beside* the mind. It is out there,

yet adjacent to here. After all, the paranoid is not antinoid, nor exnoid, nor xenonoid. It adjoins the mind, being both proximate yet quite dissimilar. Paranoia is not completely other, but a *mimic* of the noid (along similar conceptual lines as paramilitary, parapsychology, paraphrase, parallel, paranormal). It resembles the "noid," while at the same time threatening to *become* the "noid."

27. This recurring theme of exaggeration, mimicry, and excess can be viewed as a simulation, in Gilles Deleuze's sense. In an appendix to *The Logic of Sense* entitled "The Simulacrum and Ancient Philosophy," Gilles Deleuze (1990) argues that the history of Western metaphysical thought has been marked by an incessant drive to distinguish appearance from reality. In examining Platonic thought, however, Deleuze claims that this distinction is overshadowed by another sorting process. Rather than concerning itself primarily with differentiating the copy from the model, the key discrimination was made between the copy and the simulacrum. The copy, in this reading, is a well-founded faithful pretender that passes through the model, and is "guaranteed through resemblance" (p. 256). The simulacrum, on the other hand, operates without reference to the model; "it is built upon dissimilarity, implying essential perversion or deviation" (p. 256). "That to which they pretend, they pretend to underhandedly, under cover of an aggression, an insinuation, a subversion, "against the father" and without passing through the Idea. Theirs is an unfounded pretension" (p. 257). That is, the simulation is an unjust pretender, as opposed to the just pretender (the copy); it does not resemble, it dissembles, it as an image without resemblance.

Metaphysical thought, in this reading, has as its mission "to distinguish the true pretender from the false one" (Deleuze, 1990, p. 254) in order to assure the "triumph of the copies over simulacra, of . . . keeping [simulacra] completely submerged, preventing them from . . . 'insinuating themselves' everywhere" (p. 247). And why does the simulacrum need to be detected and domesticated? Quoting Nietzsche, Deleuze attributes to simulation the "power of the false. It renders the order of participation, the fixity of distribution, the determination of hierarchy impossible. . . . It assures unfounding as a joyful and positive event. It is marked by the power to affirm divergence and decentering and makes this power the object of a superior affirmation" (p. 265). That is, the simulacrum "places in question the very notation of copy and model" (p. 256). It "harbors a positive power which denies *the original and the copy, the model and the reproduction. . . .* The same and similar no longer have an essence except as *simulated*" (p. 262). Banishing the simulation would thus erase the *simulatedness* of the Same, by differentiating the simulacrum as "other."

28. This mistrust is extended by Pipes, however, to other nations. In fact, Pipes feels that some regimes, like Soviet communism and Nazi Germany, were *founded* on conspiracism (primarily because their respective leaders were paranoids).

29. This is not to say no-one appeals to direct State intervention. In much of the concern over militias there is a call for stronger laws and enforcement of them (most notably the letter from Morris Dees, head of the Southern Poverty Law Center, to Janet Reno pleading for increased surveillance powers for the FBI). In addition, the conflation of extremism with hate speech has led some watchdog groups (especially the Anti-Defamation League) to draft proposed laws and petition for harsher penalties for extremist behavior. In both these cases, however, the armed and violent character

of the activities is the target of the law-and-order boosterism, not the political positions of the actors.

30. Harking back to Harold Lasswell's early fusion of politics and psychology, this call to produce a "nonextremist" personality would "show a better way" to extremists and their potential seductees (George & Wilcox, 1996, p. 91). The objective here would be to induce higher "levels of democratic restraint," primarily through education, to produce "cadres of opposition to undemocratic excess" (p. 507).

31. This *modus* of subjectification through the problematizing of conspiracism could be assessed via Foucault's (1985) framework of the four elements of askesis:

1) *Ethical substance*: political thought itself. The style of thought as relation between rationality, freedom, and dissent.

2) *Mode of subjectivation*: Declaration of rationality of official knowledges. Announcement of trust/mistrust distribution according to regime of truth. Gatekeeping and scapegoating.

3) *Form of elaboration*: moderation in thought. Modification through hermeneutics of self-sorting, reading, suspicion/reporting of others, differentiation of narratives, and distancing self from scapegoats.

4) *Telos*: Democracy, safety and security of population. Reinventing the "American citizen." Retention of the political spectrum as reinventing reasonable politics.

32. The stakes are nonlocal, as well. They are matters of the "people," democracy, American, citizen, and the human. In the aftermath of the September 11, 2001 attacks, these stakes have intensified innumerably. Not only has dissent been managed and marginalized as anti-American, George W. Bush's call to reexamine American culture has taken the self-reflective impulse of thought to new heights of controlled consent and self-censorship. In addition, as evidenced in the national "Day of Reflection" shortly after the attacks, the turn to the self is disarticulated from the ethos of permanent criticism and rearticulated to national unity.

33. We can begin formulating the role of this scapegoating in terms of the "social." For Deleuze (1995) society is not defined by contradictions, but by lines of flight (p. 171; see also Patton, 1985, p. 65). What constitutes the consistency of the social is not causation, but its most deterritorialized forces. What holds society together is the threat. "Far from being a flight from the social field . . . these constitute the social field, trace out its gradation and its boundaries, the whole of its becoming" (Deleuze, 1977, p. 135). As one of the most public of social threats recently (to reasonable political discourse, to rational thought, to respectful and loyal critique, to common sense), conspiracy theories (and especially their concrete political actors—the militias) can be seen as an event that has put the issues of national identity and the future of political possibilities at the forefront of the social formation. See also Laclau and Mouffe (1985), especially Chapter 3, on the necessary antagonism, and expulsion-practices that infuse the formation of a social "identity."

34. And this contingency is, to reiterate Butler, endemic. Because of the very need for the scapegoat ritual to perform a regime's identity, the regime cannot erase this foundational ceremony, and thus announces its own fabricated nature. In trying

to make the simulacrum flee down the scapegoated line, the hegemonic regime cannot but show its own integrity to be always-already a result of performativity, an *effect of simulation.*

References

Barry, A., Osborne, T, & Rose, N. (Eds.). (1996). *Foucault and political reason.* Chicago: University of Chicago Press.

Brown, W. (1998). Genealogical Politics. In J. Moss (Ed.), *The later Foucault: Politics and philosophy* (pp. 33–49). London: Sage.

Burchell, G. (1991). Peculiar interests: Civil society and governing "the system of natural liberty." In G. Burchell, C. Gordon, & P. Miller (Eds.), *The Foucault effect: Studies in governmentality* (pp. 119–150). Chicago: University of Chicago Press.

Butler, J. (1997). *The psychic life of power: Theories in subjection.* Stanford: Stanford University Press.

Carpenter, J. (1964). *Extremism USA.* Phoenix, AZ: Associated Professional Services.

Dean, M. (1996). Foucault, government, and the enfolding of authority. In A. Barry, T. Osborne, & N. Rose (Eds.), *Foucault and political reason* (pp. 209–230). Chicago: University of Chicago Press.

Debord, G. (1998). *Comments on the society of the spectacle.* London: Verso.

Deleuze, G. (1977). Many politics. In H. Tomlinson & B. Habberjam, Trans.) *Dialogues* (pp. 124–147). New York: Columbia University Press.

Deleuze, G. (1986). Life as a work of art. In *Negotiations* (M. Joughin, Trans.) (pp. 94–101). New York: Columbia University Press.

Deleuze, G. (1990). The simulacrum and ancient philosophy. In *The Logic of sense.* (M. Lester with C. Stivale, Trans.) (pp. 253–266). New York: Columbia University Press.

Deleuze, G. (1995). Control and becoming. In *Negotiations.* (M. Joughin, Trans.) (pp. 169–176). New York: Columbia University Press.

Deleuze, G., & Guattari, F. (1987). *A thousand plateaus* (B. Massumi, Trans.). Minneapolis, MN: University of Minnesota Press.

Fenster, M. (1999). *Conspiracy theories: Power and secrecy in America.* Minneapolis, MN: University of Minnesota Press.

Foucault, M. (1980a). Truth and power. In C. Gordon (Ed.), *Power/Knowledge* (pp. 109–133). New York: Pantheon.

Foucault, M. (1980b). Two lectures. In C. Gordon (Ed.), *Power/Knowledge* (pp. 78–108). New York: Pantheon.

Foucault, M. (1982). The subject and power. In H. Dreyfus and P. Rabinow (Eds.) *Michel Foucault: Beyond structuralism and hermeneutics.* (pp. 208–226). Chicago: University of Chicago Press.

Foucault, M. (1983). Preface. In G. Deleuze and F. Guattari, *Anti-Oedipus: Capitalism and schizophrenia*. Trans. R. Hurley, M. Seem, & H. R. Lane. Minneapolis, MN: University of Minnesota Press.

Foucault, M. (1985). *The use of pleasure: The history of sexuality, Vol. 2*. New York: Vintage.

Foucault, M. (1988a). Politics and reason. In L. D. Kritzman (Ed.), *Politics, Philosophy, Culture* (pp. 57–85). New York: Routledge.

Foucault, M. (1988b). Practicing criticism. In L. D. Kritzman (Ed.), *Politics, Philosophy, Culture* (pp. 152–156). New York: Routledge.

Foucault, M. (1988c). The concern for truth. In L. D. Kritzman (Ed.), *Politics, Philosophy, Culture* (pp. 255–267). New York: Routledge.

Foucault, M. (1991a). Governmentality. In G. Burchell, C. Gordon, & P. Miller (Eds.) *The Foucault effect: Studies in governmentality* (pp. 119–150). Chicago: University of Chicago Press.

Foucault, M. (1991b). Questions of method. In G. Burchell, C. Gordon, & P. Miller (Eds.), *The Foucault effect: Studies in governmentality* (pp. 73–86). Chicago: University of Chicago Press.

Foucault, M. (1997a). The birth of biopolitics. In P. Rabinow (Ed.), *Foucault, ethics: Subjectivity and truth* (pp. 73–79). New York: New Press.

Foucault, M. (1997b). Polemics, politics, and problematizations. In P. Rabinow (Ed.), *Foucault, ethics: Subjectivity and truth* (pp. 111–120). New York: New Press.

Foucault, M. (1997c). Preface to the *History of sexuality, Vol. 2*. In P. Rabinow (Ed.), *Foucault, ethics: Subjectivity and truth* (pp. 199–206). New York: New Press.

Foucault, M. (1997d). What is Enlightenment? In P. Rabinow (Ed.), *Foucault, ethics: Subjectivity and truth* (pp. 303–320). New York: New Press.

Foucault, M. (1997e). On the government of the living. In P. Rabinow (Ed.), *Foucault ethics: Subjectivity and truth* (pp. 81–86). New York: New Press.

George, J., & Wilcox, L. (1996). *American extremists: Militias, supremacists, klansmen, communists & others*. Amherst, NY: Prometheus.

Gordon. C. (1980). Afterword. In C. Gordon (Ed.), *Power/Knowledge* (pp. 109–133). New York: Pantheon.

Gordon, C. (1991). Governmental Rationality: An introduction. In G. Burchell, C. Gordon, & P. Miller (Eds.) *The Foucault effect: Studies in governmentality* (pp. 1–52). Chicago: University of Chicago Press.

Goshorn, K. (2000). Strategies of deterrence and frames of containment: On critical paranoia and anti-conspiracy discourse. *Theory & Event*, 4:3. Retrieved 13/13/01 from http://muse.jhu.edu/journals/theory_and_event/v004/4.3r_goshorn.html

Grossberg, L. (1992). *We gotta get out of this place*. New York: Routledge.

Grossberg, L. (1997). Cultural studies: What's in a name? (One more time). In *Bringing it all back home* (pp. 245–271) Durham and London: Duke University Press.

Halpern, T. (1996). *The limits of dissent: The constitutional status of armed civilian militias*. Amherst, MA: Aletheia.

Hardt, M., & Negri, A. (2000). *Empire*. Cambridge, MA: Harvard University Press.

Hindess, B. (1996). *Discourses of power: From Hobbes to Foucault*. Oxford: Blackwell.

Hofstatder, R. (1967). *The paranoid style in American politics and other essays*. New York: Vintage.

Kelly, M. (1995, June 19). The road to paranoia. *The New Yorker*. (pp. 60–70).

Knight, P. (2001). *Conspiracy culture: From JFK to the X-files*. London: Routledge.

Laclau, E., & Mouffe, C. (1985). *Hegemony and socialist strategy: Towards a radical democratic politics*. London: Verso.

Lipset, S. M., & Raab, E. (1970). *The Politics of unreason: Right-wing extremism in America, 1790–1970*. New York: Harper.

Michel, L. & Herbeck, D. (2001). *American terrorist: Timothy McVeigh and the tragedy at Oklahoma City*. New York: Harper Collins.

Miller, T. (1993). *The well-tempered self: Citizenship, culture, and the postmodern subject*. Baltimore: Johns Hopkins University Press.

Miller, T. (1998). *Technologies of truth: Cultural citizenship and the popular media*. Minneapolis, MN: University of Minnesota Press.

Overstreet, H., & Overstreet, B. (1964). *The strange tactics of extremism*. New York: Norton.

Patton, P. (1985). Conceptual politics and the war-machine in *Mille Plateaux*. *Sub-Stance, 13* (3/4), 61–80.

Patton, P. (1998). Foucault's subject of power. In J. Moss (Ed.), *The later Foucault: Politics and philosophy* (pp. 64–77). London: Sage.

Pipes, D. (1997). *Conspiracy! The paranoid style and why it flourishes*. New York: Free Press.

Quinby, L. (1991). *Freedom, Foucault, and the subject of America*. Boston: Northeastern University Press.

Rabinow, P. (1997). Introduction. In P. Rabinow (Ed.), *Foucault, ethics: Subjectivity and truth* (pp. xi–xlv). New York: New Press.

Robins, R. S., & Post, J. M. (1997). *Political paranoia: The psychopolitics of hatred*. New Haven, CT: Yale University Press.

Rogin, M. (1987). *Ronald Reagan: The movie*. Berkeley, CA: University of California Press.

Rose, N. (1996). Governing advanced liberal democracies. In A. Barry, T. Osborne, & N. Rose (Eds.), *Foucault and political reason* (pp. 37–64). Chicago: University of Chicago Press.

Rose, N. (1999). *Powers of freedom: Reframing political thought*. London: Cambridge University Press.

Serrano, R. (1998). *One of ours: Timothy McVeigh and the Oklahoma City bombing.* New York: Norton & Company.

Smart, B. (1986). The politics of truth and the problem of hegemony. In D. C. Hoy (Ed.), *Foucault: A critical reader* (pp. 157–173). Oxford, UK: Blackwell.

Virilio, P. (1990). *Popular defense and ecological struggles.* New York: Semiotext(e).

Chapter 5

Bureaumentality

Jonathan Sterne

Ever since there were liberal States to think about, left intellectuals have had a variety of agonized relations with them. To draw out the broad contours of the history, Zygmunt Bauman (1992) has argued that humanistic intellectuals have moved from "legislators" who legitimized the workings of governments to "interpreters" whose work is largely irrelevant to the functioning of contemporary States. In Bauman's simultaneously tragic and comic view, the modern state started out needing its intellectuals, but by the end of the twentieth century it worked best by ignoring them.

Cultural studies scholars, meanwhile, have had a variety of theoretical and practical orientations to the State. Many of the putative father and mother figures of the field—Raymond Williams, Stuart Hall, and Angela McRobbie, to name a diverse set of three—have had various roles in organized politics and governmental policy initiatives at one time or another (see e.g., McGuigan, 1993). Yet the strongly Marxist (or at least Marxish) influence in cultural studies always carried with it a healthy and thoroughgoing suspicion of "official" State politics.

For those of us in communication studies, this split between left intellectuals and the State should sound familiar. We are used to the idea of "administrative" research that derives its funding and orientation from governmental or private interests, and "critical" research that does not. Yet even this is an exaggeration. When Paul Lazarsfeld first coined the terms in 1941, he meant them to designate ends on a continuum, two general tendencies in our field (Simonson, 2001). Today we have ossified Lazarsfeld's categories into an ontology of research methods and philosophical dispositions: "critical" intellectuals are supposedly suspicious of a State that is supposedly accepted without question by "administrative" intellectuals. But of course this is a caricature. Some of the communication scholars who most stridently self-identify as "critical" have accepted money and research agendas from governmental agencies. Some communication scholars involved in policy work are thoroughly engaged with so-called "critical" scholarship. Still, there remains considerable anxiety among left intellectuals—regardless of our field—about the terms on which we should or should not engage the state, and to what ends that work will be put.

This paper explores one particular moment when a group of Australian cultural studies scholars chose to directly engage the State and questions of policy. In the late 1980s and early 1990s, Australian cultural policy studies came together around the idea that cultural studies *should* engage policy bureaucracies. Writers in this field directly challenged what they saw as an unwarranted suspicion of the State and official politics in cultural studies. But they took a remarkably circuitous route to the policy position, using Michel Foucault's writings on governmentality to provide theoretical justification— at both the epistemological and ethical levels—for cultural studies' "move toward policy." By focusing on the work of Tony Bennett and a few of his colleagues in the late 1980s and early 1990s—in what he and others have come to call "the cultural policy debates"—I argue that their particular reliance upon Foucault's notion of governmentality requires them to bracket issues central to their project, like the problematics of political representation and specific outcomes of the machineries of power. This essay thus considers the theoretical foundations of the cultural policy school especially as they appropriate Foucault's governmentality writings.

Think of the question this way: What kinds of relationships are possible between left intellectuals and liberal or neoliberal States? Under what conditions should we seek to promote a particular policy agenda? Under what circumstances should we instead orient ourselves toward broader concerns of social transformation? Of course, the answers to these questions in practice will always depend on the context—and anxiety over relations to the State can be read as yet another replay of the neverending "reform versus revolution" debate among left intellectuals and activists. But to say that this is a practical issue is to merely defer the philosophical issues until the moment when a decision must be made. The moment when cultural policy studies first comes into its own is interesting precisely because it rightly treats the relationship of left intellectuals and the State as a theoretical problem *and* a practical problem. But, as I will argue, the move to cultural policy is shot through with an unreconciled contradiction between a humanist philosophy of political reform and liberation (however modest or modulated) and an antihumanist philosophy of power that undermines the very politics of representation the *practice* of cultural policy studies aims to effect. The result is, predictably, something of a split between theory and practice. More importantly, the split leaves unasked crucial ethicopolitical questions about the representational politics of cultural policy studies itself. If we are to intervene in state, national, and international policy, whom do we claim to represent, and on what terms? Are intellectuals in cultural policy studies to work for others' interests beside their own, and if so, how will they deal with that relationship? Foucault's governmentality writings, the primary authorizing framework for cultural policy studies in its early phase, provide little guidance to these thorny and eminently practical questions.

Tony Bennett's work is of paramount important here, because he was perhaps the most strident advocate of the Foucauldian "governmentality" position in his theoretical writings on policy. As Toby Miller points out (1998, p. 72), Bennett's curriculum vitae is relevant, since he was well known as an exponent of Gramscian cultural studies before his move to policy. In *Outside Literature* (1990) and later work, Bennett almost wholly renounces this Marxist position for a Foucauldian one, making this moment in his work a particularly rich site for the questions driving this paper. The adaptation of Michel Foucault's work by Bennett and others in cultural policy studies offers a classic case study of the uneasy relationship between poststructuralism and progressive politics rooted in a more humanist tradition, and this is why I wish to consider the problem here. Foucault's work has often been characterized as antihumanist, yet it retains a kernel of the humanist political vision. Although he refused to make programmatic statements in his books, and although one of his most significant contributions to social thought is the genealogy of subjectivity, Foucault nevertheless holds on to ideas of liberation. As Amanda Anderson argues, Foucault's work appeals "at some level to a vision of unalienated relations and undamaged forms of social life" (1992, p. 64). Otherwise, why make a critique of prison reform or so-called sexual liberation? In both cases, his criticism is that they did not do what they said they were doing. There is, then, some residual promise of liberation in Foucault's work even as he declares the "death of man" and offers a genealogy of subjectivity. This contradiction between holding on to the possibility of some form of social and subjective transformation and the desubstantialization of subjectivity is perhaps one of the most productive tensions in Foucault's work. Inasmuch as cultural policy scholars have pursued a Foucauldian position, I argue that they inherit this contradiction from him. The tension between a suspicion of the idea of liberation and a commitment to left ideals predicated on some notion of political liberation thus haunts cultural policy studies' project.

Carlo Ginzburg has argued that this tension in Foucault's thought leads to a "populism with its symbols reversed. A 'black' populism—but a populism just the same" (1980, p. xviii). Ginzburg suggests (and I extend his suggestion below as "negative populism") that by refusing to represent those people excluded by traditional history, who were *in* the institutions that Foucault analyzes, he leaves aside any *specific* ethical or political claims in exchange for a diffuse populism. In other words, instead of the classic populist position of "whatever the people do is good," Ginzburg sees Foucault's willful silence on the question of "the people" as its own kind of undifferentiated representation of "the people." Gayatri Spivak's (1988) criticism of Foucault (and Deleuze) is based upon a similar claim: the refusal to represent is itself a kind of representation. Others have argued that Foucault's politics represent a kind of poststructuralist anarchism (May, 1994). One could also make compelling arguments for strands of liberalism and Marxism in his thought, which both demonstrate his debt to humanism (e.g., Foucault, 1991b). His two final full-length studies (Foucault, 1985, 1986) also indicate a willingness to revisit the political and ethical questions posed by humanist thought.

Regardless of one's opinion of this debate on Foucault, the nature of the problem changes when his thought is applied to Australian cultural studies. Cultural policy studies began as a movement among Australian cultural studies writers who sought to engage critically with the policy apparatus of the Australian government. Like other nations responding to the massive U.S. culture industry, Australia has a ministry of culture and has at times actually engaged with academics in the humanities and "critical" social sciences. The model of cultural policy initially developed by cultural policy scholars was specific to the kind of nation that Australia represents. As Graeme Turner argues, Australian cultural policy is shaped by the fact that Australia is a "small and economically weak nation . . . torn between adjusting what it does in order to compete internationally . . . or alternatively maintaining a close relation between its activities and a sense of national identity—even when this incurs economic penalties" (Turner, 1993, p. 70; see also Miller, 1998, p. 84 on the "local flavor" debates). Turner's point is that Australia is unique in having some potential autonomy in cultural policy because of its geographical isolation, but that it is at the price of its position in the international culture industries.

So, to twist around a phrase from Marx, we ought to begin by acknowledging the "special Australian conditions." A cultural policy studies for the United States, for instance, would look different since the playing field is different in terms of what kinds of academic work are able to interface with what kinds of federal policy. It is interesting to note that in the United States, the federal government has intervened heavily in questions of "cultural policy" without calling it that. Bennett (1997, p. 7) cites Tom Streeter (1996) who prefers "law" to the term "policy" given the latter's embeddedness in "technocratic assertion" (my argument in part follows Streeter's reasoning). But policy does indeed fit. What term better describes fighting for favorable export conditions for Hollywood films, reassigning the electromagnetic spectrum, and developing a comprehensive history curriculum for public schools? All these areas could come under the cultural policy rubric in another context. A historical view would include the various schemes for destroying, assimilating, and later recovering and preserving Native American cultures by the federal government, not to mention the massive and ill-fated project of Reconstruction after the Civil War.

As Bennett (1998a, n.p.; 1997, pp. 6–7) relates it, cultural policy studies has moved from a hotly-debated research direction to a widely accepted approach among humanities scholars in Australia. He attributes this to three major differences between Australia and other countries: cultural studies experienced a major institutional boom during a period when the Labour party controlled the federal government (1983–1996) and when the government entertained a strong interest in questions of cultural policy—in contrast to the legacies of Thatcherism in the United Kingdom and Reaganism in the United States; a "permeability" of relations between universities and the Australian government; and the Australian government's explicit and intensive attention to cultural policy (in contrast to, e.g., the United States—as discussed above). In other words, Australia provided a fertile testing ground for the cultural policy studies idea in its early development because of relatively favorable conditions for humanities scholars to get involved in the policy process.

I have thus chosen to focus most heavily on writings in cultural policy studies from the late 1980s and early 1990s for two reasons: 1) the particularly favorable conditions to left humanitites intellectuals' involvement in Australian policy prior to 1996, and 2) this is the period when the move toward Foucault in cultural policy studies was most explicitly thematized and where Foucault was most strongly contrasted with Gramsci and other more philosophically humanistic inspirational figures in cultural studies. It should be noted that Bennett has modified his position somewhat since these early writings, particularly in the mid 1990s (see Bennett 1997, discussed later). To maintain the flow of this piece, I have written it in what anthropologists call "the ethnographic present" while acknowledging that Bennett has moved away from his initial position somewhat.

It should seem obvious enough that a turn toward policy in cultural studies is a good thing. The administration of culture is no small matter. Indeed, Adorno (1978) claims that *administration* is the only common factor binding together the range of artifacts and practices that exists under the sign "culture" in modern capitalism. "Culture has always been about policy" in the hierarchies of aesthetic evaluation implicit in any form of cultural production or consumption, and in its organizational or institutional existence (Miller, 1998, p. 67). This is the ground from which Bennett (1992b, p. 395) argues that all cultural studies work has a "policy horizon" (and he makes clear that this is not to say that all cultural studies work should be on policy). More recently Denis McQuail has argued that because "the agenda of cultural policy issues grows, if anything, longer and more urgent," there is a "need to revive an 'applied' version of critical cultural study which might shed continuing light on what is happening to media culture" (1997, pp. 40–41). Academics are too often content to seek some kind of pure political position, whether revolutionary or nihilistic, from which to strike a political pose. As I have argued elsewhere (Sterne, 1998), we have nothing to gain from self-imposed marginality—beyond self-imposed marginality. But cultural policy studies argues for and directly thematizes engagement with policy bureaucracies in the name of making things better, however incrementally. While I would hope for a broader vision of social transformation guiding reformist activity, there should be no question that reform politics—that is, direct political engagement with policy bureaucracies for the purpose of progressive reform—has to be a legitimate component of politically engaged scholarship.

But there are many different operations at work in the advocacy of a "policy turn." In particular, questions of representation and normative politics bracketed by Foucault become essential when academics seek to engage policy bureaucracies in order to build better policy institutions. Some vision of social justice and the good life—however provisional or partial—must underwrite the move to and through policy. Without it, there would be no ethical or political reason other than self-interest to engage policy bureaucracies. Bennett (1998b, n.p.) acknowledges as much: the analysis of culture and policy invokes "questions of an inescapably normative kind." Cultural policies inevitably promote one way of life over another; "whenever the question of culture is in play and whenever it is connected to policy, compellingly vital issues concerning how the relations between different human ways of living will be managed are always at stake."

While Foucault's governmentality work has proven inspirational for many writers, it is essential to understand the limits of the applicability of this work as an authorizing discourse for the very specific action of critically engaging policy bureaucracies. The focus on *logics* of power in Foucault's work limits its applicability in terms of accounting for one's own implication as an agent (or as part of an agent) in fields of power relations. This is because because the Foucauldian paradigm brackets questions of outcome in particular contests between particular subjects, favoring instead a much broader scope: he is interested in the production of subjects (a distinction I further develop below). The result, insofar as Bennett casts cultural policy studies in a purely Foucauldian mode, leaves one of two apparent choices: reproducing an apparatus (albeit, for Bennett and others, in some kind of "transformed" state) or refusing to participate in the logics of power upon which it functions (which is why Foucault is sometimes called an anarchist). Moreover, by refusing to engage the very issues around political representation while seeking to do the work of political representation, Bennett's earlier programmatic and theoretical version of Australian cultural policy studies more or less reproduces a bureaucratic ethos and a politics of negative populism because it refuses to directly address these issues at the theoretical level.

I am arguing two very specific issues here: the use of a governmentality approach as the sole or fundamental warrant and intellectual grounding for approaching policy bureaucracies, and its attendant bracketing of issues central to the policy enterprise. This essay is not meant as a critique of the actual policy work of people who consider themselves cultural policy studies scholars (which, to my eyes, is often very un-Foucauldian)—least of all Bennett, who has at times been quite effective at getting culture on the policy agenda both within Australia and internationally. I also have no desire to reenter the policy debate on its own terms: Bennett (1997, p. 64) writes that early critiques of Foucault within British cultural studies were essentially claims that he "wasn't Marxist enough"—they were efforts to fit him into a Gramscian paradigm. My point here is not to measure one theoretical "brand name" against another, but rather to measure Bennett's application of Foucault's governmentality work to the question of policy against the engagement with the policy field he aimed to effect. In short, Foucault's governmentality may be *useful* but not *sufficient* for policy work.

The other area in which I hope to leave behind the terms of the policy debate have to do with its inflection of the longstanding "reform versus revolution" dyad. Bennett writes that to call for reform is "a long way from some of the better known clarion-calls of cultural studies: the call to a politics of resistance, for example; the commitment to organizing an alliance of popular forces in opposition to the state." (1997, p. 61). This theme appears repeatedly in Bennett's writing. Yet this article begins from a very different place: from the ethical ground that dominant systemic power relations in our societies—capitalism, racism, patriarchy, heterosexism, ageism—are wrong and ought to be eliminated. If we start from this premise, then both calls for total social transformation *and* efforts to effect change in very specific policy domains ought to be welcomed, or at least considered on their own merits, rather than for their position in the reform versus revolution dyad.

THEORETICAL FOUNDATIONS OF CULTURAL POLICY STUDIES

That said, the reform versus revolution dyad is a founding moment for Bennett's turn to Foucaultian governmentality. The turn toward policy cast itself against several tendencies within the field of cultural studies that gained a great deal of currency prior to and throughout the 1980s. As Bennett writes, "the 'policy debate' was itself a symptom of what was an already emerging division between revisionist tendencies within cultural studies—tendencies, that is, wishing to embrace reformist rhetorics and programs—and tendencies still committed to the earlier rhetorics of revolution and resistance" (1997, p. 191). Foremost among these was the ideology and resistance model that depends on a Gramscian model of hegemony, the State, and civil society. Adopting the Foucauldian perspective of "governmentality," Bennett (1990, p. 268) argues that "the political conspectus of Gramsci's theory of hegemony is, relatively speaking, a politics of consciousness, indifferent to the specific properties of the institutional sites in which it is conducted." Of course, this says more about Gramscians in cultural studies than Gramsci's own work: to suggest that Marxism, even "Western Marxism" is fundamentally a politics of consciousness is to miss its most essential contribution to social thought. Marxism is not about the politics of consciousness alone, but rather situates consciousness against the material conditions of life and labor.

Cultural studies' innovation was to develop a kind of "cultural Marxism" that attended to culture as a significant site of struggle, *alongside* other sites. Through privileging consciousness as the primary object of study, this work winds up authenticating itself as political precisely because, as Bennett notes above, consciousness becomes the site of political struggle, or at the least the site where these scholars locate political struggle. This may well be a caricature of cultural Marxism, since it transforms the Gramscian project into an idealist exercise or achieving the properly conditioned consciousness. This is a central move in his critique: by arguing that Marxism is primarily a politics of consciousness, by turning Gramscian Marxism into a brand of idealism, Bennett is able to leave aside the large body of Marxist thought on capitalist institutions. Bennett instead claims that the Gramscian approach is itself insufficient because it cannot account for the institutional contexts in which cultural struggles emerge (see, for example, 1992a, p. 30). This methodological insufficiency then leads, for Bennett, to a practical insufficiency as well: if the Gramscian cultural studies perspective cannot conceptualize a "cultural technology," then it cannot effectively assist in "the development of practicable forms of politics capable of affecting the actions of agents within those cultural technologies" (p. 31).

In making this argument, Bennett claims that the Gramscian model takes the conditions of possibility for political struggle as given. As a result, he concludes that the Gramscian model only allows intervention in the struggle as it has been preconstituted. At the core of his critique is the issue of agency. Bennett (1992a) claims that Gramscian cultural politics has tended to promote shared perspectives among members of social groups and alliances among different social groups in anticipation of "the production of a unified class, gender, people, or race as a social agent likely to take decisive action in a moment of terminal political fulfillment of a process assigned to the task of bringing that agent into being" (p. 32). In other words, he argues that there is a revolutionary telos to Gramscian cultural politics that rejects anything short of total revolution as insufficient. Yet the theory of hegemony is precisely about piecing together contingent and sometimes inconsistent alliances in the form of power blocs. Barring a purist-anarchist political stance where actors might struggle against hegemony per se, it is a question of what classes make up the hegemonic bloc in a given society, and what the nonhegemonic classes need to do in order to achieve hegemony (e.g., a hegemony of the working class instead of the bourgeoisie—see Williams, 1977, pp. 108–115; Anderson, 1976–1977).

In his critique of Gramscian cultural studies, Bennett confuses a *horizon* of Marxist cultural politics with the *substance* of Marxist cultural politics. It is true that Marxist work (usually) holds out hope for total social transformation; but that work does not simply wait for that final moment. Rather, it understands historical process to be shaped by struggle. Bennett's confusion turns out to be a crucial move for his critique. As a result of his conflating Gramscians' end goal with their practice of cultural politics, he downplays their conceptualization of the importance of struggle and interest in political action *prior* to some kind of cathartic, apocalyptic moment of total revolution. The Gramscian notion of hegemony is well known to be predicated upon active struggle among groups whose affiliations shift. Gramscians do not generally sit around waiting for the revolution but rather give accounts of social process as a form of struggle for power and "consent" (again, see Williams, 1977, on this point); in fact, many scholars turned to the concept of hegemony because it provided a way out of simple domination-resistance models. That said, hegemony does rest upon a notion of politics as driven by the interests and intentions of actors. Bennett is right that the standard cultural studies hegemony model can be read as assuming (or at least taking from other sources) an account of the conditions of possibility for political action rather than providing its own alternative account.

So for Bennett, cultural studies scholars have to begin by understanding institutions as agents, as acting in the name of agents, and ultimately producing the conditions under which a group could come together in the name of some kind of unified interest. In understanding agency as operating on an institutional model, interventionist scholars engage with those institutions. Engaging policy agendas and operating procedures of cultural institutions, serving specific "cultural action groups," (a phrase I will consider carefully below) and impinging on the political process in such a way as to affect the kind of administrative apparatus capable of addressing specific problems would all be strategies of a policy-oriented cultural studies. "It will mean talking to and working with what used to be called ISAs rather than writing them off from the outset and then, in a self-fulfilling prophesy, criticizing them again when they seem to affirm one's direst functionalist predictions" (Bennett, 1992a, p. 32). In other words, cultural policy scholars can neither discount the state by taking it for granted nor, otherwise, mistake a diffuse model of power for the enabling condition of a kind of atomized, individualized agency (as in a resistance model).[1]

This move also warrants some reflection, because it has implicitly changed the domain of struggle. The model of power here, though semi-Foucauldian, is still resolutely top-down: one intervenes in the institution at the level of policy (i.e., at the top level). Stuart Cunningham argued that policy studies is precisely about moving away from "rhetorics of resistance, progressiveness, anti-commercialism on the one hand, and populism on the other" toward "those of access, equity, empowerment, and the divination of opportunities to exercise appropriate cultural leadership" (1991, p. 434). This is not simply to make the move of labeling Bennett a "reformist" and thereby reject his paradigm for something purer. Any serious left politics—that is, any left politics seeking to really improve people's lives in the present—must understand reform as a necessary part of the political process. But Bennett has already traded on the false dichotomy of reform/revolution: he casts the Gramscians as starry-eyed revolutionaries, waiting for the working class to take up arms. Against that he suggests that the work of cultural policy studies be addressed to the state and related institutions. In Bennett's early tales, reformist cultural policy studies plays the down to-earth pragmatist (which is not to say that Bennett is arguing for a philosophical pragmatism) to the spaced-out Gramscian idealist.

In setting up Gramscian idealism as a foil against a practical cultural policy studies, Bennett sells idealism short. As Jim McGuigan points out, so-called practicality is not necessarily the most effective policy strategy:

> In order to discover the sources of an effective and critical praxis, cultural studies must be imaginative, it must propose alternatives, different ways of ordering the social and cultural worlds. And, if this seems unrealistic, one only has to refer back to the unrealism of, say, British right-wing think tanks in the 1970s, who dared to think the unthinkable and had the opportunity to see some of their wildest dreams realized at the cost of great suffering. Cultural studies, then must be less restricted by its own space, recognizing that cognate work is going on in other spaces, aiming to reinvent the future, instead of becoming too bogged down in cataloguing the consuming pleasures of the present or merely assisting the grand pragmatics of bureaucratic and economic power. (1997, p. 153)

In other words, speculative work, idealistic work, work that holds out the possibility for radical social transformation may turn out to be incredibly useful in the long run. Rather than thinking in terms of the current policy agenda, cultural policy intellectuals should take a lesson from the British (and American) right and think in terms of changes that could happen over the course of decades.

Moreover, it is possible to engage with policy questions and retain an explicitly oppositional intellectual and political agenda. Toby Miller (1998, pp. 78–79) cites the work of Ruby Rich at the New York State Council for the Arts, Deborah Zimmerman from Women Make Movies, Ben Caldwell of the KAOS network and media critic and activist Douglas Kellner as examples of left intellectuals who did not need to abandon rhetorics of resistance, progressiveness, and anticommercialism to have significant accomplishments in the policy field. There are, in other words, a variety of ideological positions from which to approach policy. In fact, the cultural policy project itself can be read as part of a long term left project for a "rapprochement between the humanities and social life" that descends from Richard Hoggart, Raymond

Williams and E. P. Thompson down through Stuart Hall and Bennett's own earlier work at the Open University (Miller, 1998, p. 89).

Bennett's particular institutional emphasis also betrays the "special Australian conditions" informing this early work. Put simply, Bennett privileges the state as a cultural institution—probably because the Australian state was at the time a particularly amenable site for cultural policy studies. The one kind of institution noticeably absent from his analysis is the corporation. I believe this is the result of his reliance on Foucault for his theoretical authorization, since Foucault more or less takes for granted the development of capitalism as one of the backdrops against which he writes his own histories. And I use "takes for granted" deliberately. Despite Bennett's binary opposition between Gramscian and Foucauldian approaches, Foucault himself repeatedly asserts in his interviews with Duccio Trombadori that Marx's thought is central to his writings (see Foucault, 1991b). As Carrie Rentschler (2002) argues, in taking capitalism for granted, Foucault offers no account of corporate or economic power. Thus, Foucault's governmentality could be generously read as sympathetic to critiques of corporate power, but they require some supplementation for policy actors seeking to engage the economic or corporate fields. Moreover, attention to an economic analysis would reveal the complex interplay between cultural policy and these very economic conditions. Consider the ways in which work on academic labor in the U.S. has exposed the links between the politics of higher education, government funding for the arts and the humanities, the attack on the tenure system, increased reliance upon adjuncts and other undercompensated academic laborers, the movement among graduate employees toward unionization, and American labor unions' new interest in academics (see, e.g., Berube, 1998; Nelson 1997a, 1997b; Nelson & Watt, 1999; and the efforts of the on-line journal *Workplace*). One could say the same thing about any number of phenomena that should interest cultural policy scholars, from the sports-industrial complex to the repeated installation of new computers and disposal of old ones by all levels and kinds of bureaucracies.

Bennett would (and did) counter, that cultural policy studies goes beyond persuading institutions to change their policies; rather, it is oriented around the transformation of institutional *logics*. The goal is to change the rules of the game, rather than simply to help one side beat the other. This peculiar approach is best understood if we take a detour through the theoretical foundations of cultural policy studies. As Bennett writes it, the move toward cultural policy studies is founded on two primary axes: first, a reading of Foucault focusing on his "governmentality" writings; second, a critical reconsideration of the idea of "culture" in cultural studies, and especially the work of Raymond Williams through this Foucauldian perspective.

Foucault's notion of governmentality is based on his idea that power functions according to "logics"—that the "how" of power is as important as "who" has power (1991a, pp. 102–103). Governmentality becomes a political rationality not only for the state, but a whole set of relations of institutions, practices and discourses, which may or may not center upon the state (p. 104). Government is both "the conduct of conduct" and the disposition of "men [*sic*] and things." In other words, governmentality describe the logic by which everyday practice is organized through its, well, government. Governmentality, as the management of populations, distributes those populations differently through different contexts—prisons, schools, families—to different ends, but always acts on them through one instrument or another, never directly. Thus, from the perspective of governmentality, culture cannot develop in the abstract, but must rather be constructed through a variety of institutional contexts and toward contextually specific ends.

Bennett finds Foucault's governmentality is a useful contrast to Gramscian hegemony because of Foucault's particularly impersonal view of agency and because of his implicit emphasis on the bureaucratic state in modern life. The very definition of governmentality contains a totally different notion of agency as mechanical, a kind of impersonal force: governmentality itself *acts*. So in place of seeking out a "unified class, people, or race," cultural policy studies aims to identify and transform governmental logics.

The conduct of conduct and its institutionalization are Bennett's touchpoints for reconsiding Raymond Williams' conception of culture. Williams defined three major meanings of the word culture: a particular way of life, whether of a people, period or group; works and practices of intellectual and artistic activity; and the independent and abstract noun which describes a general process of intellectual, spiritual and aesthetic development (1975, p. 80). Bennett (1992a, pp. 25–27) argues that cultural studies scholars, in focusing on the tensions between the first two meanings of the words, have generally ignored the third. "Intellectual, spiritual and aesthetic development" of the individual would occur, according to Bennett's reading of Foucault, precisely under the circumstances he dubs "governmentality": these forms of "development" are at once questions of conducting conduct, the disposition of "the self" and ultimately the disposition of a population. Bennett's policy project can thus be understood through a critical rereading of Williams by way of Foucault: cultural studies writers have, thus far, focused on the relation between culture as a set of artifacts (kinds of textual production) and as a set of material practices assembled as a "way of life." By reinvoking the third term, Bennett enfolds this problematic into the larger structure of governmentality. If culture is indeed "a whole way of life" and governmentality takes as its object the population, then culture itself must be the product of various governmentalizations.

Through this logic, cultural policy studies takes culture as its object—but it understands culture as itself an object of administration. This has produced two main strands of scholarship within the field. A broadly historical and genealogical direction is exemplified by Bennett's work on museums (1995) and literature (1990). Bennett's work on museums considers at great length how they changed from private elite institutions in the eighteenth century to public, municipal institutions in the nineteenth century aimed at "culturing" the working class through a variety of regulations and practices. Similarly, Ian Hunter's (1988, 1992) work considers the uses of literary aesthetics and the study of English to produce a set of "relations to the self," to turn personality into a "vocation"—that is, the way in which the humanities (especially through literary studies) aim through their pedagogy to produce a certain type of individual. Toby Miller's *Well-Tempered Self* (1993) extends Hunter's insights in a slightly different direction, arguing that modern government and polics is aimed at producing "incomplete" subjects in need of supplementation, correction, molding, and cultivation.

The other major thrust of cultural policy studies work to date has been a more directly interventionist approach, where individuals coordinate their work with larger institutions and projects. Such work is devoted to specific policy development, involvement in government process, and consultancy. Bennett (1992b, p. 406) offers two examples: the regulation of broadcast content by bodies like the Australian Broadcasting Tribunal, and the monitoring of the cultural resources available to minority ethnic groups of the kind undertaken by the Office for Multicultural Affairs. A quick tour through the newsletters produced by the Key Centre for Cultural and Media Policy presents an impressive array of concerns such as gun control, new media, indigenous citizens' rights, land rights and tourism, and censorship (e.g., Goggin, 1996; Hippocrates, 1996; Trotter, 1997). Even these examples show the "special Australian conditions" that shaped Bennett's vision of the possibilities for cultural policy. About the same time that Bennett's example of the Australian Broadcast Tribunal appeared in print, the agency was dismantled in favor of the more deregulatory Australian Broadcast Authority, which appears to be moving Australian media regulation into line with other deregulatory approaches, like that of the Federal Communications Commission (FCC) in the United States.

So the initial mission of cultural policy studies can be described as apprehending the histories and mechanics of individual cultural institutions toward the end of influencing their functioning in the present. In these terms, cultural policy studies doesn't sound all that different from an oft-heard litany in the humanities and social sciences: "We study culture so we can change it!" Policy studies, however, understands its commitment to changing culture as one that compels it to engage with various "policy-making" institutions because it understands these institutions as primary sites of agency within culture. But writers like Bennett, Hunter, and Cunningham, while supporting the above formulation, are careful to reserve for themselves the possibility of opposition. To this end, they cite Foucault's advocacy of a "governmental logic of the left," based on the hopeful formulation that to the extent that the governed are engaged by the government, governmental rationality becomes an affair of the governed. Foucault, making a move that foreshadows much of the rhetoric of policy studies (and is frequently called upon to support it), claims that "to work with government implies neither subjection nor global acceptance. One can simultaneously work and be restive. I even think that the two go together" (quoted in Gordon, 1991, p. 48).

The result is that cultural policy studies has to walk a fine line. It wants to reserve for itself a position of dissidence while at the same time entering into dialogue with powerful cultural institutions. This, in no small part, has to do with the long tradition of socialist politics associated with cultural studies (at least in its British incarnation); Bennett is quick to point out that such major figures as Williams and Stuart Hall have themselves been active in policy questions. At issue is the relationship of academic practitioners of cultural policy studies to the institutions they hope to affect. In other words, to what extent and under what conditions can one both work with the government and be restive?

THE BUREAUCRATIC ETHOS AND NEGATIVE POPULISM: APORIAS OF CULTURAL POLICY STUDIES

This is where we begin to see the limits of Foucault's governmentality paradigm for informing policy work: in the policy context, "any attempt to uncouple the pragmatic from the ethical is dubious" at best (Miller, 1998, p. 97). While it provides a theoretical foundation for the policy turn, it cannot ground an ethic of practice on its own; nor can it begin to account for the specifics of either the internal political logics of institutions *or* the relation between cultural policy studies' position in the academy and its interventions in other institutions. This is because Foucault's work is highly specific, and because it tends toward questions of mechanics while bracketing outcomes.

While Foucault's work can certainly be read as "theory," it is also very historical, whether in its genealogical or archaeological incarnations. Yet the specificity of his work is vague: he uses terms like "the West" and "modernity" at the same time that he draws the majority of his sources and examples from France.[2] In any case his work clearly does not address itself directly or specifically to present incarnations of individual institutions. Rather, Foucault's work has always been most concerned with institutions as generalized logics or mechanisms (disciplinarity, medicine, psychiatry, prisons, sexuality).

In privileging the principles underlying the production of social contexts—questions of logics and apparatus—this orientation simultaneously brackets the question of any *specific* outcome of those logics and apparatus. Bennett illustrates the benefits of this approach through his discussion of

Nancy Armstrong's history of conduct books for aimed at domestic women. To cut to the chase:

> the domestic woman was, in short, the very model of the auto-inspecting, self-regulating forms of individuality required by liberal forms of government. The intelligibility of her functioning in this regard, however, depended precisely on her placement at the inter-section of a series of overlapping antinomies (female-male; high-low; private-public; state-civil society) and her ability, in relation to each of these, to function as part of a reformatory gradient through which that which lies outside the sphere of culture and government (male boisterousness) is to be brought into it and refashioned. (1997, p. 81)

This analysis provides an interesting account of gender in the production of subjectivity. What is does not provide is a neat way of talking about relations among particular men and women. In other words, if we were to look at a particular struggle over women's conduct in public (see, for example, Ryan, 1990, pp. 131–170), we would have to get back into questions of which women could speak in public and on what terms. These questions are in fact crucial ones—as much today as they were in the nineteenth century—for policy analysis. Of course, to ask Foucault for the latter kind of analysis (dare I say sociological?) would be to miss the point of the former; but this latter, more particularist analysis is crucial to interventions in the policy arena where there are clearly winners and losers with each major policy decision. Indigenous people are either granted certain formal rights or they aren't; women are treated as fully political subjects or they aren't. It is this smaller, contest-specific, and perhaps "sociological" sense of outcome—crucial to actually existing policy questions—that is not well explained or analyzed by the analytic of governmentality.

In other words, one can attend to the mechanisms of power and still wind up mystifying the field of differential relations produced by these mechanisms. Remember, one of the founding premises of cultural policy studies is working *with* "what used to be called ISAs." In a way, this mystification of struggle is much like the error that Bennett finds in Gramscian cultural studies: questions of immediate struggles are put aside in the service trans-forming—now—institutional logics. Questions of interest, disposition, justice, and oppression are entirely bracketed, even though these are the very political grounds upon which cultural policy studies work authorizes itself. To put it more succinctly, Foucauldian governmentality provides no mechanism for determining the difference between working *with* the government and working *for* the government.[3] "One can simultaneously work and be restive" appears in cultural policy studies work more as an axiom than an argument.

The point here is not to recover a position of authentic resistance, but rather to have some understanding of the terms of engagement in the first place. The alternative is not very promising, and is well illustrated by Christopher Simpson's (1994) work on the history of communication studies: during the 1940s and 1950s, "psychological warfare" and "communications research" were semantically identical in some contexts. That is to say, a good deal of apparently "objective" research in communication was actually defined in terms of very definite military and propaganda goals. Just as there has been a debate over the purpose of communication research, there also needs to be a debate about the ultimate purpose and shape of cultural policy studies. For all their antihumanism, Bennett, Hunter, and other advocates of the Foucauldian approach ultimately render the relations between intellectuals in cultural policy studies and policy institutions a personal, rather than a structural issue.

Foucault's assertion about government—a fairly humanistic notion that one can work with the government while being fundamentally opposed to it—relies on a notion of a (at least semi-autonomous) subject that is constituted outside the institution within which it is working. In other places, Foucault argues for a struggle against power in all its forms (cf. 1977b, p. 216).[4] It is one thing to contradict oneself—everybody does—but it is another when this contradiction is then taken up by third parties to provide ethical justification for a project. Cultural policy studies work has, to some degree, used Foucault as an authorizing discourse for its policy move—which would be fine—except that it uses Foucault's "being restive" comment programmatically. Even this would be fine if its extent were clearly delimited. Perhaps Foucault so often demurred on questions of instruction and programmatics—"what should we do?"—precisely because his work gave him no answers to such questions.

While work in cultural policy studies (and other related Foucauldian strands of cultural studies) has produced numerous and thorough critiques of cultural institutions from a "logics-of-power" perspective (literary education, the museum, libraries, schools, the regulation of pornography, etc.), there is very little discussion of the specific position of the policy practitioner,[5] nor have I found any genealogical work done on the relation of academics to policy processes and apparatuses, especially as this relation is enacted through cultural policy studies. Though Toby Miller (1998) has rightly pointed out that anxieties over engagement with policy apparatus are somewhat unique to humanities intellectuals—colleagues in the social sciences and sciences have long been doing research funded by governmental agencies—he has not gone on to consider the questions raised by left intellectuals in those fields about the status of work driven by governmental policy interests.

For his part, Bennett (1993) offers a gesture toward a genealogy, but one that locates cultural studies as an outgrowth of English, thereby effacing the development of cultural studies in other fields such as comparative literature, education, American studies, sociology, geography, and anthropology. As Stuart Hall puts it, the Centre for Contemporary Cultural Studies received hate mail from people in both literature and sociology.[6] Locating cultural studies as an outgrowth of English allows Bennett a certain set of rhetorical gestures that would otherwise be unavailable. Two are of primary concern here. His advocacy of a policy turn gestures toward an "outside" of the discipline. To the extent we allow that cultural studies is an outgrowth of literature, he is right— English professors, as a group, do not get very involved in policy (although he would also rightly point out that people like Williams and Hall *were* concerned with policy questions). Policy lies outside the theoretical-practical continuum within the discipline of English as it is traditionally conceived. But other disciplines have an ongoing connection with, and history of relations with, policy apparatus: anthropology, communication studies, geography, and even some national literatures (for instance, Russian language programs). Insofar as cultural studies emerged out of an interdisciplinary field, these other disciplinary histories have to be acknowledged, and ultimately, understood. For instance, an advocacy of policy-orientedness in anthropology has to reckon with the discipline's own history (to take one example, its role in the Vietnam War in the United States). In the case of geography, there are two sides to the policy coin: a large subfield designed to train planners, and also a tradition of radical planning scholarship. Russian language and area studies programs in American Universities were often tied to well-defined military and state department objectives. Of course, one could also find many examples of humane and progressive connections, for instance between scholars interested in educational policy and progressive changes in educational practice. But there is a huge and complicated history of engagements between intellectuals and policy institutions. By claiming that cultural studies is an outgrowth of English, Bennett, and Hunter (who has on several occasions argued for bureaucratic values over literary-aesthetic values—see Hunter, 1992b) free themselves from the burden of considering the ethical and political implications of academic work that has engaged policy over the last 60 years. While academic work on policy can lead to progressive ends, it is far from a foregone conclusion that it will, even if the academics in question have the best of intentions.

Bennett's use of the ideology of science is also rooted in a disciplinary history that presumes English as the point of origin for cultural studies. As Toby Miller argues, cultural policy studies "has an account of past and present textual criticism as a practice, but—as we shall see—no account of its own emergence in relationship to the wider domain of analyzing policy. Its autobiography continues to be articulated against aesthetic critique" (1998, p. 71). As Miller goes on to point out, Bennett takes up positions that would be impossible were he to successfully "breach the space between the humanities and social sciences." Were Bennett to locate the history of cultural studies in relation to, say, sociology or communication studies, he would have to consider the long debates within those fields about the role of "science" in social and political thought (see, e.g., Mills, 1959). Despite assurances that he is not proposing "that cultural studies aspire to the status of a science," (1993, p. 218) Bennett idealizes science through a rhetoric of meritocracy. In response to posthumous praise of Raymond Williams' personal integrity, rather than the technical merit of his work, Bennett writes,

> My purpose, then, is to ask what kind of discourse of the truth enables (indeed requires) the utterance of remarks of this kind. For it is clear that the discourse and the opposition which organizes it— essentially that between a knowledge whose truth claims are based on criteria of technical competence and one which seeks its basis in the personal qualities of the intellectual—*would have no pertinence in other spheres of intellectual inquiry: math, engineering, economics, or political science for example.* (p. 230; italics added)

The problem here is that Bennett's assertion—that prestige in science is accorded on purely meritocratic terms—is simply untenable. From the blurbs on "great mathematicians" in introductory math textbooks, to cults of personality surrounding figures like Edison and Einstein, personality—the "greatness" of the individual—is clearly an issue. (In fact, several studies have shown that prestigious journals in physics and psychology rejected articles they had previously published by well-known full professors when that work was repackaged and resubmitted as the work of unknown graduate students.)

Most importantly, Bennett's willingness to embrace an ideology of science ignores the institutional biases of the sciences surrounding major axes of difference (e.g., the mantra of gender, sexuality, race, ethnicity, and class): in the case of gender, there is no guarantee that a woman doing the same quality of work as a man will be accorded the same position in the laboratory, in the author line of a manuscript, or in the scientific profession at large. The problem with overtures to "objective" evaluation in the humanities is that they tend to mystify the very real power differentials that affect scholars and students' academic opportunities (American Institutes of Research, n.d.; Aisenberg & Harrington, 1988; Blier, 1988; Caplan, 1993; Nieva & Gutek, 1980; Parr, 1989; Peck, 1978).

Bennett's and his colleagues' emphasis on the objectivity of evaluation in scientific fields (and even the so-called "softer" social sciences like political science) suggests the continued relevance of the epistemological, methodological, and political questions that feminism has posed to cultural studies: we are not working in a "post-feminist" moment. This is not a critique unique to cultural studies. Insofar as intellectuals (regardless of field) are willing to cling to unreconstructed and needlessly abstracted indicies like "technical competence"—and mystify these concepts in an institutional structure without doing the hard work of actually ensuring equality of opportunity for everyone in the institution beforehand—their work will be unable to reconcile with, address, or "surpass" the questions posed by feminism and other politics based on the "shared experience of social groups."

Bennett's invocations of scientific language to legitimate his positions is somewhat typical of cultural policy studies work of the late 1980s and earliy 1990s. In another example, Hunter, Williamson, and Saunders (1993) claim a certain kind of objectivity for their study of pornography—a discursive position that is neither tenable in their case nor desirable in general, since both women and men are assumed to have an "interestedness" in the subject matter. In fact, this study of pornography is particularly instructive because of the authors' dismissive and monolithic view of feminism: rather than recognizing a long feminist tradition of debate around pornography and sexual representation, they erroneously take the Dworkin-MacKinnon antipornography position as representative of feminism *as such*. Far from taking an objective position on the question of pornography, Hunter, Williamson, and Saunders clumsily restate a particular position within a larger debate as if it were the debate as such. Because they have not grappled with the local and positioned struggles within what they term "the pornographic field," they are unable to truly get outside its logic to analyze them. Once again, it seems that unfinished business with feminism (and other position-based critiques) is a prior condition for cultural policy studies scholars' overtures to objectivity.

Similarly Stuart Cunningham describes his own research as "empirical," a claim that Meaghan Morris criticizes, given that Cunningham's *Framing Culture* offers exactly one empirical example, and his other case studies are in fact "thumbnail theoretical critiques of an assortment of texts" (Morris, 1992, p. 549). In fact, Cunningham's own use of the term "empirical" was to distinguish his argument about the relation of cultural theory to policy processes—which he says is based on "empirical observations"—from Tom O'Regan's (1992), which comes from "his own fine work . . ." (i.e., from personal experience).

This brings us to the vexing question of what is valued in Bennett's vision for cultural policy studies. I showed above how cultural policy studies founds its own claims on a critique of a Gramscian politics of consciousness. Specifically, he argues against understanding politics as a process that has the formation of a unified group ("class, gender, people or race") as an agent capable of taking positive action in its own interests in a "moment of terminal political fulfillment" (1992a, p. 32). At the same time, cultural policy studies appears to understand itself as an agent acting in the name of less powerful groups:

Cultural studies might envisage its role as consisting in the training of cultural technicians: that is, of intellectual workers less committed to cultural critique as an instrument for changing consciousness than to modifying the functioning of culture by means of technical adjustments to its governmental deployment (1992b, p. 406).

Similarly, in a footnote to a citation of Stuart Cunningham, Bennett (1992b) asserts that the role of the policy studies intellectual should be one of "cultural facilitation" in that "intellectuals should play more of a technical and coordinating role in enhancing the range of available cultural resources and facilitating more equitable patterns of access to those resources" (Bennett, 1992b, p. 407, n2). In other words, Bennett's ideal intellectual is the cultural technician; the cultural technician, however, is very close to the cultural bureaucrat.

Bennett's work takes up the language of bureaucratic technicism and efficiency—via a detour through its invocation of Foucault's governmentality as a logic of power—in the name of providing an alternative to a politics of consciousness. I should make clear here that this is not meant as a defense of the politics of consciousness, but rather as a critique of the terms that Bennett chooses to oppose it. As Barry, Osborn, and Rose argue, "the opposition [between the rise of the technical and aspirations to the realization of full human potential] hampers thought about our present and its ethical character—it must be refused. . . . Human capacities are, from the perspective of these investigations, inevitably and inescapably technologized" (1996, pp. 12–13). This much is clear. But Bennett in fact swings the pendulum in the other direction, rejecting the humanist model of a nontechnologized subject in favor of technique as an affirmative and desirable model of political action. In so doing, he embraces the bureaucratic model of politics: one that prizes efficiency and function—hence his frequent invocations of "technicians" and "tinkering." Far from being a positionless critique of the conditions of possibility for politics, Bennett's writing appears as a clearly *positioned* critique of politics from the perspective of a state bureaucracy. Michael Pusey (1991, p. 125) remarks upon bureaucratic officials' willingness to privilege technical considerations over political factors, and furthermore, their general assent that there are times when the technical concerns of government predominate over value and principle. As Denise Meredyth points out, these responses themselves indicate the presence of a bureaucratic ethos: a "distinctive combination of the intellectual, the technical and the ethical" (1992, p. 502). While there is certainly nothing inherently wrong with combining the intellectual, the technical and the ethical, my concern is that Bennett's invocation of technique mimics the occupational ideology of state bureaucracy. So it is to the question of bureaucracy that I turn—specifically to Max Weber's classic discussion of bureaucracy.

Weber's approach clearly resonates in Foucault's work, though Foucault diverges in important ways and almost never uses the term "bureaucracy." Bureaucracies predate capitalism for Weber (for instance, he discusses Egyptian bureaucracy), but he clearly depicts the rise of the modern nation-state as a precondition for the explosion in the size and intensity of bureaucratic forms. Like Foucault's governmentality, Weber's bureaucracy is a logic of functioning abstracted from any particular result. In fact, it is in some ways the purest expression of function abstracted from its specific manifestation; bureaucracy is by definition a mechanical, desubjectified form of social organization.

> The fully developed bureaucratic apparatus compares with other organizations exactly as does the machine with the non-mechanical modes of production. Precision, speed, unambiguity, knowledge of the files, continuity, discretion, unity, self-subordination, reduction of friction and of material and personal costs—these are raised to the optimum level in the bureaucratic administration. (Weber, 1968, p. 973)

These are, not coincidentally, the very values Bennett upholds as an alternative to the "politics of consciousness" implied by Gramscian cultural studies. Bennett's vision of the depersonified "cultural technician" equally at home in front of the literature class and in the policy apparatus is also a core element of bureaucratic reasoning in Weber's schema:

> Bureaucratization offers above all the optimum possibility for carrying through the principle of specializing administrative functions according to purely objective considerations. . . . "Objective" discharge of business primarily means a discharge of business according to *calculable rules* and "without regard for persons." (1968, p. 975; italics in original)

Insofar as we believe Weber has a relatively accurate characterization of bureaucracy and the bureaucratic ethos, Bennett—via his reading of Foucault—appears to actually argue *for* the values of bureaucracy as an alternative to other value-systems for cultural studies. But bureaucratic values are clearly consonant with the administrative apparatus; they do not in and of themselves provide an oppositional stance from which to approach policy-making organizations. On the contrary, the bureaucratic ethos is a kind of accommodation before the fact. As John Frow points out, higher level bureaucratic workers, by the very virtue of their positions, play an "ideological" role in policy shaping (1992, p. 515). For instance, carrying out the work of a bureaucracy "without regard for persons" (one possible bureaucratic value) may or may not be an ethical course of action in any given instance, but it certainly could have an ideological impact on the formation or implementation of policy. This ideological role suggests that policy work cannot operate at a purely technical level—"tinkering with mechanisms"—but must also continue in some form the "struggle over consciousness" with which Bennett wants to dispense. In other words, bracketing the questions of outcome, ethics, politics, and positionality is entirely consonant with a certain bureaucratic mentality. For Weber, it is one of the primary goals of bureaucracy.

The point is not simply to resist bureaucracy as some kind of inherent evil—the slow-moving institution can be a useful alternative to more autocratic and impulsive institutional models in many circumstances. But Bennett's advocacy of the politics of technique does not occur in a vacuum. On the contrary, unless we assume that his choice of metaphors is essentially meaningless and without context, Bennett's bureaucratic language ought to be read against bureaucracies' self-descriptions. In other words, his move to a language of technique risks uncritically reinstantiating the occupational ideologies of state bureaucracies. There may well be reason to sometimes go along with these occupational ideologies, but it is at least as dangerous to privilege a priori a politics of technique as it is to privilege a priori a politics of consciousness. Bennett is right when he says that intellectuals—and especially cultural studies writers—who think they are not already implicated in an institution are misleading themselves (1997, p. 2–3). But emphasizing our institutional groundedness is not the same thing as working through our agonistic relations with academic or policy institutions. Without a critical analysis of intellectuals' relations to the state, cultural policy risks becoming no more than "a wistful urge for intellectuals to have more importance than they actually have," to borrow a phrase from Bronwen Levy (1992, p. 553).

Whose Cultural Policy?

By engaging (or at least addressing) the policy field, cultural policy studies work portrays itself as providing a service—acting in the name of helping someone. Cultural policy studies writers can orient themselves toward service of policy institutions (e.g., "to make museums run better") or they can orient themselves toward service of the populations these institutions act upon (e.g., "to make the museum serve Native Americans better"). Notable in Bennett's invocation of "the cultural technician" is the lack of any indirect object for verbs like "facilitating." In fact, the only indirect object Bennett uses in this earlier theoretical work is the purposefully vague "cultural action groups." In other words: In whose name does cultural policy studies work act; whom *does it represent?* The issue is not that all politics should be about representation but rather that questions of representation are especially important in terms of how academics authorize themselves within the policy field. To put it another way, representative democracies always demand that policies be made in the names of constituencies (even when those constituencies may not in fact even really exist).

Bennett studiously avoids naming the object of his benevolence; cultural policy studies will work *with* policy institutions and "cultural action groups," but it is never clear *for whom* it will work. This is not to suggest that cultural policy studies scholars need to name once and for all their politics—they can, as have writers in cultural studies, work in a variety of domains toward a variety of changes. However, questions of the stakes of political representation are altogether bracketed in the work of Bennett and other influential scholars in the field. Oddly enough, Bennett does not seem to evaluate cultural policy "on behalf of those affected by it" but rather by technical criteria—how well it can be implemented by the government. "No indication is given of the ethical technology for distinguishing among cultural projects, between huge grants to ballet and small ones to street theater, no explanation of the precepts that govern the population, or of how the graduates in literature who run the institute [for cultural policy studies at Brisbane University] deem themselves qualified to do so" (Miller, 1998, pp. 73–74). Cultural policy studies offers a populist position without a populace.

Herein lies the negative populism at the base of cultural policy studies: despite the attempts to avoid questions of interest, positionality, ethics, and politics in cultural policy studies work, "cultural studies is being told to pursue the popular under the sign of governmentality and the [generalized] cultural citizen" (Miller, 1998, p. 72). Bennett's political claims are characterized by a refusal of any political positioning beyond a generic "left"; the only commitment we find in his writing on cultural policy is an unwillingness to represent the people he claims to represent. Since I have characterized him as a negative populist, Bennett's own writing on populism and "the popular" is instructive here.[7] In an essay commenting on struggles over the definition of popular culture, Bennett argues that we cannot abstractly fill in the category of "the people" or "the popular":

> I shall argue in favour of an approach which keeps the terms *definitionally* empty—or, at least relatively so—in the interest of filling them *politically* in varying ways as changing circumstances may require. (1986, p. 8)

Bennett's pragmatic answer to the philosophical problem of "the people" has an appealing ring to it, yet one must also ask at what point and by whom these terms will be filled and defined politically. Given that politics is always in process, we would expect that certain prevailing definitions exist and that some might be preferable to others. To this end, Bennett's essay explores the classic populism of socialist workerism and several other versions of "the people," all of which he rejects. Although I am very much in sympathy with a position that says we cannot simply define the protagonists of a political struggle before the fact, and that one might see multiple populations (themselves with conflicted and conflicting interests) rather than a unified "people" as political protagonists, total agnosticism on the question suggests that anything *could* fill the definition. Extending this early line of thought into his writing on cultural policy presents a real problem. If "the people" are never defined, and cultural policy scholars are to act on people's behalf in the policy field, should we simply depend on the whims of the cultural policy studies scholars as to whom they will represent in the policy field? This is, of course, a position that Bennett could propose. But it is only a plausible political position if cultural policy studies does not claim to be particularly *left* in its political orientation, and if it puts aside Foucault's critique of institutional logics in order to argue for a rational, self-knowing subject (in this case, the cultural policy scholar) who will make the decision when he or she is good and ready to do so. This is why I characterize Bennett as a *negative* populist: according to him, cultural policy studies is to operate in the name of groups whose definition will be defined later—in a final instance that never arrives. He represents "the people" as an undifferentiated whole, an anticipated constituency, by refusing to represent or differentiate them. Because cultural policy studies aims to represent someone other than itself in the policy field without specifying that someone, the very liberationist humanism it claims to reject returns through the back door. "The problem of speaking in the name of the popular is that it has not encouraged us to radically question the discourse and politics of representation" (Canclini, 2001, p. 27).

Stuart Cunningham, in his advocacy of policy, is much more willing to align himself with specific social groups:

> I strongly support the articulation of opposition when communities of interest refuse the common sense of the dominant culture—in gay and feminist cultural politics, in the politics of the disabled, of race and of youth. Some of the best outcomes in equity and access may arise from these articulations of opposition. (1992, p. 542)

But as Meaghan Morris points out shortly thereafter in the same volume (1992, p. 549), his actual theory of political representation seems to be a reproduction of the very traditional paternalistic narrative of political representation that cultural policy studies claims to reject. In other words, Morris criticizes Cunningham because his political program ultimately falls back into a kind of vanguardism, where the enlightened few will lead that many. Again, it is possible that cultural policy studies could—in theory—advance a new kind of "limited" or "strategic" vanguardism for policy intellectuals, but it has not done so. Cunningham (1993, p. 134) has gone on to argue for the value of a "social democratic view of citizenship and the training necessary to activate and motivate it"—in other words, a model of citizenship not based in consumerist or identity politics. Similarly, Jim McGuigan (1996) has argued for grounding cultural policy studies in a modified "public sphere" model. While these are clearly both normative models, both still beg the question of political representation: for whom does cultural policy studies take its stand in the policy field?

An understanding of the logic of the representative politics would seem to be essential to the cultural policy studies project. Pierre Bourdieu (1991, p. 248) argues that representative democracies (like Australia or the United States) operate through a logic of transubstantiation: since an entire group cannot act within the political field, it designates a spokesperson. But an agent with access to the political field can also "create the group that creates him [*sic*]." In other words, by speaking for a group, the speaker hails them in a particular way, and if enough people identify with the speaker (and not necessarily what is being said in their names)—or even, under some circumstances, simply fail to refute the hail, for example by ignoring it or taking an apathetic stance toward it—then that speaker can operate as though she or he was speaking *for* the entire group. The process can go either way. Even when clearly acting in their self-interest, agents within the political field must present themselves *as though they were acting in the interests of the groups they purport to represent*. Cultural policy studies work, by refusing to address the question of representation directly, ultimately cannot justify its position vis-à-vis *any* group it purports to represent. This is especially a problem given Cunningham's call for a "cultural politics that situates the power or effect of academic discourse within communities of interest where it does not have priority, but must establish its credentials" (1992, p. 542). Because cultural policy studies work offers no theory of political representation, and instead confines its discussion of politics to Foucault's governmentality, it cannot offer any kind of systematic explanation or justification for its position. The policy field into which Bennett wants to move also operates on a similar logic: it operates as though unified interest groups existed, and that political representatives could speak for them. Thus, if Marxist literary criticism has a lesson for cultural policy studies, it is a rather simple one: if you're going to play politics on the terms of the policy-making field, you need a theory of political representation.

Conclusion: Cultural Policy Studies—Moment, Movement, or More?

Through examining the ways in which early writings in cultural policy studies—most notably those of Tony Bennett—ground the move to cultural policy in a bureaucratic ethos, I have attempted to clarify the limits of their appropriation of Foucault's governmentality work and antihumanist philosophy more generally for political work. Although Bennett is able to raise questions of the institutional position of intellectual practice, and is able to address the logics of power underlying some of the disciplinary formations of English and cultural studies, he is ultimately unable to address more practical questions outcome that are directly relevant specific contests over specific policies. He offers a fairly confused ethical position concerning "staying inside" versus "getting outside" various logics of power: the political technology of the individual (as created by literary criticism) is something to be avoided, but the ideology of science—and most emphatically meritocracy—is to be emulated. The direct questions of political representation are left unasked. My concern here has not been so much to criticize Bennett for being inconsistent, but rather to use that inconsistency to point out the practical incompleteness of the theoretical paradigm he advocates. And this problem arises directly from the confrontation between antihumanism and humanism in the work of cultural policy studies.

Two qualifications are in order at this point. First, this resolute silence on the part of earlier cultural policy studies writers regarding constituencies and politics may have been an artifact of the field's emergence under a Labour government: even if specific scholars had differences with government policies, there was some sense of a shared mission (at least on questions of reform) that could be left implicit. Second, my criticism of Bennett's theoretical grounding of cultural policy studies is not meant to be a criticism of the *practice* of cultural policy studies. On the contrary, cultural policy scholars—and Bennett himself—seem to have been quite willing to engage in the wars of position and struggles over hearts and minds that Bennett criticizes in his theoretical work on governmentality and policy.[8]

In fact, Bennett's own writing in its more practical moments has never fully embraced his theoretical stance. At the conclusion to *Culture: A Reformer's Science*, Bennett responds to Richard Miller's (1984) criticism of the Open University *Popular Culture* course. Bennett's response is instructive here because he blends a governmentality approach with political analyses more properly belonging to the "pre-Foucauldian" cultural studies. For instance, when Miller criticizes the course for not allowing students to go beyond the regurgitation of facts from the course for exams, Bennett rightly points out the class basis of Miller's critique: forms of examination that favor the acquisition of knowledge from outside the classroom favor students with a middle class (or higher) background (1997, p. 225). Later, Bennett takes an explicitly antipopulist stance in responding to Miller's assertion that students' own narratives ought to be affirmed in pedagogical situations: "it supposes that all such narratives *should* be affirmed and that their being spoken will be a productive and useful activity for all concerned" (1997, p. 227). He goes on to illustrate his point anecdotally: an upper-class student of his was revolted at the idea of learning how the yobbo working classes of the north of England spent their holidays. While Bennett says these objections must be responded to in a tactful manner, we need not build a classroom around encouraging their expression (p. 228). My point here is simply that in matters of pragmatics, Bennett already makes clear that the governmentality approach, alone, is insufficient for analyzing and dealing with questions of policy (and in this case, pedagogy). Indeed, fairly classic formulations of class issues reappear and must be dealt with. The question, then, is how policy studies will move forward.

In a review of *Accounting for Tastes: Australian Everyday Culture* (Bennett, Emmison, & Frow, 1999), Ken Gelder gives the distinct impression that the Australian academy has undergone a sea change from semiotics to ethnography as the privileged models of analyzing popular culture. But cultural policy studies' promise is that it is more than a new school of criticism to replace the old and keep the ink fresh in scholarly journals. Set against the work of traditionally humanistic scholars, its promise was an actual engagement with government and policy. In that respect, we can hope that cultural policy studies is more than a scholarly moment or movement, but rather an enduing approach.

So far, the evidence is encouraging. The work of cultural policy studies has continued to grow in Australia and worldwide since the early 1990s, and has resisted a theoretical orthodoxy and monomoniacal commitment to the exclusive use of the governmentality analytic. Some of Toby Miller's writing (1993, 1998, 2001), for instance, has fruitfully continued the critical project of cultural policy studies. Other writers whose work is clearly informed by cultural policy studies have moved away from an authorizing framework that relies solely on Foucault's notion of governmentality. When Nancy Campbell (2000) confronted the implications of her own analysis of women and drug policy in the United States, she found that policy questions extended beyond Foucauldian "logics"—much more traditional questions of positionality and interest came to the fore and the outcomes of contests over specific laws were essential to her history. As a result, Campbell critiques both the mechanics of the policy field—its "institutional logic"—and the specific and repressive results of American drug policy. Her analyses of drug policy intelligently blend the questions posed by Foucauldian governmentality—the construction and management of subjects and populations—with the question of political representation. For instance, she shows how the occupational ideologies of legislators, the logics of legislative discourse, and struggles over representation U.S. Senate hearings on drug policy led to an early instance of "three strikes" law in this country. Her analysis is promising precisely because she so skillfully integrates the analytics of "culture as consciousness" and "culture as governmental logics" that Bennett opposed to one another 10 years prior. Similarly, Néstor García Canclini (2001) has forged a unique position in Latin American cultural studies by arguing for the importance of citizenship as a category of analysis *alongside* consumption rather than in simple opposition to it.

Perhaps, since scholars are able to shift between roughly antihumanist and roughly humanist positions in practice, it is time to acknowledge as much at the theoretical level. This will require a different understanding of the relationship between those questions of representation posed by humanist political philosophy and the critique of humanism elaborated in Foucault's writings and elsewhere. The crucial work of elaborating a range of social theories appropriate to cultural policy studies has really just begun. Marx, Weber, Gramsci, Foucault, Williams—these and many other names are useful for thinking through the messy work of cultural politics and cultural policy. But if our goal is political, then our loyalties cannot lie with any one of them. As we go forward in the cultural policy enterprise, our foremost responsibility is to remember *why* we are doing this work in the first place.[9]

NOTES

1. The question of Gramsci's ultimate usefulness for social theory will be left open as it is beyond the scope of this paper. Suffice it to say that the policy move has, in founding its own position, chosen to do so on a critique of Gramsci, especially as his work is taken up within cultural studies and Marxist literary theory. For a more direct comparison of Foucauldian and Gramscian approaches, see Bennett (1990, pp. 268–272 and passim) and R. Radhakrishnan (1990).

2. This is one of the primary contradictions running through Foucault's works such as *Discipline and Punish* (1977a) and *The History of Sexuality, Vol. I* (1978). For a brief discussion of his own understanding of how "specificity" plays out in his own work in terms of its domains, see Foucault (1980, 67–68).

3. This is not to say that working *with* and *for* the government are necessarily opposed, but clearly they could be—if one is opposed to the government or its policies, certainly one does not want to be working to further its ends, especially in terms of allowing the government to define the terms of the engagement.

4. For more discussion of the contradictions of humanism and antihumanism in Foucault's work, see Fraser (1989).

5. It is also interesting to note that Foucault's notion of the "specific intellectual" is generally not discussed in policy literature.

6. If we are willing to say that the CCCS is not the only or necessary point of origin for cultural studies, then we cannot reduce its history to an extension or refiguring of literary studies in British schools. This fact is acknowledged even in the histories of cultural studies that emphatically place Birmingham at the center (so to speak), such as Grossberg, Nelson, and Treichler (1992) and Nelson (1991).

7. This earlier work comes before his explicit move to Foucault and policy, but to my knowledge none of his later writing has significantly reconceptualized the positions he advances here.

8. It should also be noted the cultural policy studies takes for granted liberal, representative democracies as the form of government. Obviously, autocracies are another whole set of issues. In fact, at an international level, neoliberalism may also raise questions about the policy studies paradigm because it is a kind of corporate and super-governmental autocracy.

9. Many thanks to readers who have helped this essay along its long and winding path: Jack Bratich, Greg Dimitriadis, Larry Grossberg, James Hay, Jeremy Packer, Carrie Rentschler, Carol Stabile, the Foucault reading group at the University of Illinois, and two anonymous reviewers. Although this essay contains a critique of his work, Tony Bennett also deserves thanks for helping shape my initial thoughts about cultural policy studies and governmentality during his visit to the University of Illinois in 1994.

REFERENCES

Adorno, T. (1978). Culture and administration (W. Blomster, Trans.). *Telos, 37:* 93–111.

Aisenberg, N., & Harrington, M. (1988). *Women of academe: Outsiders in the sacred grove.* Amherst: University of Massachusetts Press.

American Institutes of Research. (n.d.). Social-educational climate affecting sex equity. *Institutional self-study guide on sex equity for postsecondary education institutions* (Section 5, pp. 1–2). Washington, DC: Association of American Colleges.

Anderson, A. (1992). Cryptonormativism and double gestures: The politics of poststructuralism. *Cultural Critique 21* (Spring), 63–95.

Anderson, P. (1976–1977). The antinomies of Antonio Gramsci. *New Left Review 100:* 5–78.

Barry, A., Osborne, T., & Rose, N. (1996). *Foucault and political reason: Liberalism, neoliberalism, and rationalities of government.* Chicago: University of Chicago Press.

Bauman, Z. (1992). *Intimations of postmodernity.* New York: Routledge.

Bennett, T. (1986). The politics of "the popular" and popular culture. In T. Bennett, C. Mercer, & J. Woolacott (Eds.), *Popular culture and social relations* (pp. 6–21), London: Open University Press.

Bennett, T. (1990). *Outside literature.* New York: Routledge.

Bennett, T. (1992a). Putting policy into cultural studies. In L. Grossberg, C. Nelson, & P. Treichler (Eds.), *Cultural studies* (pp. 23–37). New York: Routledge.

Bennett, T. (1992b). Useful culture. *Cultural Studies 6* (3): 395–408.

Bennett, T. (1993). Being "in the true" of cultural studies. *Southern Review 26* (2): 217–238.

Bennett, T. (1995). *The birth of the museum: History, theory, politics.* New York: Routledge.

Bennett, T. (1997). *Culture: A reformer's science.* Thousand Oaks, CA: Sage.

Bennett, T. (1998a). Cultural studies: Distinguishing characteristics of Australian cultural studies. In Australian Research Council (Ed.), *Knowing ourselves and others: The humanities in Australia into the 21ˢᵗ century*. Retrieved Jan. 15, 2002 from http://www.asap.unimelb.edu.au/aah/research/review/b8_bennett.html

Bennett, T. (1998b). Culture and policy: Acting on the social. Transcript of a Canadian Cultural Research Network Colloquium. Retrieved Jan. 15, 2002 from http://www.arts.uwaterloo.ca/ccm/ccrn/documents/cooloq98_Bennettt.html

Bennett, T., Emmison, M., & Frow, J. (1999). *Accounting for tastes: Australian everyday culture*. New York: Cambridge University Press.

Berube, M. (1998). *The employment of English: Theory, jobs, and the future of literary studies*. New York: New York University Press.

Blier, R. (1988). Science and the construction of Meani the neurosciences. In S. V. Rosser (Ed.), *Feminism within the sciences and health care professions*. New York: Pergamon.

Bourdieu, P. (1991). *Language and symbolic power* (G. Raymond & M. Anderson, Trans.). Cambridge, MA: Harvard University Press.

Campbell, N. (2000). *Using women: Gender and drug policy in the United States*. New York: Routledge.

Canclini, N. G. (2001). *Consumers and citizens: Globalization and multicultural conflicts* (G. Yúdice, Trans.). Minneapolis, MN: University of Minnesota Press.

Caplan, P. J. (1993). *Lifting a ton of feathers: A woman's guide for surviving in the academic world*. Toronto, Canada: University of Toronto Press.

Cunningham, S. (1991). Cultural studies from the viewpoint of cultural policy. *Meanjin* *50*(2–3): 423–434.

Cunningham, S. (1992). The cultural policy debate revisited. *Meanjin 51*(3): 533–544.

Cunningham, S. (1993). Cultural studies from the viewpoint of policy. In G. Turner (Ed.), *Nation—Culture—Text: Australian cultural and media studies* (pp. 126–139). New York: Routledge.

Foucault, M. (1977a). *Discipline and punish: The birth of the prison* (A. Sheridan, Trans.). New York: Vintage Books.

Foucault, M. (1977b). *Language, counter-memory, practice: Selected essays and interviews*. D. Bouchard (Ed.). Ithaca, NY: Cornell University Press.

Foucault, M. (1978). *The history of sexuality, vol. 1: An introduction* (R. Hurley, Trans.). New York: Vintage Books.

Foucault, M. (1980). *Power/knowledge: Selected interviews and other writings 1972–1977*. C. Gordon (Ed.). (C. Gordon, L. Marshall, J. Mepham, & K. Soper, Trans.). New York: Pantheon Books.

Foucault, M. (1985). *The use of pleasure: The history of sexuality, vol. 2* (R. Hurley, Trans.). New York: Vintage Books.

Foucault, M. (1986). *The care of the self: The history of sexuality, vol. 3* (R. Hurley, Trans.). New York: Vintage Books.

Foucault, M. (1991a). Governmentality. In G. Burchell, C. Gordon, & P. Miller (Eds.), *The Foucault effect: Studies in governmentality*. London: Harvester/Wheatsbeaf.

Foucault, M. (1991b). *Remarks on Marx: Conversations with Duccio Trombadori* (R. J. Goldstein & J. Cascaito, Trans.). New York: Semiotext(e).

Fraser, N. (1989). *Unruly practices: power, gender and discourse in contemporary social theory*. Minneapolis, MN: University of Minnesota Press.

Frow, J. (1992). Rationalization and the public sphere. *Meanjin 51*(3): 505–516.

Gelder, K. (2000, February–March). Cultural habits and practices. *Australian Book Review*. Retrieved Jan. 15, 2002 from http://home.vicnet.net.au/~abr/FebMarch00/gel.html

Ginzburg, C. (1980). *The cheese and the worms: The cosmos of a sixteenth-century miller* (J. Tedeschi & A. Tedeschi, Trans.). Baltimore: Johns Hopkins University Press.

Goggin, G. (1996). Boom time for new media. *Media and Culture Review 1*(1): 6.

Gordon, C. (1991). "Governmental rationality: An introduction." In G. Burchell, C. Gordon, & P. Miller (Eds.), *The Foucault effect: Studies in governmentality*. London: Harvester/Wheatsbeaf.

Grossberg, L., Nelson, C., & Treichler, P. with Baughman, L. (1992). *Cultural studies*. New York: Routledge.

Hippocrates, C. (1996). Policy makers to tackle violence. *Media and Culture Review 1*(1): 1.

Hunter, I. (1988). *Culture and government: The emergence of literary education*. London: Macmillan.

Hunter, I. (1992). Personality as a vocation: The political rationality of the humanities. In I. Hunter, D. Meredyth, B. Smith, & G. Stokes (Eds.), *Accounting for the humanities: The language of culture and the logic of government*. Brisbane, Australia: Institute for Cultural Policy Studies.

Hunter, I. (1992b). The humanities without humanism. *Meanjin 51*(3): 479–490.

Hunter, I., Williamson, D., & Saunders, D. (1993). *On pornography: Literature, sexuality and obscenity law*. New York: St. Martin's Press.

Lazarsfeld, P. (1941) Remarks on administrative and critical communications research. *Studies in Philosophy and Social Science 9*(1): 2–16.

Levy, B. (1992, Spring). Ruffling the feathers of the cultural polity. *Meanjin 51*(3): 552–588.

May, T. (1994). *The political philosophy of poststructuralist anarchism*. State College, PA: Pennsylvania State University Press.

McGuigan, J. (1993). Reaching for control: Raymond Williams on mass communication and popular culture. In J. Morgan, & P. Preston (Eds.), *Raymond Williams— politics, education, letters* (pp. 163–187). New York: Macmillan.

McGuigan, J. (1996). *Culture and the public sphere*. New York: Routledge.

McGuigan, J. (1997). Cultural populism revisited. In M. Ferguson & P. Golding (Eds.), *Cultural studies in question* (pp. 138–154). Thousand Oaks, CA: Sage.

McQuail, D. (1997). Policy help wanted: Willing and able media culturalists please apply. In M. Ferguson & P. Golding (Eds.), *Cultural studies in question* (pp. 39–55). Thousand Oaks, CA: Sage.

Meredyth, D. (1992). Changing minds: Cultural criticism and the problem of principle. *Meanjin 51*(3): 491–504.

Miller, T. (1993). *The well-tempered self: Citizenship, culture, and the postmodern subject.* Baltimore: Johns Hopkins University Press.

Miller, T. (1998). *Technologies of truth: Cultural citizenship and the popular media.* Minneapolis, MN: University of Minnesota Press.

Miller, T. (2001). *Sportsex.* Philadelphia: Temple University Press.

Mills, C. W. (1959). *The sociological imagination.* New York: Oxford University Press.

Morris, M. (1992). A gadfly bites back. *Meanjin 51*(3): 545–551.

Nelson, C. (1991). Always already cultural studies: Two conferences and a manifesto. *Journal of the Midwestern Modern Language Association,* 24–38(1).

Nelson, C. (1997a). *Manifesto of a tenured radical.* New York: New York University Press.

Nelson, C., & Watt, S. (1999). *Academic keywords: A devil's dictionary for higher education.* New York: Routledge.

Nelson, C. (Ed.). (1997b). *Will teach for food: Academic labor in crisis.* Minneapolis, MN: University of Minnesota Press.

Nieva, V. F., & Gutek, B. A. (1980). Sex effects on evaluation. *Academy of Management Review 5:* 267–276.

O'Regan, T. (1992). Some reflection on the "policy moment." *Meanjin 51*(3): 517–533.

Parr, J. (1989). Chilly climate—the systemic dilemma. *OCUFA Forum 6*(18): 1–2.

Peck, T. (1978). When women evaluate women, nothing succeeds like success: The differential effects of status upon evaluations of male and female professional ability. *Sex Roles 4:* 205–213.

Pusey, M. (1991). *Economic rationalism in Canberra. A nation-building state changes its mind.* Melbourne, Australia: Cambridge University Press.

Radhakrishnan, R. (1990). Toward an effective intellectual: Foucault or Gramsci? In B. Robbins (Ed.), *Intellectuals: Aesthetics, politics, academics* (pp. 57–99). Minneapolis, MN: University of Minnesota Press.

Rentschler, C. (2002). *The crime victim movement and U.S. public culture.* Unpublished doctoral dissertation, University of Illinois, Urbana, IL.

Ryan, M. (1990). *Women in public: Between banners and ballots.* Baltimore: The Johns Hopkins University Press.

Simonson, P. (2001, May 28). The centrality of Robert K. Merton. Presented at the annual conference of the International Communication Association, Washington, D.C.

Simpson, C. (1994). *Science of coercion: Communication research and psychological warfare, 1945–1960.* New York: Oxford University Press.

Spivak, G. C. (1988). Can the subaltern speak? In C. Nelson & L. Grossberg (Eds.), *Marxism and the interpretation of culture* (pp. 271–313). Urbana, IL: University of Illinois Press.

Sterne, J. (1998). Deferral, denial, disavowal and discontinuity: Leftism and the love of Academia. In The Bad Subjects Production Team (Eds.), *The bad subjects anthology* (pp. 19–24). New York: New York University Press.

Streeter, T. (1996). *Selling the air: A critique of the policy of commerical broadcasting in the United States.* Chicago: University of Chicago Press.

Trotter, R. (1997). Land rights, tourist rights: Whose rights? *Media and Culture Review* 2(1): 1.

Turner, G. (1993). Cultural policy and national culture. In G. Turner (Ed.), *Nation, culture, text: Australian media and cultural studies* (pp. 67–71). New York: Routledge.

Weber, M. (1968). *Economy and society: An outline of interpretive sociology, Vol. 2.* (G. Roth & C. Wittich, Trans.). Berkeley, CA: University of California Press.

Williams, R. (1975). *Keywords.* London: Fontana.

Williams, R. (1977). *Marxism and literature.* New York: Oxford University Press.

Chapter 6

Disciplining Mobility

Governing and Safety

Jeremy Packer

In his "Governmentality" lecture, Michel Foucault (1991) pinpoints Guillaume de La Perrier's statement in *Mirror Politique*, one of the first anti-Machiavellian treatises on government, "government is the right disposition of things, arranged so as to lead to a convenient end" (Foucault, 1991, p. 93), as the demarcator of the shift from sovereignty to governmentality. According to de La Perrier, and Foucault by extension, ruling was no longer consumed by the task of simply retaining sovereignty. Rather, it became the responsibility of rulers to employ tactics that would benefit the population as well as the State. In place of the goal simply to maintain territory and loyalty, men and territory were seen as a means to an ends, assuming they were properly disposed. According to Foucault, the metaphor often used to illustrate this point, in the governing manuals of the eighteenth century, was the governance of a ship (p. 93). This metaphor speaks to a concern with not only the men on the ship and the potential gain produced by successful shipping, but, importantly, the avoidance of catastrophes that could befall such an enterprise. It is the choice of this metaphor that I want to elucidate in this essay. It bears further elaboration because it points out the importance of mobility in the formation of thought concerning governing. In an increasingly mobile world, governing mobility consumes greater and greater amounts of mental and physical resources. A vast literature explains the structural organization, political and economic advantages, and general importance of transportation and communication systems that crisscross the globe. But more specifically, the disposition of these resources takes place not only on a global or national scale. In contemporary America, personal mobility is primarily achieved through the brute materiality of cars, trucks, buses, trains, motorcycles, and airplanes. This form of mobility plays a vital role in how individuals organize, rationalize, and inhabit their world. It is at this intersection of governance and governed (increasingly self-governed) in the realm of the microphysics of power, that the following analysis of the politics of mobility is located. Quite literally, "individuals are the vehicles of power" (Foucault 1980, p. 98). Personal mobility must therefore be seen as an act of power. An examination of the "net like-organisation" (p. 98) that binds individual aims and governmental aims can illuminate the important ways that our individual mobile conduct is implicated in, guided by, and resistant to seemingly detached political, economic, and cultural trends.

The relative importance ascribed to Foucault's work is often based on his analysis of large-scale processes such as power, discourse, or, more recently, government. The critical orientation that such generalities provide for current and future intellectual enterprises is certainly important. However, it needs to remain clear that the specificity of Foucault's research was often the microphysics of power and close discursive investigation of key texts that oriented thought at critical moments. Furthermore, thinking about mobility, like thinking about incarceration or madness, demands detours into discursive territory that is not necessarily obvious at first. In the case of this essay the notion of safety has oriented my road map for investigating how personal mobility is linked to governing. As the ship metaphor makes explicit, an important part of governing in general and mobility specifically is the avoidance of catastrophe. It is this avoidance—being safe—that comes to construct thought and ultimately self-reflection about mobility. As Foucault explains, in order for something to be governed, or imagined as governable, it needs to be problematized (1990b). This is to say that an activity to be governed needs to be thought of in terms of a problem to be overcome. In this regard, mobility, like communication (Mattelart, 1996, p. xvi), has historically been seen as an economic, cultural, and political good, but it has been problematized according to the dangers that it posed.[1] The idea of safety serves then as the solution and provides a normative orientation for mobility. Once this orientation solidifies, as I will argue it has, it disperses into a vast array of normative contexts, thereby legitimating forms of governance and self-governance that have little relation to any specific problematization.

Foucault characterizes pastoral power as a form of governing that links the individual to the state through an obligation to preserve the well-being of the citizen and attend to the needs of the population, in order to, in turn, assure a strong state. This relationship between governed and governor, as the metaphor suggests, owes much to Christianity. Ultimately, it is the conduct of the individual, not devotion and loyalty, that strengthens the state, through increased production, longevity, and population growth. The assurance of a good life here on earth replaces the reward of the afterlife as the carrot that leads the citizen down the road of proper conduct. Safety, security, and good health take the place of salvation. Just as salvation hinges on a set of undeniable truths, desire, the fear of mortality, and good conduct, so does safety.

However, in contemporary government, these truths, desires, and fears do not emanate from a single source, like the King or the Church. Foucault explains in "Governmentality" that the key issue is not so much how the State has become a force for governmentality, but rather, how governmentality has come to be the rationale for all programs of social regulation and production, State and non-State alike (1991, p. 103). Keeping this in mind, we need to approach any study of safety and the governing of mobility not simply as a social good, but as an integral part of governing across various contexts, with multiple State and non-State apparatuses taking a part in both the legitimation and dissemination of safety as social good and personal orientation. Keeping governmentality and pastoral power as the backdrop, the remainder of the essay examines the articulations that bind specific processes of knowledge, power, and subjectification with personal mobility, safety, and governance.

American Mobility—A Sacred Contract

Motorized traffic has played a tremendous role in the formation and creation of the safety discourse as it exists in contemporary America. Automobiles and motorcycles play a central role in American popular culture, a vital role in the American economic system, and an often overlooked part in the police, military, and rescue apparatuses. In order to be a "good" productive and consumptive American demands buying and driving an automobile. This entry into a "sacred contract" provides Americans their auto-mobility—meant in both the literal and figurative sense of the word. The automobile is the guarantee that one is mobile and to be mobile in America is to drive an automobile. However, even though driving is sacred to Americans, traffic fatalities have come under increased scrutiny over the past hundred years from a growing number of sources. Contradictory statements regarding the utility, devastation, and desirability of motorized mobility merge in a messy array of slogans, statistics, movies, songs, television programs, billboards, educational pamphlets, policing manuals, and educational programs to form a dispersed discourse. In the following, the key issues will be what forms of power produce and guide mobility, what type of knowledge legitimates and orients the governance of mobility, and what type of subject fulfills this sacred contract.

It has been argued for years that the automobile is the single most influential machine of the twentieth century (Patton, 1986; Rae, 1971; Whitney, 1936). It is impossible to assert in any qualitative or quantitative way that this is true, but Jacques Ellul, asserts, in contemporary society "everything (has) to be considered in terms of the machine . . . everything (is) brought into line with the machine" (1964, p. 5). So if we take the automobile, and to a lesser degree the motorcycle, as exemplary machines in this process, we come to recognize, as many have, that the social structure of postindustrial nations in the twentieth century were drastically altered at nearly every level by the automobile. From time, space, and mobility (Ellul, 1964, p. 327) to the construction of masculinity and femininity (Marsh & Collett, 1986), nearly all facets of modern life have in some way been brought into line with motorized transport and the machines used to accomplish it.[2] The American popular truths of freedom, wide open spaces, and individuality have been integrated with and altered by the mobility promised to 16-year-olds today, just as Henry Ford promised them to potential consumers of the Model T 90-odd years ago.

In the United States, cities, suburbs, and rural spaces are laid out according to a design that is automobile friendly. Commuting, shopping, dating, traveling, transporting goods, and policing are all intimately linked to the motorized vehicle network. Machines, designers, stylists, advertisers, politicians, bureaucrats, academics, and engineers, both social and scientific, all work together in a tightly orchestrated fashion in order to expand and perpetuate a network that is absolutely integral to the neoliberal capitalist state. Gilles Deleuze and Felix Guattari call this sort of network across space *striation* (1987, pp. 474–500). This conception brings to the fore the logic that produces, governs, and organizes space. Striation not only accounts for the physical structures of transportation that are readily apparent, but also for the role they play in governing and the very conceptualization of the social that governance depends upon. Andrew Barry notes that the striation of space made possible both liberalism itself and the resultant governing at a distance, primarily through communications and information technologies (1996, pp. 123–141). However, the commonsense understanding of communications is too narrow to fully appreciate the importance that it has had in establishing liberal governance. Armand Mattelart makes clear that communications, as a technique, has always focused not just on the transfer of messages, but on overcoming barriers in general in order to facilitate the transfer of people, goods, and culture (1996). Furthermore, as he points out, communications is a not only a technique, but a utopian vision of liberal democracy. The striation of space then ostensibly enacts communication in this general sense, and it is historically and conceptually linked with the techniques of governing and the utopian dreams of rulers. Techniques are not needed only to striate the space, but also to keep it well oiled and running smoothly. This is the role that safety often plays. When the human, mechanical, and conceptual components of this communications system break down, they are either fixed or disciplined according to the logic of safety. Safety experts create a set of technical knowledges that prescribe human conduct that accords with the logic of this striated space. Thus populations and activities that do not accord, or which mutiny one could say, are expelled, outlawed, or reintegrated into this striation. Disruptions occasioned by women drivers, youth, hitchhikers, truck drivers, motorcyclists, minorities, drunk drivers, and most recently roadragers have all functioned as specific forms of breakdowns. Mechanical or natural breakdowns also appear. Track-jumping trains, imploding airplanes, exploding Pintos, and somersaulting Corvairs are just a few of the mobile nemeses that sabotage striated space. As will be explained later, however, it is not necessarily a real threat in any empirical sense that automatically activates a response. Put simply, safety is not an absolute by any means. Just as the rules for entering the gates of heaven have changed, so do the rules for staying alive.

Merging Safety and Technique: Disciplined Mobility

Paul Virilio's thesis in *Speed and Politics* (1986) is that the power of the State is primarily that of the police: the management of the public ways. He follows this with a combative assertion on thinking about knowledge. Virilio states in his study, "the related logic of knowing-power, or power-knowledge, is eliminated to the benefit of moving-power—in other words the study of tendencies, of flows" (p. 47). An examination of this statement will make it apparent that although Virilio does provide impetus to think about the importance of mobility and its control, his dismissal of the relationship between power and knowledge not only weakens his claims but forces his hand regarding notions of power and freedom. Foucault, according to Virilio, is the thinker of confinement and disciplinarity. Power/knowledge according to Foucault describes the coconstitutive capacities of knowledge and power to produce apparatuses of control, regulation, and production. The important insight that power/knowledge provides is that discourses such as science, medicine, or psychology, through their monopoly on truth claims, exert the power to determine the relative face of "reality." For instance, Foucault in *Madness and Civilization* (1965) explains how, through the creation of the descriptive category of madness, a whole series of material effects were carried out upon those deemed mad by medicine and psychology. Knowledge then is not simply descriptive, but productive. It produces, among other things, normative categories, prescriptions for proper conduct, and relations of power: for instance the relationship of doctor-patient or highway patrolman-driver.

Virilio, by dismissing the power/knowledge thesis, demonstrates that his understanding of power is in line with traditional Marxism in which power is wielded by the State and is exerted upon an unsuspecting proletariat, with negative effects.[3] His discussion of freedom begins to reveal his notion of the negative effects that the power of speed has, namely the loss of freedom. Freedom for Virilio is something innate to individuals rather than the product and necessity of certain forms of government. Furthermore, speed is a correlate of freedom within conceptions of mobility: more speed is said to equal greater freedom. In *Foucault and Political Reason* (1996), Andrew Barry,

Thomas Osborne, and Nikolas Rose critique this understanding of freedom and its relation to a top-down conception of power. The following quote sums this up:

> Freedom is neither an ideological fiction of modern societies nor an existential feature of existence within them; it must be understood also and necessarily as a formula of rule. Foucault's concern here might be characterized as an attempt to link the analysis of the constitution of freedom with that of the exercise of rule; that is, with the extent to which freedom has become, in our so-called "free societies," a resource for, and not merely a hindrance to, government. (p. 8)

If we are to take Foucault's notion seriously we need not simply look for instances in which something, in this instance speed, leads to a loss of freedom, but instead reveal the types of freedom produced by speed, the types of regulations placed on speed and its purposes, and the necessity of freedom as a constitutive element of the very notion of speed. Speed after all is always relative; it is measured against what is considered the normative rate.

Freedom and mobility, one of its material corollaries, must be understood then in their specificity and in their necessity to current forms of governing, State and otherwise. This demands a recognition that as the potential for mobility is increased, the subject of governing must change in accordance. A "more free" or at least "more mobile" citizen becomes necessary to partake actively in a differently striated space. Thus the goal of governing is not to simply guard against too much freedom, but to produce the type of freedom that accords with the expansive demands of culture and economy. Governing at a distance across striated space takes the place of direct control. A proper deployment of power requires enabling and activating "men and things" (Foucault 1991, p. 93) in a manner that allows them to and in fact demands that they move outside of confined and continuously surveyed arenas. It also means striating space in such a fashion that rule can still be exercised. Depending upon what perspective drives one's analysis, one could view the directly surveyed subject as far less dangerous to the State than the mobile subject, and thus more free, in that once it is surveyed, its perceived ability to do harm to the state is minimal and thus not taken as seriously. Mobile subjects, on the other hand, must be highly disciplined, because they are not under continual surveillance, are not always within the immediate scope of state interaction, and are depended upon to execute the goals of State and non-State institutions when the State per se is not present to do so. Thus, to be mobile is to be free to govern oneself, across a vast territory, but it is always in accordance with governing in so far as it coincides with "convenient ends" (p. 93).

Contrary to Virilio, Deleuze argues (1988) that Foucault's global project is apparent in his discussion of the naval hospital found in *Discipline and*

Punish (1979) which is to say his understanding of networks of power in space, is made clear. Deleuze argues that it is necessary to look at Foucault's notion of discipline not simply as a singular form of power or means of control. Discipline is just one of many forms of power, and it is essential to also take into account not only knowledge, which Virilio dismissed, but also subjectification (which, as it relates to mobility, will be elaborated in the last section of this essay). At this point I want to consider the value of the notion of discipline for the analysis of automobility.

Turning to Foucault's analysis of the naval hospital, we find that very little is made obvious regarding mobility. In fact, the naval hospital merely serves as an example of what Foucault calls "functional sites" which are only one of four techniques related to "the art of distributions" (1979, p. 143). The others are: enclosures (monastic model of places separated from the rest of world), partitioning (each individual has its own place and each place its individual), and rank (each place is fixed by classification). "The art of distribution" is itself only one of four structures that together perform the deed of producing disciplined subjects; docile bodies. As such the naval hospital is only an example of a small part of the disciplinary process.

The insight that the naval hospital does provide is that particular spaces serve as crossroads of several potentially dangerous trajectories. The naval hospital, for instance, was located at the crossroads of disease, weapons, armies, and commercial goods. By serving as a "filter, a mechanism that pins down and partitions" (p. 144), the military was able to control all of these dangerous trajectories and re-deploy them for productive purposes or eradicate them. The notion of the "functional site" may serve as one spatial form through which mobility is regulated and redirected, but it certainly can not fully explain the process of regulating and producing mobility all together. Foucault suggests later that what is needed is not an analysis of architecture, but of engineering. Instead what is needed is an understanding of how "docile bodies" can be made into "docile mobile bodies."

Lawrence Grossberg hints at something resembling this in a footnote to "Identity and Cultural Studies: Is That All There Is?"

> It is here that we can understand Foucault's distinction between different machines of power: societies of sovereignty and disciplinary societies—as different ways in which agency is itself constituted. In the former, agency is constructed on the materiality of the body. In the latter, through vision (surveillance) and structure (normalization). In disciplinary societies, the individual is placed into a mass space and monitored. Life is organized through enclosed environments. I might add a third category here—societies of disciplined mobilization—in which agency is organized through the control of mobility. (1995, p. 27)

This last assertion provides a starting point for the conception of disciplined mobility, although Grossberg takes an alternate approach to what I want to suggest. Grossberg's account deals with mobility and mobilization at a more metaphorical level than that which I am describing. His analysis of disciplined mobilization entails a detour through affect and everyday life. He argues that everyday life has been disarticulated from politics and that this is largely an effect of changes in groups' "mattering maps." This is to say that potentially politicized cultural formations, such as rock music, have increasingly failed to compel mobilizations outside disciplined spaces and into places of their own. Instead mobility itself has become the norm. This negates the possibility for the production of places that could ground political affect. The result is "an apparatus which produces spaces with no places, mobility with no stability, investments with no permanence, belonging with no identity, authority with no legitimation" (Grossberg 1992, p. 296). To a degree, the understanding of mobility that I outline in this essay is both more general, in that it attempts to situate mobility itself within a long historical process of liberalism, and more specific, in that it will explain the micromechanisms of discipline which organize individuals' mobility as opposed to the potential mobilizations of social formations.

Disciplined mobility then may be a very specific machine of power that operates across striated spaces and is aimed at particular populations. As Grossberg notes, disciplinarity is a different form of power than sovereignty, and Foucault in his "Governmentality" lecture makes clear that government can be added to, though it by no means replaces, other forms of power: producing a triangular power of sovereignty, disciplinarity, and government. The primary target of this triangle is population and "its essential mechanism the apparatuses of security" (p. 102). The examination of this notion of security has generally taken the route of an investigation into the governmental formation of welfare and urbanism (Rabinow 1989), insurance and risk management (Castel, 1991; Defert, 1991; Ewald, 1991; O'Malley, 1996) and health (Osborne, 1996; Petersen & Bunton, 1997). This work tends to focus upon the formation of expert knowledges that produce normative standards that support the enactment of policy that insures the general "well being" or security of populations in liberal societies. These accounts tend to prioritize expert knowledge over popular knowledge as most of their concern is with the element of governing. However, the production of mobile subjects and their implication in self-governing is often more attentive to popular knowledge than expert knowledge. Furthermore, safety campaigns have often begun with nongovernmental institutions and special interest groups, which respond to and depend upon popular sentiments of fear and stereotyping, and the popular culture that transmits them. Toby Miller (1998) goes so far as to say that popular truth (knowledge) has become a key element in the formation of governmental power. Thus the mapping of popular truth bears considerable importance when it comes to safety. As will be shown, the specific disciplinary and biopolitical formations that correspond to mobility respond to both popular truth and expert knowledge.

Disciplined mobilization is necessary for many of the social and economic changes said to characterize neoliberal capitalist societies. On a global scale the nature of the world economy demands vast mobilizations of populations.[4] When these mobilizations are nomadic, as with refugees and illegal aliens, new sites are created in order to monitor and redirect migratory patterns, much like Foucault's naval hospital. What may prove more important though is the possibility that certain places, like the United States, have been societies of disciplined mobilization from the outset. Governmental initiatives to settle the West have always depended upon creating mobile populations to accompany economic investment in transportation systems that striated new territories often before European populations had moved in.[5] A highly mobilized, yet less than nomadic, population is needed in order to adapt and migrate from old urban centers to new jobs in suburban sites of production. Post-Fordism has led to a less centralized form of production in which both technologies of production and populations are increasingly under the gun to mobilize quickly in order to meet new market shifts. These movements occur not only in local areas, but also across regions of the United States, from the Northeast and Midwest to the Southwest and Southeast. The ever increasing demand for lengthy job related automobile commutes in the United States is just one other current example of the importance of a highly mobilized population. In this way Virilio's claim that Foucault has been the thinker of confinement and closed spaces may speak more to the fact that he chose prisons to elaborate his discussion of power, his call to examine "territory, communication, and speed" (Foucault, 1989, p. 264) has not been dealt with in any extensive fashion, and his specifically French project, due to the formation of modernity after, not before, European spacial striation, is historically and contextually contingent. The more important question is, To what extent can Foucault's understanding of discipline provide insights into something which might be called disciplined mobilization?

As noted above in the quotation from Grossberg, the historical shift from sovereignty to discipline denotes a shift from a focus on the power over life to the power of creating productive populations and individuals. Foucault distinguishes between the technologies of control corresponding to the individual and the population. The first focused on "the body as machine" that took the form of "discipline: an anatomo-politics of the human body." The second concerned the "species body" in what Foucault called "a bio-politics of the population." The former dealt with disciplining the most minute actions of individual bodies through various apparati, the most notable being the prison, the school, the military, the hospital, the asylum, and the factory. The latter focused upon the health, propagation, and longevity of the population through medicine, sexuality, and the social sciences. The two technologies work together, reinforcing each other in the various spaces in which both individuals and populations find themselves. Both technologies are needed to fully understand disciplined mobility as it is being described here. Mobilization and mobility correspond respectively to discipline and biopolitics. Mobility is generally a more individualized capacity to move from place to place, and it is here that discipline enters the picture as its focus is upon individual bodies. Mobilization, on the other hand refers to the movement of populations, their deployment for particular purposes. While Grossberg's "disciplined mobilization" is largely a matter of population biopolitics, disciplined mobility involves both population biopolitics and anatomo-politics.

A caution regarding the notion of disciplinarity is in order here. In *Discipline and Punish*, (1979) Foucault makes clear that his research was specific to the French penal system as far as its history was concerned. Yet this has not stopped numerous authors from "finding" panoptica nearly everywhere. I do not want to simply find new panoptica scattered across the landscape, but I also do not want to dismiss the fact that panopticism is a key element of disciplined mobility. It does bear mentioning that disciplinarity cannot be simplified to panopticism, and thus it is toward other techniques that I want to turn first.

Foucault describes the creation of the "disciplinary society" as the culmination of a shift from the "discipline-blockade" to the "discipline-mechanism." The discipline blockade is exemplified by the enclosed institution on the edges of society, which focused its disciplinary power upon an institutionally separate group of individuals. The prison, asylum, school, and hospital are the best examples. The disciplinary mechanism, on the other hand, is directed at the population in general and depends upon surveillance as its primary coercive tool. It is less obtrusive and stringent but according to Foucault, more effective. The disciplinary mechanism is best understood as a technology or diagram of power that reappears with regularity across the social plane, reasserting itself in various sectors, creating a grid of possibilities not primarily aimed to limit actions, but to speed up and standardize specific actions. In this sense the disciplinary mechanism is not exactly aimed at mobile populations, but individuals in various institutional spaces, who are not in and of themselves institutionalized—as with the ill, the mad, or the criminal.

Before advancing too far in a description of the disciplinary mechanism, it may be of use to quickly outline the key features of the disciplinary blockade which eventually are disarticulated from their specificity, only to gain a life of their own for rearticulation across the social plane and in this instance in regards to mobility. The basis of disciplinary power, in both cases, is a microphysics of power, which is to say that discipline operates in a minute, particular, and meticulous fashion upon "docile bodies." Foucault sees this as a general form of domination, different from slavery, service, or vassalage, and ultimately part of the disciplinary apparatus that produces individuals who desire the very actions that benefit modern governing apparatuses. The following techniques are those which have transferred across disciplinary sites most effortlessly and remain in operation in the creation of mobilized as well as confined populations. These can be broken down into four techniques aimed at docility and three techniques aimed at training. Techniques of docility are distribution of individuals in space, control of activity, capitalization of time, and the composition of forces. Hierarchical observation, normative judgement, and examinations comprise techniques of training.

The first technique of docility dealt with by Foucault is "the art of distributions," mentioned earlier in the discussion of the naval hospital. It entails the distribution of individuals in space provided through the enclosure of populations, the partitioning of individuals within that space, the creation of specialized spaces in which only singular activities took place, and the rank of arrangements through which individuals move. This last point is particularly important in that individuals are never given a fixed location, but rather their purposefulness is dependent upon the relative location that they occupy at any given moment. This allows for mobility, yet only in a very predetermined fashion. For instance, there are very particular places in which one can operate motor vehicles: primarily the road system, with some ever-decreasing number of off-road areas. The roads themselves only connect certain places, and the quickest routes generally only connect places of political and economic importance. Furthermore, only certain types of vehicles and modes of transportation are allowable in these spaces.

The second technique is "the control of activity," which primarily depends upon the allocation of time and the efficient connection of actor and tools, through the use of time-tables, the standardization of time allowed for actions, the partitioning of actions, and exhaustive use of time. The control of activities on the road can in a simple way be understood as the rules of the road: one-way streets, stop signs, turn signal use, speed limits, and so forth. In the name of efficiency an entire traffic engineering apparatus has been set up to minimize time spent on roads in order to command the most efficient use of resources. As drivers we merely serve as transporters of our own resources: time, money, and labor. This creates the third technique of docility, capitalization of time. It entails the repetitive but gradual acceleration of proficiency. Thus the Highway Commission is constantly under pressure to produce more proficient drivers through the use of traffic engineering. Whether automobiles or other forms of public transportation are involved, the often divergent goals of personal mobility and population mobilization frequently derail any plans to satisfy both desires with one system as Bruno Latour (1996) notes.

The last technique described by Foucault is "the composition of forces." It entails the response to a new demand for social efficiency, which is to "construct a machine whose effect will be maximized by the concerted articulation of the elementary parts of which it is composed" (Foucault, 1979, p. 164). Thus the techniques listed above are said to elevate the effectiveness of simple actions into a comprehensive activity. In this instance it is paramount that the mobility produced must service other sectors of the social order, most notably the economy and government. Put simply, these techniques of docility must enable individuals to get to work, transport goods, go on vacation, get to shopping malls, and go to school in an efficient manner. Furthermore, the road system needs to operate to keep particular, often less docile, populations off the streets, away from middle-class suburbs, and without access to quick group mobilization.[6]

Tactics aimed at training primarily function by "making" individuals through treating them "both as objects and as instruments of its exercise" (Foucault, 1979, p. 170). Foucault calls these three techniques of training "simple instruments," and as such their use has spread beyond their original home in the discipline blockade. Hierarchical observation, the first technique, coerces through observation. New architectural plans and spatial organizations were created in order to more easily observe multiplicities of individuals. Continual surveillance allows power to be both discreet and omnipresent, since it is known to be everywhere, but rarely is called upon directly. To an extent this model was replaced by panopticism, discussed below. However, for a largely middle-class population, the road system operates as the primary passage through which the gaze of heirarchical observation passes, in the form of traffic police. As Foucault notes, there is an attempt in social planning to construct neighborhoods that can easily be monitored (1979). The grid structure of inner-city neighborhoods is much more amenable to this form of mobile surveillance than the curvy, cul-de-sac laden suburbs. Those with the power to regulate behavior thus have access to observe.

The second and third techniques of training are closely linked and they are the "normalizing of judgment" and "the examination." Five microtechniques operate in the normalization of judgment: 1) each and every misbehavior is punished; 2) not reaching the required level of proficiency in any task is considered an offence and thus punishable; 3) punishment takes the forms of training, most notably repetition of the task ill performed; 4) there is not only punishment, but a double system of punishment-gratification and; 5) rank and grade serve both hierarchizing and punishment-gratification.

Finally, there is the examination which serves both as a "deployment of force and the establishment of truth" (Foucault, 1979, p. 184). The examination is the place where observation and judgement are combined to both help organize individuals, for instance a medical examination determines who is placed where within the hospital, and the school examination works in the deployment of truth. Examination also works to stratify and organize the placement of individuals and to determine access to previously closed spaces.

Two essential components of accessing mobility are the driver's license and automotive insurance. The driver's license serves as the pass-to-freedom for middle-class teens, but it comes accompanied by extensive drivers training. This training serves to normalize judgment on the road. Paramount to this is testing, repetition of driving tasks, and ultimately either success or failure. Insurance, on the other hand, operates more as a ranking device. Through actuarial practices populations are ranked according to their probable capacity to destroy property. In coordination with population ranking, personal punishments, such as proving one's lack of proficiency by accumulating moving violations, are taken into account in order to place a relative price on one's access to mobility. Thus drivers are punished for lack of docility and rewarded for compliance.

Actuarial practices have also created new types of populations: risk groups. An effect of this is that populations that are said to pose a risk to themselves are collectively denied easy access to "fast" mobility. Automobiles and motorcycles considered sports models are charged greater insurance fees, while populations that have been considered social risks outside the realm of mobility, youth and motorcyclists,[7] find that the label is applied to them in matters of mobility as well. Most recently, there has been an attempt on the part of the Automobile Association of America (AAA) to situate every driver as potentially risky through the creation of a new category of deviance, road rage.

Panopticism is the most notorious example of a discipline mechanism. It is the culmination of many earlier techniques of power outlined above. Panopticism as a system derives from Jeremy Bentham's design for a prison system in which all inmates are potentially under continual monitoring. The prisoner is never sure whether he is being surveyed, but knows that he is always within view. Foucault calls this the "eye of power." Panopticism demands that prisoners behave at all times. The main difference, according to Foucault, between this and earlier examples of discipline-blockade is that "whatever use one may wish to put it to, produces homogenous effects" (1979, p. 202). In other words, panopticism is a free floating mechanism with countless applications. Furthermore, its primary function is to inscribe within individuals the gaze of power, so that one becomes both the object and the subject of constraint. A self restrained citizen who does not act merely out of fear of being surveyed, which would imply a desire to break free of repression. Rather, panopticism ensures that "the individual is carefully fabricated in [the social order], according to a whole technique of forces and bodies" (Foucault, 1979, p. 217). This reduces the need for actual surveillance. Disciplinary power then in this ultimate form reaches the point of noncoercive regulation that Foucault considers "a perpetual victory that avoids any physical confrontation and which is always decided in advance" (p. 203).

Panopticism is the most discussed technique of disciplinarity, and it appears to be a key element for understanding traffic control as well. For instance, training manuals for police operate implicitly on the repressive hypotheses and employ a version of panopticism in order to repress a perceived desire for speed and lack of constraints. In other words, the manuals assume that if set free of surveillance and regulations, drivers and riders would "go crazy," drive "too fast," and lose any sense of responsibility for their own safety, not to mention that of others. A brief quote from *Traffic Supervision*, a police training manual, helps sum up these assumptions.

> Enforcement measures generally are repressive. *They aim to deter the potential violator by making the outcome of committing a violation an unpleasant experience.* (Vanderborsch, 1969, p. 104; italics in original)

They recognize that there are other apparatuses working to produce compliance, but that police are a required last line of defense.

> Traffic enforcement is a total police effort aimed at obtaining compliance with traffic regulations after safety education, driver training, traffic engineering and similar programs fail to do the job. (p. 103)

According to this model, police serve the function of repressing a sublimated desire to break the law simply through their continual surveillance and the negative effects which accompany violations. This repressive model is carried out through observation and reputation. Observation is just what it sounds like. It is panopticism. In its most concrete form we have what officers call "off-the-street-patrol," which is essentially police parked in cars looking for speeders and other offenders. But the real issue here is to what extent observation is internalized. To what extent are drivers always aware of how thoroughly the streets are being monitored and the possibility that at any particular moment they may be under surveillance? The traffic supervision manual states that "This reminder of the police presence will linger after the police vehicle is no longer in sight" (Vanderborsch, 1969, p. 105). Yet the length of duration is said to depend upon two things. First, the symbol of enforcement authority is paramount. This is said to be ensured by a vigorous and focused enforcement policy. In other words, officers must hand out violations continuously. Second, motorists must see the symbols frequently. Hence, off-the-street patrol cars must station themselves along highly traveled routes. This observation plan is summarized as follows:

> A long-range, comprehensive traffic enforcement program seeks to generate voluntary compliance. When enforcement practices are uniformly and extensively conducted over a long period of time, drivers become aware of the risks and no longer depend on seeing

a police officer to be reminded of enforcement practices or his own driving behavior. (p. 105)

But what type of compliance is called for? Ultimately, traffic regulators state that compliance is not merely for repressive purposes in and of themselves. Instead the police are doing their job to ensure the safety of the mobile population. According to James L. Malfetti, executive officer of the Safety Education project at Columbia University in the 1960s,

> In each of us is a desire for calculated risks of excitement. Our daily activities may provide little of this excitement and indeed may represent a series of minor frustrations . . . so that, consciously or not, we sometimes enjoy taking a little risk, such as speeding and cutting in and out of traffic. (1958, p. 98)

It must therefore be recognized that, according to safety and police officials, there is an inherent desire to violate traffic regulations. Ultimately, however, "many motorists develop safe driving habits simply because they are aware of the consequences suffered by those apprehended for traffic violations" (Vanderborsch, 1969, p. 104). Thus, the police are supposedly merely public health officials, ensuring motorists' safety against their own destructive desires.

The link then between panopticism and the internalization of the gaze depends, at least in this instance, upon the internalization of a particular discourse, safety. In order to address the question of how safety is internalized and produced we may benefit by looking at another practice in which the repressive model flourished, namely, sexuality. *The History of Sexuality: An Introduction* (1990a), overturned the notion that there existed an innate sexuality that was held in check and repressed by mores and morals. Instead, Foucault argued, sexuality, needed to be created through the proliferation of discourse about sex. In a similar manner, safety and its other, risk, are not simply natural states, as argued by the police; rather, they too are produced discursively. Furthermore, the safe rider/driver is produced, not repressed: they come to desire safety and safe driving practices.

KNOWLEDGE: WHAT IS THE TRUTH OF SAFETY

Safety is often considered to be a buffer between technology run rampant and the sanctity of human life; a zone that protects humanity from the modernization machine, the greed of corporations, speed, the crash, the insensitivity of the bureaucratic monster, and breakdowns in the moral order. There is no doubt that safety serves the needs of many institutions and plays a large part in many discourses. However, can it so simply be seen as the panacea to the myriad threats that the postindustrial poses? It is impossible to live in our technological society and not feel the effects of the safety discourse in many facets of our life. Safety as a discourse produces "truths" (Foucault, 1980) that have material effects in such various arenas as the speed and boundaries of our movement, the form and flavor of our diet, and the variety and range of our sexual practices.

Another effect of this discourse is much more subtle. Safety does not simply offer protection against the modern technological monster: it serves the monster. It is often the mask behind which the human face of technology hides. Safety is a reterritorializing machine, as it reorganizes the ways in which we construct, think about, and move through space. It serves as a vital tool to all modern social mechanisms, an apparatus that outlaws unwanted activities and expels populations that threaten the mechanism's smooth operation. If we go back to the original metaphor of the ship, we realize that securing the successful passage of the ship's passengers is not in and of itself the goal and duty of the shipmaster. His goal is to ensure that this type of mobility is properly disposed of in a productive, efficient, and profitable fashion. The avoidance of disaster is a means to an end, not an end in itself. The lives of the citizenry are only important insofar as they can be transported in a productive fashion. Safety, then, can be defined in several functional ways: the positive steps taken to avoid the loss of production; the insurance of profitability; the maintenance of efficiency; or most generally any technique used in the disposition of things and wo/men that avoids loss.

Safety is not a thing, but a relative state of being in relation to health and risk. Health itself is a discursively constructed term that is organized around a set of practices and knowledges concerning the standard operation of physical bodies and social populations and the policies used to shape individuals' conduct within the sphere of activities that it circumscribes (Osborne, 1997). Safety then is one discourse used to legitimate practices that pertain to health at both the personal and social levels. Its other in most cases is risk. Risk too is discursively produced. The vast literature on risk has grown tremendously over the past two decades, following Douglas' and Wildavsky's germinal text *Risk and Culture* (1982). Risk is something to be avoided, while safety is the positivity that organizes conduct. Risk management is something that specialists assess and police, but as a discursive regularity it has a very limited scope of operation. In a sense both risk and safety refer to the same techniques and forms of governing, but at the level of self-governing, in the everyday, in how we conceive of ourselves, we think in terms of safety. There are safety campaigns, safety pamphlets, and safe citizens, not risk-managing citizens. The goal of safety policy, as one of the earliest driver's education manuals, Youth at the Wheel, made evident in 1937, "This book is not intended to make young drivers danger-conscious but rather to instil into them a deep safety-consciousness" (p. 7). Yet, operating behind and alongside all of the cultural definitions of safety and risk are normative assumptions regarding the acceptance of injury or death for specific activities. For example, a greater acceptance of injury is assumed in a state of war than in a state of peace. Somewhat ironically, leisure activity is often imbued with a greater acceptance of risk than necessary activities such as work or transportation. Mountain climbing, skiing, scuba diving, and sex are all considered risky activities these days. But it must be emphatically stated that risk and safety are both part of multiple, highly contextual discursive networks.

There is no ground-zero against which either safety or risk can be judged. Instead acceptable limits are created to validate or invalidate different activities. These limits are quite variable from one time period to another and across different activities and different cultural contexts. Different justifications are used to validate some activities that result in immense loss of life (e.g., war) while others that result in very little loss of life (e.g., electrocution by bathroom appliance) are regulated heavily. The bottom line, though, is that these varying logics are accompanied by technical expert knowledges, popular truths, and differing assumptions about the value of the lives of different populations.

Biopower as it operates in the United States is dependent upon the safety discourse. This is the political/social arm of biopower in which populations are taken as a whole, invested with productive possibilities and normalized according to new knowledges that create systems of assessment and diagnosis. What is unique about biopolitics is that it depends first, upon the production of knowledge to validate the normative standards by which populations can be measured and second, upon policy initiatives that are mandated to bring the population up to snuff. In the scenario of disciplined mobility the real question is, what specific knowledge is deployed in order to legitimate the normative practices of mobility, and furthermore, how has this knowledge been transferred into everyday practices and self-reflection?

Biopolitics attempts to control and produce mobilizations of particular populations, such as motorcycle gangs or youth. At times the safety discourse itself accounts for the very creation of these populations. Actuarial practices depend upon the production of very specific categories, while insurance companies over the past seventy years have continuously been guilty of using scare campaigns that depend upon just such stereotypes, which serve not only to validate their actuarial tactics, but also actively to disenfranchise some populations from mobility altogether. More generally, the very same populations historically denied social mobility often have their mobility curtailed through safety campaigns. Women were considered a problematic addition to the driving environment in the early 1950s due to their supposed inability to deal with the technical demands of the automobile. After insurance companies reformulated the normative driver using women drivers of middle age as their actuarial yardstick, campaigns were aimed more specifically at women's supposed desire for a safer driving environment in order to reorient the mobile environment. During the Depression when itinerant laborers used it as a means of mobility and later when larger numbers of youth began hitchhiking, this form of mobility was increasingly surveyed, regulated, and outlawed. "Driving While Black" is another example of the fairly repressive ways in which the mobility of minority populations are regulated. In particular, police profiling sanctions and initiates this form of surveillance. Safety campaigns of this sort limit and redirect these populations' mobility, because their *mobile activities* are said to be dangerous, although this does not raise the question of whether their very mobility itself is dangerous to social-political orders.

A potentially more insidious outcome of the proliferation of the safety discourse is that it has increasingly served as a free-floating legitimator. The claim that some activity, product, or form of conduct is unsafe automatically legitimates public concern, media worthiness, litigation, and governmental involvement. The space for public debate about nearly any topic is limited not by what is the just, the good, or the democratic, but rather by what is safe. As I have shown, what is safe remains an abstraction, but it is treated as though it were not only an automatic good, but something definable, measurable, and controllable. Goodness, justice, and democracy are also abstractions, but ones which have a long history of intellectual debate. I am not trying to assert that these other abstractions should be the end point or absolute grounds for every policy decision or public discussion. However, the safety discourse, due in large part to its appearance of objectivity, colonizes discussions concerning how to mange things properly and reduces all other issues to epiphenomena.

Furthermore, safety concerns can be brought in as justification for any specific social policy in such a fashion that it hides more nefarious means, desires, and ends. Thus debates over the Internet, education, gun use, mobility, sex, television programming, and myriad others have been territorialized by safety. Yet safety is a free-floating discourse, witness that it can be used as justification for both private ownership of handguns and their abolition. Safety minded citizens would assert that one side must be correct; it is either more safe or less safe to allow or not allow private handgun ownership. But, either assertion puts its faith in the measurement, definability, and infallibility of an abstraction: an abstraction that at its core serves the needs of liberal governance, not those of the individual. These needs may be mutually agreeable, but it is this very agreeability, this desire to conduct oneself according to the goals of governance, that is most troubling. As Foucault has pondered, what is it "that causes us to love power, to desire the very thing that dominates and exploits us?" (Foucault, 1983b, p. xiii). Why do we want to be safe?

Safe Citizens

Being a good driver requires the same qualities that are needed if you are to be a good citizen, a good neighbor, a good son and a good brother. That would mean that *learning to drive must be closely connected with learning to live*. That is exactly so, and accounts for the fact that you cannot teach people to be good drivers without teaching them the same kind of things that make them good citizens, good neighbors, good sons and good brothers. And, as a matter of fact, the converse is true: one very effective way of learning what it takes to live acceptably in the modern world is by discovering these things through learning to drive! (*Man and the Motorcar*, 1936, p. 59; italics in original)

Why is it that learning to be a good driver, or to be a mobile subject, is the same as learning to be a good citizen, and how is this all connected with learning how to live? Governing a mobile society, I have argued, demands disciplining individuals differently. Furthermore, this disciplining and governing depend upon and are organized by the logic of safety. It follows then that being mobile, safe, and a citizen under liberalism would entail largely homologous expectations and demands. The goals of government are closely intertwined with the training of its citizenry, not simply in terms of the most simple tasks like driving, but insofar as driving itself, or at least being mobile, is inherently a part of citizenship training. Because governing at a distance demands mobile citizens, an integral part of successful disposition is training citizens to be "good drivers." One of the shortcomings of the governmentality literature in general is that it has failed adequately to articulate the relationship between governing and the subject. This last section will briefly attempt to provide a few lines of articulation between governance, mobility, and the "safe subject."

I have dealt with power and knowledge. The third dimension according to Deleuze's understanding of Foucault's "philosophy" is the subject (Deleuze, 1988), though not the subject as it was classically understood, but rather the product of processes of objectification and subjectification. Different ways of existing are established through "the forms and modalities of the relation to self by which the individual constitutes and recognizes himself qua subject" (Foucault, 1990b, p. 6). Foucault was trying to provide not simply a better model of the subject, as the subject itself is not an a priori, but rather an understanding of the "different modes by which in our culture human beings are made subjects" (Foucault, 1983a, p. 216). Barry Smart (1986) claims that it is "governmentalization" and the pastoral form of power accompanying it that have produced a "matrix of individuation" which has focused power upon producing self-reflexive subjects (pp. 161–163). Given this individuation of power, resistance often takes place in battles regarding subjectivity and the struggle to deny modes of objectification and the "truths" about ourselves that they demand (p. 171). Three lines of enquiry need to be followed, then. First, what does Foucault mean by objectification and subjectification? Second, how is this tied to pastoral forms of power? Third, what types of resistance, via the subject, are possible?

Foucault articulates three modes of objectification: 1) modes of inquiry that give themselves the status of science, 2) "dividing practices," and 3) the self turning itself into a subject (Foucault, 1983a, 208). Foucault's early writings deal most directly with the first two modes and the examples he provides make this apparent. The speaking subject of linguistics, the productive subject of political economy, and the "living" subject of natural history and biology are just three forms of objectivizing the subject by producing a "truth" for what it means to be human. By dividing the subject inside itself or from others, the second form of objectivization normalizes conduct and the body. In the division of the mad from the sane, the sick from the healthy, and the criminals from the "good boys," the human being is forced into a grid of assessment. One is either properly human or not, and institutionally determined relations of power make these assessments and are organized to rehabilitate the insane, criminal, or sick subject. In these examples the "truth" of the subject in general and in each specific case is continually being assessed and altered.

Foucault describes the third type of objectification as "the way a human being turns him- or herself into a subject" (p. 208). In *The Use of Pleasure* (1990b) and *The Care of the Self* (1990c) Foucualt calls this activity subjectification and seems to leave behind the language of objectification, though his reading of such classical authors as Plato, Galen, and Aristotle, among others, does show how modes of inquiry such as philosophy and medicine did produce truths and divide the subject in various ways. However, for the Greeks these truths did not approach scientificity and were not explicitly tied to any specific institutions. Foucault articulated the links between objectification and subjectification in his "Introduction" to *The Use of Pleasure* in which he first outlined the project to write a "history of the experience of sexuality, where experience is understood as the correlation between fields of knowledge, types of normativity, and forms of subjectivity in a particular culture" (1990b, p. 4). He attempted to do this by focusing upon the "games of truth by which human beings came to see themselves as desiring individuals" (p. 7). Just as he had previously examined the games of truth that led man to see himself as mad, insane, ill, or whereby "he judge(ed) himself and punish(ed) himself as a criminal" (p. 7), Foucault would now articulate the relationship between truth and sexuality.

In "The Subject and Power" Foucault (1983a) asks that we take "the forms of resistance against different forms of power as a starting point" (p. 211) in our analysis of power relations. Foucault provides six commonalities of these oppositions. Briefly, they are: 1) not limited to one country or form of government, 2) focused upon power effects, 3) immediate struggles over power that directly acts upon individuals, 4) "struggles which question the status of the individual" (p. 211), 5) opposed to the privileges of knowledge, and 6) centered by the question, Who are we? As a whole they are more interested in the specific technique of power that

> applies itself to immediate everyday life which categorizes the indi-
> vidual, marks him by his own individuality, attaches him to his own
> identity, imposes a law of truth on him which he must recognize and
> which others have to recognize in him. It is a form of power that
> makes individuals subjects. (p. 212)

Foucault sees these struggles as largely replacing earlier forms of struggle against domination and exploitation. He in no way dismisses the earlier forms, but makes sure to insist that these contemporarily popular forms are not reducible to the others. They are instead a response to the emergence and expansion of pastoral power with its individualizing properties.

With the Christians, the originators of the pastoral model of power, life and death were linked by salvation. In the contemporary context of governmentalization we find that safety, not salvation, marks out this terrain. Safety articulates our relationship to life and death and ultimately, the "truth of ourselves." Safety is etymologically linked to salvation and this relationship becomes brilliantly apparent when the shining light of pastoralism is shed upon the life of its subjects. In the Christian pastoral, salvation, a life after death, is of paramount concern; in contemporary forms of state pastoralism it is safety, the staving off of death, that takes center stage. Furthermore, once power takes life as its objective, as it does in the pastoral model, it must necessarily give rise to a life that resists power (Foucault, 1999, p. 94). Subjects within the pastoral model of Protestantism since the Renaissance must have the freedom to choose to be a moral subject as salvation demands it (Foucault, 1983a, p. 251). One must not simply follow a code, but choose to be moral, to reflect upon oneself as an ethical subject. What I want to argue, then, is that there is such a thing as a "safe subject": a self that reflects upon various practices and discourses regarding safety in the construction of its ethical subjectivity. There are guidebooks, prescriptions, codes, warnings, guilt producing car commercials, education programs, and so forth, which help individuals prepare a regimen that will ensure that they are free from risk. It certainly is not as tightly configured as Greek sexuality, although even that was a somewhat contentious field. However, the issues associated with objectification and subjectification in this concluding discussion will focus most specifically upon the safety practices of motorcycle riders.

A common narrative thread runs through the logics of salvation and safety. This thread ties the subject to an epiphanic experience or moment that is said to produce a profound change in the individual. The most famous of salvation narratives is that of Saul blinded by the blinding light of God on his way to take part in the persecution of Christians in Damascus. His epiphanic experience enlightens him, shows him the truth, and produces the model for the epiphany. Mobile subjects, and especially motorcyclists, have their own epiphanic narrative that is told over and over again in magazine articles, letters to the editor, and the popular genre of motorcyclist autobiographies. In this narrative the motorcyclist experiences a near-fatal crash, which points out the errors of his or her previous unsafe motorcycling habits. This experience then proves the truth of a safety regimen, thus producing its own form of salvation through enlightenment.

Motorcyclist's productive epiphanies provide an example of Deleuze's claim that "The folding or doubling is itself a Memory: the 'absolute memory' or memory of the outside" (1988, p. 107). The memory of the near fatal crash that needs to be narrativized in order for it to take on a truth value. As Deleuze states, "everything is knowledge, and this is the first reason why there is no 'savage experience'" (p. 109). It is the folding of this epiphanic narrative upon one's experience which creates the memory in a specific form. It articulates the memory to a specific knowledge of oneself as a newly produced safe subject. So what possibility exists to reorient memory? Hunter Thompson in *Hell's Angels* (1966) describes a different relationship to the crash. Rather than the crash being folded into the safety discourse, it is folded into an ethic that validates the crash as a badge of honor and a reminder of the precarious nature of mortality which further validated one's choice to ride, and, thus, live "on the edge."

Forgetting is the possibility. Ultimately it is the struggle over memory that organizes the subject. "Memory is the real name of the relation to oneself, or the affect of self by self" (Deleuze, p. 107). Deleuze plays memory not against forgetting, but against forgetting that one can forget. Forgetting allows for an unfolding. Forgetting that the experience is supposed to be profound for instance unhooks the articulation between the crash and the truth of safety. Forgetting also demands the production of a new memory, a newly directed fold upon the experience. Forgetting that one can forget, however, "dissolves us into the outside and constitutes death" (p. 108), a death of possibilities or new lines of flight. Forgetting, then can be thought of as a strategy of disarticulation, a way of denying the easy narrative placement of our experiences, of our memories. If we want to struggle for our "selves," we must learn to forget. Forget that fear is bad, that new possibilities are scary, and that safe answers are always best.

Foucault asserts that it is the everyday struggles of individuals against forms of power and objectification that make them into resistant subjects. Motorcyclists, due to the claimed degree of risk involved in their form of mobility, have been the focus of the most intense forms of objectification in the realm of vehicular mobility. As Foucault's thesis would suggest, the intensity of disciplinary activity has produced an intense reaction. Motorcyclists have spearheaded some of the most vocal and politically active movements against mandated safety procedures. Political activism against safety legislation often fails to "get outside" the telos of safety and instead simply attempts to prove the inconclusiveness of statistical data. This may have a legislative effect, but it reinforces the very logic that legitimates the mandates in the first place. More importantly, motorcyclists have produced a vast array of practices of the self that place in question the legitimacy of safety as the only meaningful organizing telos of one's relation to self and to mobility. This leads me to look at counter forms of subjectification that do not take for granted the relationships between life and death, risk and safety, that pastoral forms of power assume.

Of primary concern is the relationship that safety plays in our conceptions of the self. Safety in its most literal sense means to be free from hurt, injury, danger, and risk. So safety isn't a desirable thing in and of itself, but, rather, a freedom from something undesirable. But what is so undesirable about risk? Risk is not simply the opposite of safety. Risk implies new possibilities. It often demands stakes that are of equal or greater value than any loss could negate. A loss after all produces new possibilities, has effects just as much as a gain. So how is it that we could be so facile as to want to be free from risk? What kind of relation with oneself allows for a negation of new possibilities? Because of this we must interrogate this relation with safe practices: this regimen of staving off pain, injury, suffering, and death. In our regimens we may be free from a certain "oppression," but are we free to do that which is desirable, that which may be politically useful, that which may simply be part of "the good life"?

It is ultimately the processes of objectification and subjectification that seem most politically compelling. I would suggest, given Foucault's conception not only of governmentality—that it is merely one point of the "triangle of power"—but of knowledge and of the subject, that it is important to keep in mind the many sites and forms of potential resistance. More specifically, if disciplined mobility is to be taken seriously and safety questioned, then how we orient ourselves as safe subjects must also matter. In other words, how we conduct ourselves as mobile subjects and how we construct mobilizations is related to how we inhabit ourselves as citizens, neighbors, and intellectuals.

NOTES

1. For instance, dystopian rhetoric has always accompanied new communication technologies. This rhetoric generally concerns itself with the potential disruptive effect the new technology will have on the social or political fabric said to bind the nation.

2. While cars are of course used in other countries, this essay focuses upon governing auto-mobility in the United States.

3. Todd May's *The Political Philosophy of Poststructuralist Anarchism* (1994) draws clear lines between Marxist understandings of power and the accompanying understandings of freedom. Furthermore, he clearly separates the work of Foucault, as well as that of Lyotard and Deleuze, from such conceptions of power and freedom.

4. See Harvey (1990), Lash & Ury (1989), Massey (1984, 1994), and Soja (1989) for some of the most comprehensive discussions of these changes.

5. Montana for instance was entirely mapped out and connected by railroad lines before the government and railroad companies could initiate legislation and propaganda to entice settlers to move there mostly from 1911–1915. Migrations of these settlers further west followed successive droughts and were aided by the advent of the widespread use of inexpensive automobiles.

6. It is always the streets and highways that are fought over, partitioned off, and redirected during protests, marches, and riots. The streets then are not only the arteries of production, but also the pressure points for cutting off the circulation of resistant uprisings. See Foucault, 1977, p. 219.

7. There is a long history of demonizing motorcyclists that began in earnest in the mid-1950s. This was primarily the result of hyperbolic magazine stories about the horrors committed by motorcycle gangs. The stereotype grew with the release of *The Wild Ones* and reached its peak in the early 1970s following 5 years of B-movie saturation.

REFERENCES

Barry, A. (1996). Lines of communication and spaces of rule. In A. Barry, T. Osborne, & N. Rose (Eds.), *Foucault and political reason: Liberalism, neo-liberalism and rationalities of government* (pp. 123–142). London: University of Chicago Press.

Benedek L. (director). (1954). *The Wild One* [film]. Kramer/Columbia.

Burchell, G., Gordon, C., & Miller, P. (Eds.). (1991). *The Foucault effect: Studies in governmentality*. Chicago: University of Chicago Press.

Castel, R. (1991). From dangerousness to risk. In G. Burchell, C. Gordon, & P. Miller (Eds.), *The Foucault effect: Studies in governmentality*. Chicago: University of Chicago Press.

Defert, N. (1991). 'Popular Life' and insurance technology. In G. Burchell, C. Gordon, & P. Miller (Eds.), *The Foucault effect: Studies in governmentality*. Chicago: University of Chicago Press.

Deleuze, G. (1988). *Foucault* (S. Hand, Trans.). Minneapolis, MN: University of Minnesota.

Deleuze, G. (1995). *Negotiations: 1972–1990.* New York: Columbia University Press.

Deleuze, G., & Guattari, F. (1987). *A thousand plateaus: Capitalism and schizophrenia.* Minneapolis, MN: University of Minnesota Press.

Douglas, M., & Wildavsky, A. (1982). *Risk and culture: An essay on the selection of technical and environmental dangers.* Berkeley, CA. University of California Press.

Ellul, J. (1964). *The technological society.* New York: Vintage Books.

Ellul, J. (1971) *Propaganda: The formation of men's attitudes* (K. Keller & J. Lerner, Trans.). New York: Knopf.

Ewald, F. (1991). Insurance and risk. In G. Burchell, C. Gordon, & P. Miller (Eds.), *The Foucault effect: Studies in governmentality* (pp. 197–210). Chicago: University of Chicago Press.

Foucault, M. (1965). *Madness and Civilization: A history of insanity in the age of reason.* New York: Random House.

Foucault, M. (1979). *Discipline and punish: The birth of the prison.* New York: Vintage.

Foucault, M. (1980). *Power/knowledge: Selected interviews and other writings 1972– 1977.* New York: Pantheon Books.

Foucault, M. (1983a). The subject and power. In P. Rabinow, & W. Dreyfus (Eds.), *Michel Foucault: Beyond structuralism and hermeneutics.* Chicago: University of Chicago Press.

Foucault, M. (1983b). Preface. In G. Deleuze, & F. Guattari. *Anti-Oedipus: Capitalism and schizophrenia* (pp. xi–xiv). Minneapolis, MN: University of Minnesota Press.

Foucault, M. (1988). The ethic of care for the self as a practice of freedom. In D. Rasmussen, & J. W. Bernauer (Eds.), *The Final Foucault* (pp. 1–20). Boston: MIT Press.

Foucault, M. (1989). *Foucault live.* New York: Semiotext(e).

Foucault, M. (1990a). *The history of sexuality: An introduction* (Vol. 1). New York: Vintage Books.

Foucault, M. (1990b). *The use of pleasure: The history of sexuality* (Vol. 2). New York: Vintage Books.

Foucault, M. (1991). Governmentality. In G. Burchell, C. Gordon, & P. Miller (Eds.), *The Foucault effect: Studies in governmentality* (pp. 87–104). Chicago: University of Chicago Press.

Foucault, M. (1994). *Birth of the clinic.* New York: Vintage Books.

Foucault, M. (1999). Pastoral power and political reason. In J. Carrette (Ed.), *Religion and Culture.* New York: Routledge.

Grossberg, L. (1992). *We gotta get outta this place: Popular conservatism and postmodern culture.* New York: Routledge.

Grossberg, L. (1995). Identity and cultural studies: Is that all there is? Unpublished manuscript.

Harvey, D. (1990). *The condition of postmodernity.* Cambridge: Blackwell.

Lash, S. & Urry, J. (1989). *The end of organized capitalism.* Madison, WI: University of Wisconsin Press.

Latour, B. (1996). *Aramis, or, The love of technology.* Cambridge, MA: Harvard University Press.

Malfetti, J. (1958). Human behavior-factor X. *The annals of the American Academy of Political and Social Science.* November.

Marsh, P. & Collet, P. (1986). *Driving passion: The psychology of the car.* Boston: Faber and Faber.

Massey, D. (1984). *Spatial divisions of labor: Social structures and the geography of production.* New York: Methuen.

Massey, D. (1994). *Space, place, and gender.* Minneapolis, MN: University of Minnesota Press.

Mattelart, A. (1996). *The invention of communication.* Minneapolis, MN: University of Minnesota Press.

May, T. (1994). *The political philosophy of poststructuralist anarchism.* University Park, PA: Pennsylvania State University Press.

Miller, T. (1998). *Technologies of truth: Cultural citizenship and the popular media.* Minneapolis: U, MNniversity of Minnesota Press.

O'Malley, P. (1996). Risk and responsibility. In A. Barry, T. Osborne, & N. Rose. (Eds.), *Foucault and political reason: Liberalism, neo-liberalism and rationalities of government* (pp. 189–208). London: University of Chicago Press.

Osborne, T. (1996). Security and vitality: Drains, liberalism, and power in the nineteenth century. In A. Barry, T. Osborne, & N. Rose. (Eds.), *Foucault and political reason: Liberalism, neo-liberalism and rationalities of government* (pp. 99–122). London: University of Chicago Press.

Osborne, T. (1997). Of health and statecraft. In A. Petersen, & R. Bunton (Eds.), *Foucault: Health and medicine.* New York: Routledge.

Patton, P. (1986). *Open road: A celebration of the American highway.* New York: Touchstone.

Petersen, A., & Bunton, R. (Eds.). (1997). *Foucault, health and medicine.* New York: Routledge.

Rabinow, P. (1989). *French modern: Norms and forms of the social environment.* Chicago: The University of Chicago Press.

Rae, J. (1971). *The road and the car in American life.* Cambridge, MA: MIT Press.

Soja, E. (1989). *Postmodern geographies.* New York: Verso.

Smart, B. (1986). The politics of truth and the problem of hegemony. In D. Couzens Hoy (Ed.), *Foucault: A critical reader* (pp. 157–174). London: Basil Blackwell.

Thompson, H. S. (1966). *Hell's Angels: A strange and terrible saga.* New York: Ballantine.

Vanderborsch, C. G. & The International Association of Chiefs of Police. (1969). *Traffic supervision*. Washington DC: Library of Congress.

Virilio, P. (1986). *Speed and politics: An essay on dromology*. New York: Semiotext(e).

Whitney, A. (1936). *Man and the motorcar*. New York: J. L. Little and Company.

Part II

Policy, Power, and Governing Practices

Chapter 7

Unaided Virtues

The (Neo)Liberalization of the Domestic Sphere and the New Architecture of Community

James Hay

An increasing number of sociologies about the 1980s and '90s have come to describe developments in that period as a new form of liberalism. In many explanations of "neo-liberalism," the term refers to the emergence of the New Right, particularly in countries such as Britain and the United States. These explanations often emphasize that political government in these nations became deeply committed to policies of deregulation, to "free-market" ideology, and to the disassembling of a welfare state and its centralized model of governmental administration. *Neo*liberalism is seen to build upon a long-standing tendency in nineteenth- and early twentieth century liberalism to bring government *indirectly* into projects of social improvement, while rejecting all forms of *direct* State control, particularly forms of socialism that emerged in Europe during the 1920s and '30s.[1] Much of the writing about neoliberalism has understood it as a political and economic philosophy. Some of the writing about it also rightly understands it as a political-economic practice by pointing out its relation to a mode of production, consumption, and trade—to a general economy—that is global and "post-Fordist."

An important intervention into discussions about neoliberalism has been a fairly recent body of writing that draws upon the work of Michel Foucault, particularly his conception of "governmentality" and his writing about "care of the self" and "technologies of the self" (see Barry, Osborne, & Rose, 1996; Burchell, Gordon, & Miller, 1991; Dean, 1999; Rose, 1996, 1999). In this, Foucault's later writings, he contended that one of the primary challenges to Western societies in the nineteenth century was not only how to govern populations and resources over increasingly extensive territory (beyond the city-state or the model of household as economy) but also how to rationalize the role of government as it came to rely less upon political institutions of the state ("structures of sovereignty" associated with the Prince) and to develop techniques for *governing at a distance*, relying increasingly upon a pluralization of forms of governing and of technical, organizational, and administrative knowledges—a whole range of practices that "constitute, define, organize, and instrumentalize the strategies that individuals *in their freedom* can use in dealing with each other" (Foucault, 1997c, p. 300). Governing at a distance and acting freely both require an implicit contract or *arrangement*—procedures, techniques, and rules of conduct across different spheres of life. In this sense, freedom (living and governing at a distance) pertains to a new political and governmental rationality, to rules of conduct that are not purely juridical but that decidedly make freedom political and ethical, an ongoing process of governing oneself, properly applying oneself, and acting responsibly across every sphere of life. Governing, therefore, does not occur through an absolute state of domination and coercion (since absolute domination precludes the possibility of freedom) but through practices of freedom, among different spheres and on different scales (i.e., arrangement as a dispersion of resources and powers through which bodies and populations become active and mobile in different ways). Foucault's writing about freedom and governing thus points to the relation between economy (management) and the moral—to a *moral economy* and (what Nikolas Rose has called) an *ethico-politics*.

For Rose and others who have discussed neoliberalism through Foucault's writing about governmentality, neoliberalism is neither a new political philosophy nor simply a new form of mercantilism that can be explained in the traditional terminology and problematics of political economy. These authors focus instead on the reasons for constituting government and on liberalism as a political and governmental rationality—as the multiple and dispersed techniques of management that collectively comprise the current reasons for and rationales of state government. Their argument accepts that there have been new forms of governing that could be described as "neo-" or "advanced" liberalism, but (after Foucault) they view this trend less as a new philosophy of governing and democracy than as a governmental rationality for a social arrangement that relies upon new kinds of citizen-subjects and new techniques for governing them.[2] After Foucault's writing about care of the self and technologies of the self, their view of neoliberalism emphasizes its tendency to encourage ever greater reliance upon self—self-expertise and self-governing as necessary components of a political rationality affecting all aspects of life. Because a neoliberal form of governance assumes that social subjects are not and should not be subject to direct forms of state control, it relies upon mechanisms for governing "through society," through programs that shape, guide, channel—and upon *responsible*, self-disciplining social subjects. As Nikolas Rose puts it: "It has become possible to actualize the notion of the actively responsible individual because of the development of new apparatuses that integrate subjects into a moral nexus of identifications and allegiances in the very processes in which they appear to act out their most personal choices" (1996, pp. 57–58).

This view of neoliberal forms of governing not only emphasizes the relation between the political and the technical dimensions of Modern life, but it also understands the technological (i.e., the "new" apparati of rule) as mediating a kind of State control that values self-sufficiency and a kind of personal freedom that requires self-responsibility and self-discipline. Although this view of a neoliberal apparatus of rule thus emphasizes that "human capacities are inevitably and inescapably technologist" (Burchell, Gordon, & Miller, 1991, p. 13), it does not view technology per se as *determining* the possibilities of freedom and/or social integration. That is to say, neither is technology a *telos* (i.e., the preeminent cause or motor of Modern social formations) nor is technologization inherently a process that frees or enslaves. Foucault's importance to this conception of technology is in part his recognition of the productive relation between "molecular" (specific, situated, corporeal, and technical) procedures and a distribution of power, wherein "technologies are at once both relatively autonomous of power and act as its infinitesimal elements."[3] For Foucault, how or whether technologies facilitate and limit the exercise of power is never guaranteed because, while power may be everywhere, it must be *practiced, exercised, and carried out through conduct* and through technical procedures and the deployment of particular technologies at and across specific sites. The *effectivity* of a technology thus depends both on its local applications and on the network that is articulated through the local performances of technical procedures: "Individuals are the vehicles of power, not its points of application" (Foucault, 1997b, p. 98). Power, conversely, depends upon individuals' competence or expertise at particular sites, upon one's access to and ability to act through a particular technology and technological assemblage or *apparatus*. In Foucault's lecture on governmentality, this view about the relation between technology and power informs his discussion about the paradox of Modern government that is a basis for Rose's perspective on neoliberalism: how Modern States must devise ways of governing "at a distance" and must rely upon technologies of management that lie outside the purview of the state.

While those who have written about neoliberalism as a governmental rationality have acknowledged the importance of *media* as a technology or power and as the kind of apparatus that Rose refers to in the passage above, their account of media has remained generalized.[4] This essay is therefore interested in amplifying and rethinking Foucauldian accounts of neoliberalism, considering more carefully than they have a particular way that "media" and "communication systems" operated as technologies of governing in the United States during the 1980s. Such an account however involves working toward a new conception or logic of *mediation*. Specifically, I want to consider how the convergence of media and other technologies during the 1980s contributed to the formation of a new social arrangement that depended upon a particular model of domesticity. My focus on the domestic sphere as a space of self-governing organized through multiple technologies is, in part, intended to take up the spatial problematic that is central to Foucauldian critiques of neoliberalism (i.e., how the domestic sphere was integral to a broader social *arrangement*).[5] More specifically, however, I want to discuss how communication technologies, in their relation to other household technologies, came to support and to rely upon a particular model of the domestic sphere during the 1980s—one that I refer to as a (neo)liberalized domestic sphere. Although this is a model that had been taking shape for some time, it became crucial to neoliberal forms of governing over the 80s. Its endurance and strengthening over the 90s affirms that neoliberalism has less to do with political philosophy than with the emergence of new practices and new environments of governing in the last part of the twentieth century. Furthermore, even though writing about neoliberal governance recognizes that the neoliberal state exercises power indirectly, it tends to have focused upon the practices of state government rather than on the spheres (such as the domestic sphere) that operate separately yet interdependently through state power. It therefore is crucial to figure out what sort of mechanism and sphere accomplish these latter tasks. Mapping the formation of networks of power "up through" the spheres and mechanisms that cannot be explained as primarily a function of State governance is, after all, the thrust of Foucault's writing about Modern apparati of power and about governmentality. If in fact neoliberalism is a mode of governance that decenters the State, then it is incumbent upon those interested in these developments to begin from positions outside State forms of power and then to consider their paradoxical relation to State governance.

In order to understand how the domestic sphere came to constitute a site and a set of technologies for a neoliberal form of governing, it is necessary to recognize its implication in both a new *regime of mobility* and a new *regime of privacy*. The term "regime" is intended to capture Foucault's sense that power relies upon specific (prioritized) technical procedures that, within a particular context and through interlocking institutions, actualize and regulate/regularize social subjects' conduct as regimen and program.[6] To say that power is exercised or practiced, therefore implies that power involves discipline and regularity as well as the activity and freedom of individuals.[7] Foucault's references to "regimes of truth," although central to his critique of Modern forms of rationality and his argument about self-governing, only indirectly concern mobility and privacy. My intention therefore is to extend these terms, maintaining the spirit of Foucault's argument about Modern forms of governing while considering their importance (in ways that Foucault never quite addressed) to late-Modern technologies of power. To do so involves turning slightly in another direction, to Raymond Williams' notion of "mobile privatization."

In *Television: Technology and Cultural Form* (1974/1992), Williams offered the term "mobile privatization" to explain how the emergence of television was predicated upon a widespread and profound social reconfiguration. While Williams does not mention either Foucault or neoliberalism, his view of television as a technology that became instrumental for a new social arrangement does make it a useful position to think about "regimes" of mobility and privacy. Furthermore, Foucault, for the most part, remained silent about (communication) technologies in the twentieth century, and as the writers about neoliberalism point out, his work primarily critiques early forms of liberalism. Although there are numerous differences between Foucault's and Williams' understanding of power, which lie beyond the scope of this paper, Foucault's arguments about technologies of power offer an interesting way of thinking about (indeed of amplifying Williams' brief remarks about) how a technology such as television historically filled a "need" in a new environment's intersecting regimes of mobility and privacy—and, as historical and social necessity, in a new economy of value.

For Williams, television was part of a social reconfiguration that was *material*; he understood social relations to be organized through the convergence of "communication systems" and other technological practices.[8] Williams' book, however, criticizes the technological determinist thesis, refuting the notion that communication systems created a new society or new social conditions (1974/1992). His "cultural materialism," furthermore, was not interested in understanding social history (or the history of television) as determined by State institutions or economic conditions or as unfolding in a unilinear fashion. And in this sense, Williams' view bears little resemblance to "classic" expressions of dialectical materialism. His view of television as social practice and as cultural form emphasized that television was not just a system of communication, that it was deeply imbricated in other social practices, that its uses and effects were contingent upon its relation to other practices (i.e., that television and the social arrangement depended upon one another), but that it did perform a necessary and technical role within a changing social configuration.[9] For this latter reason, Williams described television as a technology whose utility and effectivity can only be understood with considerable difficulty as part of a widespread "social investment." Although he proposed that technologies respond to historical needs, his book is less about "the need itself than about its *place* in an existing social formation" (p. 13; italics added). *Locating* the historical necessity for television within a social formation is particularly crucial in Williams' account, given his emphasis upon the spatial definition of the social formation that became so invested in television. For Williams, the historical necessity of television developed through a society "characterized at its most general levels by a mobility and extension of the scale of organizations: forms of growth which brought with them immediate and longer term problems of operative communication" (pp. 12–13). That Williams sees television as a technology of social integration and for managing (in Williams' sense, coping with) increasingly extensive social organization makes his project at least pertinent to Foucault's (1991) view that Modern forms of governing develop primarily in response to new distributions of populations and resources over expanding territory.[10]

Mobile privatization is central to Williams' description of how television developed when it did and as part of a broad set of social investments—"a social complex of a new and central kind":

> Socially, this complex is characterized by the two apparently para-doxical yet deeply connected tendencies of modern urban industrial living: on the one hand mobility, on the other hand the more apparently self-sufficient family home. . . . Social processes long implicit in the revolution of industrial capitalism were then greatly intensified: especially an increasing distance between immediate living areas and the directed places of work and government. . . . Yet this privatization, which was at once an effective achievement and defensive response, carried, as a consequence, an imperative need for new kinds of contact. The new homes might appear private and "self-sufficient" but could be maintained only by regular funding and supply from external sources, and these . . . had a decisive and often disrupting influence on what was nevertheless seen as a separable "family" project. This relationship created both the need and the form of a new kind of "communication." (Williams, 1974/1992, pp. 20–21)

As a feature of Modernity's industrialization and urbanization, which Williams traces to the nineteenth century, mobile privatization refers to a long, slowly emerging social arrangement that lay the groundwork for a fairly rapid and widespread "investment" in television in the late 1940s. There are three issues that bear reflection here: one concerning regimes of mobility and privacy as a spatial problematic, another concerning how television's relation to regimes of mobility and privacy was implicated in a form of governing, and the third concerning their duration and their relation to the 1980s. I will take them up in this order.

First, to the extent that "mobile privatization" refers to the historical relation among television's situatatedness, its circulation, the development of communication networks and transportation systems, and the mobility of social subjects, the broad social reconfiguration that accompanied them is decidedly a *spatial* issue. Mobile privatization referred to a changing set of spatial distinctions and definitions, most notably for Williams (and others who have cited him) between the public and private sphere. Also, mobile privatization involved a material repositioning—a spatial redefinition—of the home, increasingly situated "at a distance" from other sites, from its earlier locations, and from earlier concepts and material embodiments of the city, yet conjoined through broadcasting and other kinds of "flows" among places (such as automobile travel on newly constructed highway and freeway systems). In this regard, mobile privatization—the convergence of regimes of mobility and privacy—concerns the spatial distribution and arrangement of social subjects. Television, as *social* and *cultural technology*, becomes a valuable technique for living within this social arrangement and material environment.[11]

But "living within" this arrangement involves, as Williams repeatedly suggests, issues of power, control, and governance. Williams' explanation of mobile privatization thus shares Foucault's sense that modern forms of governing have involved developing ways to manage the distribution of people and resources over increasingly greater territory (as an *arrangement*), increasingly at a distance through new systems of mobility and transfer. Television, as institution and practice, was instrumental to the overall reproduction and maintenance of the social formation at its most general and local levels. Its instrumentality, however, was never a matter of direct government control, nor, for that matter, of direct control by the broadcasting industry. Similarly, Williams refused to see the widespread social investment in television as an indication that it was a "mass" form. Mass communication, he notes, is a concept and practice that was a rarity and that ran counter to mobile privatization's relation to transformations of social space and modes of governing these new social arrangements. "'Mass' uses of radio," he declares, were confined to the example of Nazi Germany as a form of governing through broadcasting (i.e., a form of "direct political and social control") and through "public" social space ("public listening groups and . . . receivers in the streets"). The instrumentality of television was more germane to the art/culture of self-government, more a matter of living and governing at a distance. (And in this sense, it is entirely appropriate to discuss television as a technology integral to *regimes* of mobility and privacy.) Williams acknowledges as much in the passage above when he refers to the "*self-sufficiency* of the family home . . . [and] an increasing distance between immediate living areas and the directed places of work and *government*" (p. 20; italics added). So, if greater mobility and privatization could be said to have "created a need," this was a need of governing and self-sufficiency, of the sufficiency of self-government, of satisfying the needs of governing and the need to be free and self-sufficient. Television may have allowed individuals to "cope" with living at a distance, but as a technological assemblage crucial to maintaining the regimes of mobility and privacy.

For Williams, television's emergence was somewhat facilitated by early forms of telephony and radio broadcasting, but it quickly emerged when it did through relatively advanced and sophisticated regimes of mobility and privacy, and as an indispensable mechanism for regulating these regimes and everyday life within them. His view of mobile privatization thus underscores the *longue duree and* the specific historical convergence. Television was a form and practice produced within, modulating, and converting (spatially and historically) residual and emerging social arrangements. The last chapter of his book is concerned with a number of technological developments that began to call into question not only what one means by "television" but also its effectivity. As he notes, "Many of the contradictions of capitalist democracy have indeed come out in the argument about television control"—particularly, he adds, in Britain and the United States (1974/1992, p. 126). As an intervention into this argument, this chapter obliquely touches upon whether the technological developments surrounding television in the 1970s might be articulated through the current democratic forms of government and citizenship or into new or alternative ones. Strangely, his commentary about emerging uses of cable and satellite broadcasting, video cassettes, and VCRs never recovers his initial point about mobile privatization. While he holds out the possibility that "independent, democratic organizations" may effect a broad struggle (the "long revolution") for "free communications," he also holds onto the conviction that, even though people may resist a regimen of programmed possibilities, "as the size of effective decision-taking communities gets so much larger, and as the scale and complexity of interlocking agencies makes identification let alone struggle more difficult, it is not enough to rely on *unaided virtues*" (pp. 145–146; italics added).

In the last part of this paper I want to reflect on the tenor of Williams' expression "unaided virtues" and to rethink its implications for the context—the crossroad—that he describes in 1974. Certainly the forms of broadcasting that he discusses in relation to mobile privatization are examples that lend themselves particularly well to his concluding characterization of an environment and regimen of programmed possibilities that need be resisted. Television and radio, while not "mass" forms (as Williams rightly points out), were up until the mid-1970s vivid and commonly cited examples of the "programming" of the everyday lives of their audiences. Discussions of them commonly dwelt upon the potential passivity of their audience and the need to restore activity—by resisting and/or not engaging them. These assumptions continue to inform Williams' distinction between "reactive" and "interactive" televisual technologies—the former which he views negatively and the latter positively as an improvement over traditional forms of broadcasting. Individuals have always interacted, however, with television and radio. And that interaction has always been part of their everyday lives, their organization of their households as a form of self-governing, and their connectedness and sense of connectedness to other spheres of sociality. So, in that sense, interactivity is a condition and technique of "self-governing" societies. In the 70s, however, a myth of interactive media—as an "unaided virtue"—was becoming crucial to a social arrangement that differed from the one wherein television had emerged so rapidly. As I explain below, this new configuration emerged out of a form of mobile privatization that had sustained and relied upon broadcasting and telephonic systems but was rapidly coming to depend upon a new set of technologies—particularly in the home—that pertained to new regimes of mobility and privacy. This new arrangement was not produced by neoliberal political philosophy ("the Reagan years") or by policy alone but was decidedly given to a neoliberal form of governing and its reliance upon a liberalized domestic sphere as a space of unaided virtue. The liberalized home (as a concept that came to be articulated to unaided virtue) and household (a space of self-governing) were also produced by and for a particular social class and taste culture, often referred to as the "professional managerial class."

The technological developments that most deeply styled the liberalized domestic sphere during the 80s were those that were programmable, generally through digital computer hardware and software. By the early 80s, television companies had begun to distinguish their newest models from earlier ones by emphasizing the sets' "intelligence." In 1983, Zenith's Smart Set TV featured "Zenith's exclusive Computer Brain" that was "smart enough to give you 178 channel capability," remote control, Zenith's exclusive space phone, and "self-monitoring" picture control (fig. 7.1). Although articulating television to intelligence attests to an emerging, rehabilitated identity for television (since the 50s widely regarded as the antonym of intelligence), this articulation also contributed to a new identity and arrangement of the home—at least for those who recognized and desired the domestic environment to which an "intelligent" TV pertained.[12] As part of an emerging arrangement of the domestic sphere—a new regime of privacy and of mobility to, from, and at home—television rapidly became appended to an array of programmable devices such as the VCR, remote controls for video and audio units, and the video camera. Although there are many ways to account for their fairly rapid emergence over the 1980s, their programmability did have several implications for the emerging formation and regimes that I am describing.

The domestic screen became a mechanism for conducting and monitoring multiple tasks, not only for programs and applications pertaining to the machine to which the screen was attached (e.g., TV sets with multiple programming capability) but also for devices that could be appended to that machine (e.g., the VCR). During the 80s, the screen was increasingly referred to as a "monitor"—a designation that refers to the screen as a technology for managing a system of components. As accouterment and concept, the monitor became integral to a new regimen for managing a household dependent upon programmable, self-governing appliances. The programmable capabilities of the monitor (i.e., those features internal to a machine and displayed on its screen) were akin to and dependent upon the concept, techniques, and technologies of "remote control." Although the remote control had been a feature of the most expensive television sets since the 1960s, it became standard equipment for managing the functions of video and audio units (as well

FIG. 7.1.   "The New Freedoms of 'Smart TV' "

as garage doors) during the 80s. As a tool for operating domestic appliances at a distance, it also became the most recognized metaphor and metonym of the self-directed household.[13] The monitor and remote control thus comprised mutually supporting instruments of self-governing subjects and objects. Furthermore, they brought domestic video and audio systems into a new relation with other household appliances—an ensemble of programmable technologies that could be utilized to temporally and spatially regulate a household.

They accompanied, for instance, the fairly rapid and widespread consumption and use of telephonic equipment, such as the "portable" telephone and the telephone answering machine.[14] These "communication" technologies generally became part of a complex of other, increasingly inexpensive, domestic technologies that were marketed and widely perceived as "time-saving" devices. The microwave oven, the programmable coffeemaker and electric blanket (e.g., Sunbeam's "Blanket with a Brain"), digitally metered "fitness systems," "talking" clock radios for kitchens and bedrooms, and time-regulating devices for lighting (not to mention the standardization of programmability in more established machines such as dishwashers, clothes washers and dryers, stoves, and alarm clocks) all were domestic appliances that, while not always hardwired with computer chips, were rapidly adapted to the organization and stylization of a domestic sphere, one of whose predominant "virtues" was self-governance.[15] The promise of self-regulating appliances included a 1983 Whirlpool refrigerator that featured a "new no-fingerprint" exterior surface and "monitored itself to help protect food." Also, General Electric's "counter-intelligence team"—appliances such as microwaves, coffeemakers, and clock radios—could be mounted underneath kitchen cabinets and thus off kitchen counters (fig. 7.2). That is to say, their users could rely upon these devices to achieve both greater flexibility and greater management of the household and everyday life. These were machines that could be seen as self-governing, for households that were self-governing. The domestic sphere itself became a mechanism that "freed" their users to do other tasks.

Home fitness technology, particularly for aerobic exercise—walking, jogging, and climbing simulators—often combined many of the programmable applications of these technologies. Home fitness technology routinely became equipped with audio and visual meters for monitoring movements of the body over a virtual terrain—a stationary mobility. Moreover, home fitness technology was designed to facilitate integrating exercise (managing one's body) into other domestic and extradomestic routines. Advertising and manuals often emphasized the freedom of self-directed movement (exercising as monitored activity and as part of a domestic routine) afforded by the surveillance and management of oneself within programmable complexes. *Good Housekeeping*'s 1983 guide to "electronic living" featured the "aerobics joystick [that] makes exercise fun" by coordinating exercise with remote control of television and music systems (see fig. 7.3). The home fitness technologies thus wed the programmatic procedures of "aerobic exercise" with the programming of exercise equipment (as in the advertisement for the Vitamaster treadmill that claims, "nothing works out better at home." The concept and

FIG. 7.2. "Programming Domestic Appliance: The Kitchen as Self-Regulating Space" (1982)

FIG. 7.3. "The *Good Housekeeping* Program for 'Electronic Living'" (1983)

activity of home fitness became a dimension of the new regimes of mobility and privacy, not only through the application of interdependent programmable devices for physical exercise in the home but also through the portability of audio devices such as the Walkman, which linked jogging or walking for exercise outdoors to indoor forms of exercise. In these ways, the activity and meaning of "exercise" became conjoined to a regimen (a regularity of everyday life) sustained through programmable, self-monitoring techniques and technologies.

While the "personal computer" developed as part of this domestic complex, its widespread use did not occur as rapidly over the 1980s as for these other domestic technologies. As a technology that was available/accessible strictly to the households of a professional managerial class during the 1980s, it did become instrumental to the institution of the self-governing home as a concept and sphere of sociality. But its fairly rapid domestic installation over the late 80s and particularly the 90s, as part of a redefinition of the professional managerial class and of the domestic sphere as a site of work and leisure, also bespeaks how much its development depended upon the kind of self-governing household that already was being constituted through these other technologies during the 80s. The common usage (indeed the interchangeability) of the term "*soft*-ware" for "program" since the early 80s was crucial to the self-directed features of home or "personal" computer use. Programs/software could be applied (i.e., directed, customized, personalized by a user) as well as relied upon precisely because they helped with programming problems and were a feature of a personal computer's self-monitoring system.

The programmability of domestic technologies was not simply a feature of computerized hardware—or of a "computer revolution" (the technological determinist's thesis)—but a mode of simultaneously freeing and governing oneself through an investment in an arrangement (a model and economy) of domestic space that could be managed at a distance. To see these technologies as part of a new domestic complex entails, as I suggested earlier, recognizing their role as mechanisms in a changing regime of mobility and privacy. While a robust explanation of these regimes would take me beyond the editorial limitations of this essay, it is important to emphasize how these developments contributed to and relied upon the domestic complex and the myth of "unaided virtue" that I have been describing. As part of a new set of procedures for moving about—from one part of the house to another, from the house to other sites—or for not having to move, these devices became crucial to the installation of a regime that actualized and organized other spheres. They became techniques for rationalizing where one could go and how one could get there. Of course this mobility was instrumental to a particular social class that possessed or was acquiring the economic and cultural capital to achieve this kind of mobility. These techniques also were part of the restructuring of men's and women's mobility within that social class. In fact, it is impossible to understand the "virtue" of the self-governing household without acknowl-edging how these devices accompanied the redefinition of women's work in and outside the home, and to a certain extent men's changing everyday rela-tion to the household (see Reed, 2000). Notwithstanding these issues of class, however, these developments affirm a new *arrangement*—at once a *distribu-tion* and a *disposition* within and among households in the 80s. To the extent that the freedoms of the neoliberal household depended upon the household's spatial organization and the disposition of subjects to living (exercising power, managing their lives and their space) on a daily basis through these technolo-gies, the household as arrangement became integral to the formation of a broader social arrangement.

As Williams noted about mobile privatization in the years following World War II, one of the central contradictions of industrial capitalism had to do with reconciling mobility and privacy. This new regime of mobility and the virtue of unaidedness (of the self-governing household) needed to be reconciled with a contemporaneously emerging regime of privacy. The prac-tice of "living at a distance" in the 80s in the self-governing household made matters of privacy a threat to the new regime of mobility. For if the self-governing household was predicated upon technologies that supposedly fa-cilitated movement, through new techniques for rationalizing domestic work and leisure and for restructuring the regimen of everyday life, this move-ment—the multiple flows within, to, and from the home—relied upon a sense of security. There are a number of ways of thinking about the issue of security in a new regime of privacy that, again, lie beyond the limitations of this essay. But let me quickly touch on a few of them. One way would be to consider the changing environment of the professional managerial class during the 80s, particularly in the changing constitution of U.S. suburbs and the migra-tion of this class to areas of gentrification. Another, which may bear more directly upon the developments of media practices, concerns issues of surveil-lance. The self-governing household is one that came to rely upon various mechanisms for surveying both the inside and outside of homes (particularly in "gated communities"). But the very flows that organized, rationalized, and resituated the self-governing household also became part of concerns about privacy, about being surveyed.

One of the most significant frictions at the intersection of the new re-gimes of mobility and privacy has occurred over the distribution of and access to pornography. Not only did the domestic sphere become a primary site for the consumption of pornographic material over the 1980s (through many of the video and telephonic technologies that I mention above), but the political debate over pornography has been the one most tightly linked to the de-/regulation of personal or home uses of video and computer technology.[16] Consider, for example, the longevity of the Communications Decency legis-lation since the early 90s and that the first Supreme Court ruling about the

Internet was an effort to legislate home consumption of pornographic material. While the Cable Communication Policy Act of 1984 provided the
legislative support for "deregulating" the distribution of television programming—as well as later reports and court decisions (e.g., the Meese Commission Report on Pornography in 1986 and the Supreme Court's ruling to
uphold Section 505 of the Telecommunication Act of 1997)—it also supported or required the implementation of various devices for scrambling
material deemed offensive by adult members of a household. Although cable
and satellite broadcasting were thus technologies for bringing the household
into a new relation with the state regulatory apparatus, this was a relation that
demanded an "ethics of access" by cable company and citizen *programmers* and
that emphasized the "responsibility of viewing" through new programmable
technologies. Home video hardware became a technology for monitoring and
regulating access from the home of material from outside the home, for de-
/regulating the household and the family as citizen-subjects.

The conflicted and contradictory discourse (among the main users of
these technologies) about the relation of pornography to the domestic sphere
vividly demonstrates both the importance of home to neoliberal forms of
governing and the difficulties and ambivalence of linking the (neo)liberalized
household to/through new regimes of mobility and privacy. "Unaided virtue"
may have been a necessary myth to the marketing of domestic technologies
and to achieving a model of a self-governing home during the 80s. See, for
instance, this Norman Rockwell-esque advertisement from 1983 for Atari
home computing (fig. 7.4), or ads from 1983 for Armstrong designed flooring
that insinuates new programmable appliances into a room with nineteenth-
century styled furnishings. Both ads articulate these appliances to/through a
design scheme based on chronotopes of the pre-80s home that *naturalizes* the
appliances' utility for the *contemporary* home. But to describe unaided virtue
merely as myth simplifies the practices that contributed to a self-governing
household, its importance to a changing social arrangement, and techniques for
governing "at a distance." The "virtue" of living "unaided" has been a hallmark
of a neoliberal ideology, but it is not confined to the political values of the left
or the right, which makes recognizing its practice through sites such as the
domestic sphere so important for imagining and conducting any political project
since the 80s. To the extent that neo- or advanced liberalism refers to a governmental rationality (a mode of reasoning, an arrangement, a disposition), that
runs through the life of social bodies, it is incumbent upon those interested in
understanding it to consider how its rearticulation has occurred through changing mechanisms and social spaces that may be coordinated with state power but
that operate outside its direct control. My account of the household is one
way—one site—for thinking about governmentality, and in a way that does not
begin with the State. Furthermore, given that Foucault's account of
governmentality in terms of a historical passage from premodern "economy"

FIG. 7.4.   "Computing As Domestic Appliance" (1983)

(the management of one's household) to modern "economy" (the science of managing populations and resources), it is worth rethinking the mattering of household as a sphere of management integral to contemporary technologies of government.[17] In this respect there is a connection between governmental rationality and knowing how to run one's home (how to run one's life from home and in one's mobility to and from home).

To describe self-directed-ness ("unaided-ness") as a virtue for and within neoliberal governance raises another issue: how the household, as an assemblage of technologies and technological exercises ("domestic appliances") that freed individuals and families by conjoining them to a regimen of programming, became an important site and conversion mechanism for a *moral economy* and an *ethico-politics* (i.e., a mode of governance and of governing virtue) that depended upon the formation of self-disciplining, ethical citizen-subjects.[18] This moral economy and ethico-politics have occurred on many scales, and mapping their interdependencies is a project well beyond the constraints of this paper.[19] While this essay outlines how this politics operates through domestic applications (domestic *appliance)* and programmable households, I want to indicate one way that such households have become integral to other spheres and scales comprising the new sociospatial arrangement and its implication in new regimes of mobility and privacy, and I want to do so in a way that addresses Rose's (1999) argument that a new discourse about community has become integral to an ethico-politics.

For Rose, community has become a site through which political actor-subjects are formed as government comes to rely upon ways of shaping ethical citizen-subjects whose lives are not managed directly by the state. Community becomes a terrain for building trust, not only among citizens but also by state government in citizens' ability to manage themselves. The state's reliance upon community as a new field of governing that produces ethical citizen-subjects is concomitant not only with a new political discourse about community but a new relation of community to governing that allows states and citizens to govern through community. This has occurred amid a proliferation of communities claiming certain degrees of cultural and political autonomy. As Rose points out, for communitarians a fundamental question is: "How can *virtue* [fixed standards which allow conduct to be judged in moral terms] be governed in a multi-cultural society in accordance with the liberal presuppositions of individual freedom and personal autonomy?" (1999, p. 183) Given the proliferation of communities claiming cultural and political autonomy, an answer to this question cannot appeal to a generalized conception of community. Instituting and representing community—defining its space and purview and defining values as virtues—are thus political issues.

At one point in his discussion of community, Rose proposes a rereading of Bentham's preface to *Panopticon*, whose benefits Bentham cited as: "Morals reformed—health preserved—industry invigorated—instruction diffused—public burthens lightened—Economy seated, as it were, upon a rock—the Gordian-knot of the Poor-Laws not cut, but untied—all by a simple idea in *architecture*" (Rose, 1999, p. 187; italics added). Rose suggests that now this statement should be rewritten as: "virtue regenerated—crime reduced—public safety enhanced—institutionalization banished—dependency transformed to activity—underclass included—democratic deficit overcome—idle set to work—political alienation reduced—responsive services assured—economy reinvigorated by seating it, as it were, within networks of trust and honour—the Gordian-knot of State versus individual not cut but untied, all by a simple idea in politics: *community*" (p. 187; italics added). Rose is right to note that community, as a new/liberal governmental rationality, is "not primarily a geographical space, social space, or sociological space or space of services, although it may attach itself to any or all such spatializations" (1999, p. 172). Still, in order to understand how these "attachments" or articulations have been occurring in the United States does need to account for how community has becomes a primary objective for the "production *of* space"[20] and how the organization of social spaces has been a mechanism for governing community and governing through community.

Two issues particularly pertain to this perspective about community and space. One is that, in the new politics of community, the question of how to govern virtues (fixed standards which allow conduct to be judged in moral terms) amidst the proliferation of communities and "in accordance with the liberal presuppositions of individual freedom and personal autonomy" (Rose, 1999, p.183) is also a question of governing the emplacement of community and governing through the production of space (precisely in a society such as the United States which values automobility and the free development of the residential/commercial spaces). Furthermore, as Doreen Massey (1994) has noted, places are often identified, wrongly, as "communities." This is the essentialist view of place and community, which assumes that places are discrete and self-enclosed rather than intersected by various flows and networks that connect places—through space—to other places and that make a particular place a convergence of multiple communities. Conversely, as Massey and others have pointed out, community can be (and arguably is increasingly) spread out over multiple places. While Rose's point that community may attach itself to particular spaces affirms this point, in spirit at least, his rationale does not address how communitarianism has become a spatial program and definition about stabilizing and governing values and identity or how community (as moral economy) occurs through a social arrangement organized through a new regime and new intensities of mobility.

A second issue concerns the new relation of architecture and community, and how neoliberal governance has been predicated upon new "architectures of community." Rose contends that community, as a "space of *emotional relationships*" and a "moral field binding persons into durable relations," represents a new "third space" of governing ("third" because it represents neither a pure form of state socialism nor a pure form of laissez-faire capitalism) and that making this new space involves emplacing boundaries and distinctions: "These spaces have to be visualized, mapped, surveyed, and mobilized" (1999,

p. 189). While Rose rightly accepts that "a whole array of little devices and techniques" (p. 189) have been invented to emplace communities, his explanation understands community emplacement and new forms of governmental rationality primarily in terms of procedures of calculation, such as market research, opinion polls, and surveys of attitudes and values.

Without rejecting Rose's view about emplacing community, his revision of Foucault's statement might be formulated in a third way—one that recognizes the implication of architecture and urbanism as part of a new governmental rationality. Rose's revision of Foucault's statement actually restates an argument made by Foucault about the relation of architecture to a modern political rationality (Foucault, 1997b). According to Foucault, a discourse about the aims of government began to occur during the eighteenth century through a "very broad and general reflection" about architecture and urbanism—with the city and the house becoming models for governing the territory (as the "extensive space") of nation-states.[21] By the nineteenth century, however, the model of enclosed space (regulated as *polis*) was supplanted by "technics of space," such as networks of communication, transport, and energy (e.g., electricity). A technics of space whose central variables were territory, communication, and speed (*more than architecture*) thus became the basis for a new governmental rationality (i.e., liberalism).[22] In this sense, freedom and the art/science of governing that Foucault associates with liberalism, became integral to the production and practice of social space (i.e., freedom/mobility as sociospatial practice and production).[23]

Rose's revision of Foucault's statement gestures toward the rather contradictory way that liberal government relies upon the separate and relatively self-enclosed institutional rationalities and architectonics of factories, prisons, and asylums, while it relies increasingly upon technics of space precisely for governing more effectively at a distance. The architect is not, as Foucault points out, like the doctor, priest, psychiatrist, or prison warden, nor is freedom determined or guaranteed by the *arrangement of objects* (as Modernist architectural projects often attempted to demonstrate). Still, techniques of power have been invested in and have operated through architecture and urbanism to the extent that they have played *a* role in the production of social space through the practice of freedom/mobility. *Technics* of space, in this sense, refer to techniques and technologies of mobility that have been articulated to and through liberal governmental rationalities and that during the twentieth century gradually became techniques of automobility and the mobile self—technics, in other words, of the new space and arrangement of mobile privatization. Therefore, if community acquired a political salience in the late twentieth century, it has done so through technics of space that negotiate not only the relation between a new discourse and practice of the self and a new regime of mobility, but also their relation to new discourses and practices of architecture and urbanism. Furthermore, in that the economy of the house-

hold (its arrangement and management) and its value for neoliberal governance have occurred through what Rose has called a new ethico-politics of
community, a linkage has formed between governing through the household
and through community—two separate but interdependent spheres. The discursive, technical, and material organization/management of these two different spheres has contributed in turn to a political reasoning about the role of
architecture and city planning in a kind of household and community suited
to new technics of space and a new regime of mobility.

One way to historicize how the discursive and material organization/
management of different spaces and different scales began to contribute to a
political reasoning about architecture and city planning as technologies of
community that are suited to the new technics of space and a new regime of
mobility would be to consider a Norman Rockwell illustration that appeared
on the cover of the *Saturday Evening Post* in 1949 (fig. 7.5). Published barely
2 years after commercial television broadcasting had begun, this illustration
depicts the attachment of the television antenna to a dormer of the kind of
turn-of-the-century residential architecture that Rockwell's illustrations mythologized. During the 1950s, this architecture (and its representation through
the circulation of Rockwell illustrations) was coming to represent a version of
village and domesticity for the rapidly emerging regime of mobility and privacy that Williams has discussed. Both Rockwell and television contributed
to defining parallel neighborhoods—the former pertaining to a pretelevisual
arrangement, and the latter instituted increasingly through suburbanization.

I invoke the Rockwell illustration also to reconsider the 1981 advertisement for Atari home computers that I have mentioned previously (fig. 7.4).
In the Atari ad's effort to represent the new personal computer as suitable
indoor work and play for kids, it defines a new/familiar (or neo-traditional)
relation between inside and outside—between a domestic sphere (a *home*
shaped by elements of Rockwell's style) and a *neighborhood* where this style
fits. Neighborhood is an extension of (imagined through) the interior tableau;
the kids at the window extend the neighborhood into the domestic sphere,
with the personal computer as the site where that transaction occurs.

Since the 1980s in the United States, forging a new relation between the
domestic sphere and neighborhood has become the point of a politics of
community and has become integral to a new moral economy. One of the
most prominent ways that this relation has been imagined and organized and
that this politics is being collectivized in the United States has been through
the New Urbanism—a program through which redesigning the urban and
suburban environment into "neighborhoods" is tantamount to restoring "community."[24] For Philip Langdon (1994), "the building block" of community is
neighborhood, and "lessons about how to build better communities can be
extracted from the nation's successful older communities," as represented in
the design of older houses and residential spaces (see pp. x, 217, & 243). For

FIG. 7.5.   "Installing Television in Norman Rockwell's America"

Peter Calthorpe, "the traditional American town still demonstrates many . . .
principles which can be adapted to the contemporary situation" (1993, p. 21).
Calthorpe particularly emphasizes the propinquity of "the traditional American town"—its small scale, walkability, increased possibility of face-to-face

interaction, and "diversity of use and users" through proximity (p. 21). New Urbanism is thus often described as "neo-traditionalist" in that it seeks to recapture a spatial practice *and* sociability lost to suburbanization. One proponent of New Urbanism, Todd Bressi, claims that "by isolating people in houses and cars and by segregating households into homogenous enclaves, the late twentieth century suburban metropolis has done little to replace the urban vitality it so aggressively replaced, and little to foster desperately needed civic responsibility" (1994, p. xxx). For Bressi, "civic responsibility" was not only lost during the era of suburban development but is (tautologically) both a necessity and consequence of the New Urbanist program. For Vincent Scully, another proponent of the New Urbanism, the restoration of community is fundamentally what is at stake for the New Urbanism. As he states in "The Architecture of Community": "It now seems obvious to almost everybody . . . that community is what America has most conspicuously lost, and community is what the [automobile and the] canonical Modern architecture and planning of the middle years of this century were totally unable to provide" (1994, p. 223). New Urbanists presume therefore that the inducement and civic responsibility for converting the suburban environment lies in the widespread desire for community through neighborhood. In the words of the planners of Seaside, Florida: "If they [the inhabitants of suburban areas] can be shown that future development will provide them with a gratifying public realm—narrow tree-lined streets, parks, a corner grocery, a cafe, a small neighborhood school—they may even embrace growth" (Duany, Plater-Zyberk, & Speck, 2000, p. 42). Calthorpe, however, makes more explicit the commercial dimensions of the impetus for the New Urbanist project. He reasons that reinstituting a "commons" (a social space and a conviviality which he associates with the traditional American town) not only should be the primary technique for "recentering" life in a postsuburban environment but also an integral technique of "commercial life": "The Commons once gave identity to the larger community and acted as the physical glue between residential neighborhoods, commercial center, and civic services" (p. 24). In its communitarianism, New Urbanism is nothing short of a program for *shaping* the relation among residential spaces as ethical collectivities and for giving a spatial definition (a definite shape) to community and its virtues. (See Appendices 1, "The Ahwahnee Principles" and 2: "Preamble to the Charter of the New Urbanism.") As Duany, Plater-Zyberk and Speck, & Calthorpe's statements above indicate, this moral economy relies upon refashioning the relation of oneself to a neotraditional space of neighborhood/community, itself fashioned as a neotraditional agglomeration of commercial space, civic space, and residential space.

If the New Urbanist village/community is supposed to be a collective space where responsible, civic-minded citizens can interact outside—in a public sphere—how does this public sphere operate as a site of governance and what is the relation of this public sphere to the management of the domestic sphere? One way to begin addressing these questions is to recognize that, as a program of civic improvement, New Urbanism is a technical *and* ethical discourse conducted by architects and urban planners as communitarians (or a discourse formed through the converging objectives of communitarians and planners). In this respect New Urbanism represents a new reasoning about government, not only with professional designers and planners as guides for shaping the postsuburban neighborhood into communal—diverse and egalitarian—space, but with neighborhood as the small-scale, neotraditional object of neoliberal governance for a post-suburban environment. As a discourse and rationale about the relation between housing and community, however, New Urbanism circulates widely—beyond the literature and associations of city planning and architecture. It has figured prominently in journalistic accounts of housing, ranging from cover-story descriptions about the state of housing in the United States by news magazines such as *Newsweek* (Bye-bye surburban dream, 1995) to technical evaluations of the housing market by *Consumer Report* (Homes that make sense, 1996)—accounts whose assessment and description about value in the housing market are just as much about the loss of community as how a New Urbanist program can correct it. In very profound ways, New Urbanism has thus been part of a discussion about the relation between liberalized growth and a program for liberalizing the economy/management of housing.

The connection between the emergence of the New Urbanism and neoliberal governance has been particularly evident in attempts to distance government projects involving housing from traditional forms of state welfare. The New Urbanism represents a reason for government by the state to govern through the "community-building" of citizens and it represents a kind of project whose aim is to display (to make public through citizen involvement and the spatial practice/representations of neighborhood restoration) citizen responsibility. The U.S. Department of Housing and Urban Development (HUD), in a 1996 initiative called Hope VI, adopted New Urbanist design guidelines and rationale about "community participation" to "assist residents" in redesigning public housing and its relation to surrounding zones. Echoing the New Urbanist commitment to "reestablishing the relationship between the art of building and the making of community through citizen-based participatory planning and design," HUD director Henry Cisneros stated at the 1996 Congress for the New Urbanism that the role of government is to "combine features of traditional community planning with new ways of organizing daily life in a rapidly changing world." For government, New Urbanism therefore represents a means of rearticulating the state's involvement in public housing, represented by projects erected during the suburban boom years. Cisneros's statement underscores that Hope VI intends to rely upon "traditional community planning" rather than direct government funding and management. Public housing projects in the 90s, however, are just one way that a New Urbanist discourse informs the broad objectives of neoliberal governing, tying the *economy* (effective management) of residential space and community to a new market economy. This relationship is underscored by Vice President Al Gore's statement (reprinted in the *Charter for a New Urbanism*): "While the blight of poor development and its social consequences have many names, the solutions, pioneered by local citizens, are starting to coalesce into a movement. In the future, *livable communities will be the basis of our competitiveness and economic strength*" (quoted in Lecesse & McCormick, 2000, p. 3; italics added). In language underscoring the economic benefits that could result from improving the *appearance* of public housing, *Principles for Inner City Neighborhood Design: Hope VI and the New Urbanism*, a pamphlet produced jointly by the Congress for the New Urbanism and by HUD, also states that "the economic health and the harmonious evolution of neighborhoods can be improved through graphic urban design codes that serve as predictable guides for change" (1999, pp. 5, 32). In this policy pamphlet, instituting "design codes" and "pattern books" (architectural proportionality and continuity as key to calculating, engineering, and demonstrating civic improvement) are articulated to a new rationality about both economic well-being and the proper use of the regulatory apparatus of municipal and federal government.

Beside being a rationale about a new relation between government by the state and government through community in the zones of public housing, the New Urbanist project became a distinctive component of a more encompassing federal policy in 1999 outlined in the White House Task Force on Livable Communities and their production of a Livability Agenda for "building livable communities."[25] In framing this agenda, Vice President Gore described architects as purveyors and technicians of "an architecture of community" and defined their stake in designing "livable community": "places where young and old can walk, and play together; places where we not only protect historic old neighborhoods, but where farms, green spaces, and forests can add life and beauty to the newest of suburbs . . . a way of life in which economic dynamism, green spaces, and friendly civic streets all coexist." As a policy agenda that links aestheticism, "economic health," public safety, and community as a site/means of self-government, and that entrusts architects and planning professionals to be the technical and moral guides for a citizenry, the Livability Agenda also avoids (indeed promises to "remedy") another legacy of government by the state: regulation through zoning. The *reason* for government, in this sense, lies in the "mistakes that decades of bad zoning and planning have imposed" and the ravages of urban sprawl—as the reason for the "crime and disorder" of urban neighborhoods and for the transformation of suburbs into "lonely cul-de-sacs" where "the freedom of the open road can explode into commuting-induced road rage."[26] Particularly over the late

1990s, the Clinton-Gore administration cast their initiatives for "building livable communities" as forms of "smart growth"—a moral and rational policy that has promised a path between no-growth and unfettered growth ("sprawl"), that has encouraged collaboration ("partnerships") between citizens, local government agencies, and planning experts, and that has posited *livability* (in these terms) as a new basis for governability.[27]

Notwithstanding the public housing initiatives, the more broadly directed policies such as the Livability Agenda, or the claims by planners or those in government (such as Gore) that New Urbanist projects are and should be "pioneered by local citizens," New Urbanism thus far has been a program of civic improvement adapted for privately developed suburban enclaves of a new professional managerial class—Seaside and Celebration in Florida, Laguna West in California, and Harbor Town in Tennessee being some of the most cited (and in the case of the Florida developments, caricatured) examples of New Urbanism. That major weekly magazines such as *Newsweek* have framed accounts of recent housing trends in the language of the New Urbanism also affirms its relevance to suburban lifestyle clusters and taste cultures. In policy proposals such as the Livability Agenda, the benefits of redressing the broadly detrimental consequences of urban sprawl fall particularly to the residents of suburbs. Where New Urbanist projects have involved "in-fills" of previously deserted urban tracts, these projects also have been integral to a program of gentrification. In these projects as well as in less distinct and fully completed zones of gentrification since the 1980s, New Urbanism is about a new relation between the city and suburb—the New Urbanism as a New Suburbanism. This new relation rests upon at least two contradictory objectives. One is that designing and *developing* community is an antidote to planned suburban development. In aspiring, however, to provide an alternative to an earlier regime of mobility and privacy (to the lack of sociability accompanying the organization of suburban space and the dependence upon automobility) and in promising to make unnecessary the security practices of "gated communities" in favor of "open" and "public" spaces, New Urbanism assumes that community and a public sphere are and should be desired for their own sake. This contradiction about planned community is related to one pitting the old suburban formation against a "new" (neotraditional) rationale about governance: whereas the suburban environments lacked community and public spaces, the New (Sub-)Urbanist neighborhood's restoration of public interaction frees residents from their homes and cars so that they can enter a space governed/disciplined through the household's new relation with neighborhood, as a collectivity of responsible, civic-minded citizens and of spaces where trust can be produced and used to govern in very local ways. This new mode of governance is no less dependent than was post-World War II suburbanization or the village upon an "architecture of community." Now, however, the neighborhood, village, and

"community" have acquired a salience for the new political rationality that
Rose has described as ethico-politics—the practice of governing through
community as discourse and as spatial arrangement. The spacious front porch,
a leitmotif of the New Urbanist dwelling as "mirror of the self" and as
restoration of lost community, was after all a technology of surveillance in
village life. Other New Urbanist techniques for modifying the relation between house and neighborhood, such as reviving the practice of installing
windows on and around doorways to avoid representing the house as bunker,
also make surveillance a key feature of the New Urbanist neighborhood.
Furthermore, in that the New Urbanist program for restoring "town life'" and
community seeks to reform both the public sphere and the domestic sphere
and to redefine the relation between them, it is particularly valuable to a
mode of governing that requires interdependent spheres and scales of self-
governing collectivities. For New Urbanism, this interdependence rationalizes
redesigning the trappings of suburban home as a key strategy for a new
"architecture of community" while assuming that the neighborhood can be
designed to provide structural incentives for drawing people out of their
houses and into localized public spaces governed by the rationalities of neighborhood and community. As Calthorpe argues, "the more privatized our technology and social forms become, the more isolated and defensive we are"
(1993, p. 37).

Although the New Urbanism has formulated a program of civic improvement through a binary logic that opposes the virtue of community and
the negativity of the domestic sphere (with the aim of restoring community
in suburban zones previously organized through private and thus noncommunal
spaces), this program has occurred through a technical expertise of *domestic
appliance* supporting a new regime of privacy and new techniques for household as self-governing spheres. In order to consider domestic appliance as a
technology of power and governance, one would need to ask how neoliberal
governance and the New Urbanism have been so readily articulated to/through
a particular arrangement of the domestic sphere and so dependent upon the
new technologies of domestic appliance. How have technologies of Home
come to matter within the new definition and deployment of community and
within an ethico-politics that works through community? In concert with a
discourse about family, such as Hillary Rodham-Clinton's (1996) writing about
how family/household management can be a means for restoring "the village"
in American life, the New Urbanist discourse has deemed television to be a
symptom of suburbanization (the regime of mobility and privacy) that should
be condemned. Creating a more walkable and interactive neighborhood of
porches and town squares out of the suburban legacy involves turning off
the TV set, with one of the more woeful justifications for New Urbanism
being the diagnosis by clinical behaviorists about the psychic and social
"unhealthiness" of TV watching. "Freeing" households of television is even

viewed by some New Urbanists as necessary to the ethico-aesthetic formation of residents and community—a conviction particularly pronounced in James Kuntsler's (1993) argument (reminiscent of the Mass Culture thesis from the 1950s) that TV "degrades" community and culture because it has "filtered" the outside, has prevented inhabitants of suburban houses from connecting their lives to the outside in an "active way," and has thus degraded aesthetic sensibility (which cultural critics of the American landscape, as moral exemplars, should correct).[28] Invoking Neil Postman, Langdon argues that the domestic sphere is typically a state of greater confusion, instability, and anxiety than the neighborhood precisely because "modern technology has flooded the household with more stimuli, more information, than people can digest" and because (citing Postman) "when the supply of information is no longer controllable, a general breakdown in psychic tranquility and social purpose occurs" (1994, p. 152).

There are several contradictions to this reasoning that are worth mentioning, particularly given my description of the programmable household in the first part of this essay. One is that the New Urbanist discourse about the domestic sphere simplifies how freedom has come to depend upon programmable technologies in the domestic sphere and how the New Urbanist vision of everyday life is governed through a moral economy connecting neighborhood and the domestic sphere. Second, its faith in the freedom and simplicity of a new "village"-life—a neotraditional public sphere—requires self-directed citizens who can leave their homes up and running while they are away and who can manage risk through domestic appliance rather than through the control mechanisms of "gated communities," though there is nothing about New Urbanist projects that is inherently anathema to the technologies of contemporary gated residential developments (fig. 7.6). Developing trust depends as much upon a technical expertise/competence about domestic appliance (programming a VCR) as it does about conducting oneself as a neighborhood. The rationale that TV is a symptom of suburbanization and that both have produced inactive and controlled citizen-subjects misses not only how interactivity (from the domestic space to the outside) depends upon a technical expertise/competence but also how the transaction between the self-governing and self-directed neighborhood/ "community" and household/ "home" has become integral to neoliberal governance. Furthermore, the New Urbanist discourse is mostly silent about the kind of domestic technologies and practices that I have described above, choosing instead to focus on televisuality as a pernicious symptom of a residual suburbanization, automobility, and the lack of conviviality accompanying living at a distance.

In repudiating automobility and television as twin ills of living at distance and as the primary spoilers of a public sphere, the New Urbanism not only implies a connection between them but also implies that sociability depends upon technologies of mobility and privacy. The New Urbanist rationale about

FIG. 7.6.   The Remote-Controlled Household

automobility and television, and about the relation of community, freedom, and governance to architecture/urbanism *and* technics of space, rests however upon a contradictory understanding of mobility and privacy. According to New Urbanists, television and cars have contributed, in different ways, to a formation of social space that has destroyed the *propinquity* of the traditional American town. Whereas television has contributed to a hyperimmobility and to a predilection for remaining indoors, the suburban environment's development around the automobile has contributed to an overreliance upon technologies of personal transport, a distancing of destinations in everyday life, and a redundancy of traditional forms of mobility such as walking. Compared to walking, the hypermobility of driving oneself is not therefore unlike the hyperimmobility of watching television, since both of the latter activities are assumed to involve a sedentary subject closed into a privatized space.

The New Urbanist communitarianism moreover makes mobility (as a practice and display of freedom) intricately linked to governance even though New Urbanism understands cars, TVs, and the privatization accompanying suburbia to have thwarted or imperiled liberal democratic governance. For Calthorpe, automobility has produced an environment that is undemocratic in that it limits the "independence" of those who are unable to drive, such as the working poor, the elderly, and children (1993, p. 17). Richard Moe and Carter Wilkie (1997) carry this rationale a bit further: "a complete dependence upon the automobile to move around poorly planned sprawlscapes is said to give us more freedom and mobility, but it may actually give us less [because] Americans spend more time driving vaster distances in the car (p. 71). In both senses, redesigning cities and suburbs for diversity of use and more equitable access is seen to be a matter of enhancing physical mobility for all residents and to be a prerequisite for restoring a public sphere, as a space that—unlike the domestic sphere or the automobile—is productive of citizenship (and consumerism, in "commons" designed to mix commercial and civic uses).

Another contradiction of this rationale is that its remedy lies as much in redesigning cities and suburbs for pedestrians as in assuring freedom by "liberating" drivers (and TV watchers) from their sedentary, privatized enclosures. In this respect, a new practice of freedom and mobility is linked to new spaces of governance—whether they be streets designed for pedestrians, multi-use "commons," or households and car use suited for that kind of neighborhood design. The New Urbanist project is not, after all, about eliminating the use of automobiles but of rearticulating their relation to neighborhoods organized to maximize access to small-scale, mixed-use ("public") spaces. As Calthorpe has proposed, "the goal of community planning is not to eliminate the car, but . . . to accommodate the car and still free the pedestrian" (1993, p. 17). Designing small-scale neighborhoods suited primarily to walking and secondarily to driving oneself also assumes that the fewer the *technologies* of mobility the greater an equity of access and mobility. It does not acknowledge that walking and driving both pertain to new modes of governing in a new regime of mobility and privacy. The New Urbanist communitarianism, for all its valuing of freedom (or an equity of freedom) through a "commons," envisages a return to a form of governing through architecture and the city, but for a society already profoundly organized through advanced technics of space. By reasserting architecture and the space of localization as the primary objectives of liberal governance, the New Urbanist strategy thus reaffirms but also slightly reformulates Foucault's account that liberal governance has involved a transition from a space of localization to a technics of space.

The New Urbanist communitarianism unequivocally emphasizes the rootlessness of the post-suburban society. It more or less agrees that "as habitats for community have eroded, so too has the true meaning of the word" (Moe & Wilkie, 1997, p. 73), and thus it often draws a distinction between authentic (presuburban) community and postsuburban psuedocommunity. In its most neoconservative variants, represented by statements such and Moe and Wilkie's, the New Urbanism conflates community and place and assumes that community is only ever about the fixing of values and the rooting of people in places that display "centers" and "commons" ("where people [are] tied by fellowship or even kinship to one another, to a shared past, and to a common interest in the future"). The New Urbanist communitarianism, in this regard, does not recognize that such places always have been based on unequal distribution of access and have been linked to other regions and governed through technics of space. Still, the New Urbanist project of "*re*-building" community is about designing small-scale social spheres with greater equity of access than occurred in post–World War II suburbanization, though their conception of freedom, equity, access, and diversity of use has much to do with making commerce and shopping integral to the neotraditional spaces of sociality where civic responsibility can be displayed. Nor is New Urbanism entirely about the rootedness and circumscription of dwelling, neighborhood, or city. Precisely in its effort to design or map small scales of equal access that are linked to other urban and suburban regions (in part through interdependent technologies of dwelling and transport), it is about bringing propinquity to governing at a distance. For the New Urbanism, the domestic sphere represents an impediment to its vision of a "commons" and of neighborhoods suited for equity of access and mobility, but I have tried to suggest a few ways how the very model of the domestic sphere rejected by the New Urbanism is compatible with and instrumental for practicing freedom and for self-governance within a new regime of mobility and privacy. New technologies of the domestic sphere (some of which are increasingly integral to automobile design), and the technologies of community dear to New Urbanists, are about articulating "livability" to governability, about both insulating and connecting habitat to other scales of sociality, and about governing through mobility and privacy. In other respects, the New Urbanist project is about designing new mechanisms for governing the domestic sphere/privacy and automobility. I have considered some of the contradictions of the New Urbanist communitarianism (precisely *in* its relation to the technologies of domesticity) in order to provide an alternative way of thinking about its binary logic about freedom and governance, especially as its model of neighborhood improvement (as a more equitable space of access and mobility) has become integral to a governmental rationality that relies upon techniques for governing community and governing through community.

Considering the interdependencies between the New Urbanism and the technologies and new arrangements of the domestic sphere is one way to consider the interdependence of two spheres/scales of ethico-politics: how one of the most contemporary programs in city planning and architecture has been instrumentalized through *domestic appliances*. Rose is right to note that *community*, as a governmental rationality for advanced liberalism, is "not primarily a geographical space, social space, or sociological space or space of services, although it may attach itself to any or all such spatializations (1999, p. 172). In this essay I have attempted to suggest some of the ways that these attachments or articulations have been occurring in the United States and particularly how the discursive and material organization/management of different spaces and scales have contributed to an emerging political rationality about place and cultural technology. Considering the relation between cultural technology and domestic appliance (of managing community and household, of governing through community and household, and of shaping community through the self-governing household or vice versa) requires a different way of thinking about media and communication technology and a different logic of mediation than have driven modern conceptions of media-culture and technoculture, and certainly than have guided a New Urbanist discourse. This is not to say, however, that the urban, suburban, neighborhood, or domestic environments have become only spaces of control. On the contrary, their relevance to a discussion about advanced liberalism has to do with their assemblage and articulation through agents whose mobility and conduct through these spaces depends upon certain kinds of technical expertise and a technological practice—some of which no longer requires an individual to stay at home to manage the home. Nor do I want to suggest that community is not desirable or valuable. Instead I want to call attention to some of the technological and spatial practices that underpin the virtue of community and home for a political rationality that emphasizes self-governance and self-sufficiency.[29]

Appendix One: The Ahwahnee Principles, 1991

Preamble:

Existing patterns of urban and suburban development seriously impair our quality of life. The symptoms are: more congestion and air pollution resulting from our increased dependence on automobiles, the loss of precious open space, the need for costly improvements to roads and public services, the inequitable distribution of economic resources, and the loss of a sense of community. By drawing upon the best from the past and the present, we can, first, infill existing communities and, second, plan new communities that will successfully serve the needs of those who live and work within them. Such planning should adhere to these fundamental principles:

Community Principles:

1. All planning should be in the form of complete and integrated communities containing housing, shops, work places, schools, parks and civic facilities essential to the daily life of the residents.
2. Community size should be designed so that housing, jobs, daily needs and other activities are within easy walking distance of each other.
3. As many activities as possible should be located within easy walking distance of transit stops.
4. A community should contain a diversity of housing types to enable citizens from a wide range of economic levels and age groups to live within its boundaries.
5. Businesses within the community should provide a range of job types for the community residents.
6. The location and character of the community should be consistent with a larger transit network.
7. The community should have a center focus that combines commercial, civic, cultural and recreational uses.
8. The community should contain an ample supply of specialized open spaces in the form of squares, greens, and parks whose frequent use is encouraged through placement and design.
9. Public spaces should be designed to encourage the attention and presence of people at all hours of the day and night.
10. Each community and cluster of communities should have a well defined edge, such as agricultural greenbelts or wildlife corridors, permanently protected from development.

11. Streets, pedestrian paths and bike paths should contribute to a system of fully-connected and interesting routes to all destinations. Their design should encourage pedestrian and bicycle use by being small and spatially defined by buildings, trees and lighting; and by discouraging high speed traffic.
12. Wherever possible, the natural terrain, drainage, and vegetation of the community should be preserved with superior examples contained within parks or greenbelts.
13. The community design should help conserve resources and minimize waste.
14. Communities should provide for the efficient use of water through the use of natural drainage, drought tolerant landscaping and recycling.
15. The street orientation, the placement of buildings and the use of shading should contribute to the energy efficiency of the community.

Regional Principles:

1. The regional land use planning structure should be integrated within a larger transportation network built around transit rather than freeways.
2. Regions should be bounded by and provide a continuous system of greenbelt/wildlife corridors to be determined by natural conditions.
3. Regional institutions and services (government, stadiums, museums, etc.) should be located in the urban core.
4. Materials and methods of construction should be specific to the region, exhibiting continuity of history and culture and compatibility with the climate to encourage the development of local character and community identity.

Implementation Strategy:

1. The general plan should be updated to incorporate the above principles.
2. Rather than allowing developer-initiated, piecemeal development, local government should take charge of the planning process. General plans should designate where new growth, infill or redevelopment will be allowed to occur.
3. Prior to any development, a specific plan should be prepared based on these planning principles. With the adoption of specific plans, complying projects could proceed with minimal delay.
4. Plans should be developed through an open process and participants in the process should be provided visual models of all planning proposals.

Appendix Two: Preamble to the Charter of the New Urbanism

The Congress for the New Urbanism views disinvestment in central cities, the spread of placeless sprawl, increasing separation by race and income, environmental deterioration, loss of agricultural lands and wilderness, and the erosion of society's built heritage as one interrelated community-building challenge.

We stand for the restoration of existing urban centers and towns within coherent metropolitan regions, the reconfiguration of sprawling suburbs into communities of real neighborhoods and diverse districts, the conservation of natural environments, and preservation of our built legacy.

We recognize that physical solutions by themselves will not solve social and economic problems, but neither can economic vitality, community stability, and environmental health be sustained without a coherent and supportive physical framework.

We advocate the restructuring of public policy and development practices to support the following principles: neighborhoods should be diverse in use and population; communities should be designed for the pedestrian and transit as well as the car; cities and towns should be shaped by physically defined and universally accessible public spaces and community institutions; urban places should be framed by architecture and landscape design that celebrate local history, climate, ecology, and building practice.

We represent a broad-based citizenry, composed of public and private sector leaders, community activists, and multidisciplinary professionals. We are committed reestablishing the relationship between the art of building and the making of community, through citizen-based participatory planning and design.

We dedicate ourselves to reclaiming our homes, blocks, streets, parks, neighborhoods, districts, towns, cities, regions, and environment.

Notes

1. This view of neoliberalism is particularly germane to policies supported by the Clinton administration that have promised a "third way" between traditional forms of state welfare ("socialism") and laissez-faire capitalism. In the U.S. context, neoconservatism has rejected "liberalism" as too bound to traditional forms of State welfare and as socialistic and has aimed (in its libertarianism) to institute a kind of government that works indirectly, through local government or through institutions

---

Charter of the New Urbanism, M. Leccese and K. McCormick (Eds.) for the Congress of the New Urbanism (2000), New York: McGraw-Hill.

and mechanisms that have no direct connection to the State. Therefore, while "neoliberalism" may contradict the traditional terms used to distinguish/identify Democrat and Republican government in the United States, the policies of both political parties certainly share the objectives of neoliberalism, particularly as a new relation of government to the responsibilities of "free citizens" and as new techniques for governing through the free and responsible citizen-subject.

2. Whereas the term "neoliberal" dramatically captures the historical category as rhetorical strategy (the effort to redefine the role of the State), the expression "advanced" liberalism emphasizes the intensification of nineteenth and early twentieth century forms of governmental rationality and acknowledges that contemporary forms of State government are organized through both a recent and residual governmental rationality.

The relation between late-twentieth-century and nineteenth-century liberal government is also important and complicated precisely because neo- or advanced liberalism is not merely an issue of trade and markets—not, in other words, only an "economic" matter (at least in the narrow way that economy is understood scientifically, as a distinct practice with its own rules). For Foucault, in his writing about governmentality, the modern practice of government involved how to introduce economy into political practice, of making "economy" a political rationality (or science)—instrumental—for governing populations, territory, and resources. For Foucault, economy is less *the* basis for understanding political practice; it became nonetheless an important problematic in governing since the eighteenth century. For Rose, advanced liberalism is about governing not simply through economy but through society and through freedom.

3. See Foucault's explanation of power in his lecture, January 14, 1976:

> One must . . . conduct an *ascending* analysis of power, starting, that is, from its infinitesimal mechanisms, which each have their own history, their own trajectory, their own techniques and tactics, and then see how these mechanisms of power have been—and continue to be—invested, colonized, utilized, involuted, transformed, displaced, extended, etc., by ever more general mechanisms. . . . I believe that the manner in which the phenomena, the techniques and procedures of power enter into play at the most basic levels must be analyzed . . . ; but above all what must be shown is the manner in which they are invested and annexed by more global phenomena and the subtle fashion in which more general powers or economic interests are able to engage with these *technologies that are at once both relatively autonomous of power and act as its infinitesimal elements.* (Foucault, 1977/1980, p. 99; italics added)

In Foucault's lecture on governmentality, written two years after the lecture cited above, this view of power informs his discussion about governing. He places greater emphasis upon techniques of governing and offers a more elaborated explanation about the paradox of modern government that is a basis for Burchell, Gordon, and Miller's perspective on neoliberalism: how modern states must devise ways of governing "at a distance" and must rely upon technologies of management that lie outside their purview. See Foucault (1991).

4. Toby Miller's *The Well-Tempered Self* (1993), while not directly taking up neoliberalism, is one of the few examples of work that more carefully addresses some of the issues concerning media raised by discussions about neoliberalism as a project for developing and relying upon a new kind of ethical subject.

5. The term "arrangement" here is intended to capture the connotations of the French *dispositif*—a technology (i.e., something that regulates), the connection of positions/people over territory (i.e., the arrangement of military forces on a battlefield), and a contract/agreement about positions that is the basis for a disposition/inclination.

6. For Foucault's discussion of "truth regimes," see "Truth and Power" (1980) and "On the Government of Living" (1997c).

7. Foucault elaborates this point in "The Ethics of the Concern of the Self as a Practice of Freedom," *Ethics, Subjectivity, and Truth*, Paul Rabinow (Ed.), New York: New Press, 1997.

8. Williams was decidedly less invested in describing television as a "medium" than as "a system of communication." The former term only appears in (and is the point of) his brief critique of Marshall McLuhan (1992, p. 120), while the latter term pertains to his interest in television's historical relation between community and technology. As Williams stated in *Culture and Society* (1958), "Any theory of communication is a theory of community" (p. XX). Here Williams' emphasis upon the development of technologies for overcoming and managing the *extensiveness* of Modern forms of *community* (a term that conjoins culture and social organization) makes his work consonant with Foucault's writing about "governmentality" and (to a greater extent) with Armand Mattelart's (1996) account of "communication" as a Modern concept and practice imbricated in the development of systems of conveyance and circulation for new social arrangements. Williams' inclination to describe television as communication and to emphasize the relation between communication and community implies that television is a "cultural technology"—a technology that came to matter in defining, shaping, and managing community/culture.

9. To say that television is not just a system of communication needs to be qualified by Williams' view that, as I note above (endnote 7), a system of communication relies upon a broad array of technologies for producing and maintaining "community" in modern societies.

10. Foucault (pp. 100–101), "Governmentality."

11. Williams uses the term "social technology," but his discussion of television as "technology and cultural form" tempts me to develop a third term—"cultural technology"—in order to acknowledge television's linkage to other technologies/appliances (e.g., the microwave oven, the remote garage door opener, or the refrigerator) while emphasizing its technical role in representing technologies and social spaces (something that refrigerators or microwave ovens are not designed to do). The concept of cultural technology allows us to ask which technologies most come to matter in organizing and representing spheres of sociality and sociability. Furthermore, cultural technology is a way of emphasizing the technical mechanisms and procedures upon which *community* is instituted, redefined and reinstated—the cultural (in Williams' sense) being in part about the formation of community. Cultural technology is a useful

application of Foucault's understanding of political economy as a way of governing through the distribution of population and resources over territory. What kind of cultural capital as technical expertise is required for the formation and maintenance of social arrangements? What is the relation of a political economy to a cultural economy (i.e., the distribution of populations and cultural resources over territory)? One problem, however, in conceptualizing cultural technology is its reification of "technoculture"—an expression that is potentially just as generalized as "mass culture" or "postmodernism" (e.g., the '90s as a technoculture). For my project, the challenge of thinking about and trying to understand technoculture is not only the articulation of these two terms historically but how specific technical competencies and technological assemblages have come together in the production, differentiation, and disciplining of particular social spaces.

12. Defining this taste culture lies beyond the scope of this essay, but it is worth noting that the concept of an "intelligent" TV emerges concurrently with the critical acclaim of TV series produced for the kind of "quality" demographic described in *MTM: Quality TV* (1987). The "intelligence" of TV thus became a quality associated with both the twin technologies of ("niche") programming and programmability (an "asset" of the neoliberalized home).

13. The increasing commonality of the remote control device for video and audio units during the '80s was deeply contradictory with respect to the emerging regime of mobility and privacy. On one hand, the remote control was an instrument that "freed" users to perform multiple tasks and with less movement and expenditure of energy. On the other, the device became the object of considerable concern and derision about the immobility of its users (the "couch potato").

14. The transportation of vision and sound over greater distance (efforts to engineer simultaneous viewing and listening among increasingly numerous and dispersed locations) had made television and telephony interrelated projects since the late nineteenth century. Not until the 1980s, however, did the programmability/storage of television and telephone reception, the rapid reliance upon coaxial cable TV via telephone grids, and the emergence of TV programming such as "home shopping" which integrated telephonic conversation into broadcasting did the link between broadcast TV and telephony begin to sustain the kind of "interactive" procedures that defined the neoliberal home. While the concept of a portable TV was common in advertising for television sets since the mid-1950s, TV sets capable of being carried easily by one hand did not become common until the period of the portable telephone. Their contemporaneity further contributed to the relation between a new regime of mobility and privacy.

15. Recognizing the interdependence of these domestic technologies has not always been easy for mass communication studies and media studies, whose disciplinary disposition to treat media and communication as if they were distinctive objects or sets of practices brackets their reliance upon and their implication in technological assemblages. They assume, in other words, that "media" are the most important form of mediation. Mark Levy, for instance, begins *The VCR Age* (1989) with an essay entitled "VCR's Aren't Pop-Up Toasters." Beside being a justification for the rest of the book, the essay is also a semiserious apology to a referee of an academic commu-

nications journal who had criticized an earlier submission on VCRs for not having explained sufficiently why VCRs mattered. According to Levy, the reviewer asked: "Is it [the VCR] only significant because of widespread diffusion? That could lead to a rash of studies of electric toasters." Levy recounts how he had fumed over the criticism: "Electric toasters? Give me a break. Why not electric coffeepots or electronic water-piks while you're at it?" He goes on to explain how some time later, after having reflected upon the criticism, he recognized the wisdom of its reasoning: "What if thirty-five years ago, I had submitted a research paper to a journal, dealing with what was then the new home communication technology—television. And what if a referee then had asked, 'Why investigate the role of *television* in the mass communication process, after all it's nothing more than another electrical appliance?'" Both the reviewer and Levy's statements presume that television or VCRs matter primarily in their role as "mass communication" and as objects of mass communication research. Why indeed aren't the toaster and the water-pik viable ways of understanding the "mass communication process" (or its value, as paradigm, to communication studies or media studies as a discursive formation)?

This is an argument that I develop more fully in "Locating the Televisual," *Television and New Media*, vol. 2, no. 3., August 2001.

16. Foucault notes that political economy, as a "science of government," developed out of (and, to a certain extent, against) an earlier conception of economy as the art of managing family and household. The problem confronting modern, western societies becomes one of "how to introduce economy—that is to say, the correct manner of managing individuals, goods, and wealth within the family (which a good father is expected to do in relation to his wife, children and servants) and of making the family fortunes prosper—how to introduce this meticulous attention of the father towards his family into the management of the state" (Foucault, 1991, p. 92). For Foucault, governmentality thus comes to depend upon the family and household more as an instrument of government than (as was the case of the Prince) as a model for government.

17. See Juffer, *At Home With Pornography: Women, Sex, and Everyday Life*, (1998). Chapter One, "Home Sweet Pornographic Home?" particularly concerns the contradictions of legislating home consumption of pornography.

18. In many respects I agree with Nikolas Rose's (1999) argument about a "new ethico-politics," though I want to emphasize how this politics operates differently on different scales, comprising a new socio-spatial arrangement wherein *domestic appliances* and programmable households are integral to the larger scale of a ethico-politics of community that his book takes up.

19. This essay pertains to a book-length project that I am completing wherein I develop a critique of neoliberalism through a discussion about cultural technology, governmentality, and social space in the United States and wherein I am able to map these interdependencies of scale more thoroughly and carefully.

20. I invoke Henri Lefebvre's notion that social space is both produced and productive. Representing and shaping community occur on a terrain that is always, already organized by the representational and material production of spaces. See Lefebvre, *The Production of Space*, London: Blackwell, 1991.

21. In "Other Spaces: The Principles of Heterotopia" (1997a), Foucault describes the transition from medieval space (the "space of localization") to a space of "extension"—"the assertion of an infinite and infinitely open space."

22. Deleuze, "Postscript on the Societies of Control" (reprinted in Leach, 1997).

23. "I think it is somewhat arbitrary to try to dissociate the effective practice of freedom by people, the practice of social relations, and the spatial distributions in which they find themselves. If they are separated, they become impossible to understand. Each can only be understood through the other" (Foucault, 1997b, p. 372).

24. New Urbanism is a discourse that became formalized and was articulated to a political rationality about government over the 1990s, though many of the projects (residential developments) that served as models for the New Urbanist discourse were carried out during the 1980s. The first formal statement of New Urbanist ideals was developed in 1991 at a meeting convened by California's Local Government Commission at the Ahwahnee Hotel in Yosemite National Park. In 1993, the first Congress of the New Urbanism convened in Alexandria, Virginia and has been followed by other congresses. For more on the New Urbanism, see Peter Katz, *The New Urbanism: Toward an Architecture of Community* (New York: McGraw-Hill, 1994); Andres Duany, Elizabeth Plater-Zyberk, and Jeff Speck, *Suburban Nation: The Rise of Sprawl and the Decline of the American Dream* (New York: Farrr, Straus, & Giroux, 2000); and *Charter of the New Urbanism*, Michael Leccese and Kathleen McCormick (Eds.) for the Congress of the New Urbanism (New York: McGraw-Hill, 2000). The official bibliography of the Congress of the New Urbanism can be found at <http://www.cnu.org/>

25. This agenda was presented formally by Vice President Al Gore in an address before the American Institute of Architects on January 11, 1999.

26. The Livability Agenda proposed four initiatives: 1) "Better America Bonds," tax credits for state and local bonds to "help communities reconnect to the land and water around them"; 2) grants "to help communities develop alternatives to building more clogged highways"; 3) subsidizing a Regional Connections initiative "to aid in the development of truly regional game plans for smarter growth"; 4) grants targeted at specific localities "to encourage school districts to involve the whole community in planning and designing new schools . . . , to provide communities with . . . information and technical assistance to develop strategies for smarter growth . . . , to promote the sharing of crime-data across jurisdictions." On one hand, this program governs through community, directing resources to localities, while providing a framework for overcoming (through regional and national networks) the potential ungovernability of that kind of rule.

27. See particularly *Building Livable Communities: Sustaining Prosperity, Improving Quality of Life, Building a Sense of Community*, a report from the Clinton-Gore Administration, June 2000.

28. After having complained about the practice of decorating lawns with painted cutout plywood figures, Kunstler (1993) confesses that he "can't pass these cartoonlike displays without thinking of television . . . of how much television has to do with the way houses look in the present landscape" (p. 167). More generally, the book's comments about "yard art" and television rests upon a rationale about the ethical

responsibility by cultural critics of the suburban landscape to condemn such forms. Rebuking sociologies of the suburban landscape, such as the one by J. B. Jackson, Kuntsler states that "a Jacksonian student of landscape can observe a Red Barn hamburger joint . . . and never arrive at the conclusion that the Red Barn is an ignoble piece of shit that degrades the community" (pp. 123–124). See Kuntsler, *The Geography of Nowhere: The Rise and Decline of America's Man-Made Landscape*, New York: Simon and Schuster, 1993.

29. I want to thank Jack Bratich, John Clarke, Jane Juffer, Lawrence Grossberg, Cameron McCarthy, and Jeremy Packer for their suggestions about this project. A significant part of this essay first appeared as "Unaided Virtues: The (Neo-) Liberalization of the Domestic Sphere," *Television and New Media*, vol. 1, no. 1., February 2000 (Thousand Oaks, CA: Sage).

REFERENCES

Barry, A., Osborne, T., & Rose, N. (Eds.). (1996). *Foucault and political reason: Liberalism, neo-liberalism, and rationalities of government.* Chicago: University of Chicago Press.

Burchell, G., Gordon, C., & Miller, P. (Eds.). (1991). *The Foucault effect: Studies in governmentality.* Chicago: University of Chicago Press.

Calthorpe, P. (1993). *The next American metropolis: Ecology, community, and the American dream.* New York: Princeton Architectural Press.

Homes that make sense. *Consumer Report* (1996, May) pp. 21–30.

Dean, M. (1999). *Governmentality: Power and rule in modern society.* Thousand Oaks, CA: Sage.

Duany, A., Plater-Zyberk, E., & Speck, J. (2000). *Suburban nation: The rise of sprawl and the decline of the American dream.* New York: Farrar, Straus, and Giroux.

Fever, J., Kerr, P., & Vahimagi, T. (1984). *MTM "Quality television."* London: BFI Publ.

Foucault, M. (1977, 1980). *Power/knowledge: Selected interviews and other writing* (C. Gordon, Ed.). New York: Pantheon.

Foucault, M. (1991). "On Governmentality." *The Foucault Effect.* Chicago: University of Chicago Press.

Foucault, M. (1997a). Of other spaces: Utopias and heterotopias. In N. Leach, (Ed.), *Rethinking architecture: A reader in cultural theory.* London: Routledge.

Foucault, M. (1997b). Space, knowledge, and power. In N. Leach (Ed.), *Rethinking architecture: A reader in cultural theory.* London: Routledge.

Foucault, M. (1997c). *Ethics, subjectivity, and truth* (P. Rabinow, Ed.). New York: New Press.

Hay, J. (2000). "Unaided Virtues: The (Neo-) Liberalization of the Domestic Sphere," *Television and New Media*, pp. 53–74. *1*(1).

Hay, J. (2001). "Locating the Televisual," *Television and New Media*, pp. 205–234. 2(3).

Juffer, J. (1998). *At home with pornography: Women, sex, and everyday life*. New York: New York University Press.

Katz, P. (1994). *The new urbanism: Toward an architecture of community*. New York: McGraw-Hill.

Kuntzler, J. (1993). *The geography of nowhere: The rise and decline of America's man-made landscape*. New York: Simon and Schuster.

Langdon, P. (1994). *A better place to live: Reshaping the american suburb*. Amherst, MA: University of Massechusetts Press.

Leccese, M., & McCormick, K. (Eds.). (2000). *Charter of the new urbanism*. New York: McGraw-Hill.

Lefebvre, H. (1991). *The production of space*. London: Blackwell.

Levy, M. (1989). *The VCR age*, Thousand Oaks, CA: Sage.

Massey, D. (1994). *Space, place, and gender*, Minneapolis, MN: University of Minnesota Press.

Mattelart, A. (1996). *The invention of communication*. Minneapolis, MN: University of Minnesota Press.

Miller, T. (1993). *The well-tempered self*. Baltimore: Johns Hopkins University Press.

Moe, R., & Wilkie, C. (1997). *Changing places: Rebuilding community in the age of sprawl*. New York: Henry Holt.

Bye-bye suburban dream: Fifteen ways to fix the suburbs. *Newsweek* (1995, May 15). pp. 40–53.

Reed, L. (2000). Domesticating the personal computer, *Critical Studies in Mass Communication*. Vol. 17, no. 2. June 2000. pp. 159–185.

Rodham-Clinton, H. (1996). *It takes a village: And other lessons children teach us*. New York: Touchstone.

Rose, N. (1999). *Powers of freedom: Reframing political thought*. London: Cambridge University Press.

Rose, N. (1996). *Inventing ourselves: Psychology, power, and personhood*. London: Cambridge University Press.

Report from the Clinton-Gore Administration. (June 2000). *Building livable communities: Sustaining prosperity, improving quality of life, building a sense of community*. Washington, D.C.: U.S. Government Printing Office.

U.S. Department of Housing and Urban Development and Congress for New Urbanism (2000). *Principles for inner city neighborhood design: Creating communities of opportunity—Hope VI and the New Urbanism*. Washington, D.C.: (HUD) and San Francisco, CA (CNV).

Williams, R. (1974, 1992). *Television: Technology and cultural form*. Hanover and London: Wesleyan University Press.

Chapter 8

From Nation to Community

Museums and the Reconfiguration of Mexican Society under Neoliberalism

Mary K. Coffey

Introduction

Mexico's shift from State-sponsored capitalism toward neoliberalism in the 1980s occasioned a reconfiguration of government vis-à-vis Mexican society. Throughout most of the postrevolutionary period, Mexican society has been imagined through the totalizing identity of a national-popular. This hegemonic identity has been critiqued from a number of positions, and increasingly "community" is emerging as the privileged formation of social identity. Within this latter formulation, the national aggregate is re-imagined as an atomized network of indigenous or subnational groups. This re-imagination is both a response to the specific history of postrevolutionary nationalism in Mexico and its preeminent figure, the *mestizo*, and a general effect of social mobilization following the advent of privatization and austerity—the much-lamented "state withdrawal from the public sector"—under neoliberalism.

The tendency to view this withdrawal as a withdrawal rather than a reconfiguration of the relations between State and society has led to a number of assumptions about the politics of community, particularly with respect to the establishment of community museums. These regional and local institutions, inaugurated by, administered, and representative of the communities they serve, are understood by their supporters as resistant and even revolutionary sites. As I will argue, the development of a politics of community in Mexico is not an alternative formation that eludes the influence of the state, but rather a product of the reconfiguration of government in the wake of the collapse of the postrevolutionary model of a centralized state. Rather than reify community as a form of natural social organization that either precedes the formation of the state or that automatically exists in opposition to state interests, I demonstrate how, as a newer figuration of society, community enables the processes of "governing at a distance" that have characterized liberal forms of government from their inception (Barry, Osborne, & Rose, 1996; Hindess, 1996). Thus the shift from a national-popular to a kind of multiculturalism made up of subnational identities signals not a withdrawal of government from the affairs of everyday life, but rather, new governmental processes that attempt to constitute autonomous and self-governing communities, as well as national citizens who conduct themselves as modern, enfranchised political subjects.

Commenting on the effects of decentralization throughout Latin America, George Yúdice has argued that social and political actors must recognize that decision-making is taking place in varied, and often changing, sites, which necessitate new strategies for political targeting (Yúdice, 1998). An important effect of this dispersion of power has been the emergence of civil society as the privileged paradigm for political struggle. Under this new paradigm, ideological struggle is expressed through difference rather than through an articulation to the "kind of imaginary totalizing national identity presumed in the era of the popular" (Yúdice, 1998a, n.p.). Thus culture, as a mechanism of difference, assumes a significant role in the elaboration of antagonisms and rights. Moreover, the museum, the preeminent space for the codification of culture, has become an important strategic locus for group organization. As sites for the legitimation of culture, these dispersed centers of decision-making seek to rectify the injury of "misrecognition" that Nancy Fraser has argued is as significant as distributive injury in the struggle for social justice (1997). Consequently, the community museum offers a potential opportunity to strengthen civil society in the interest of effecting democratic citizenship. However, in order for this potential to be exploited, the cultural politics of the museum need to be reoriented, from a commitment to adequate representation toward an understanding of how these institutions constitute social identities.

Throughout the postrevolutionary period, the museum has been a crucial governmental apparatus for regulating conduct and objectifying the abstract domains—"man," "nation," "community," and so forth—necessary for conceptualizing society. By tracing the history of museums in Mexico, particularly the postrevolutionary consolidation of a centralized, federal, institutional infrastructure and more recent attempts to decentralize national culture through regional and community initiatives, this essay is concerned with the problems and potentialities presented by the museum as an agent for social domination and/or resistance in Mexico, and by analogy other national contexts within the current configuration of global economic restructuring.

Following the roundtable held by UNESCO in Santiago, Chile in May 1972, museums have increasingly been incorporated into a cultural politics of resistance throughout Latin America (Martínez & Puig, 1977). The UNESCO manifesto, *Cultural Rights as Human Rights* (1970), has now drawn culture into the naturalizing logic of liberal humanism concerned with codifying an individual's relation to power. As Graham Burchell notes, "it is in the name of forms of existence which have been shaped by political technologies of *government* that we, as individuals and groups make claims on or against the *state*" (1991, p. 145; italics in original). The articulation of a claim to a culture through the language of rights requires the arbitration and affirmation of a sovereign power in order to be realized. Thus, culture cannot be understood as a reflection or manifestation of a mythical social organization that precedes or is independent of the state. Furthermore, culture itself is a product of governmental processes—those apparati, techniques, knowledges, institutions, and practices that have constituted the reality of the *idea* of society since the late eighteenth century (Bennett, 1992a, 1992b). The museum, as Tony Bennett has demonstrated, is one such technology, and its "birth" in the late eighteenth century is constitutive of culture as both a product of human achievement and a field of naturalized social relations (Bennett, 1995). The "cultural rights" that have motivated the commitment to the development of community museums in Mexico (and elsewhere in Latin America) need to be understood in their relation to government if they are to be at all effective in strategizing a collective politics for change.

In what follows I begin with a discussion of Foucault's governmentality in order to establish a theoretical framework for understanding the relationship between government and society and the role of the museum in their articulation. I then situate the rapid development of museums in Mexico with respect to the broader orchestration of national culture in the postrevolutionary period, in order to elaborate the specific characteristics of the national-popular in the Mexican context. Following the insights of Foucault's governmentality studies, I discuss postrevolutionary nationalism as a governmental project that configured relations between the Mexican state, society, and individual through the welfare model of a centralized state, a *mestizo* society, and individual subjects of need. The advent of neoliberalism, I argue, has not only decentralized the mythic unity of the state, but also has exploded the imagined unity of the national-popular into variegated communities comprised of self-advocating subjects of choice. This process is being effected, in part, through the agency of the museum. In my analysis, the National Museum of Anthropology and a local museum in Tláhuac (currently under construction in a suburb of Mexico City) serve as paradigmatic examples of how the museum has produced different conceptions of population and different ethics of citizenship at two different moments in Mexico's political transformation. The implications of this for both a politics of resistance and the cultural analysis of power will be elaborated in the conclusion.

THEORIZING LIBERAL GOVERN*MENTALITIES*[1]

Conceptions of population are central to the problem of government; thus an analysis of the historical emergence of government vis-à-vis the question of society will help to clarify the significance of the shift from nation to community at the heart of this essay. Governmentality, as a cultural logic, emerged in the late eighteenth century as a result of the crisis of sovereignty or "reason of the state." Foucault traces the elaboration of an "art of government" through the historical transition from absolute sovereignty to the administrative states of the fifteenth and sixteenth centuries and the rise of mercantilism in the seventeenth century (Foucault, 1991). As the legitimation of rule through a theory of divine right waned, a counterdiscourse about *how* to rule gained greater purchase. By the late eighteenth century, liberal theories of rational rule took hold of the political imaginary and established the historical conditions for both a science of politics and a newly objectified field of social relations as the object of that rule (Burchell, 1991; Gordon, 1991). Arguing that the idea of "society" was a discovery of political theory at the end of the eighteenth century, Foucault asserts that political rule is no longer solely concerned with securing territory and the loyalty of its subjects in order to maximize the power of a sovereign or state, but rather that it takes on an ethical and technical dimension as it endeavors to manage this new domain of social actors dispersed within a complex field of relations. He writes:

> government not only has to deal with a territory, with a domain, and with its subjects, but . . . it also has to deal with a complex and independent reality that has its own laws and mechanisms of disturbance. This new reality is society. From the moment that one is to manipulate a society, one cannot consider it completely penetrable by police. On must take into account what it is. It becomes necessary to reflect upon it, upon its specific characteristics, its constants and variables. (Foucault, 1989, p. 261)

The discovery of society marks the birth of new fields of knowledge concerned with objectifying this complex reality for the purposes of proper management. While concerned with the questions of authority, discipline, and regulation, governmentality is not a theory of state domination. In fact, Foucault argues that liberal theories of government emerge just as the juridical state, as a historical form of rule, becomes problematized and reconfigured from a model of absolute sovereignty to a diffuse form of power that seeks to "govern at a distance." Governmentality, then, refers to

> the ensemble formed by the institutions, procedures, analyses and reflections, the calculations and tactics that allow the exercise of this

very specific albeit complex form of power which has as its target population . . . resulting, on the one hand, in the formation of a whole series of specific governmental apparatuses, and on the other, in the development of a whole complex of *savoirs*. (Foucault, 1991, p. 103; italics in original)

Thus, liberal forms of government hinge upon the question of the population which has become identified as a natural phenomenon, a species, datum, or a general *system* of living beings. As Colin Gordon explains, "Foucault's analysis of early liberalism indicates the ways in which our political objectification as living beings who are part of a population, as members of society. . . sought to render us *governable*" (1991, p. 144). As a consequence, population and society are not seen as empirical realities or natural orders that preexist government; rather, they have been historically produced in order to make government more effective. "The supposed separation of State and civil society," write Barry, Osborne, and Rose, "is the consequence of a particular problematization of government, not of a withdrawal of government as such" (1996, p. 9). Furthermore, this problematization yielded a whole series of technical knowledges, or expertise (namely the field of the social sciences), which sought to render cognizable and thus manageable this new, ostensibly natural domain.

Rob Watts has suggested that rather than maintain a commitment to theorizing the separation of political authority and society and the proper relation between them, we turn our attention to "the intellectually trained whose interventions bind the sites of social action conventionally distinguished between state and civil society in an ironic yet mutually reliant relationship" (1993/1994, p. 157). Arguing that governance is central to the project of modernity, Watts asserts that "the age of modernity has seen the wholesale discursive constitution of disciplines and subjects in which the conjoint urge to know and to govern are evident" (p. 157). It is the intellectual, after all, who does the social science research that helps to constitute cultural images of the object to be governed: the field of population. Thus cultural apparati are important technologies of government insofar as they help to objectify abstract concepts such as "man," "nation," or "ethnicity," through discursive practices both verbal and visual, for the purposes of more effective government. Following Bennett, I am arguing that the positive knowledges that comprise museology have been critical intellectual and discursive practices in the constitution of society for the purposes of knowing and governing.

Like the idea of society, the birth of the modern museum is also a late-eighteenth-century phenomenon. In his genealogy of the public museum, Bennett has convincingly argued that the museum is a technique of power wherein "culture," defined as "the aesthetic," is deployed for the improvement of the manners and behaviors of "cultures," defined as specific groups of targeted populations (Bennett, 1992a). Bennett eschews the heroic history of the modern museum, which locates its birth in the enlightened secularism of the French Revolution, and concentrates instead on its "political rationality," a component better discerned within the late-eighteenth-century debates in Britain over "rational recreations" (Bennett, 1995). Thus the museum is ushered forth not as a democratic space of egalitarian public access, but rather as a highly contentious space for modeling refined behavior, and enjoining acquiescence to proper modes of political and social participation.

As a social space of representation and regulation, the modern museum is distinguished from its various predecessors in two important ways. First, the formation of the modern museum broke with the principles of "private ownership and restricted access" by transferring cultural and scientific property into "public ownership where they were housed within institutions administered by the state for the benefit of an extended general public" (Bennett, 1995, p. 73). Second, while cultural institutions formerly sought to wow a limited audience with uniqueness or rarity, the modern museum seeks to instruct the many by organizing its objects according to an evolutionary historicism that makes each one "representative" within chronological narratives of progress, at some times universal and at others national.[2] These differences, Bennett argues, marked a "changed orientation to the visitor—one which was increasingly pedagogic, aiming to render the principles of intelligibility governing the collections readily intelligible to all and sundry" (1995, p. 41). Just as governmental reason rearranges the objects of sovereignty (territory and subjects) into a field of productive and cognizable relations, the modern museum reorganized the contents of former royal and elitist collections into an ordered and knowable domain of objects and a rational and proper set of relations. Within the great exhibitionary complex of the late eighteenth century, objects of wonder and curiosity are converted into representative cultural and historical artifacts that signify and stand in for abstracted social concepts. Through this new exhibitionary logic, social concepts, like the modern nation-state, become naturalized as social realities, while their constituent populations are targeted and regulated through the narratives and architectural arrangement of these new social technologies.

THE MUSEUM AND MEXICAN SOCIETY

In Mexico, the birth of the museum coincided with the birth of the nation. The National Museum of Mexico was founded in 1825 by presidential decree just 4 years after Mexico won its independence from Spain. While the museum, as a particular kind of cultural institution, had been around since the period of Independence, after the Revolution of 1910 (1910–1920) museums began to proliferate at a greater pace. At the close of the Revolution there were two public museums in the country. By 1964 there were at least 40 museums of various types open in Mexico City alone. In 1985 the National Institute of Anthropology and History (INAH)[3] oversaw 106 public museums. Of those, 6 were national, 25 were regional, 55 were local, and 20 were heritage sites distributed throughout the country. By 1991, after the inauguration of the community museum initiative in the 1980s, INAH counted an additional 33 community museums in the states of Chihuahua, Hidalgo, Guerrero, Yucatan, and Baja California, with 21 more in progress. Today so many community museums pop up and disappear that an accurate count is impossible (Cimet et al., 1987, p. 33; Department of Community Museums, 1990, p. 28; *INAH Anteproyecto*, 1985, p. 9; http://www.arts-history.mx/museos/muse.html).

Over the nineteenth and twentieth centuries, the museum in Mexico has evolved from a fairly crude storehouse of antiquities and "pagan" objects to a highly organized space of regulation, education, and citizenship (Fernández, 1987; *INAH Anteproyecto*, 1985; Morales-Moreno, 1994; Reyes—Palma, 1987). Cultural institutions have been indexed to education and national initiatives since the birth of the Mexican nation. With the establishment of the Ministry of Public Education (SEP) in 1921 during the post-revolutionary presidency of General Obregón (1920–1924) and the cultural and educative policies elaborated by its first Secretary, José Vasconcelos, an institutional structure for the diffusion of culture was set in motion. Along with his public arts initiative, most significantly manifested in the commissioning of artists to paint murals on public walls, Vasconcelos brought the fine arts under the umbrella of the SEP, not only by enfranchising the National Museum of Archeology, History, and Ethnology, but also by advocating the creation of new museums for the conservation, protection, and diffusion of Mexico's artistic and monumental patrimony (Reyes—Palma, 1987, pp. 20–21). Historian Augusto Urteaga Castro-Pozo argues that with the creation of the SEP, museums were included within the federal education system and utilized as "cultural spaces through which the ideology of revolutionary nationalism, the product of the popular movement of 1910–1917, would be diffused" (1995, p. 291).[4] This ideology placed an emphasis on the indigenous past in order to formulate a "national historical consciousness" forged in Mexican values and symbols.

From Vasconcelos' establishment of a national culture project in 1921 through the inauguration of the National Anthropology Museum in 1964, Mexican museology has organized its exhibitions around a concept of national identity predicated on assimilation or *mestizaje* (racial and cultural mixing). *Mestizaje*, as a figure of Mexican nationality, was a specific response to the psychological and historical conditions of Spanish conquest and colonialism (1519–1821), U.S. and French military intervention (1846–1948 and 1862–1867), and finally U.S. economic imperialism during the *Porfiriato* (1876–1911).[5] While multiple social and intellectual actors participated in the elaboration of *mestizaje*, Vasconcelos' pseudoscientific tract of 1925, *The Cosmic*

Race, is the putative source for the postrevolutionary elevation of the *mestizo* (a person of mixed Indian and Spanish heritage) as the iconic Mexican. In *The Cosmic Race*, Vasconcelos transformed racial miscegenation, a sign of Mexico's backwardness and historical condition of colonization, into a transcendent principle of future promise. Arguing that "a mixture of races accomplished through the laws of social well-being, sympathy, and beauty" will lead to a *cosmic race*, "infinitely superior to all that have previously existed," Vasconcelos predicted that "we in America shall arrive, before any other part of the world, at the creation of a new race, fashioned out of the treasures of the previous ones" (1925/1979, pp. 31, 40).

While this hoary rhetoric has lead some critics to celebrate Vasconcelian *mestizaje* as a prescient symbol of multiculturalism, his concept was an explicit figure of assimilation that was instrumentalized through the postrevolutionary development of the SEP and subsequent cultural initiatives enacted by INAH and INBA (the National Institute of Fine Arts). The constitution of the nation as a *mestizo* nation necessitated the improvement of its indigenous "element"—a "lower breed" in Vasconcelos' estimation (1925/1979, p. 100). Consequently, postrevolutionary national discourse and policy were obsessed with the "Indian Question," which became the primary raison d'être for the bulk of governmental programs.

Manuel Gamio, the founding father of Mexican anthropology whose canonical study of Teotihuacán[6] was published under the revealing title *Forging a Fatherland*, routinely advocated for the necessity of "official institutions" to study Mexico's indigenous populations for the purposes of both understanding and government (Gamio, 1926b, p. 173). "Cultural fusion, linguistic unification and economic equilibrium," he argued, were integral for a "coherent and definite nationality and true fatherland" (p. 173). In a lecture entitled "Incorporating the Indian into the National Population," he made his governmental agenda clear, writing, "It is unquestionably urgent, most urgent, to investigate the indigenous population of Mexico scientifically, for until this is done thoroughly, social contacts cannot be normalized and oriented authoritatively. . . . This, and only this, can place the Mexican nation as a nation, upon a solid, logical, consistent, and permanent base" (1926a, p. 127).

This intellectual and governmental concern for Mexico's indigenous population has been termed "official *indigenismo*" because it resulted in the state promotion of pre-Hispanic culture and indigenous populations as the foundation of Mexico's national "originality," while at the same time these very same groups were undergoing a forced "modernization" that effectively obliterated the remaining vestiges of the practices and affiliations identified as "indigenous" (Brading, 1988). As the examples of Vasconcelos and Gamio suggest, more often than not the most influential voices of indigenous valorization were also the most vocal proponents of assimilation and forced modernization. While some have scratched their heads at this seemingly contradictory logic (Brading, p. 89), I maintain that it is consonant with the fundamentally disciplinary phenomenon of nationalism and that it makes manifest the relationship between intellectual activity (knowledge) and the processes of governance (power) (Coffey, 2000).

Recognizing the constitutive relationship between *indigenismo* and *mestizaje* is critical to any analysis of community in Mexico today. The postrevolutionary production of the indigenous as a population for the purposes of government provided the foundation for subsequent attempts to advocate for indigenous rights and to reorient nationalism toward a *Mexico profundo* (deep Mexico).[7] The shift from a unified category of the indigenous to a more variegated concern with multiple ethnic communities merely refines the work inaugurated by these (and other) postrevolutionary figures. This is not to assert that Indian communities do not exist, but insofar as they have become recognizable political identities, they are products of the governmental processes of this century. Unlike in the United States where community, when it designates a locality, conjures up the social form of the neighborhood (a form with no necessary racial or ethnic coherence), in Mexico, community is almost always synonymous with indigenism. In this respect it is more congruent with identitarian formulations of community in the U.S. (the queer community, a community of women); however, as an identity formation, community in Mexico has an a priori status that eschews the volunteerist and pragmatic inflections of its U.S. counterparts. Any defense of community in Mexico is a tacit defense of the indigenous population, which has been the preeminent figure of political resistance since the Revolution of 1910. Thus the turn toward community as a preferable social imaginary is neither a recovery of a prelapsarian past, nor is it a corrective recognition of a legitimate civil society independent of the activities of the postrevolutionary state. Rather, it is a reorganization of the national population, and potentially a more effective organization for the purposes of governmentalization.

THE APOTHEOSIS OF THE NATIONAL-POPULAR: THE NATIONAL MUSEUM OF ANTHROPOLOGY

The museum has been a crucial site for the construction of the *mestizo* as the national-popular and for the incorporation of indigenous populations into the national imaginary. The governmental commitment to the use of culture to promote social progress has always been oriented toward the production of subjects who understand themselves as participants in the nation and whose participation in cultural life is encouraged as an appropriate mode of civil conduct. As Iker Larrauri, former Director of Museums for INAH, explains:

> museums should be viewed as factors in the development of social
> awareness, helping to train individuals to play an active and effective
> part in the processes that affect their personal lives, their social re-
> lations and their relationship with their environment. (Stellweg, 1976,
> p. 37)

Larrauri's statement betrays the liberal logic that undergirds Mexican
museology. As Nikolas Rose suggests, under liberalism the subject of government is reformulated as active in their own government. "From this time
forth," he writes, "liberal governmentalities will dream that the national objective for the good subject of rule will fuse with the voluntarily assumed
obligations of free individuals to make the most of their own existence by
conducting their life responsibly" (Rose, 1996, pp. 45–46).

This understanding of the museum was developed and refined in the
National Museum of History and the National Museum of Anthropology,
arguably the nation's two most popular cultural institutions. But it is also
evident across the spectrum of public institutions of culture in Mexico, from
the National Museum of Art to regional museums like the Museum
Cuahnuahuac in Cuernavaca. The postrevolutionary development of a national culture infrastructure reflects the rise of a centralized form of rule that
sought to integrate the individual into a social formation. The presidency of
Lázaro Cárdenas (1934–1940) nationalized Mexico's oil industry and established the *latifundo* initiative, two hallmarks of the social welfare state in
Mexico that have been dismantled under neoliberal reform. Not only did the
Cárdenas administration signal the onset of a socialized form of rule, but it
also founded the Institutional Revolutionary Party (PRI), the ruling political
party that dominated Mexican politics, at every level, for 60 years. Thus, the
Cárdenas years augured the onset of the "cold monster" of the Mexican state
while simultaneously enacting the protectionist measures that to this day are
the yardstick for most demands for a revival of the state's responsibility toward its citizenry.

Regarding the phenomenon of social welfare states, Rose cautions that
the development in the early twentieth century of a social form of rule indicates "not so much a process in which a central state extended its tentacles
throughout a society, but the transformation of the state into a center that
could program—that is shape, guide, channel, direct, [and] control—events
and persons distant from it" (1996, p. 40). Simultaneous with the development of centralized welfare states, the liberal subject was reformulated from
an individual moral being into a subject of need (p. 40). This reformulation
has important implications for how we characterize the consolidation of the
Mexican state, because it takes into consideration the empowerment of various professionals to elaborate the truth claims by which this need could be
administered. Not least among these professionals are museum directors,

curators, and policy makers. In what follows, by describing the policy agenda, architectural solutions, and content of the exhibitions in the National Museum of Anthropology, I demonstrate how the expertise generated by the disciplines of anthropology, ethnography, and museology have constituted the national-popular in this very governmental space.

Arguably the crown jewel in Mexico's cultural complex, the new National Anthropology Museum, inaugurated in 1964, has come to embody "Mexicanness" (fig. 8.1). As the most visited museum in the country, its success has been attributed to its spatial organization and displays that assert that national culture originates in the indigenous sectors of Mexico's population. However, as Néstor García-Canclini (1995b) has argued, it does this by marking the limits of the ethnic through a separation of ancient and contemporary cultures. This separation is instantiated through the display of the archaeological wealth of Mexico's pre-Hispanic cultures on the first (and more frequented) floor and ethnographic displays purporting to represent contemporary indigenous groups on the second floor. The museum gives pre-Hispanic culture much greater emphasis; however, as I will demonstrate, both display strategies construct the indigenous as an antiquated or premodern category. García-Canclini describes the displays' absence of modern appliances and the restriction of indigenous culture to "authentic" crafts and practices, which deny the hybrid realities of the products and peoples that continue to manufacture them (p. 130).

FIG. 8.1. The "crown jewel" of Mexican museums, Mexico's National Anthropology Museum was inaugurated in 1964 as a state-of-the-art institution of national patrimony.

The museum's collections are distributed across two floors of galleries that form a rectangle around an open patio (fig. 8.2). While patrons are free to enter each gallery from this patio, there is a clearly marked place to begin their experience in an introductory hall that explicates the museum's mission and articulates its objects to and through the science of anthropology or the study of "man." In his statement about the "origins, aims and achievements" of this museum, Ignacio Bernal, director of INAH during the period of the museum's construction and throughout the 1960s, makes explicit the significance of the science of anthropology to the Mexican nation. He writes:

The diverse indigenous cultures of Mexico, both those which flourished in prehistoric times and those which have persisted until the present day, present anthropology with a vast field for study while providing museums with rich and valuable materials for display. . . . Keeping this in mind, those who planned the new National Museum of Anthropology decided to include an initiatory hall that would justify the Museum's name and at the same time present a universal framework into which the Mexican cultures could be fitted in space and time, as well as allowing visitors to compare their cultural contributions with those of other peoples. (Bernal, 1968, p. 14)

FIG. 8.2.   Interior patio of the National Anthropology Museum demonstrating its organization into two floors of exhibitions distributed among galleries that progress chronologically in a counterclockwise movement around the courtyard and from the first to second floor.

This initiatory hall opens with a mural depicting the *Cosmic Race*[8] and proceeds to explain the science of anthropology through didactic presentations of its physical, linguistic, archeologic, and ethnographic methods. Presenting a progressive narrative that moves from prehistoric animal and plant life to the emergence of humans, the display culminates with "civilization" and the concept of "horizontal cultures." As the origin of the museologic journey, it prepares the viewer to understand the objects in subsequent galleries as both national in content and universal in significance. The galleries that follow are organized according to the chronological emergence of particular meso-American cultural groups, with special emphasis on the Toltecs and the Mexica (Aztecs)—the pre-Hispanic populations that have been retrospectively crafted as the pinnacle of cultural achievement before the Conquest and thus as the "deep Mexico" that undergirds modern civilization (fig. 8.3). The less sophisticated

FIG. 8.3.   View of the first-floor gallery dedicated to Tula and Toltecan culture. The monumental sentinel figures and dramatic lighting convey the magisterial display of archeological objects within the galleries devoted to Mexico's most revered pre-Columbian cultures.

exhibitions on the second floor are organized geographically and present generic mannequins in regional dress posed in dioramas or sets that replicate the housing and ceremonial activities "typical" to these regions (fig. 8.4).

While the introductory hall instructs the visitor before they proceed, the final hall, in its original form, punctuated their experience with an invitation to utilize their new knowledge by becoming proper modern citizens. Entitled "Modern Autochthonous Mexico," this last exhibition represented, in the words of Bernal, a "synthesis of the process of social and cultural change taking place in Mexico today" (1968, p. 193).[9] Unlike the rest of the institution, which cements indigenous cultures into seemingly ahistorical formations, "Modern Autochthonous Mexico" represented the synthesizing processes of modern Mexico through a photomosaic in which images of various ethnic groups were montaged into a progressively assimilated and modernized image of the national populace. Bernal describes this mosaic as an inducement for the "participation of the native peoples" in national life (p. 193). The museum, he writes, is a governmental site, "through which the National Indigenist Institute is trying to integrate the various ethnic groups into Mexican national life" (p. 193). Functioning as bookends to the museum experience, the introductory and final halls convert the viewer's progress through the exhibitions into an evolutionary performance that begins in a glorified past and

FIG. 8.4.   Ethnographic display of the Otomi peoples from the second floor exhibitions. The genericized mannequins dressed in typical clothing, juxtaposed with traditional crafts and wares, and placed in front of documentary photographs from the region, exemplify the anachronism of the ethnographic exhibitions as well as their visual poverty relative to the exhibitionary strategies in evidence on the first floor.

looks to the future. This organization implies that the synthetic vision of the nation's future is the fulfillment of a promise embodied in the culture of the nation's past, and it configures Mexican society as an assimilated *mestizo* population.

As one of the only public museums in the country to receive its own building designed specifically to facilitate its didactic message, the National Museum of Anthropology is a unique but paradigmatic public museum. The 4 years of planning that went into its construction not only were concerned with architectural design, but also the development of audience focus groups who were marshaled through mock-exhibitions and then surveyed in order to determine the efficacy of each display. The resultant dossier on these activities testifies to a positivist attitude toward social programming, which is now somewhat quaint but nonetheless revealing of the governmental concern for the thought and conduct of museum patrons (Marquina & Aveleyra, 1962). If this museum marks the apex of Mexico's cultural project, however, it also signals the onset of doubt about the relationship between the museum and its public. Occasioned as much by critical discourses developing within the social sciences as by the political turmoil surrounding the 1968 massacre of students at Tlatelolco, the version of Mexican society constructed in public museums like this one underwent criticism and reformulation.

CRISIS AND CRITIQUE: THE EMERGENCE OF COMMUNITY

The 1968 mass murder of protesting students at Tlatelolco[10] threw into doubt the populist claims of the PRI. Along with the recognition of totalitarian elements in the ruling party's hold on political power, intellectuals and interest groups lodged a complaint against the cultural hegemony of its public institutions (Cimet et al., 1987; Martínez & Puig, 1977). Far from reflecting the "people," public museums were accused of addressing their patrons with an official mandate to, in the words of García-Canclini, "convert yourself into what you are" (1995b, p. 135). An increased awareness of the "cultural hegemony" of federal institutions accompanied growing concerns about the power of the postrevolutionary state and its ability to enforce a homogenizing vision of industrial modernity on a people that remained deeply stratified along lines of class and race. Additionally, critics felt the celebration of the Indian through "official *indigenismo*" to be ideologically motivated and therefore in the service of the ruling elites.

These concerns were given impetus by UNESCO in 1972 when a Latin American delegation put together a roundtable discussion in Santiago, Chile to address the problem of "cultural politics" and to put forth resolutions for its constituencies. In Mexico the SEP began implementing a new and integrated plan throughout its departments from the period of 1977 to 1982.

This plan sought to put public culture more firmly in the service of the development of "justice, independence and liberty" (Martínez & Puig, 1977, p. 67). Recognizing the "impossibility of formulating a project of cultural politics based on a single world view" (p. 67), the architects of this project spearheaded attempts to develop a diverse concept of patrimony that would reflect the multiplicity of Mexico's populations, traditions, and influences.

A 1985 report published by INAH retrospectively summarizes the problems with what they termed "Museologic Centralism" (*INAH Anteproyecto*). Its authors assert that the ethnocentric version of national history codified in these institutions had "deformed or occulted the regional diversity of the country" (p. 7), while the emphasis on preserving the past through a progressive narrative organized around "precious" objects, which no longer had a vital connection with living populations, failed to adequately reflect "the continuities and ruptures of the social and historic formation of Mexico" (pp. 7–8).[11] The concentration of Mexico's cultural wealth in Mexico City and the lack of public participation in museological activities were identified as contributing causes, and a new national plan was drawn up. To rectify the problem of cultural hegemony, INAH instituted a new Direction of Museums charged with developing local museums dispersed throughout the nation. This plan attempted to "democratize" culture through dispersion and the incorporation of nonprofessional individuals into the practices of museology (Galicia, 1978, p. 41). It is fair to assume that along with a genuine desire to democratize representation and reach a more diverse public, museum professionals also recognized that the didactic messages of their displays were rarely as effective as they had originally thought. A series of reception studies inaugurated in the 1970s revealed the idiosyncrasies of taste and habitus that Bourdieu has theorized in a different national context (Bonfil-Castro & García-Canclini, 1990; Bourdieu, Darbel, & Schnapper, 1990; Cimet et al., 1987; Eder, 1977; Kerrious, 1981; Villafranca & Barra, 1994).[12] Thus, the subsequent enfranchisement of individuals into the processes of knowledge production was also a concerted attempt to make the museum a more effective technique of government. By acculturating people at the local and community level, these initiatives make better museum citizens who are more likely to patronize and properly understand their heritage on display in Mexico's national institutions. Whether this is the intention of every local organizer or not, it has to be acknowledged as a likely effect of their activities.

The first local museum was established in 1973 in Pénjamo, a municipality of the State of Guanajuato. The primary objective of this initiative was to locate the specific issues facing the community and to address them through temporary exhibitions and related projects. An initial problem that the Pénjamo organizers identified was community apathy in advocating for change on its own behalf (Galicia, 1978, p. 46). Furthermore, the locals demonstrated little interest in museums in general, let alone a desire to build their own. Recognizing that this was in large part due to the extreme poverty of the area and a general perception that museum culture was unrelated to their everyday lives, the organizers targeted these attitudes in an initial exhibition that sought to demonstrate objectively the museum's social role. They gathered photographs, crafts, and historical documents from the local residents so that they could present their own image of the community (p. 47). Once the museum was in place, they used the institution to foment broader community development. For example, the financial proceeds and local labor were utilized to build new roads that connected Pénjamo to other nearby municipalities, thus facilitating commerce and establishing the local museum as a regional tourist and heritage site. Ultimately, they exploited this organized social unit to develop a literacy campaign and a new school. Through this example we can see not only how the museum helped to codify a distinct local identity, but also how that identity and sense of community solidarity were instrumentalized to foster other kinds of development.

In 1986 this initiative was converted into the Program of Community Museums as part of a pan-Latin American movement to develop better links between museums and civil society. Community museums are founded by local citizens in conjunction with an INAH "promoter." Like the local museum initiative, this program also capitalized on the institutional form to foster cultural identity and development. However, the community museum program has refined its agenda and placed a greater emphasis upon the relationship between community *cultural* identity and citizenship. As the Department of Community Museums explains, "the community, in order to assume its historic responsibility, needs to be the subject of the educative process and as such the subject of critical and reflexive action" (1990, p. 21).

The first objective of the community museum is to incorporate communities into the project of preserving, protecting, and diffusing cultural patrimony, now defined more broadly as the "conjunction of material, natural, and spiritual wealth of all peoples and ethnicities of the past and present" (Department of Community Museums, 1990, p. 10).[13] Cultural patrimony, by this account, is represented by historical monuments and popular traditions as well as local ecology and oral culture (pp. 10–11). With this expanded definition of heritage INAH has addressed the "ethnocentric" bias of "Museologic Centralism." A second objective is to affirm the cultural values that structure Mexican identity "in its diverse levels: national, regional, local, and ethnic" (p. 9).[14] And, finally the community museum is designed to create an expressive, dialogic space in which the community members interact and through which the changing needs of the group can be articulated. Culture becomes dynamic; the museum becomes a civic center for the diffusion of art and history as well as the strengthening of civil society. Furthermore, the new community museum accomplishes a vital connection between the present and "precious" objects from the past by enlisting the museum patron/local citizen as the author of that connection.

This initiative places the "responsibility" on the community to foster its own social well-being. It operates by making the community a historical subject in the museum, which becomes a space not only of representation, but also of national participation. As its promoters argue, the community museum is a "social organizer" and an "educator" that helps social groups improve their own conditions of life; "that is," they write, "to know in order to transform and to transform in order to obtain a better social well-being" (Department of Community Museums, 1990, p. 16).[15] In this respect, the local and community museums are examples of what Graham Burchell (1996) has dubbed "responsibilization" to describe the ways that forms of liberalism seek to integrate individuals into the practices of their own government. He writes that "liberalism, particularly in its modern versions, constructs a relationship between government and the governed that increasingly depends upon ways in which individuals are required to assume the status of being the subjects of their lives, upon which they fashion themselves as certain kinds of subjects, upon the ways in which they practice their freedom" (pp. 29–30). The neoliberal permutations of the individual amount to a transformation of the somewhat passive subject of welfare, the subject of need, into a partner in their own government. Rose describes this new governmental subject as the subject of *choice*, thus emphasizing the agency attributed to the individual under neoliberalism (1996, pp. 57–61). This "autonomizing ethics" of the self is congruent with the consumerist orientation to power that Yúdice (1995) has so deftly theorized as an increasingly important characteristic of civil society in the contemporary United States and Latin America.

Responsibilizing the Community: The Tláhuac Community Museum

Most theorizers of governmentality draw their examples and consequently their models from Europe and the United States. As a result, they emphasize the individual and the various "techniques of the self" that have arisen since the advent of Thatcherism and Reaganism in England and the United States respectively. The utility of these concepts for Mexico requires that they be tailored to fit a decidedly different set of political and historical realities. The relatively weak form of democracy in Mexico and the idiosyncrasies (when measured against European precedents) of its liberalism render a different unit of neoliberal "responsibilization." Rather than dispensing with social groups in the interest of fostering individual agency, neoliberalism in Mexico seeks to empower community as a way of aligning the political aspirations of state and civil society. Rose has noted that as a challenge to the rise of individualism in the wake of welfare reform, a " 'third way' of governing," has emerged that promotes the "third space" of community as its exemplary figure (1999, p. 167). In the political rhetoric of the "third way," community is paradoxically asserted as a natural, prepolitical zone yet also as a key terrain for the successful actualization of the goals and aspirations of government. This paradoxical attitude, while specific to the United States and Britain where the battles between the political left and right have dictated the discursive necessity of a "third way," provides an apt description of governmental interest in community in Mexico since the advent of neoliberal economic policy. This new understanding of community is distinct from the nineteenth century formulation of community as a historical set of moral bonds fragmented by industrialization or the welfare concept of community as a set of professional services. Rather, community as a "third space" between the authority of the state or the amoral whims of the free market and autonomous individuals "is a space of *emotional relationships* through which *individual identities* are constructed through their bonds to *micro-cultures* of values and meanings" (Rose, 1999, p. 172; italics in original). In Mexico, community still evokes its nineteenth century formulation, as indigenous communities are often promoted as a recovery of the historical bonds that preceded the twentieth century projects of *mestizo* nationhood. Nonetheless, insofar as these indigenous communities are being objectified and instrumentalized through governmental initiatives like the museum, they need to be understood as apparatuses of "third way" government.

While attempts to convert the museum into an agent of local community development dates back to the early '70s following the aforementioned cultural and political crises, its conversion into the Program of Community Museums corresponds exactly with the privatization of State-owned enterprises and the deregulation of markets that characterizes neoliberalism in Mexico. While the program cannot be entirely attributed to a State-led initiative, the major restructuring of Mexican political policy throughout the '80s and '90s has capitalized on social programs like these to make neoliberal government more effective. Mexico's neoliberal transformation began in 1982 when it defaulted on its international loans after the bottom fell out of the oil market (the source of Mexican prosperity and speculative investment throughout the preceding decade). President Miguel de la Madrid (1982–1988) initiated macroeconomic stabilization measures through the trade liberalization that culminated in the North American Free Trade Agreement (NAFTA) (Castañeda, 1995; Haber, 1997). De la Madrid's successor, Carlos Salinas de Gortari (1988–1994), deepened the state's commitment to neoliberalism, in part by initiating political programs that sought to squelch the popular appeal of a powerful and growing opposition.[16] The National Solidarity Program (PRONASOL)—the first official act of his presidency—

was the policy enactment of the neoliberal ideology Salinas elaborated in his
Harvard dissertation (Salinas de Gortari, 1982). An attempt to soften the
social burden of neoliberal reforms, PRONASOL instituted a move away
from state "paternalism" toward social "solidarity" with four main objectives:

> respect for the will, initiatives, and organizational forms of individuals
> and communities, . . . full and effective participation and organization
> by the communities, . . . co-responsibility [in project management] and
> transparency [in the handling of resources]. (Fox, 1997, p. 1360)

The Salinas administration increased social spending 20% from the former
administration's budget and inaugurated local projects around the country.
PRONASOL transferred 95% of its resources to state and municipal governments for them to invest in education, health services, food subsidies, electrical service, potable water, sewage systems, and so forth. While solidarity
did amount to a state reinvestment in the social infrastructure, subsequent
analysis has revealed that far from corresponding with Mexico's most impoverished regions, spending patterns targeted middle-income states, and typically
those where opposition to the PRI had been strongest in the 1988 elections.
Clearly, solidarity was as much an ideological attempt to shore up flagging
support for the ruling party as it was an attempt to absorb the social shocks
incurred by the nation's economic restructuring (Cornelius & Fox, 1994).

Discussions of neoliberal transformation in Mexico in general, and
PRONASOL in particular, tend to frame this development through the orthodox opposition between state and civil society with all of its attendant
assumptions about the politics that inhere in the public and private sectors.
While critics lament the cuts in state aid under neoliberalism in general, they
also chastise solidarity as yet another example of state manipulation of the
public. These discussions routinely invoke "popular sectors" as unproblematic
and empirical domains, without recognizing the links between the emerging
understanding of these populations and the governmental restructuring of
state and society (Chalmers, Vilas, Hite, Martin, Piester, & Segarra, 1997;
Conniff, 1999; Cook, Middlebrook, & Horcasitas, 1994). The general logic
of solidarity (state/society partnerships) expounded by Salinas and set in motion
by PRONASOL helped to consolidate community as a neoliberal social
configuration. Moreover, the labor of intellectuals, particularly museum promoters, has contributed to this process by codifying community as a political
identity and incorporating individuals into governmental activities.

The Tláhuac Museum provides an illuminating example of how the
neoliberal logic of solidarity has permeated community organization, even in
the absence of any direct state intervention (fig. 8.5). The museum was founded
in 1997 after five ceremonial urns dating from the postclassical era of pre-
Hispanic Mexico were discovered in a local farm field. It is particularly inter-

FIG. 8.5. The Tláhuac community museum, located in a former municipal building near the central plaza of Tláhuac, a suburb of Mexico City.

esting because it was not inaugurated by an INAH promoter, but rather was generated by local residents who actually fought INAH for possession of their cultural heritage and then brokered a partnership with the organization. After the discovery of the urns, a community alliance was formed to keep the statues in Tláhuac (a southern suburb of Mexico City), rather than see them off to the capitol where they would form part of the National Museum of Anthropology's collection. The association then began developing a permanent site to house these valuable objects along with exhibitions detailing the region's history and the traditions of its inhabitants from pre-Hispanic times to the present. Currently only two rooms are open with temporary exhibitions describing the museum's eventual goals. One ceremonial urn is on view along with a few archaeological fragments and an ethnographic display of "typical" clothing, activities, and crafts from the area (figs. 8.6 & 8.7). While comparatively crude, the organization and style of presentation are no different from those strategies found in the National Museum of Anthropology (i.e., the use of generic mannequins, the separation between anthropology and ethnography, the reliance upon representative objects to signify a particular group or population).

Unlike its model, this museum does not endeavor to tell the story of the nation; instead, it is devoted to the particularities of Tláhuac, and the nation appears only where its story intersects with that of the community. Above all, it is the location that makes this site matter to its community. Jesús Galindo Ortega, the president of the local alliance, explained to me in an interview in

FIG. 8.6.   An exhibition of one of the five preclassic ceremonial urns discovered in a local field that comprise the archeological collection of the community museum. These objects were claimed as communal patrimony in the struggle that ensued between Tláhuac and the National Institute of Anthropology and History over their ownership and display.

1998 that rather than having to trek to the capital city, the area's inhabitants could stay in their own environs and actually participate in the production of knowledge about their heritage. Ortega was clear that he did not view the strengthening of local identity as a critique or disavowal of national identity; rather he argued that the history and culture of Tláhuac are an important component of the larger Mexican history and culture.

FIG. 8.7. Ethnographic displays of traditional Tlahuican dress, implements, and foods. The use of generic mannequins, traditional clothing and cultural artifacts, as well as documentary photography mimics the exhibitionary paradigm established by the National Anthropology Museum.

Ortega's assertion is meted out in a booklet (González, 1998) published by the alliance to drum up local support and finances for the museum. In this pamphlet the authors detail the work accomplished by the alliance, the value of the ceremonial urns, the significance of the Church of San Pedro in colonial history, and the historic visit of Independence hero Vicente Guerrero to Tláhuac in 1828. It is pitched to a low level of literacy and combines educational information with activities that steer the reader toward an appreciation of the history and customs of Tláhuac (connect-the-dot pictures of local monuments, fill-in-the blank exercises, multiple-choice quizzes, etc.). However, while encouraging the community to know its own particular history and to promote its uniqueness "to the world," the Tláhuac pamphlet is still thoroughly saturated with the patriotic sentiments promoted throughout the national culture project. For example, a recounting of the visit of Independence hero Vicente Guerrero to the region in 1828 is accompanied by his famous slogan—"Patria es Primero" (The Fatherland First)—in bold-face (in this respect it quotes directly from the exhibitions at the National Museum of History). The authors ask, "Have you heard this story before?" and suggest that readers annotate the story on their own (p. 12).

The sense of participation encouraged by repeated use of the second person is enhanced by the different kinds of activities the pamphlet offers. Museum patrons/community members are not only educated about their past but also are invited to contribute their own ideas to their museum's future. Through varied textual strategies, the Tláhuac pamphlet reveals the subjectifying practices at play in the modern museum. Like the pamphlet, the didactic exhibitionary strategies of museums address the patron as both the object and subject of its displays. Just as the Tláhuac pamphlet seeks to incorporate its reader into directed acts of authorship, the museum seeks to incorporate its patron into specific modes of conduct. In contradistinction to traditional museologic strategies, which relied almost entirely on exhibitions executed by museum professionals offered up to a public, this museum (and pamphlet) invite the public to enter into the acts of compiling, archiving, and presenting the museum's content. Through the museum, the community gains agency as a producer of knowledge about itself. The rationalizing and professionalizing processes involved in becoming competent historians and curators help to construct autonomous groups better equipped to self-govern.

In community museums like this one, the citizen is construed as an individual with aspirations to self-actualization and self-fulfillment. However, he or she is no longer conceived in terms of a national society, but rather as a member of heterogeneous communities of allegiance. The affective bonds fostered by the intimacy of community (as opposed to the more abstract anonymity of the national subject) obliges an ethical concern for the self and others that is a significant feature of "third way" government.[17] However, to imagine that these communities strengthen civil society in opposition to the state is to miss their function as governmental apparati. As Rose notes, the dismantling of the social welfare state under neoliberalism has mutated the notion of the "social" into that of community, which is now a new way of administering personal relations. He writes, "the relation between the responsible individual and their self-governing community comes to substitute for that between social citizen and their common society" (1996, p. 56). Furthermore, it is intellectual activity that has articulated the particularly prepolitical characteristics of this formation. Watts states that it is through the liberal intellectual tradition that "community . . . became associated with a normative nostalgia for a world we have lost at the same time as it supplied a focus for new forms of management and administration" (1993/1994, p. 141). The formulation of this social unit enables:

> new agencies and agents (from community leaders, local politicians, community and social workers to corporations that build shopping centers) [to] lay possession to the categorical territory that community is supposed to inhabit and claim to speak on its behalf or to act so as to sustain it . . . here the category itself supplies something of a binding, useful, yet ultimately fictitious sense of integration to a set of social relations that are actually dispersing. (p. 141)

In essence, community museums attempt to reconstruct the social relations that purportedly existed before the modernizing initiatives of the postrevolutionary governmental projects took hold. Community, in contemporary Mexico, is now a pluralizing concept. As such, it is understood to counterpose the concept of a national community figured as an assimilated *mestizo* population. But this does not mean that these institutionally enabled identities elude government. As Bertha Chávez, the promoter for the Museo Comunitario *Asalto a las Tierras* in Baja, California, explains:

> the role of the museum has been educative, understood as formative or modifying of attitudes and conducts that contribute to the personal development of the society . . . the community museum has permitted the recuperation and revalorization of the history and traditions of the region and the country . . . the community has been converted into a diffusing agent of the culture and history of the municipality and the state. (Department of Community Museums, 1990, p. 21)[18]

While the community museum initiative itself stresses the desire to strengthen civil society, it transforms communities into active agents of their own progress.

THE POLITICAL POSSIBILITIES OF COMMUNITY?

The prior discussion of the museums' possible roles in civil society might well lead us to ask, what kind of politics is imaginable under neoliberalism?

Furthermore, given community's constitutive links to government, should we abandon the idea that community can be a viable site for resistance and social change? The answers to these questions are complex and not entirely clear. But one place to begin would be to question the assumptions that prevail in the critical disciplines devoted to describing, analyzing, and promoting resistance through culture, especially given the rise of an often divisive cultural politics of difference in the '80s and '90s. Some of these assumptions are: that community is always already a site of resistance; that the local is always a preferable social unit to totalizing or globalizing ones; that participation in the production of culture is a fundamental human right; and that when communities promote "their culture" they are expressing something that is authentically their own and thus outside of the hegemonic forces of State-power. Questioning these assumptions is particularly urgent lest we aid in reifying subject positions amenable to the most pernicious forms of neoliberal responsibilization. The subjectifying strategies of neoliberal government produce and require self-governing citizens, and the community museum, as we have seen, is an optimal site for this production. However, all is not lost. Remarking on the conjuncture of neoliberal subjects and cultural technologies of government, Rose suggests that with the development of the subject of choice under neoliberalism, "we can witness the 'reversibility' of relations of authority—what starts off as a norm to be implanted into citizens can be repossessed as a demand which citizens can make of authorities" (1996, p. 59). This reversibility is precisely the case with the development of social movements in Mexico, particularly the Zapatistas in Chiapas, who have identified themselves with a normative indigenism and utilized this as the foundation for the rights they are demanding. Yet, as the example of the Tláhuac museum makes evident, it is far from clear that any necessary politics follow from fostering communal cultural identities. To the contrary, Tláhuac illustrates the tendency for identitarian communities to organize around symbolic consumption rather than around productive processes that might contribute to structural changes at the macropolitical level (García-Canclini, 1995a). All of the organizers' resources (labor, finances, etc.) are being mobilized for the construction of a respectable institution to house their repatriated heritage. While this can lead to economic gain for the community through tourism or even financial partnerships with the state for infrastructural improvements, it remains to be seen if the site will become anything more than a source for securing an atavistic identity or a storehouse for antiquities. As a form of representation the Tláhuac museum's exhibitions betray no resistant strategies. Yet one could imagine a defense of this or any other community museum based on its subtle subversion of the "master narrative" of the National Museum of Anthropology, or through an uncritical appeal to the value of community and the significance of location: arguments that derive from a "politics of representation" and classic political economy. However, these kinds of arguments are fairly useless, insofar as they rely on relatively naive models of power and culture. Any assessment of symbolic politics needs to take into consideration how the institution or practice is linked to political and economic concerns. It needs to ask, what kind of citizenship is being produced? How is it being mobilized? For what ends? These concerns exceed the parameters of textual analysis just as surely as they force consideration beyond the celebration of "cultural rights" as an end in and of itself.

Similarly, these concerns also require a more subtle theory of political economy than the Marxian and Gramscian forms that prevail in cultural studies. One of the most crucial insights of Foucault's governmentality is his assertion that the academic left has tended to overvalue the problem of the state. This overvaluation has attributed a reductive functionality to the State that paradoxically renders it essential as a "target" to be "attacked" as well as a " privileged position" that needs to be "occupied" (Foucault, 1991, p. 103). The left's obsessive focus on the State—its history, abuses, and power—generates a misguided politics because it mistakes the "composite reality" of the State for a unity. Rather than targeting the diffuse mechanisms of power, this kind of cultural politics seems to assume that the goal is to appropriate State power by controlling its functions. Foucault opposed this juridical model of power to the disciplinary and governmental forms that constitute the diverse centers of calculation, regulation, and subjectification that characterize the modern period. It is the sovereign or juridical model of power that informs most studies of institutions (whether they are deemed "ideological," "hegemonic," or "resistant"). Thus, determining the political effects of a particular institution often amounts to little more than determining who "controls" the institution, its funding, its exhibitions, and so forth. From this, a politics is often generalized: "community ownership good"; "State ownership bad;" "national culture dominates," "communal culture resists." Foucault's work not only helps us to see how the museum is part of what he called the "governmentalization of the state," but it also helps explain why community ownership does not necessarily avoid the regulatory effects of governmental power. It is not the link to the State (via INAH or any other state agency) that makes the community museum amenable to neoliberal political agendas. It is the museum-form itself. As a narrative space for showing and telling, with a particular historical development as an apparatus of social regulation, the museum is not essentially an agent of self-expression or freedom, nor a neutral storehouse for culture. Replacing national culture with community culture does not question the governmental utility of culture. In order to do this, we might begin by recognizing the museum as what Deleuze and Guattari would call a "state form of thought," a machine for objectification and subordination through representation (1987, pp. 424–474).

The question, it seems to me, is how can we construct a politics that understands the implications of all of this? If liberalism, rights, and identity are tied up with subordination, rationalization, and a "State form of thought," how are we to theorize resistance, autonomy, and social welfare? I think that the first step is to recognize the inadequacies of the orthodox State/civil society opposition, and a sincere grappling with the subordinating component of identity as a force of subjectification. With regard to the latter, we need to continue to ask what kinds of identity positions are being constructed, what are their mechanisms of exclusion, and are they being calcified into atavistic and/or essentialized systems of representation and affiliation? We need to analyze the "power effects" of the current configuration of government and citizenship in their particularities. I do not advocate abdicating any analysis of coercion or oppression that might proceed from the centers of calculation that comprise the state. However, I am suggesting that we can not simply appeal to a metatheory that holds in every case and at all times when trying to explore the relations of power between the state and cultural institutions. Museums do articulate individuals to the State. Efforts to foment community development in the interest of inculcating a sense of cultural ownership or rights qualify dubiously at best, as resistance per se. Using the museum to bolster civil society in order to elude State control simply misrecognizes the historical constitution of each. Finally, intellectuals are implicated in these processes in ways that beg scrutiny before strategizing commences. This chapter provides a preliminary analysis of the problematics of government and the museum in the hope that it will inform cultural politics in Mexico as well as intellectual analyses of the museum in Latin America. The new social movements that have arisen in response to privatization and the dismantling of the social welfare state are, in part, an effect of the governmental production of new forms of identification. And while this might be sobering to those who want to view identity and collective organization as radically opposed to State power, it can also make us take note of the productive potential of governmental processes. It is this potential that has to be harnessed, if the museum is to become what its supporters claim it to be: an agent of democracy.[19]

NOTES

1. In emphasizing the latter half of Foucault's term, I follow the example of Colin Gordon and Nikolas Rose who both stress that in addition to naming a "problematics of rule," governmentality also denotes a form of thought that "seeks to render itself technical" (Gordon, 1991; Rose, 1996, p. 41). Foucault's coupling of the words "govern" and "mentality" signals the extent to which the reflection of experts participates in the regulation of individual and group conduct. This helps to clarify the decentralized nature of governmental power while also indicating the part that thought plays in the translation of general political goals into effective and realizable practices.

2. Bennett notes that the art museum is something of an exception in that it continues to promote the rare, but nonetheless does not elude evolutionary and chronological logic in its display (1995, pp. 163–173).

3. While I have translated the names of all of Mexico's museums and national institutions into English, I have maintained their Spanish acronyms.

4. My translation from the original Spanish, "como espacios culturales a través de los cuales se difundiría la ideología del nacionalismo revolucionario producto del movimiento popular de 1910–1917."

5. The *Porfiriato* refers to the 30-year dictatorship of Porfirio Díaz. During this period, Mexico underwent the most rapid process of industrialization of any time in its history. This "progress" was accomplished, however, through massive human-rights abuses and the courting of international corporate investment that effectively sold Mexico's most valuable resources (mines, oil, cotton, sugar, rail roads, etc.) to U.S. and European capitalists.

6. Teotihuacán, or the "place of the gods," is the pre-Columbian city located just north of Mexico City. Flourishing between 500 B.C. and 700 C.E., it was a sprawling metropolis with a population of over 200,000 at its zenith. Its major architectural monuments (the famed Pyramids of the Sun and Moon) and cultural achievements were renowned throughout much of meso-America. After its abandonment the city was claimed by the Mexica (Aztecs) and converted into the birthplace of their deities. Manuel Gamio's (1926b) multivolume study of the archeology, natural environment, and contemporary populations inhabiting the area is still one of the most comprehensive studies of Mexico's pre-Columbian patrimony. Today, along with the Templo Mayor in Mexico City, Teotihuacán is a premier national symbol and ritualized heritage site. It is also a primary tourist destination, and any time of the year one can see hundreds of people, Mexican and foreign alike, clambering up the massive pyramids or making their way down the vast Avenida de los Muertos (Avenue of the Dead).

7. The term *Mexico profundo* is drawn from Guillermo Bonfil Batalla's influential rewriting of Mexican history in which he asserts the indigenous, or "deep Mexico," as the essential nation in an attempt to reorient representative politics around Mexico's most subjugated populations (Bonfil-Batalla, 1987).

8. This mural by Jorge González Camarena was executed in 1964. It depicts abstracted female figures with Asiatic, Indian, African, and Caucasian physiognomies and symbolic attributes metamorphosing into a single, racially amalgamated, central figure. While in keeping with the spirit of Vasconcelos' idea of a *cosmic race*, Camarena's image is far more egalitarian than the resultant being Vasconcelos describes. In the latter's conception, the new *mestizo* was, in the final analysis, a Hispanic figure, who through selective inter-breeding would "redeem" the blood of the "lower breeds." That is, through a process that Vasconcelos called "aesthetic eugenics," the cosmic race would be a hybrid of only the best and most desirable traits of each racialized group. Camarena's mural differs from Vasconcelos' treatise in a number of subtle ways; however, most significantly, it diverges from Vasconcelos' racist attitude toward the "African race." The author devotes scant attention to this "race," only mentioning it in order to disparage it mercilessly and argue, in essence, that it had absolutely nothing to contribute to his *mestizo* ideal.

9. The "today" of the quote refers to 1968. This gallery no longer exists. It was dismantled in the '80s and has been replaced by a space for temporary exhibitions. The first time I visited the museum in 1997, a UNESCO display about the abuse of children's human rights around the world was running. The museum is currently undergoing major renovations, particularly with respect to its ethnographic displays on the second floor. In order to facilitate tourism, English text panels are being added to all of the displays. With respect to content, there are attempts to address the static presentation of indigenous life that Canclini describes (García-Canclini, 1995b). For example, one of the new displays dedicated to the Mayans presents a photograph of an indigenous man at work on a personal computer while seated in a traditional dwelling. The accompanying text panel explains that the Mayans have been active in sustaining their ethnic identity in the face of a homogenizing national identity. This statement resonates with the Zapatista takeover in Chiapas, a Mayan region, while the computer signals one of the primary mechanisms of their transnational organizational efforts (Yúdice, 1998b). In 1998 this computer was the only sign of modern technology in the entire museum, and it was clearly the result of institutional attempts to incorporate the insights of cultural critics as well as respond to the political and cultural crises I discuss in what follows.

10. About 2,000 people were arrested, but accounts vary as to how many were killed. The Mexican government claimed 49 protesters were killed, while the *New York Times* correspondent claimed that 200 was a more accurate figure. Today, 300 dead is the standard statistic for this terrible event (Stevens, 1974; Young, 1985).

11. My translation from the original Spanish, "los museos ha sido mas una secuencia cronológica de sucesos y hechos aislados, ilustrada por objetos artisticos, que una reflexión sobre las continuidades y rupturas de la formación histórica y social de México."

12. It is important not to overstate the utility of Bourdieu's work in the Mexican context. Following a series of studies of the public response to art museums, Canclini has argued that the relationship between various social strata and "elite culture" in Mexico differs in important ways from that in France. Most significantly, researchers found that the formal and functional qualities associated with pre-Columbian artifacts and *artesanías* (popular arts and crafts) inform the aesthetic appreciation of "high culture" in Mexico. Furthermore, what in Europe would be relegated to "low culture" or exhibited in nonart contexts—crafts, popular artforms, and artifacts—comprises a significant part of what is considered "high culture" in Mexico. Therefore, Bourdieu's groundbreaking analysis, insofar as it relies on a rigid distinction between these domains, cannot be mechanically applied to Mexican society (Cimet et al., 1987).

13. My translation from original Spanish, "al patrimonio cultural como el conjunto de bienes materiales, naturales y espirituales de todos los pueblos y etnias del pasado y del presnete."

14. My translation from original Spanish, "Contribuir a la afirmación de los valores culturales estructuradores de nuestra identidad en sus diversos niveles: nacional, regional, local y étnico."

15. My translation from original Spanish, "Es así como el museo comunitario se convierte en un organizador social y en un educador que busca que los grupos sociales generen procesos autogestivos encaminados a mejorar sus condiciones de vida, es decir de conocer para transformar y de transformar para alcanzar un mejor bienestar social."

16. The economic crisis that ushered in neoliberal reforms, coupled with the legacy of Tlatelolco, resulted in the most successful oppositional bid for power since the instantiation of the PRI, until the recent victory of opposition candidate Vicente Fox. In the 1988 elections, Salinas won by the narrowest margin of any postrevolutionary president amidst accusations of voter fraud lodged by his primary opponent Cuauhtémoc Cárdenas, son of Lázaro and leader of the Democratic Revolutionary Party (PDR). Cárdenas' presidential campaign was founded upon a critique of neoliberalism and called for a return to the national populism that characterized his father's presidency.

17. In its challenge to individualism, Rose finds grounds for optimism in the ethico-politics of "third way" community (1999, pp. 187–194). Self-government through community obliges one to develop an ethical concern for the self *and* others. As a form of subjectification that proceeds through the particularities of a group, it offers up possibilities for creative new forms of subjectivity. Furthermore, the atomistic nature of community (as opposed to national or broader formulations of the social) belies any orthodox moral code and, at least, allows for the possibility of debate over basic social virtues. The recent revival of fundamentalism in U.S. political and cultural life reveals how easily this "agonistic politics of ethics" can produce and help to legitimate a return to a normalizing moralism. In Mexico, however, the ethical dimension of "third way" community hasn't been exploited for these ends. The emphasis continues to be more on secular civics than morality. This is due in part to the domination of the PRI, which maintained the anti-clericalism of revolutionary social movements. However, with the recent election of Vicente Fox—the opposition candidate from the conservative National Action Party (PAN), which has made a return to Catholic morality a pillar of its political ideology—the particular dynamics of "third way" government in U.S. and Mexico may become less distinguishable.

18. My translation from original Spanish, "Sin duda el papel del museo ha sido educativo, entendido como formativo o modificador de actitudes y conductas que contribuyen al desarrollo personal y de la sociedad.... En el aspecto cultural la comunidad se ha visto fortalecida, ya que el Museo Comunitario ha permitido recuperar y revalorizar la historia y tradiciones de la región y del país.... La comunidad se ha convertido en agente difusor de la cultura e historia del municipio y estado."

19. In addition to the editors and contributors to this volume, I would like to express my gratitude to Jonathan Fineberg, Marie Leger, Katherine Manthorne, Michael Palm, and George Yúdice for reading and commenting on earlier drafts of this essay. Furthermore, I want to acknowledge the Center for Latin American and Caribbean Studies at the University of Illinois and the Tinker Foundation for the travel grants that enabled my research as well as the brown-bag lecture series that provided an early forum for the presentation and discussion of the argument I elaborate here. Finally, I want to relay my indebtedness to Cameron McCarthy and my colleagues in the original "Foucault Reading Group." Without Cameron's willingness to lend us faculty support and personal enthusiasm, the work in this volume might never have found the encouragement it needed. The intellectual community that developed among the members of this group over a period of years was truly unique within contemporary academia. The intellectual engagement of my colleagues sharpened my understanding of Foucault's work and shaped my scholarship in profound and innumerable ways.

References

Barry, A., Osborne, T., & Rose, N. (1996). Introduction. In A. Barry, T. Osborne, & N. Rose (Eds.), *Foucault and political reason: Liberalism, neoliberalism and rationalities of government* (pp. 1–19). Chicago: University of Chicago Press.

Bennett, T. (1992a). Putting policy into cultural studies. In L. Grossberg, C. Nelson, & P. A. Treichler (Eds.), *Cultural studies* (pp. 23–37). London and New York: Routledge.

Bennett, T. (1992b). Useful culture. *Cultural Studies* 3(6): 395–423.

Bennett, T. (1995). *The birth of the museum: History, theory, politics.* London and New York: Routledge.

Bernal, I. (1968). *The Mexican National Museum of Anthropology.* London: Thames and Hudson.

Bonfil-Batalla, G. (1987). *México profundo* [Deep Mexico]. Mexico City: SEP.

Bonfil-Castro, R., García—Canclini, N., (May 28–June 2, 1990). *Memorias del simposio: Patrimonio, museo y participación social* [Symposium proceedings: Patrimony, museum, and social participation]. *Colección Científica,* 272.

Bourdieu, P., Darbel, A., & Schnapper, D. (1990). *The love of art: European art museums and their public* (C. Beattie & N. Merriman, Trans.). Cambridge, England: Polity Press.

Brading, D. A. (1988). Manuel Gamio and official indigenismo in Mexico. *Bulletin of Latin American Research* 7(1): 75–90.

Burchell, G. (1991). Peculiar interests: Civil society and governing "the system of natural liberty." In G. Burchell, C. Gordon, & P. Miller (Eds.), *The Foucault effect: Studies in governmentality* (pp. 119–151). Chicago: University of Chicago Press.

Burchell, G. (1996). Liberal government and techniques of the self. In A. Barry, T. Osborne, & N. Rose (Eds.), *Foucault and political reason: Liberalism, neoliberalism and rationalities of government* (pp. 19–37). Chicago: University of Chicago Press.

Castañeda, J. G. (1995). *The Mexican shock: Its meaning for the U.S.* New York: New Press.

Castro-Pozo, A. U. (1995). Museums and expositions. In O. Negrete, J. César, & B. Cottom (Eds.), *INAH: Una historia, antecedentes, organización, funcionamento y servicios* [INAH: A history, antecedents, organization, function, and services, Vols. 1 & 2]. México, DF: Consejo Nacional de Antropología e Historia.

Chalmers, D. A., Vilas, C. M., Hite, K., Martin, S. B., Piester, K., & Segarra, M. (Eds.). (1997). *The new politics of inequality in Latin America: Rethinking participation and representation.* Oxford: Oxford University Press.

Cimet, E., Dujovne, M., García Canclini, N., Cullco, J., Mendoza, C., Reyes Palma, F., & Soltero, G. (1987). *El público como propuesta. Cuatro estudios sociológicos en museos de arte* [The Public surveyed: Four sociological studies in art museums]. Mexico City: INBA.

Coffey, M. K. (2000). The "Mexican Problem": Nation and "native" in Mexican muralism and cultural discourse. In N. K. Denzin (Ed.), *Cultural studies: A research annual* (pp. 147–189). Stamford, Connecticut: JAI Press.

Conniff, M. L. (Ed.). (1999). *Populism in Latin America*. Tuscaloosa and London: University of Alabama Press.

Cook, M. L., Middlebrook, K. J., & Horcasitas, J. M. (Eds.). (1994). *The politics of economic restructuring: State-society relations and regime change in Mexico*. La Jolla, CA: Center for U.S.-Mexican Studies, University of California, San Diego.

Cornelius, W. A., Craig, A. L., & Fox, J. (Eds.). (1994). *Transforming state–society relations in Mexico: The national solidarity strategy*. La Jolla, CA: Center for U.S.-Mexican Studies, University of California, San Diego.

Deleuze, G., & Guattari, F. (1987). 7000 B.C.: Apparatus of capture. In *A thousand plateaus: Capitalism and schizophrenia* (B. Massumi, Trans.), (pp. 424–474). Minneapolis, MN and London: University of Minnesota Press.

Department of Community Museums. (1990). El museo comunitario, un espacio alternativo de rescate y preservación del patrimonio cultural [The community museum: An alternative space for the rescue and preservation of cultural patrimony]. *Antropología: boletín oficial del Instituto Nacional de Antropología e Historia* [Anthropology: Official bulletin of INAH], *32* (Suppl.), 1–28.

Eder, R. (1977). El público de arte en México: Los espectadores de la exposición Hammer. *Plural, 4*(10): 51–65.

Fernández, M. A. (1987). *Historia de los museos de México* [History of Mexican museums]. Mexico City: S.A. de C.V.

Foucault, M. (1989). An ethics of pleasure. In S. Lotringer (Ed.), *Foucault live* (pp. 257–76). New York: Semiotext(e).

Foucault, M. (1991). Governmentality. In G. Burchell, C. Gordon, & P. Miller (Eds.), *The Foucault effect: Studies in governmentality* (pp. 73–87). Chicago: University of Chicago Press.

Fox, J. (1997). Solidaridad, Programa Nacional de (PRONASOL) [Solidarity, National Program for (PRONASOL)]. In M. S. Werner (Ed.), *Mexico: History, society & culture* (Vol. 2) (pp. 1360–1362). Chicago and London: Fitzroy Dearborn.

Fraser, N. (1997). *Justice interruptus: Critical reflections on the "postsocialist" condition*. London and New York: Routledge.

Galicia, Y. R. (1978). Museo y comunidad [Museum and community]. *Antropología e Historia* [Anthropology and History] *3*(21): 41–52.

Gamio, M. (1926a). Incorporating the Indian into the Mexican population. In M. Gamio & J. Vasconcelos (Eds.), *Aspects of Mexican civilization: Lectures on the Harris Foundation* (pp. 105–128). Chicago: University of Chicago Press.

Gamio, M. (1926b). The United States and Mexico. In M. Gamio & J. Vasconcelos (Eds.), *Aspects of Mexican civilization: Lectures on the Harris Foundation* (pp. 158–188). Chicago: University of Chicago Press.

García—Canclini, N. (1995a). *Consumidores y ciudadanos: Conflictos multiculturales de las globalization* [Consumers and citizens: The multicultural conflicts of globalization]. Mexico, DF: Grijalbo.

García—Canclini, N. (1995b). *Hybrid cultures: Strategies for entering and leaving modernity* (C. L. Chiappari & S. L. López, Trans.). Minneapolis, MN: University of Minnesota Press.

González, M. T. (1998). *Tláhuac: "Un pasado vigente"* [Tláhuac: A forceful past].Tláhuac, Mexico: Técnicos en Artes Gráficas.

Gordon, C. (1991). Governmental rationality: An introduction. In G. Burchell, C. Gordon, & P. Miller (Eds.), *The Foucault effect: Studies in governmentality* (pp. 1–53). Chicago: University of Chicago Press.

Haber, P. L. (1997). Neoliberalism. In M. S. Werner (Ed.), *Mexico: History, society & culture* (Vol. 2) (pp. 1014–1019). Chicago and London: Fitzroy Dearborn.

Hindess, B. (1996). Liberalism, socialism and democracy: variations on a governmental theme. In A. Barry, T. Osborne, & N. Rose (Eds.), *Foucault and political reason: Liberalism, neoliberalism and rationalities of government* (pp. 65–81). Chicago: University of Chicago Press.

INAH. (1985, August). *INAH anteproyecto del programa nacional de museos* [INAH preliminary project plan for the national museum program]. Mexico City: INAH.

Kerrious, M. A. de. (1981, February). *Los visitantes y el funcionamiento de Museo Nacional de Antropología de México* [The visitors and function of the National Museum of Anthropology in Mexico]. Mexico City: internal memo.

Marquina, I., & Aveleyra, L. (1962). *Consejo de planeación e instalación del Museo Nacional de Antropología. Informe general de las labores desarrolladas durante, del 1° de enero al 31 de diciembre de 1961* [Council for planing and installing the National Museum of Anthropology. General report on work developed from January 1 to December 31 of 1961]. Mexico City: INAH, CAPFLE, SEP.

Martínez, E., & Puig, J. (1977). *Políticas culturales de México* [Cultural politics in Mexico]. Paris: UNESCO.

Morales-Moreno, L. G. (1994). History and Patriotism in the National Museum of Mexico. In F. E. S. Kaplan (Ed.), *Museums and the making of "ourselves": The role of objects in national identity* (pp. 171–186). London and New York: Leicester University Press.

Reyes-Palma, (1987). Acción Cultural y Público de Museos de Arte en México [Cultural Action & the Art Museum Public in Mexico]. In E. Cimetetal El publico como propvesta. Cuatro estudio sociológicos en museos de arte [The Public Surveyed: Four Sociological Studies in art museums] (pp. 17–47). Mexico City: INBA.

Rose, N. (1996). Governing "advanced" liberal democracies. In A. Barry, T. Osborne, & N. Rose (Eds.), *Foucault and political reason: Liberalism, neoliberalism and rationalities of government* (pp. 37–65). Chicago: University of Chicago Press.

Rose, N. (1999). *Powers of freedom: Reframing political thought.* London: Cambridge University Press.

Salinas de Gortari, C. (1982). *Political participation, public interest and support for the system: A comparative study of communities in Mexico*. La Jolla: Center for U.S. Mexican Studies, University of California, San Diego.

Stellweg, C. (1976). Mexico, museum country, extracts from a conversation with Iker Larrauri, Director of Museums, National Institute of Anthropology and History, Mexico City, *Artes Visuales*, *11*, 36–37.

Stevens, E. P. (1974). *Protest and response in Mexico*. Cambridge: MIT Press.

UNESCO. (1970). *Cultural rights as human rights: Studies and documents on cultural policies* (Vol. 3). Switzerland: UNESCO.

Vasconcelos, J. (1979). *The cosmic race: A bilingual edition*. (D. T. Jaén, Trans.). Baltimore and London: Johns Hopkins University Press. (Original work published 1925)

Villafranca, J. C., & Barra, R. W. (Eds). (1994). *Memoria del simposio patrimonio y politica cultural para el siglo XXI* [Proceedings from the symposium on patrimony and cultural politics for the 21st century]. Mexico City: Instituto Nacional de Antropología e Historia.

Watts, R. (1993/1994). Government and modernity: An essay in thinking governmentality. *ARENA Journal*, *2*, 103–157.

Young, D. J. (1985). Mexican literary reactions to Tlatelolco. *Latin American Research Review*, *20*(2): 71–85.

Yúdice, G. (1995). Civil society, consumption, and governmentality in an age of global restructuring. *Social Text*, *45*(14): 1–25.

Yúdice, G. (1998a, March). From the popular to civil society. Paper presented at the conference "New Perspectives in/on Latin America: The Challenge of Cultural Studies," University of Pittsburgh, PA.

Yúdice, G. (1998b). The globalization of culture and the new civil society. In S. E. Alvarez, E. Dagnino, & A. Escobar (Eds.), *Cultures of politics/politics of cultures: Revisioning Latin American social movements* (pp. 353–379). New York: Westview Press. http://www.arts-history.mx/museos/muse.html

Chapter 9

Designing Fear

How Environmental Security Protects Property at the Expense of People

Carrie A. Rentschler

Around the corner of Matthew Street and Oregon Street in Urbana, Illinois, a doorway stands secured behind red-painted grating. Everything about this corner on the University of Illinois campus suggests safety and openness, except for the locked and gated door leading into the basement of the School of Social Work building. On Halloween night 1995, university employee Maria Pia Gratton was dragged through this doorway, raped, and strangled to death. Her attack became a flashpoint for the fear many women have of being assaulted, both on and off campus. After Gratton's death, news coverage did little to calm women's fears of assault by representing the perpetrator as a stranger. Police and university officials withheld information (by order of the state attorney general, John Piland) on their prime suspect, James Radic, a 29-year-old sophomore in the College of Liberal Arts and Sciences, until 9 days after Gratton's murder, encouraging members of the university to assume the assailant was still at large (Bauer, 1995a). The front page of the University of Illinois student newspaper, the *Daily Illini*, placed the first story on Gratton's murder directly above a story detailing James Radic's suicide, which he committed by walking in front of a moving locomotive shortly after Gratton's murder (see two Nov. 2, 1995 stories, "UI Worker Murdered" and "Locomotive Strikes UI Student on Champaign Railroad Tracks"). The *Daily Illini* drew no connections between these events. Police soon discovered Radic's fingerprints all over the duct tape used to bind Gratton's arms and mouth, and DNA evidence later confirmed him as her attacker. Combined with university Police Chief Oliver Clark's comment that the police had no suspects despite their suspicions of Radic, encouraging students and faculty to report "suspicious activity on campus," the official refusal to talk about the investigation and the subsequent security measures that were instituted on campus speak to the ways institutions mystify violence against women.

Maria Pia Gratton's rape and murder on campus highlights a number of assumptions about violence against women implicit in some of the University of Illinois' security measures. The attack crystallized a number of changes in security at the university that were publicized as anti-assault measures, but that actually fail to address most violence committed against women. University planners' and risk-management assessors' use of what are termed "environmental" security measures, as well as the publicity of crime data based on police reports, use the fact of violence against women to represent a generalized fear on campus. At the same time, planners and administrators put into place safety measures that address property crimes and other "crimes of opportunity," which they suggest address sexual assaults. However, as I will demonstrate, environmental security simply cannot thwart sexual violence. It is not designed to do so, and saying that it stops sexual violence only mystifies the realities of this violence. These security measures *might* work to some degree when strangers perpetrate assaults against women, but the reality is that the majority of assaults against women are perpetrated by someone the woman knows (Gordon & Riger, 1991; Warshaw, 1994).[1] While environmental security can deter "crimes of opportunity," such as theft, vandalism, and trespassing, it is much less successful in dealing with premeditated crimes, such as rape, murder and bias-related assault (author interview with UI risk manager John Benberg, August 11, 1997).[2]

The gate erected after Gratton's murder (see fig. 9.1) provides the perfect symbol of the gap between the stated and probable effects of environmental security. The use of the gate makes certain presumptions that demonstrate this gap. It assumes that threats of violence come from outside the university, and that blockading doors to university buildings will directly thwart physical threats to university members. After the attack on Gratton, the university began to revisit its approach to security, opting for less visible security measures that draw less attention to safety problems. By adopting a holistic approach to security known as Crime Prevention Through Environmental Design (or CPTED, pronounced "sep-ted"), the university began addressing the problem of gendered violence with a set of security practices that are known to prevent property crimes, but not premeditated or interpersonal forms of violence such as sexual assault and harassment. CPTED presents an image of naturalized security that makes it harder to see the conditions in which sexual violence occurs. As a result, the university's image of security misrepresents risks women face for sexual violence.

Environmental security planning operates under masculinist and institutional assumptions, in which risks to property come to stand in for all risks, including women's risks of personal assault. This essay addresses the specific workings of the relationship between violence and environmental security

FIG. 9.1. Gated response to violence at the University of Illinois, School of Social Work.

within the University of Illinois. Since CPTED principles were recently adopted there, the university provides an excellent case study of the rhetoric of security accompanying changes in physical and social protocols within large institutions. As a marriage of state and private interests, public universities are forced to concern themselves with their marketability while still appearing to serve the public at large. Crime reports and safety campaigns have become a central channel through which universities cultivate the appearance of security and communal unity, creating a public image that best attracts new students, faculty, and corporate money. Additionally, readers should not underestimate the economic resources of undergraduates. Most university budget reports and publicity materials suggest that undergraduate students are a primary revenue source. Simultaneously, graduate students are becoming more of a revenue source, as tuition waivers are being undervalued and out-of-state students' in-state residency costs, and in-state tuition prices, are being raised.[3] Students are universities' "customer" base, and school after school has begun referring to undergraduate students as customers.

While campus publicity material represents campus life as harmonious, actual social relations at the University of Illinois suggest otherwise. The university's approach to campus security measures is consistent with its approach to other conflicts on campus—the *image* of unity becomes synonymous with peaceful social relationships on campus. At the University of Illinois, the power of building maintenance, copying services, and food-service unions is being consciously undermined through off-campus contracting policies. Students are increasingly identified as consumers of university services and of banks within the campus town area. The university has finally agreed to a union election for graduate employees, but only after a several years-long legal battle with the Graduate Employees Organization. Conflicts over the university's mascot, "Chief Illiniwek," pit minority students and supporters against alumni who contribute to the athletic department. The university represents itself as a harmonious social milieu, while at the same time it feeds antagonistic relations between workers, between the administration and campus unions, between staff and students, and between activists and alumni.

I explore the contradictions between the university's image of security and the realities of sexual violence on campus to demonstrate that environmental security measures make invisible the realities of violence perpetrated against women. The use of environmental security to address interpersonal violence speaks to a rhetorical collapse between the protection of property and the identity of university community. As a pseudo-public corporate institution, the university's interests lie in protecting its corporate and state funding. Fulfilling these economic needs requires, at least in the minds of administrators, a concomitant vision of a unified university community, distinguishable from town residents and that appears conflict-free. The reality of violence against women within the context of this university, and universities in general, suggests that this image of unity is pure fiction. It is a fiction that speaks very clearly to the incommensurability of preventing physical violence to people through practices of property protection.

This study is therefore framed as a demonstration of what Foucault terms "governmentality," or the institutional regulation of conduct, and the workings of its logic through safety practices. The university attempts to govern the conduct of members and non-members alike through its security—what Foucault would call "governing at a distance." It is a "state of government" that corresponds to a vision of society as "controlled by apparatus . . . of security" (1991, p. 104). The university attempts to govern members of its community by shaping perceptions of safety through environmental measures and the publication of safety documents. I see the university's security corpus as the combined expression of pastoral and territorial power. Pastoral power is

> exercised not so much over a fixed territory as over a multitude in movement toward a goal; it has the role of providing the flock with its sustenance, watching over it on a daily basis, and ensuring its salvation; lastly, it is a matter of power that individualizes by granting, through an essential paradox, as much value to a single one of the sheep as to the entire flock. (1997, p. 68)

Territorial power manages economic and boundary relations: it is military (or police security in the case of the university), diplomatic, and self-regulating. It manages external relations by fortifying internal mechanisms of order and control (p. 69). Universities are both feudal and modern. They manage their populations, and the relations among their members, through the combination of force, public relations, and self-monitoring. The university tells its subjects: "Take care of yourself. We are doing our part to fortify our borders, but you must also do your part."

This chapter examines the injunction to take care of our own safety through an analysis of the means the university makes available to do that. To keep ourselves safe, we need accurate information on violence against women and how to ward off attack. The practices of security I describe set up "a whole range of practices that constitute, define, organize, and instrumentalize the strategies that individuals . . . can use in dealing with each other" (Foucault, 1997, p. 300)—strategies which are, for the most part, not useful for responding to violence against women. Environmental security delimits the options members of the university perceive they have for structuring their conduct—how safe or unsafe they feel, how they perceive other university members and town folk. They suggest and prescribe to individuals "techniques of the self" based upon fear in relation to others which in turn is based upon the recognition of public university spaces as unsafe (Foucault, 1997, p. 87). Fear is the primary affect mobilized by security measures and used by university members to identify as possible targets of violence. It is a form of fear directed at "outsiders," namely Black residents of Champaign-Urbana, and intensified for women on campus. The university tells us: "Be careful, university spaces aren't safe," which means, "Be careful, nonuniversity people aren't safe." In reality, it is relations within the university that are not safe. So environmental security enables one form of safety consciousness—strangers are dangerous—by largely disabling another: university members are dangerous.

THE CONFLATION OF PROPERTY PROTECTION
WITH PERSONAL PROTECTION

Security has recently become a major public concern across university campuses. The occurrence of high-profile attacks against women, such as the local
attack on Maria Pia Gratton, has fed public attention to the perceived lack
of security on university properties.[4] In 1996, following the murder, University of Illinois planners and risk managers adopted the principles of Crime
Prevention Through Environmental Design to redress problems of violence
on campus. The adoption of CPTED combined physical planning, crime
prevention, and risk management into a systematized approach to security.
The university had used other crime prevention measures prior to 1996. In
1983, a Rape Awareness and Prevention Committee (RAP) had been formed
on campus to address sexual assault, which it did by focusing on assaults by
strangers. RAP undertook a number of initiatives, including a million-dollar
lighting plan, installation of 32 emergency telephones, the trimming of bushes
and shrubbery, the distribution of 6,000 whistles annually through the Whistlestop program, and the publication of a number of public information bulletins (O'Shaughnessey & Palmer, 1990, p. 1). At the same time women working
on campus were organizing around the rampant problem of acquaintance
rape. In 1985, the Committee on Acquaintance Rape Education (CARE)
formed in response to criticisms of RAP's focus on stranger attacks. CARE
took responsibility for acquaintance rape education programs on campus, and
they currently run a required workshop on acquaintance rape for all first-year
students (CARE, 1998).

The year 1996 marked a distinct change on the University of Illinois
campus in physical security measures, and how they would work in relation
to the publicity of campus crime reports. Environmental and urban planning
decisions now had to be filtered through the risk manager's office, so that all
planning decisions included security considerations. These changes were related to a beautification and crime prevention plan, the "Campustown 2000"
initiative, which I will discuss later. Crime prevention measures now included
environmental security considerations in all building projects at the university,
as well as systematic physical changes across campus based on the principles
of Crime Prevention Through Environmental Design, also known as "defensible space" (see Newman, 1972, 1996).

CPTED began as a movement in architecture and urban planning in the
early 1970s (National Crime Prevention Institute, 1996b). C. Ray Jeffery's book
Crime Prevention Through Environmental Design introduced the term. Jeffery
argued that security must focus on preventing criminal activity by focusing on
"direct controls" that affect criminal behavior, such as perceptions of safety, how
visible a site is to outside surveillance, and how many people use the space at
any given time (Jeffery, 1971; National Crime Prevention Institute, 1996a).

CPTED, then, is an architectural-behavioral model of security; it assumes "crime is located in the environment, not in the individual. There are no criminals, only environmental circumstances which result in criminal behavior. Given the proper environmental structure, anyone will be a criminal or noncriminal" (Jeffery, 1971, p. 177). CPTED thus enacts a theory of criminality based upon environmentally induced behavior rather than individual pathology (Ekblom, 1995, p. 115). It seeks to elicit conformist (noncriminal) behavior from authorized users of a space and to discourage use by unauthorized users, based upon the idea that crime is a result of environmental engineering rather than systemic social inequality (Jeffery, pp. 167–188). Human aggression is understood as a behavioral response to environmental stimuli, so CPTED assumes that altering environmental cues will discourage criminal activities. Crime can be prevented by "decreasing the reinforcement available from criminal acts and increasing the risk involved in" committing them, through environmental engineering (p. 178).

CPTED operates on the principles of natural surveillance, natural access control, territorial reinforcement, and maintenance.[5] Use of the term "natural" signifies three basic principles: the unobtrusiveness of the security, the visibility of public spaces and access ways, and the unquestioned embodiment of surveillance practices users of the space will ideally inhabit as a result of environmental security. Its security design operates on a panoptic principle, making public spaces very visible to surveillance while making security mechanisms invisible (Foucault, 1979, pp. 195–228). Its naturalness is therefore judged by how the security feels. While CPTED security measures encourage participation by users of the space, they should not *feel* like they are exerting effects. It is a systemic approach to security that emphasizes control over the physical environment, the behavior of people, the "productive" use of space and loss prevention. It signifies a mentality of "holistic security" in which all aspects of the environment are available for manipulation in the name of crime prevention.[6] Since the program was initiated, the University of Illinois has erected berms and fences along its borders, removed rows of hedges along parking lots and sidewalks, installed additional lighting throughout campus, and instituted "traffic calming" procedures to deter skateboarders from skating in high traffic areas and to slow traffic by raising pavement around intersections, changing the texture of pavement, and decreasing speed limits. The first official project utilizing CPTED principles fortified the new university president's office, for an estimated $750,000. A silent alarm system, security doors, a cell phone and bulletproof vest were all provided for University President James Stukel to address his fears of student uprisings (which he had dealt with at the Chicago campus) (author interview with John Benberg, August 11, 1997).

CPTED's goal is to produce and maintain environments where authorized users will feel more comfortable about the spaces they use and those likely to commit crimes will go elsewhere. According to Oscar Newman, "Design can make it possible for both inhabitant and stranger to perceive that an area is under the undisputed influence of a particular group, that they dictate the activity taking place within it, and who its users are to be" (1972, p. 3). In one study, it was found that the number of property crimes committed in a suburban neighborhood (Miami Shores, FL) that had recently made use of CPTED design principles stayed relatively constant, while surrounding neighborhoods saw an increase in police reports of property crimes. The Miami Shores data suggests that CPTED practices do not prevent crime, but they may physically displace it into other geographic areas (Atlas & LeBlanc, 1994; Blakely & Snyder, 1995). The point of CPTED's risk-management mentality is not to get rid of crime, but to make it someone else's problem.

Environmental security is therefore premised on altering perceptions of the most common users of a physical space. For this to work, people must begin to see their own personal interest in safety as complementary to the university's desire to protect its properties and profitability. Universities are liable in some cases for the personal safety of their members, so the adoption of programmatic security practices helps deflect legal responsibility.[7] In fact, each of the court cases establishing university liability for campus safety regarded sexual assaults against women, one in which the victim was murdered (Fisher, 1995). Security speaks to the legal and public relations needs of the university, which require that the university appear safe and that its members believe that violence originates from social intercourse between university members and nonmembers. Thus, the overall goal of CPTED practices is propagandistic. They encourage the university population to identify with the economic interests of the university and come to see those interests as their own. According to Henri Lefebvre, one of the central contradictions appearing in the physical spaces of for-profit economic systems is that between the appearance of security and the constant threat of violence (1991, p. 57). The management of physical space does not just inhibit certain kinds of thought and action, it produces actions and perceptions that are more manageable within the space. The university presents itself as a secure set of buildings and operations, though the murder of Maria Pia Gratton and more recent assaults on women show that a real contradiction exists between the appearance of security and the concrete forms violence takes within the university community.

Securing university space is an economic concern for the university administration in terms of its need to attract students, high-profile faculty, and grant monies. Like corporations, educational institutions address risks in a way that protects profits first, and people second. According to security executives, corporations tend to fear employee theft, property crime, and unauthorized access the most, followed by workplace violence, computer security, parking lot security, and burglary (in that order; see Zalud, 1998). Campus security executives rank their top "risks" in similar fashion: theft and burglaries top the list, followed by computer security, unauthorized access, alcohol and drug problems, and vandalism ("Campuses Bridging Gap," 1998).[8] While the safety of technology and information can easily be translated into profits, human safety becomes an issue of public image. According to Rob White, professor of criminology at the University of Melbourne, the primary motivations for "adopting exclusionary policies, to sell 'security,' and to enforce a particular kind of spatial code are shaped by 'commercial' decisions and corporate balance sheets, rather than sociological or political considerations" (White, 1995, p. 37). CPTED principles are another way that universities more closely resemble the corporate sector.

Environmental security measures at the university operate under unquestioned assumptions about race and class, presuming authorized users (e.g., university members) to be middle to upper class and white. While white teenage skateboarders have been identified as a big problem on campus (because they destroy cement and marble work), and exclusionary policies have been directed against them, they do not produce the same level of perceived threat as people of color do. Criminal threats are addressed as people who do not belong on campus—the poor, the indigent, the homeless, and for the University of Illinois, residents living north of University Avenue; residents who, to a large extent, are both black and poor. The use of CPTED supports the identity of the campus as a white and middle-class institution needing protection from black others by consciously considering race in planning decisions. All new buildings built along the edges of campus, especially facing the north side of town, have no doors facing north and have symbolic and real barriers between the building and the outside community, including berms and 6-foot steel fences (interview with John Benberg, August 11, 1997). The College of Communications' new WILL-TV and radio station on the north edge of campus was built with doors facing south and an outside picnic table area on the south side of the building, apparently to discourage residents from the north side of Champaign from using WILL's facilities. The university's risk manager, John Benberg, implied that members of the university do not reside on the north side of town, so the university does not need to provide doors and other access points to university property from the north (author interview, August 11, 1997). The majority of Champaign-Urbana's poor and African American citizens, however, do reside on the north side of town.

The Beckmann Institute, which houses the National Center for Supercomputing Applications, provides another example of fortified north-facing buildings on the edge of campus (see fig. 9.2). When it was built in the early 1990s, community residents were outraged by its fortress mentality. It is surrounded by 6-foot fences and rows of bushes on the north side. The fences surround an outside eating area only accessible from the inside of the building. Security cameras follow activity around the building, and users can only

Fɪɢ. 9.2.   Gated communities? The Beckman Institute: securing university and industrial interests on campus.

access Beckmann from the south and east. The WILL and Beckmann buildings physically signify the mentality of the university toward north-side residents of Champaign-Urbana: "You don't belong here."[9]

The university's attempt to present a unified, harmonious representation of its spaces comes at the cost of making them exclusive and heavily fortified. This picture of unity depends upon social antagonisms and inequalities, such as the CPTED groupings of "authorized" and "unauthorized" users. CPTED principles function similarly to other risk management responses to social threats in that they collapse the differences between social threats and the populations they effect into a larger category of "risk" (Beck, 1992; Burchell, Gordon, & Miller, 1991; Furedi, 1997). According to sociologists Ulrich Beck and Frank Furedi, the more available knowledge on social, economic and health hazards becomes, the more people most likely to benefit from this knowledge (white middle classes) tend to perceive that they are at risk (Beck, pp. 19–50; Furedi, pp. 15–44).

Ultimately, the conflation of property protection measures with personal protection from violence fails. The presentation of the campus as a centralized, harmonious social milieu through the management of physical spaces is undermined by evidence of sexual violence. While physical planning decisions organize physical spaces to present the university community with feelings of safety and harmony, systemic violence against women continues.

CONSTRUCTING THE IMAGE OF UNITY:
WELCOME TO THE UNIVERSITY

A lot of work goes into creating the physical illusion of unity. Highly visible mythologized symbols on campus need the backing of police, anti-panhandling and other anti-poor ordinances and corporate boosterism to produce even partially believable representations of campus as conflict-free. Take, for instance, the former entrance to the University of Illinois which stands at the corner of Wright Street and Green Street, right on the border of Champaign and Urbana.[10] The Alma Mater, a statuesque berobed woman standing with arms outstretched, welcomes students and official visitors to the university: "To thy happy children of the future those of the past send greetings." (See fig. 9.3). The Alma Mater suggests a closed-circle family unit, where alumni

Fig. 9.3.   Welcome to the University of Illinois.

and current students share collective good feelings about the university. The Alma Mater is particularly important to the image of the university. Many a protest is held here, since Alma Mater holds such symbolic weight for the university's public commitment to educating its citizens. Postcards capture her solemn greetings for tourists and undergrads writing home.

Alma Mater also stands at the entrance to a walking campus. One cannot drive up to her on campus. One can only inspect her on foot and continue on into the pedestrian quad, flanked by the architecture of the foundational arts and sciences: philosophy, history, languages, chemistry, anthropology, English, rhetoric, and lastly, the administration and University of Illinois Foundation. Park-like and fully visible, the quad serves as a general meeting ground for students to lounge and interact, for all members of the university to walk from destination to destination, and as a symbolic central space for holding demonstrations and press conferences. In contrast to what Kenneth Jackson calls the "drive-in culture of contemporary America," the University of Illinois, like many other universities, still maintains centralized spaces geared towards pedestrians (Jackson, 1985, pp. 246–271). The quad represents a central meeting ground for pedestrian interaction on-campus. The heart of campus appears serene, peaceful and orderly because spatial management is at work. As university promotional material explains, "The center of the campus, the quad combines the best of campus traditions with the dreams of every Illinois student" ("Choosing Smart," 1997, p. 22).

The university is an odd mix of private and public land relations. Green Street, which cuts through the heart of campus, provides an excellent example of the interrelation of public and private ownership and management on campus. A 3-foot high sign at the corner of Green and Matthew states: "This entrance to the Campus of the University of Illinois is not a public highway. Vehicles may enter if operated with due regard to the rights of persons and property" (See fig. 9.4). The sign states that the university owns and controls access to Green Street. The Illini Union offers a similar warning:

> Use of the Illini Union is limited to students, faculty, staff, alumni, retirees and guests of the University of Illinois. Visitors to the University must be accompanied by a student, faculty/staff member or alumnus, or must have scheduled business in the building.

Yet with recent contracts signed by Blimpie Subs and McDonald's, and a proposal to sell first floor space to national retail chains, the Illini Student Union looks more and more like the privatized "public" space of a suburban shopping mall.

Despite its dependence on public funding, the university operates like a members-only club. Members of the public, especially homeless people, are often evicted from university buildings (Smith, 1999, p. 5). The university physically

FIG. 9.4.   Signifying private property, Green Street on the University of Illinois campus.

reproduces a sense of belonging for alumni and current students, faculty and staff through its environmental security measures and its symbolic representation. For everyone else, the university signifies inaccessible privilege and racism.[11]

In this combination of public and private spaces, the university is like a lot of other pseudo-public institutions, such as public parks in inner cities, city sidewalks, skyways, public highways and roads, and gated communities. All these spaces are managed through members-only policies, whether explicit and formalized or not (Blakely & Snyder, 1995; Ellin, 1997). As Mike Davis argues in *City of Quartz*, "Today's upscale, pseudo-public spaces—sumptuary malls, office centers, culture acropolises, and so on—are full of invisible signs warning off the underclass 'Other.' Although architectural critics are usually oblivious to how the built environment contributes to segregation, pariah groups—whether poor Latino families, young Black men, or elderly homeless white females—read the meaning immediately" (Davis, 1990, p. 226). Perceptions of university space as for members only, buttressed by city panhandling ordinances which make it illegal for homeless people to be stationary and ask for money on city sidewalks, serves to create a false sense of security within university spaces. At the same time, members-only understandings of privatized public spaces reproduce segregationist behavior and fuel irrational fears about poor local town residents. Outsider status becomes associated with the potential for criminal action. The perceptual and actual segregation of university and city space thus leads to contradictory and misleading understandings of crime and violence.

The "Campustown 2000" initiative—a development project to renew the dining and shopping district surrounding the campus, to beautify the Boneyard Creek that passes through campus, and to beautify the campus itself—encourages members of the university to perceive themselves as at risk from crime. Security measures are a central part of the initiative, and the "Truth or Dare" campaign is the most visible part of the campaign. The campaign focuses most specifically on publicizing police crime statistics, and consequently, members of the university are encouraged to understand risk as police represent it and through the campaign's own public relations. The "Campustown 2000" initiative also instituted the "Put Your Change Where You Can Make One" program, modeled on similar programs in Baltimore, MD and in Oregon. Restaurants and businesses in the campustown area post flyers encouraging their customers to place money for homeless people in a provided cup to be donated to a local charity, rather than interact directly with homeless people in the area. This program seeks to rid the part of town surrounding the campus from signs of poverty and inequality by demonizing homeless people as "untouchables."[12] As a result of these campaigns, my students understood that they were prey to attack by local townspeople for their electronics, cars, and cash. Yet a professor confessed to me that students perpetrate most property crime around campus (where she lives). While the truth is probably somewhere in between, these are radically different understandings of who perpetrates property crimes on and around campus. Feelings of safety will differ based upon who you are and how you are positioned within and through the university, whether as woman, "person of color," homeless person, or town resident. Overall, the security mentality pervading the university creates competing senses of security and encourages continued segregation between townspeople and university members. The continued problem of sexual violence on college campuses provides the impetus for this "us versus them" security mentality.

SECURING UNIVERSITY SPACE: HOW THE CAMPUS RESPONDS TO VIOLENCE AGAINST WOMEN

Asked if she felt safe after Maria Pia Gratton's murder on Halloween 1995, University of Illinois student Christie O'Connell reported to the school newspaper, the *Daily Illini*, "I do. I feel the recent incidents are isolated. I feel as safe as I did my junior, sophomore and freshman years." (Johnson, 1995) O'Connell's sentiments register the population management effects of intentional security-oriented spatial design. That she could understand a series of sexual assaults on campus as isolated instances suggests that the management of university space reproduces false feelings of security and inadequate knowledge of the realities of sexual violence.

Not only is sexual violence a common occurrence on college campuses, environmental security against sexual violence is nearly impossible. Acquaintance assaults often occur in contexts where the victim and perpetrator share a certain level of trust and/or expectations of honesty. The usual publicized warnings—like being wary of strangers and avoiding dark places—offer no solution to most violence against women. The media and university public relation responses to Gratton's murder operated under the assumption that attacks on university members would come from outside the university community. Media coverage of Gratton's attack emphasized it as a stranger assault, even after police knew it technically was not. These media representations encouraged readers to understand violence as committed primarily by strangers, even strangers who are also members of the University community (see the following stories from the *Champaign-Urbana News-Gazette* and the *Daily Illini*: Bauer, 1995a, 1995b, 1995c; Cetera, 1995; LaLande, 1995; Smith & Wasag, 1995). While both the local and school newspaper represented violence as perpetrated by strangers both on and off-campus, the university's PR campaigns represented violence as perpetrated by strangers from off-campus. Neither addresses the possibility that sexual violence that appears as random violence may in fact be better defined as acquaintance assault.

That the assailant was found to be 29-year-old university student James Radic, who committed suicide less than two hours after he murdered Gratton, did not seem to affect the security responses or how sexual violence has been addressed on campus. The university administration's response served to present a public perception of itself as safely managed from violence, despite the obvious failures of stranger-oriented security measures to deal with acquaintance violence.[13] Radic existed within Gratton's social milieu—as a biochemistry major, he took classes in Noyes Lab, the building in which she worked. He did not fit the stereotype of the dangerous stranger who comes from another social class or social context into another one to commit violence. Kim Lonsway, a graduate student in psychology specializing in sexual violence, addressed these contradictions in a letter to the *Daily Illini*:

> If there is a possibility that Gratton was murdered by someone she knew, we must wonder: Of what use would the "personal safety tips" have been in preventing this particular attack? Assuming that, as a woman, I remain aware of my surroundings and do not use headphones as advised when someone I know approaches me, I would respond as any other individual would in such a situation. I do not blow the safety whistle the University has provided me with as a panacea for my personal safety. Rather, I *greet* the person. I generally respond to people I know with trust rather than suspicion, and it is exactly this trust and vulnerability that is so frequently taken advantage of by men who commit violence against women. (1995, p. 8)

The CPTED-based security measures after the murder were more appropriate for stranger attacks, usually in the form of robberies: increased lighting along walkways, more police presence at 5 P.M. when university offices close, installing more public emergency phones, handing out 10,000 whistles, and locking dorms between 7 P.M. and 7 A.M. (a practice in place before the murder) (Challos, 1995). Included in the security measures were fairly common safety prevention tips: walk in groups at night; if being followed, go to a public and well-lit space and get help; don't wear headphones when out alone; be aware of your surroundings and who is near you; use well-lit pathways; blow your whistle if you're being followed.[14] In announcing these security measures, university chancellor Michael Aiken admitted, "I know there is great anxiety among the members of this community. This tragedy serves as a reminder that it is important for all members of our community to continue to take every precaution possible for their personal safety" (Challos, 1995).

By setting out rules for women to follow, the university—indeed, most crime prevention in general—deflects responsibility for safety onto individuals' own behaviors as targets of violence. Rule-based prevention measures (e.g., don't walk alone, never wear headphones) make women feel solely responsible for protecting themselves against violence, while also increasing the emotional burden of feeling personally at fault if they are assaulted (Cotler & Bowman, 1999).

University security measures make more sense as management mechanisms for its own population than as deterrents to violence. Like gated communities in wealthy suburbs, the University of Illinois projects an image of its environment out to the rest of the community while simultaneously imposing regularity on its members within university confines. Environmental security measures isolate the university community from the rest of Champaign-Urbana, and they maintain divisions among members, such as the divides between faculty, grad students and undergrad students (all academic workers) and support staff (nonacademic workers).[15] The contradictions fueled by a unifying but differentiating bureaucratic management of University relations reproduces the appearance of public safety while dismissing the violence at the core of university relations, violence based on rank, gender, and other power differentials. The university encourages people to invest in the belief that they have common interests and a common community (albeit a commonality opposed to the rest of the town), while, as I will suggest, it reinforces the social hierarchies within the institution. Unless security measures can help redistribute power on campus, and provide a way for all university members to have a binding say in decision-making, most violence on campus will continue unabated.[16]

MAKING SEXUAL VIOLENCE INVISIBLE: THE "REAL" IMPACT OF ENVIRONMENTAL SECURITY

The securing of university property through "naturalized" protective measures focuses women's fears of attack on public spaces in particular, without redressing these fears through more accurate knowledge of violence against women, and most importantly, how to deal directly with physical threats of violence. Women are more likely to be assaulted in their own homes than in public. Roughly 80% of attacks occur within women's own residences, while only 20% occur outside of the home (Koss, 1982; Warshaw, 1994). Yet fears of personal assault are still focused largely on public spaces, where women are taught to most clearly identify being a woman with being a target of sexual harassment and violence.

As a result, women disproportionately perceive public spaces as dangerous, despite the relatively low likelihood of being attacked outside of the home or workplace (Gordon & Riger, 1991; Madriz, 1997). Our level of fear of public space is quite high—49% of women interviewed in a study of 299 U.S. cities said they felt "very" or "somewhat" unsafe when out alone at night (study cited by Pain, 1991). In a study conducted in London, 75% of respondents "often or sometimes felt frightened" when out at night (cited in Pain, 1991, 420).

Although the fear of violence in public space is out of sync with the actual spatial locations of violence against women, fear of harassment is not.

> [A]ll the sources of information from which women learn about sexual danger suggest it is a public sphere phenomenon; and, . . . although sexual violence mainly takes place in private space, the common occurrence of sexual harassment in *public* space acts to remind women of sexual danger. In other words, sexual harassment evokes fear of more severe sexual attack through routinely creating a state of insecurity and unease amongst women. (Pain, 1991, p. 421)

Discourse on space and women's experiences of harassment in public combine to make women insecure about going out into public spaces. As feminist geographer Gill Valentine argues, women's sense of security has less to do with changes in the environment of "threatening locations" than it has to do with the social relations supported by those locations (Valentine, 1990, 1992). Most women seem to fear particular spaces when others' behaviors in those spaces are unregulated. Valentine's research in Reading, England suggests that youth gathering spots and areas surrounding drinking establishments, open park spaces and parking lots constitute spaces women frequently mention as threatening. Women's fear, it seems, is based on the perception that men dominate public space. These fears are born through experience with harassment, leering, and men's mocking of women's engagement in leisure activities (e.g., playing pool in a pool hall). Women rightly interpret these behaviors as aggressive and potentially dangerous. They feel subject to, rather than subjects in, public spaces.

As an institution combining private residence and public space with highly informal learning and work environments, the academy provides a particularly ripe context for the perpetration of sexual violence. Additionally, many young people get their first taste of freedom away from their parents within the social setting of the university (Koss, 1982; Warshaw, 1994). This university setting also often encourages young people to reenact harmful sexual relationships. One example of this is the reproduction of aggressive hetero-sexual masculinity in fraternities and intercollegiate athletics. In 1990, the Sexually Stressful Events Survey reported that 63% of sexual assaults and 71% of sexual abuse cases on the University of Illinois campus were commit-ted by members of fraternities (O'Shaughnessey & Palmer, 1990, p. 12).[17] To put the numbers in perspective, this means that the 25% of men on campus who belong to fraternities commit roughly two-thirds of all cases of violence against women on campus. Also, a majority of victims of sexual assault belong to sororities: 45% of women victims of sexual assault belong to sororities; 31% of women on campus belong to sororities (p. 12). The culture of sorority life helps foster the heterosexual hypermasculinity of fraternities through shared parties and the establishment of "sister" sororities for each fraternity. In ad-dition, most attacks occurred either at a fraternity house (25%), in a woman's residence hall (22%), or in a man's house or apartment (16%), further dispel-ling the myth that most attacks against women occur out in public (p. 9). A study conducted by Towson State University's Campus Violence Prevention Center in 1991 also found that 55% of all admitted acquaintance rapes were committed by members of athletic teams, even though they made up only 16% of the male student body (see Gmelch, 1998, p. 203). All this suggests that sexual assaults tend to be fostered by hypersexualized, masculinist male cultures. According to Eugene Kanin's research on date rapists, rapists were found to be "very heterosexually active men who had been socialized into a hyper-active male culture that views sexual success as the main way to estab-lish manhood and maintain self-esteem. . . . They also belong to a subculture (which includes fraternities and sports teams) that treats women as sexual targets" (p. 201).

Yet sexual violence is invisible on campus because those responsible for security privilege a male population. In part, this is a result of the number of assaults on men reported to police. Men are more likely to report assaults than women, and they are more likely to be assaulted by strangers than women (50% of attacks on men are perpetrated by strangers; see Leung, 1991). Assaults on men are therefore less likely to result in male victims blaming themselves for their assaults, since they often do not know their attacker and are often attacked in public places, where the context is not that of an intimate relationship. At the University of Illinois, the "Truth or Dare" safety campaign posts bulletins emphasizing that men are more likely to be victims of assault than women. It is true that men are more likely to be victims of aggravated assaults and battery. Between September 1995 and August 1997, 81% of victims of aggravated assaults and battery were men, while 96% of victims of criminal sexual assault were women ("Campus Crime Increase," 1997, p. 1). The "Truth or Dare" campaign attempts to counteract the assumption that women are more likely to be assaulted by framing assaults as "battery." While there are more *reported* cases of aggravated assaults and battery on campus, that does not mean that women are less likely to be sexually assaulted or to be victims of domestic violence. Most women do not report sexual assaults and abuse to the police because they feel shame, they may have been threatened with reprisal by their abuser, they may blame themselves for the attack, or they may think the police will not believe them. It is safer and more realistic to assume that there are far more sexual assaults occurring on campus than are reflected in police statistics and official university policy. As a result, the *appearance* of security measures on campus tends to make women's perceptions and experiences of violence largely invisible. While gendered violence motivates the adoption of environmental security measures and safety campaigns, these measures do not directly address violence against women perpetrated by acquaintances, lovers, friends, and family members.

Due to public pressure and new federal requirements, the university began publishing campus crime reports in the early 1990s. In 1990, the U.S. Congress passed the *Student Right-to-Know & Campus Security Act*, requiring colleges and universities receiving federal financial aid funding to compile and publish statistics on crime on campus.[18] All violent crimes reported on the University of Illinois campus, both "attempted" and "completed," totaled 46 in 1993, 34 in 1994, and 42 in 1995. Nearly half of the total for each year were aggravated assaults. Forcible rapes ranged from three to five per year, considerably lower than the reported number of assaults and robberies.[19] However, Rape Crisis Services (RCS) in Urbana documents many more sexual assaults from reports women make directly to them. In September and October of 1997, 20 to 30 cases of sexual assault were reported to RCS each *month*. According to Eileen Orzoff of RCS, "In my opinion, the University tries to cover up a large amount of the sexual assaults. . . . [University officials] want to keep statistics low so it's not scary for incoming students" (quoted in Balsley & Clifford, 1997, p. 9).

Violence against women occurs in other settings within the university besides fraternities and athletic contexts. The training of graduate students, for instance, often entails highly intense personal relations between faculty and students that can lead to sexual relationships in which the power inequalities between faculty and student are not addressed.[20] These and other sexualized power relations within the university can be explained, in part, through the way safety measures that actually empower women are deemphasized in university management. One simple alternative measure to the emphasis on the built environment would be to publish statistics on how many women successfully ward off attacks on their person, helping women to both avoid and survive assaults. Rather than focusing on the few reported cases of criminal sexual assault, publicizing knowledge on how successful women are and can be in keeping themselves safe changes the whole tenor of discussions of safety on campus. It puts the power of safety in women's hands, rather than in the hands of planners and administrators.

Antiviolence education, I suggest, can offer a better response to violence against women than a security approach "governing as a distance." Environmental security measures fail to create emboldened, knowledgeable subjects who can defend themselves from violence with knowledge and physical know-how. What I am suggesting is a kind of self-defense education that creates more able-bodied, able-minded subjects than environmental security techniques. Through consciousness-raising efforts—a form of self-care and self-relation that focuses on one's possibilities rather than one's potential to be targeted by violence—women can learn to respond to violence in ways that do not reproduce the dependent subjectivity produced by external property crime prevention measures.

I do not suggest women should focus their fears on private spaces instead of public spaces. The problem is fear itself, and the reproduction of it through institutionally produced knowledge that explicitly encourages women to fear the world around them. There is, in fact, a lot for women to fear. Women are targeted for particularly humiliating and terroristic forms of violence. At the same time, several collective movements of women, most notably the women's self-defense movement, have developed amazingly empowering and effective tools for dealing with violence in our daily lives. Women can and do educate themselves on how they can make their lives safer; for instance, by knowing how to recognize signs of potential violence and how to verbally and physically respond to violence. "Self defense," according to Martha McCaughey, "transforms what it means to have a female body" (1998, p. 279). Self-defense offers a way of unlearning passive and brutalized femininity and replacing it with a physical feminism (see McCaughey, 1997; Rentschler, 1995, 1999). McCaughey calls self-defense the act of deconstructing femininity, enabling women to "internalize a different kind of bodily knowledge." Learning self-defense is a "pleasurable process" engaging women mentally, physically, and emotionally, instilling "a new bodily comportment" (1998, p. 281).

> Women's self-defense is a reprogramming regimen for the body. Here, women—regardless of their conscious political beliefs about gender—rehearse a new script for bodily comportment. The body [] is not simply the locus of patriarchal power, ideology, or brutality; it is a potential locus of resistance. In self-defense classes, women make their aggression, and the femininity that prevents it, conscious. They develop a new self-image, a new understanding of what a female body can do, and thus break out of the expectations under which they have acted—expectations that have cemented themselves at the

level of the body. In this way, a feminine bodily schema is supplanted by a fighting bodily schema, or what some self-defense instructors call the "fighting spirit." (p. 281)

Women create a new bodily memory in self-defense. They actively shape new perceptions of their physical and mental abilities—particularly the belief that women can be aggressive and can fight off attack. Yet it is unfortunate that so much attention focuses on what women can do to protect themselves rather than on the perpetrators responsible for harassment and violence. Without systemic changes and the eradication of sexism in all its forms, women are thrust into the position of critic and defender at the same time. Self-defense is a necessary step in the process of dismantling sexism, on the level of its embodiment.

Physical planning's shortcoming is in not being able, nor perhaps willing, to address experiences of sexism as experiences of physical space. The threat of sexual violence stems not from the configuration of space itself, but from sexist social relations grounded in women's oppression and devaluation. Until social relations on campuses and other public spaces express equality and freedom from domination for women, physical security measures will most likely fail to create completely safe environments for women and men. The more women see personal attack as a real possibility (or the less likely they are to deny that sexual violence only happens to other women) the less likely we are to venture out into public space. Women then become more dependent upon men and larger social networks to create a semblance of safety and protection (Valentine, 1989). Ideally, we should be able to depend upon ourselves for accurate knowledge on crime and for safety and prevention skills. The security mentality at the University of Illinois has tended instead to increase women's dependence upon university police for knowledge of crime, analysis of safety, and physical protection.[21]

Rather than using violence against women as an excuse to fortify university property against property crimes and "crimes of opportunity," universities could publicize accurate information on the realities of violence against women, such as the 1990 report of the "Sexually Stressful Events" survey and the recent campus report, "Campus Climate: The Effects of Gender, Race and Sexual Orientation" (Fitzgerald, n.d.; O'Shaughnessey & Palmer, 1990). According to Koss's study of acquaintance rape, only 5% of acquaintance rapes are reported to police, so it is safe to assume that there are far more (95% more!) acquaintance assaults than official sources report. Universities could help make available anonymous stories women have to tell of the violence they have dealt with (harassment and "uncompleted" and "completed" assaults, for example).[22] Campus rape education programs could be one avenue for sharing this knowledge with women who want it in a caring and safe context. University judicial boards have also hindered many victims from getting justice. They often fail to really deal with sexual violence because they pit victims against their attackers, as if they somehow occupy the same position ethically, legally and physically (Warshaw, 1994, pp. 147–150). Stories across the literature on sexual violence report unjust judicial board resolutions, such as requiring a rapist to write a paper on sexual violence. According to the director of student life at the University of Rhode Island, "date and acquaintance rapes are the most difficult cases to handle in a disciplinary hearing just as they are in a court of law. . . . It's her word against his" (quoted in Warshaw, pp. 149–150).

To really deal head on with violence against women, institutions need to be willing to deal substantively with known sexual harassers and rapists and to eradicate the social conditions that perpetuate sexism (Nelson & Watt, 1999). This means putting binding responsibility for violence on those who perpetrate it (Gordon & Riger, 1991; Warshaw, 1994). But institutions can also be more proactive by funding programs that have proven to deal more effectively with violence; for instance, by helping develop women's own capacities to deal with violence. Women need to know that institutions will not tolerate sexism, and that they will be supported with policy, advocacy, and counseling when and if they are put into the position of being victimized by violence. Additionally, universities and other institutions can fund women's self-defense courses taught from a feminist perspective, which means they highlight the options women have for dealing with violence, avoid scare tactics and rule-based prevention measures, and ideally create the conditions for a community of women who work and learn together to keep themselves safe. Women need to experience their safety as an effect of choices they make. Seeing safety as personal choice has been shown to increase women's ability to ward off attack and heal more effectively after attacks (Bart, 1981; Levine-MacCombie & Koss, 1986). Research also demonstrates that women are very successful at warding off and surviving attacks. One study found that 81% of women who ran escaped rape, 62.5% of women who yelled escaped successfully, 68% who used physical force avoided rape, and 83% escaped when someone intervened (Bart 1981, pp. 18–19; cited in Leung, 1991).

Groups across the nation teach self-defense in this manner (see Leung, 1991; McCaughey, 1997). Women train women students to become teachers themselves, to share what they know with other women. Building networks of women armed with physical and practical knowledge of the types of violence we are most likely to face is a proven way women have found to be and feel more safe. These groups tend to be severely underfunded and relatively unknown to most of the public. Universities could be one funding source that makes this education more accessible.

The institutions we work and learn within have an ethical responsibility to avoid scare tactics and promote accurate and practical information on violence. To do otherwise simply uses women's victimization to increase fears of violence and scapegoat nonuniversity community members. We all have options for being and feeling safer.[23] It's time to start exploring them.

NOTES

1. Most information on acquaintance rape comes out of a body of research sponsored by *Ms.* Magazine and the National Institute of Mental Health, and directed by Mary Koss, Ph.D. The research took 3 years to complete (the impetus for the project resulted from overwhelming response to a 1982 article on date rape), culminating in survey data from 32 college campuses and 6,100 male and female undergraduate students. This research demonstrated that very few acquaintance rapes are ever reported (roughly 5% are reported to police), that one in four college-aged women have been raped, and that in 84% of the cases, the woman knew her attacker. Robin Warshaw's book *I Never Called It Rape* (1984) uses Koss' statistical findings to present this research to a wider audience. See also Ellen Sweet's October 1985 *Ms.* article on date rape.

2. Benberg is responsible for training police and University of Illinois planners in the principles of Crime Prevention Through Environmental Design, and he oversees all planning decisions and their adherence to environmental security procedures.

3. For recent budget information at the University of Illinois, see the Campus Profile online at www.dmi.uiuc.cp.

4. Gratton's rape and murder in 1995, as well as recent attacks on women in the campus area by a group of three white, college-aged men, have drawn media attention to violence against women on campus. After James Radic's attack on Gratton, two other cases of sexual assault tied to a serial rapist that had occurred in campus residence halls received media coverage. Before Gratton's attack, the media made no mention of these assaults. See Bauer, 1995d, 1999; Jiang, 1999; LaLande, 1995; "UI Murder Not Tied to Rapes," 1995; Zeman, 1999.

5. The first three principles are the key concepts taught by the National Crime Prevention Institute; the fourth was added by the Sarasota City Administrative CPTED Task Force as a result of its field surveys. See "Crime Prevention Through Environmental Design Task Force," 1996.

6. According to Timothy Crowe, a criminologist who has worked with CPTED since the early 1970s, "CPTED is based on the theory that the proper design and effective use of the built environment can lead to a reduction in the fear and incidence of crime and an improvement in the quality of life." See his "Understanding CPTED," *Planning Commissioners Journal*, Fall 1994, 5.

7. As a field that is part of "security management," CPTED is an effect of legal decisions, which hold property owners responsible for activities that occur on their premises. Environmental security measures are a way to protect universities, businesses and cities from litigation. In the 1970s and 1980s, student crime victims won negligence suits against universities, making universities liable for crimes committed on their property if the universities were aware of prior crimes committed there. Four

seminal cases established the duty to warn students about known risks and the duty of universities to provide students with adequate security protection. The cases establishing the duty to warn students of risks were *Durate v. State of California* (1979) and *Peterson v. San Francisco Community College District* (1984). The cases establishing the duty to provide adequate security were *Miller v. State of New York* (1984) and *Mullins v. Pine Manor College* (1983). The plaintiffs in these cases were all female sexual assault victims, one of whom was murdered during her assault. See Bonnie Fisher, 1995.

   8. Violence ranks significantly higher for secondary schools. One article in *Security* magazine's June 1996 special report "School Security" ranked gang problems as the third-highest ranked threat, with computer security coming in first and vandalism second. In August 1998, *Security* magazine's special "Focus on School Security" ranked student violence as the second threat, following theft and burglary.

   9. For a historical understanding of the racial segregation of Champaign-Urbana, see Jonathan Sterne, 1998.

   10. In 1997, the formal entrance to the university was moved to the eastern edge of campus. The new admissions building as well as a historic archway, the Hallene Gateway, now welcomes visitors through a more driver-friendly part of campus.

   11. University researchers have had difficulty attracting local African American residents to the university for participation in research. Professor Bruce Williams discussed with me that many local black residents see the university as a foreign place inaccessible to them. For members of the university, this racial reality of the university is submerged under the public symbolism of openness and public access that the university reproduces. Personal correspondence with Professor Williams and researcher Eric Pearson, April 1997, University of Illinois.

   12. For a brief description of the campaign, see the University of Illinois' website at www.oc.uiuc.edu/oc/ps/summary.html

   13. Since Radic was a student of Chemical Sciences and worked in the same building as Gratton, Radic would count as an acquaintance. Some people reported to the *Daily Illini* that Radic attempted to establish a relationship with Gratton, though Gratton is said to have deflected his attempts. Enrico Gratton, Maria's husband, publicly denied that Radic knew his wife, in an apparent attempt to establish Radic as a stranger and diffuse rumors that his wife may have been promiscuous. While Enrico Gratton's response appears to be an attempt to deflect blame from his wife for the violence she suffered, it also implies that women who have sexual relations with more than one partner are to blame for their victimization. Whatever a woman's sexual practices, she never deserves nor is to blame for her victimization.

   14. The whistle measure provides little if any security against assault. A former student of mine once related that when a man chased her down a university street, she blew on her whistle over and over again, only to have nearby apartment residents peer out their windows. No one came to her rescue. In part, this is because a whistle blow is a very unclear message. In addition, the use of whistles in other assault situations, like hate and bias crimes, has more community support and a stronger assault prevention knowledge base. Whistles in gay and lesbian communities and hang out areas are a clear sign and sound of bias attacks. At the University of Illinois, with 36,000

students, a whistle blow could signify a prank, a sporting event, or any of a number of things, because the knowledge of violence and whistle responses isn't widespread. Thanks to Grace Giorgio for pointing out the appropriation of whistles from gay and lesbian bias crime prevention measures, and the distortion of knowledge about violence in which this appropriation has resulted.

15. Shortly after Gratton's murder, AFSCME local 3700 negotiated with University administration to change office hour closing times from 5 to 4:30 P.M. AFSCME was thwarted in their attempt to negotiate by the administration and the *Daily Illini*, which charged that AFSCME was callously using the murder to negotiate over nonrelated issues. In opposition to their point, AFSCME's actions appear instead as proactive measures to increase feelings of safety among clerical workers, who, since the change over to a 37.5 hour work week, now must go to their cars alone because of staggered work schedules. See *Daily Illini* editorials ("UI responsive to tragedy," and "seek real solutions to crime," November 3, 1995) and Stoll and Hetman's letter to the editor, November 10, 1995.

16. The university's incompatible mission to serve the public good while making profit intensifies conflict-based social relations on campus. Within this conception of the university, administrators and heads of departments have managerial control because they participate in maintaining social and physical divides among job categories and social statuses. In many academic departments, the chairs of the department have final control over decisions made in the department, from hiring, firing, wage and salary levels to the public face of the department. The Board of Trustees, populated by CEOs and self-made business people, carry out university policy in the name of profit and growth. Trustee Susan Gravenhorst recently said that the board is open to input from students and staff, but only in an advisory role (quoted in a documentary film on the University of Illinois' mascot Chief Illiniwek, "In Whose Honor," broadcast on WILL-TV, July 12, 1997, 8–9 P.M.). In other words, university policy is decided by people we do not elect, and those who are affected by policy have little formal voice in university decision-making.

17. Criminal sexual abuse is defined differently from criminal sexual assault in that the victim was not penetrated by the perpetrator.

18. A current congressional campaign, called the *Accuracy in Campus Crime Reporting Act*, would close numerous loopholes universities have for deflating their crime statistics and channeling certain criminal prosecutions, such as felonies and misdemeanors, through confidential disciplinary committees. Two of the major offenses channeled into these committees are alleged sexual assaults and cases of sexual harassment; in other words, gendered violence. The *Family Educational Rights and Privacy Act* (FERPA) of 1965 provides protections for students from damaging "criminal larks." Perpetrators of sexual violence on campus are legally protected from criminal procedures by FERPA. Essentially, universities maintain legal rackets to protect the reputations of its students and faculty and to prevent publicity trials.

19. Campus Safety Crime Statistics, published on World Wide Web at: http://www.uiuc.edu/safety/resources/safety/crime_statistics.html

20. Women scholars have spoken out about their victimization by sexual harassment, and many report not feeling like they had any institutional support for stopping

the harassment. See Nelson & Watt, 1999, pp. 232–257. Nelson and Watt include excellent policy recommendations for universities in dealing with sexual harassment. Within my own field, Communications, two particular articles written by women scholars detail their experiences with sexual harassment. See Blaire, Brown, & Baxter (1994); "Telling Our Stories" (1992).

21. One police officer teaching a self-defense course suggested that women only needed knowledge of self-defense on vacation, because the University of Illinois police would protect them when they're on campus (Officer José Ortiz, National Organization of Women Self-Defense Workshop, Urbana, IL, April 1996).

22. The language of calling an assault "attempted" or "uncompleted" is highly problematic for the simple fact that these "attempts" can be experienced as highly traumatic. Calling them "attempted" makes them appear insignificant.

23. The following people have provided valuable comments, conversations, and perspectives on this chapter and the issues addressed herein: Jody Baker, Alice Crawford, Katherine Coyle, Kelly Happe, Mark Harrison, James Hay, Donna Hoeflinger, Allen Larson, Diane Long, Andrea Press, Dawn Schmitz, Jonathan Sterne, and Mike Willard.

References

Atlas, R., & LeBlanc, W. G. (1994). Environmental barriers to crime. *Ergonomics in Design*, 9–16.

Balsley, K., & Clifford, K. (1997, May 2). Survey to test rape rates. *Daily Illini*, p. 9.

Bart, P. (1981). A study of women who both were raped and avoided rape. *Journal of Social Issues*, *37*(4), 123–37.

Bauer, S. (1995a, November 8). Suspect in UI murder called quiet, reliable, *Champaign-Urbana News-Gazette*, p. A1.

Bauer, S. (1995b, November 10). Fingerprint solves UI rape-killing, *Champaign-Urbana News-Gazette*, p. A1.

Bauer, S. (1995c, November 10). No known link between killer, victim, *Champaign-Urbana News-Gazette*, p. A10.

Bauer, S. (1995d, November 11). Mayor: Could officials have said something earlier? *Champaign-Urbana News-Gazette*, p. A1.

Bauer, S. (1999, November 4). Crime on campus nothing new. *Champaign-Urbana News-Gazette*, p. A14.

Beck, U. (1992). *Risk society: Towards a new modernity* (M. Ritter, Trans.). London: Sage.

Blaire, C., Brown, J. R., & Baxter, L. A. (1994). Disciplining the feminine, *Quarterly Journal of Speech*, *80*, 383–409.

Blakely, E., & Snyder, M. G. (1995). *Fortress America: Gated and walled communities in the United States*. Cambridge, MA: Lincoln Institute of Land Policy.

Burchell, G., Gordon, C., & Miller, P. (Eds.). (1991). *The Foucault effect: Studies in governmentality.* Chicago: University of Chicago Press.

Campus crime increase. (1997, October 1). *Daily Illini*, p. 1.

Campuses bridging gap between police powers, security systems. (1998, February). *Security*, pp. 22–23.

Cetera, M. (1995, November 8). University student linked with murder. *Daily Illini*, p. 1.

Challos, C. (1995, November 3). Restoring safety: University officials initiate measures to increase security on campus. *Daily Illini*, pp. 1, 6.

Choosing smart. (1997). University of Illinois at Urbana-Champaign promotional material.

Committee on Acquaintance Rape Education (CARE). (1998). First year CARE workshop. Office of Women's Programs, University of Illinois at Urbana-Champaign.

Cotler, S., & Bowman, M. (1999, June 18). Methodologies: Women's self-defense. Presentation at "Express Your Power, Special Training 1999" National Women's Martial Arts Federation, St. Catharines, Ontario.

Crowe, T. (1994, Fall). Understanding 'CPTED.' *Planning Commissioners Journal, 16*, 5.

Davis, M. (1990). *City of quartz: Excavating the future in Los Angeles.* New York: Vintage.

Ekblom, P. (1995, May). Less crime, by design. *Annals of the American Academy of Political and Social Sciences, 539*, 114–129.

Ellin, N. (Ed.). (1997). *Architecture of fear.* New York: Princeton Architectural Press.

Fisher, B. (1995, May). Crime and fear on campus. *Annals of the American Academy of Political and Social Sciences, 539*, 85–101.

Fitzgerald, L. (n.d.) Campus climate: The effects of gender, race and sexual orientation. Report, Chancellor's Committee on the Status of Women, University of Illinois at Urbana-Champaign.

Focus on school security. (1998, August). Special Report. *Security, 22–23*.

Foucault, M. (1979). *Discipline and punish* (A. Sheridan, Trans). New York: Vintage Books.

Foucault, M. (1991). Governmentality. In G. Burchell, C Gordon, & P. Miller (Eds.), *The Foucault effect: Studies in governmentality* (pp. 87–104). Chicago: University of Chicago Press.

Foucault, M. (1997). The ethics of the concern for self as a practice of freedom. In P. Rabinow (Ed.), *Michel Foucault: Ethics, subjectivity and truth, Vol. 1* (pp. 281–301). New York: New Press.

Furedi, F. (1997). *Culture of fear: Risk-taking and the morality of low expectation.* London: Cassell.

Gmelch, S. B. (1998). *Gender on campus: Issues for college women.* New Brunswick, NJ: Rutgers University Press.

Gordon, M., & Riger, S. (1991). *The female fear: The social cost of rape.* Urbana, IL: University of Illinois Press.

Jackson, K. T. (1985). *The crabgrass frontier: The suburbanization of the United States.* New York: Oxford University Press.

Jeffery, C. R. (1971). *Crime prevention through environmental design.* London: Sage.

Jiang, J. (1999, March 29). Three men sexually assault local woman. *Daily Illini,* p. 1.

Johnson, L. (1995, November 13). Do you feel safe on campus? Why or why not? *Daily Illini,* p. 11.

LaLande, J. (1995, November 13). Clues point to Radic as Gratton's killer. *Daily Illini,* p. 1.

LaLande, J. (1995, November 13). Police timing questioned. *Daily Illini,* p. 1.

Lefebvre, H. (1991). *The production of space* (D. Nicholson-Smith, Trans.). Oxford: Blackwell.

Leung, D. (1991). *Self-defense: The womanly art of self-care, intuition and choice.* Tacoma, WA: R&M Press.

Levine-MacCombie, J. and Koss, M. (1986). Acquaintance rape: Effective avoidance strategies. *Psychology of Women Quarterly, 10,* 311–320.

Locomotive strikes UI student on Champaign railroad tracks. (1995, November 2). *Daily Illini,* p. 1.

Lonsway, K. (1995, November 8). Acquaintance rape demands attention. *Daily Illini,* p. 8.

Madriz, E. (1997). *Nothing bad happens to good girls: Fear of crime in women's lives.* Berkeley, CA: University of California Press.

McCaughey, M. (1998). The fighting spirit. *Gender & Society 12*(3), 277–300.

McCaughey, M. (1997). *Real knockouts: The physical feminism of women's self-defense.* New York: New York University Press.

National Crime Prevention Institute. (1996a). Crime prevention through environmental design task force report. Training manual. Louisville, KY: University of Louisville.

National Crime Prevention Institute. (1996b). "History of crime prevention through environmental design." Training manual. Louisville, KY: University of Louisville.

Nelson, C., & Watt, S. (1999). *Academic keywords: A devil's dictionary for higher education.* New York: Routledge.

Newman, O. (1972). *Defensible space: Crime prevention through urban design.* New York: Macmillan.

Newman, O. (1996, April). *Creating defensible space.* U.S. Department of Housing and Urban Development, Office of Policy Development and Research.

O'Shaughnessey, M. E., & Palmer, C. J. (1990, January 22). Summary report of the sexually stressful events survey. Urbana, IL: University of Illinois at Urbana-Champaign.

Pain, R. (1991). Space, sexual violence and social control: Integrating geographical and feminist analyses of women's fear of crime. *Progress in Human Geography*, *15*(4), pp. 415–431.

Rentschler, C. (1995, October). Perpetrate my fist. *Bad Subjects*, *22.* Online at http://www.eserver.org/bs/22/rentschler.html. Last retrieved on August 13, 2002.

Rentschler, C. (Spring/Summer 1999). Women's self-defense: Physical education for everyday life. *Women's Studies Quarterly*, *27*(1/2), 152–161.

Seek real solutions to crime. (1995, November 13), Editorial, *Daily Illini*, p. 10

School security. (1996, June). Special Report. *Security*, 12–17.

Smith, L. (1999, March 21). Restrictions limit use of university. *Daily Illini*, p. 5.

Smith, R.E., & Wasag, B. (1995, November 3). Connection? Members of the university community speculate on the coincidence of the murder and apparent suicide. *Daily Illini*, p. 1.

Sterne, J. (1998). Scratch me and I bleed Champaign: Geography, poverty and politics in the heart of east-central Illinois. In Bad Subjects Production Team (Eds.), *The bad subjects anthology* (pp. 83–88). New York: New York University Press.

Stoll, J. and Hetman, P. (1995, November 10). Harsh attack on AFSCME unjustified. Letter to the editor, *Daily Illini*, p. 8.

Sweet, E. (1985, October). Date rape: The story of an epidemic and those who deny it. *Ms.,* 54–56.

Telling our stories: Sexual harassment in the communications discipline. (1992, November). Special issue of *Journal of Applied Communication Research*, *20*(4).

UI murder not tied to rapes. (1995, November 3). *Champaign-Urbana News Gazette*, p. A1.

UI response to tragedy (1995, November 3), Editorial, *Daily Illini*, p. 8.

UI worker murdered. (1995, November 2). *Daily Illini*, p. 1.

Valentine, G. (1989). Geography of women's fear. *Area*, *21*(4), 385–390.

Valentine, G. (1990). Women's fear and the design of public space. *Built Environment*, *16*(4), 288–303.

Valentine, G. (1992). Images of danger: Women's sources of information about the spatial distribution of male violence. *Area*, *24*(1), 22–29.

Warshaw, R. (1994). *I never called it rape: The* Ms. *report on recognizing, fighting and surviving date and acquaintance rape.* New York: Harper Perennial.

White, R. (1995, February/March). The forbidden city: Young people and public space. *Arena Magazine*, 34–37.

Zalud, B. (1998, January). Whose advantage? *Security Distributing and Marketing*, 68–73.

Zeman, E. (1999, March 30). Investigation continuing of student rape. *Daily Illini*, p. 1.

Chapter 10

Creating a New Panopticon

Columbine, Cultural Studies, and the Uses of Foucault

Greg Dimitriadis and Cameron McCarthy

The Panopticon . . . must be understood as a generalizable model of functioning; a way of defining power relations in terms of the everyday life of
men [sic]. . . . It is polyvalent in its applications; it serves to reform prisoners, but also to treat patients, to instruct school children, to confine the
insane, to supervise workers, to put beggars and idlers to work. It is a type
of location of bodies in space, of distribution of individuals in relation to one
another, of hierarchical organization, of disposition of centers and channels
of power, of definition of the instruments and modes of power, which can
be implemented in hospitals, workshops, schools and prisons. . . . Panopticism
is a general principle of a new "political autonomy" whose object and end are
not the relations of sovereignty but the relations of discipline.

—Foucault, *Discipline and Punish*, pp. 207–208

INTRODUCTION

In this chapter, we draw on the concepts of discipline, surveillance and
panopticism, concepts developed by Michel Foucault in books such as *Discipline and Punish* (1979), in order to articulate a critical assessment of current
approaches to the topic of school-based youth violence in cultural studies and
education. We should say right off that we do not intend to offer a developed
exposition of Foucault's thought on these matters. Instead, we deploy these
concepts in an overall assessment of the status of youth violence in this
emergent area of radical educational research paradigms. We look at these
approaches to youth violence in the light of policy initiatives in schooling in

the aftermath of the Columbine School massacre in Littleton, Colorado. The Columbine massacre precipitated policy responses that led to the intensification of the surveillance of American youth and a pattern of deeper incorporation and commodification of school spaces and environments.

We specifically call attention to the strengths and limitations of an emergent body of work in the subgenre known as cultural studies in education, in which radical scholars such as Henry Giroux (1996), Alan Block (1997), and John Devine (1996) offer sharply divergent accounts of youth violence and the social and pedagogical responses to nonconformist youth practices. We conclude by pointing readers beyond the central opposition that animates current educational approaches to school youth: the opposition between the field of popular cultural texts in which young people seem so deeply immersed and the lived reality of classroom practice and the organization of knowledge in schooling.

SCHOOLS, TECHNOLOGY, AND SURVEILLANCE AFTER COLUMBINE—WHAT DO RADICAL SCHOLARS *KNOW*?

As Meaghan Morris (1996) has argued for some time now, a fundamentally debilitating feature of contemporary radical scholarship in cultural studies and in the social sciences—education included—is its seeming inability to conjure up the world in a manner that has both rhetorical efficacy and explanatory power. Critical theorists, critical pedagogues, and the like, have failed, it seems, to present programmatic alternatives to dominant sociocultural imperatives that might persuade relevant constituencies to act for transformative social change. Critical scholarship seems to have collapsed into what Nancy Fraser (1997) calls "weak publics." Indeed, we live in a time of the rampant pessimism of the will, a sort of postsocialist, postutopic moment in which critical writing has reached a sort of narrative implosion. The gulf between theory and practice is becoming an ever-more expanding void. Again and again, critical pedagogues seem to be outfoxed by the cunning of history and the complexities of the present. Again and again, educational theorists seem inadequate to the task of interpreting and intervening in public life.

This scenario of intellectual inertia in education was sharply fore grounded on April 20, 1999, when two students at the Columbine High School in Littleton, Colorado, Eric Harris and Dylan Klebold, killed 15 people (themselves included) in what was the worst school shooting in the nation's history. The enormity and significance of this horrible tragedy left educators speechless. The silence of radical scholars on Columbine was particularly deafening. By contrast, however, dominant conservative responses have been decisive and interventionist. As a result of this silence on one part and stridency on the other, the massacre at Columbine—the most visible in a series of recent such shootings—has been met with public and policy responses of the most impoverished and reactionary kind. Targeted at the disciplining of youth, these policies have aimed at a completeness of surveillance in which increasingly diverse student populations would be regulated by a massive intensification of technological control. Within this disciplinary framework, the bodies of today's school children have been usurped from the classroom teacher and delivered to a new panopticon apparatus composed of metal detectors, surveillance cameras, security guards, and school bouncers. School security systems and metal detectors proliferate. Young people signifying difference—those straying from an increasingly narrow and increasingly policed norm—are labeled "deviant." Popular culture—from the music of Marilyn Manson to the video game Doom—is targeted. In sum, an overwhelming array of disciplining practices and procedures have emerged quickly in the wake of Columbine.

This trend shows no signs of abating. As the *PR Newswire* reported, 39% of middle and high schools in the United States were scheduled to be equipped in 1999 with electronic security systems (Samsung Camera, 1999). By the 2003–2004 school year, that number is expected to jump to 62%. Like the Internet, security systems are now seen as an immutable fact of life for schools today, encouraging increasingly common alliances between education and industry. This same article documents a deal between Secaucus High School and Samsung Camera for security equipment, the latter offering for donation,

- 32 indoor and ultra-low light outdoor color CCD cameras (Model SDC-2304 indoor color cameras and Model SHC-710 ultra-low light outdoor color cameras)
- 2 digital color duplex multiplexers (16 channel) (Model SMD-1600)
- 2 21" color CCTV monitors (Model SAM-21M)
- 2 14" color CCTV monitors (Model SAM-14K)
- 2 VHS time lapse video cassette recorders (Model STR-960)

Secaucus High School Principal Patrick G. Impreveduto said of the gift, "On behalf of the entire community, and especially the students and faculty of Secaucus High, we thank Samsung Camera for being our Partner in Progress. Their generosity will enable all those who use our facility to work and play in an even safer and more secure environment." As with technology, one expects similar such "partnerships" to flourish in years hence.

This Samsung Camera partnership is but one example of the furious expansion of regulatory media technologies into the nation's schools begun in the latter part of the last century. One might recall here the Channel One invasion of schools in the early 1990s, in which the company's president, Chris Whittle, offered schools who signed on to his cable programming a quid pro quo. "Appealing to cash-hungry schools, Whittle provides $50,000 in 'free' electronic equipment, including VCR's, televisions, satellite dishes, on the condition that the schools agree to broadcast a ten-minute program of current events and news materials along with two minutes of commercials" (Giroux, 1994, p. 53). The Whittle project along with the Samsung and many other corporate "partnerships" use mass media forms to penetrate the audio-visual systems of schooling (cable feeds, textbooks, etc.), in order to mobilize media environments as vehicles of consumer normalization and regulation. With security systems, as with other technologies, the range of possible critique seems usurped a priori. To be against security measures is to be against the safety of the young, pure and simple. In the Foucauldian sense discussed by Jeremy Packer in this volume safety and security are being integrated into the process of government and, by extension, the regulation of school youth. Surveillance has become a proliferating technology and discourse, generating new powerful psychosocial needs for safety and thereby facilitating an expanded corporate integration and occupation of school environments.

Concomitant to increases in security measures there has been a marked increase in the surveillance of "deviant" or nonconformist cultural practices. As became common knowledge soon after the shooting, both teens were heavily influenced by the "goth" subculture—marked by a romanticizing and aestheticization of death—and were also fans of industrial music groups like KMFDM as well as video games such as Doom. Educators and pop psychologists came to call these investments in popular culture "warning signs," and their diagnoses encouraged a general moral panic that criminalized young people who strayed from an imagined norm of healthy teenagerdom. The normative gaze of peers and teachers alike became a counterpart to the surveillance equipment that proliferated in schools across the nation. In each of these cases, school practices were brought into greater synchrony with broader cultural forces specifically around the demonization of youth. The popular responses—as evidenced on television and radio talk shows as well as everyday school life—assumed the problem with young people was one of control, that young people needed to be contained as violent and dangerous, that ever-sharper scrutiny was important above all else.

Following Foucault and his notion of governmentality, we argue, this increase of policing in schools is not to be understood as the stuff of top-down state planning, but rather indexes the ways that these discursive constructions of outsider youth came to infuse themselves in institutions as such, orchestrating cohesion and elaborating affect, sensibility, and association in complex ways. This is, to echo Foucault, "rule at a distance": "power at its extremities, in its ultimate destinations . . . those points where it becomes capillary, that is, in its more regional and local forms and institutions" (1980, p. 96). The simultaneous marginalization and surveillance of young people is carried out in public policy (including discourses on new, harsher youth sentencing, assaults on welfare benefits, etc.), popular culture (including discourses on much rap music as well as films such as Larry Clark's *Kids*), as well as in contemporary school life, all of which increasingly work in concert. As we have argued elsewhere, these connections between power and schooling have been largely ignored in recent work in education, which has remained locked into either Durkheimean or post-state models of social reproduction (McCarthy & Dimitriadis, 2000).

No wonder educators seemed so ill prepared to deal with Columbine and its fallout. Indeed, after the massacre one had the very real sense that critical theorists and researchers—including those in cultural studies—had no compelling response post-Columbine, no compelling vision for what education might look like, how schools might look different, how this kind of violence might be prevented in the future. It would not be an understatement to say that Columbine threw a very large, very challenging shadow over the annual American Educational Researchers Association conference held that very week in Montreal.

In recent work, work that has taken on new relevance since Columbine, Giroux, Block, and Devine have interrogated the fraught topic of youth and violence from the point of view of cultural studies of education. Giroux, in *Fugitive Cultures* (1996), Block, in *I'm Only Bleeding* (1997), and Devine, in *Maximum Security* (1996) collectively maintain that school has become a site of both symbolic and physical violence and that young people experience this violence in multiple ways. They experience—as both perpetrator and victim—physical violence inside and outside the classroom. They vicariously experience violence in the seductive realms of television, film, and popular culture. They are forced to take part in a schooling system and curriculum that do violence to their psyches and that discipline and regulate their bodies and their social conduct. And they exist—most importantly—in a political climate where the terms "youth" and "violence" have become near-synonyms. Yet, all three critics resist this all-too-easy conflation, fighting bravely against a *realpolitik* that has demonized young people, most notably in relation to education and education-related policy.

In this chapter, we will look at these quite different texts as exemplars of an emergent body of literature in the subfield of cultural studies in education. Proponents of cultural studies are, generally speaking, pedagogical populists whose principal project is to translate and apply complex social and philosophical ideas for a large and diverse educational audience. These radical educational theorists argue for a more contextualist and relational approach to education. Specifically, theorists like Giroux, Block, and Devine seek to disseminate neo-Gramscian, psychoanalytic/humanist, Frankfurt school, and even Foucauldian perspectives to the broader educational community. They are working in a post-Marxist moment, with and among those who insist on a continual revision of the neo-Marxist approaches that have virtually dominated the genre of critical pedagogical analysis of education since the 1960s.

In the texts mentioned above, Giroux, Block, and Devine all address the issue of young people and violence, a topic that provokes our minds and bodies in equal measure and does not lend itself to ready-made answers from either end of the political spectrum. We will see what each offers us in our understanding of school violence, post-Columbine. And we will see, ultimately, the uses of Foucault for this project.

Fugitive Cultures and *I'm Only Bleeding*, are highly engaging, if utopian, theoretical texts. Giroux's volume is a collection of essays on a broad range of popular and children's media forms, including film, television, and radio. He offers a vision of a broadly democratic education, rooted in a rigorous critical pedagogy. *I'm Only Bleeding* elaborates a cultural humanist perspective that integrates psychoanalytic theories (object relations take on a particular salience here) in exploring the process of schooling itself and how it does violence to young people. Like Giroux, Block offers a vision for education, but one rooted in the imagination and the ability of the child to reinvent him- or herself through play. We thus see the elaboration of two distinct positions in this field of inquiry: for the former, a neo-Gramscian position that looks to intellectual work in public spheres, especially vis-à-vis popular culture; for the latter, a more traditionally humanist position that holds out hope for "deep selves" that transcend social context and positioning.

Finally, Devine's *Maximum Security* details the day-to-day efforts of participants in the Stay in School Partnership Program (SSPP), a collaborative program for "at-risk" teens languishing at the bottom of New York City high school system. By employing ethnographic methods and empirical work in ways that blur the line between research and service, this text puts us "close to the action," a fresh and invigorating take on an issue tempting to deal with from a practical and theoretical distance. Devine compellingly deploys the work of Michel Foucault, that prophet of surveillance, using his notion of the panopticon to help explain school violence and surveillance. The panopticon is, for Foucault, the preeminent governing device of modern disciplinary institutions and networks. Originally designed by Jeremy Bentham, the panopticon is an architectural model composed of a large central tower that stood in the middle of a surrounding prison. The guard who occupied this tower could look out onto the prisoners, though no one could see into it. Hence, much of the power of this model lies in the fact that prisoners do not know when they are being watched and thus must regulate themselves. Foucault sees this individually sustained and produced mode of surveillance resonating across various modern institutions. Devine's understanding of the panopticon is perhaps counter-intuitive. One might expect a more whole-cloth critique of surveillance itself, one that theorizes school security as a device to encourage students to regulate themselves. Yet, *Maximum Security* argues for a clearer interrogation of the *purposes* of surveillance. For Devine, it is a question of how surveillance is used and to what ends. His reading moves beyond the restrictive interpretations one often sees fore grounded in critical cultural studies. As we will argue, his deployment of theory is useful but like much work in a utilitarian spirit, needs extension in key ways. While the most useful of the three texts that we will examine is Devine's, we will also call attention to its limitations. We will pay special attention to some of the contradictions in Devine's theorizing of youth cultural practices and their effects, particularly as we reflect on the legacies of the Columbine massacre and their ramifications for the world in which we live.

Indeed, Devine's work seems very much locked into a kind of Frankfurt school relationship with technology and the popular, one that fetishizes face-to-face human interaction at the expense of broader kinds of analysis and critique. Though compelling, in the ashes of Columbine it seems a bit narrow. Quite simply, we cannot elide any dimension of young people's lives—popular culture especially—if we are to understand the complex dynamics that played out among and between Harris and Klebold. One recalls here that Eric Harris, on a videotape recorded before the massacre, boasted, "tick, tick, tick, tick . . . Ha! That f___ing shotgun is straight out of Doom." One recalls, as well, that these teens were motivated by the desire for fame (which they, ironically, achieved) and discussed which director—Quentin Tarantino or Steven Spielberg—would tell their story (Gibbs & Roche, 1999, p. 42). These young people lived a reality immersed in popular culture and all its multiplicities—movies, music, computer games, and so forth.

In sum, while Giroux, Block, and Devine allow us to understand contemporary schooling in neo-Gramscian, humanist, and Frankfurt School terms, they do not point us sufficiently toward the discursive functions of school institutions as one node in a larger elaboration of modern systems of regulation and control. The issue of school violence of the type that erupted at Columbine forces us to think beyond their formulations. We must, for instance, more systematically think the connection between difference (not simply in terms of the well-worn identity matrix of race, class, and gender, but however produced), disciplinarity, and the institutionalization of knowledge in the body. What Foucault's theory of discipline allows us to begin to conceptualize is precisely the microphysics of power in the institutional setting of schooling, even as we try to understand its more macrosociological effects in wider society. In so doing, we work to break down the split that still exists in neo-Gramscian and humanist cultural studies models between popular cultural practices and the world of institutional and social policy and practice. And, further, we work to break down the unwarranted separation of texts and discourse, the domains of immanent critique, from their necessary coarticulation to young people's lives. This would lead us more decisively onto the terrain of cultural policy and cultural institutions and away from the endless oscillation between the demonization of popular culture and its celebration. For if schooling is the site par excellence for the installation of the disciplinary apparati and practices that regulate the body of the adolescent, then schooling might also be the most critical institutional site in which societal regulation might be transformed and the bodies of young people might be recuperated.

Let's first take a look at Giroux's discussion of youth violence in *Fugitive Cultures*.

CULTURAL STUDIES AND SCHOOL VIOLENCE

In *Fugitive Cultures*, Giroux (1996) explores the crisis of youth and youth violence by way of now-ubiquitous popular cultural forms, such as film, radio, and music. As Giroux notes, these media forms are critical sites for understanding young people and their particular historical condition. They are, increasingly, providing the narratives—albeit violent, oppressive, and simplistic ones—in which and through which young people come to inhabit particular subjectivities. These media forms are, in his memorable phrase, dispersed and multiple "teaching machines," which young people invest with tremendous affective energy and meaning. These are the sites where much of the most important pedagogical work is taking place for young people today. Against a backdrop of failing and irrelevant schooling systems, "youth make sense of themselves and others" in the spaces opened up by media cultures (p. 15).

Film is a particularly powerful, though often regressive, "teaching machine" for wide groups of youth and must be explored as such. Many popular youth-oriented films, he notes, demonize young people, offering a poverty of images and narratives for them to inhabit. Films about young Whites (e.g., *Kids* [1995], by Larry Clark and *River's Edge* [1986], by Tim Hunter) and urban Blacks (e.g., *Boyz N the Hood* [1991], by John Singelton and *Juice* [1992], by Ernest Dickerson), present gratuitously violent images of youth, images cut off from broader social processes and forces. *River's Edge*, for example, presents young teens as bored and alienated, existing in a perpetual state of despair, and plagued by casual violence—"a spectacle which in the end flattens the complex representations of youth while constructing their identities through ample servings of pleasure, violence, and indifference" (Giroux, 1996, p. 35). Such films lack complexity. They present young people as irredeemably deviant and morally vacuous, offering no broader social context in which to understand their actions.

Indeed, films like *River's Edge* and *Juice* do an injustice to both Black and White youth and certainly do not provide them with any way to contest their often marginalized situations. "Missing from these films," Giroux notes, "is any sense of the larger political, racial, and social conditions in which youth are being framed, as well as the multiple forms of resistance and racial diversity that exist among different youth formations" (1996, p. 38). They draw young people in simplistic, asocial, and ahistorical ways, separate in their pathologies but united in their deviancy and ultimate antipathy to dominant middle-class culture. These films, though loved by many young people, play into insidious conservative forces, that ultimately and destructively marginalize young people.

In response to the reactionary force of popular culture, Giroux calls upon researchers and educators to expand their notions of pedagogy, both in definition and in location. Young people learn in a variety of sites and it is important for those on the left to meet them there, with emancipatory visions and pedagogies. If the left fails to do so, the right will go unchallenged in co-opting masses of people into its uncritical and oppressive socioeconomic project. Giroux stresses the importance of "political education" throughout *Fugitive Cultures*, education that does not simply indoctrinate, but opens up spaces for critical reflection about power, knowledge, and identity.

> Political education, which is central to critical pedagogy, advocates being attentive to the historical and ideological formations that shape the politics of one location as a teacher and cultural worker. Rather than abstracting politics from education, political education exercises a critical self-consciousness regarding how power operates in the classroom to produce knowledge, arrange teacher-student relations, and challenge oppressive structures of power. Political education embraces the inescapable political nature of education while always being suspicious of any politics that is dogmatic, doctrinaire, or closed to critical examination. (1996, pp. 182–183)

His work here seems heavily influenced by Gramsci and, in a more recent essay, Giroux talks of the compelling links between "culture, pedagogy, and power" in Gramsci's work and posits the latter—especially his foregrounding of culture in relation to the material—as a model for critical pedagogues (1999, p. 2). In a Gramscian tone, Giroux asks us to rethink the idea of nationality not as immobilized in a stable body of books or facts but as a process that we constitute and reconstitute through dialogue rooted in difference. Political education is the key to such a radical democracy that invites the broadest and most intense kinds of popular participation. Popular culture, in a Gramscian sense, is a terrain of struggle over consent.

Giroux holds out a utopian vision in these highly theoretical essays. Breadth of scope and intensity of theoretical engagement are strong features of this text. In his relentless interrogation of how the affective investments of young people are interpellated into wider hegemonic projects, his work shares much with the best of cultural studies. Further, he is one of the clearest and most articulate voices calling for a meaningful encounter between cultural studies and pedagogy. He is explicitly concerned with how academics can intervene in the processes outlined above. However, what Giroux gains in macrotheory, he loses in an appreciation of situated interaction. His theoretical abstractions limit his work's usefulness, and his language and constructs are noticeably vague at points. It is difficult to attach real bodies and voices to his otherwise quite appealing pedagogical vision. The essays in *Fugitive Cultures* are not grounded in a contextualized treatment of situated sites in which real people "speak back" in concrete ways. One has little sense of how particular young people with particular (and especially marginalized) life histories live through the texts and social processes upon which Giroux so brilliantly elaborates.

This is an especially paralyzing elision post-Columbine. Understanding the forms of popular culture that these young people drew on is crucial, and even more crucial is to understand how and why they lived through these texts in the ways they did. We need to understand how popular culture has redefined "the real" for young people. As Henry Jenkins noted in his testimony before the U.S. Senate Commerce Committee in Washington, D.C. on May 4, 1999,

> Media images may have given Harris and Klebold symbols to express their rage and frustration, but the media did not create the rage or generate their alienation. What sparked the violence was not something they saw on the internet or on television, not some song lyric or some sequence from a movie, but things that really happened to them. When we listen to young people talk about the shootings, they immediately focus on the pain, suffering, and loneliness experienced by Harris and Klebold, seeing something of their own experiences in the media descriptions of these troubled youths, and struggling to understand the complex range of factors which insure that they are going to turn out okay while the Colorado adolescents ended up dead.... If we want to do something about the problem, we are better off focusing our attention on negative social experiences and not the symbols we use to talk about those experiences. (1999, n. p.)

Jenkins points to the necessity of looking beyond a mode of analysis that seems to have taken hold among the left as well as the right. However, contra Jenkins, we see a proliferation of textual approaches from a range of critics working in cultural studies, media studies, and education today (e.g., Kellner, 1995). These and other left-wing critics have assumed a kind of neo-Gramscian stance towards the relationship between popular culture and the public sphere—one which is provocative but has remained locked, ultimately, into textual exegeses.

If the world of Giroux is abridged outside the texts of television, film, and radio, the world of Block implodes in pre-adolescent and adolescent schooling. In this world, violence rules the teaching machine and the teaching machine is ever-present and all-pervasive. The routinized operation of contemporary arrangements in education kills creativity and the work of the imagination in children. Like *Fugitive Cultures, I'm Only Bleeding* offers a radically utopian vision for education and educators. But, as with Giroux's book, the analysis here could also benefit from a sustained, situated ethnographic check. Block argues that dominant educational processes themselves do violence to young people, stating from the outset:

> I would like to discuss the violence that is practiced upon the child psychologically by the educational system that presently functions in the United States and that consequently denies the development of self and world which is the birthright of every individual in our society and which ought to be the primary activity of every person. (Block, 1997, p. 3)

Drawing on a psychoanalytic tradition, Block contends that the child's "self" emerges through his or her interaction with different "objects," which can be diverse, including books and toys. Even the self can eventually become an object for the young person to reflect upon, thus giving birth to "subjectivity."

According to Block, schools should allow young people unfettered access to a wide range of such objects, allowing a wide range of "selves" to emerge. Block's self is a postmodern self, one constantly defined and redefined through concrete experience:

> The postmodern decentered self is not a fragmented subjectivity but a complex structure that may be expressed in relationships with objects that evoke separate and distinct selves. Subjectivity is the meaningful interpretation of self in experience. Subjectivity is founded in object relations. (1997, p. 23)

"Dream" and "play" are the ideal ways in which these subjectivities emerge. In "dream," the "self is evoked in its engagement with objects, events, selves, and persons elected because they have been psychically charged within the environment" (p. 43). In "play," these dreams are realized in material contexts. Indeed, while we construct a "dream space" in our sleep, re-making selves with charged or invested objects, "the ability to use an object depends on the ability to play" (p. 60).

Invoking a Vygotskian tradition, Block notes that play is perhaps the single most important activity in which young people can engage, allowing selves to emerge in unfolding material contexts. Play is denied in school, which has come to function in loco parentis, in idea inherently odious and repressive to Block:

> The traditional role of the family in the education of the child was
> given to the schools presided over now not by the mother but by her
> surrogate who would be taught to treat other people's children as she
> would never treat her own. Children were sent to school to be made
> into adults who might benefit the State; until that time the children
> were safely entombed within the school's walls. (1997, p. 139)

This kind of discipline is inherently odious for Block, who notes, "The discipline of school that has invented children denies the act of creation and in
that denial commits an execrable act of social violence" (p. 171). Thus, both
the concepts of "children" and "schooling" were created in a spirit of violence
and denial that is perpetrated to this day and will continue to thrive if conservative notions of education persist.

I'm Only Bleeding is a passionate text, one that provides a global vision of
schooling and its failures, and looks forward to a more humane future. Yet,
like Giroux, Block lacks any kind of situated ethnography to help ground this
work. He approaches the problems of schooling with an extremely broad
brush, eliding the voices of children as well as the very real social constraints
they face. As in Giroux's text, there are no faces or bodies to attach to his
theories. Despite its humanist spirit, his work marginalizes and silences the
specificities of schooling and childhood.

Block draws on a "universal child" throughout this text, faceless and
without subject position, betraying his essentially humanist position. In doing
so, he ignores, like many humanists, the specific problems of the marginalized.
Indeed, there is barely a mention of the specificities of race, gender, and class
in *I'm Only Bleeding*. In the tradition of liberal humanism, Block ignores these
issues and questions in the name of "universal"—and implicitly privileged—
cultural imperatives. Block's child-centered approach to education presupposes a world where psychological constraints reign supreme, and the lived
reality of marginalized identity is invisible. His humanist vision perceives
institutions such as schools to occlude of our "deep" and "true" selves. His
vision is of a world without constraint, either internal or external.

In many ways, this book is helpful for understanding the dynamics at
play in Columbine, a middle-class institution. To a large degree, the problems
that Harris and Klebold seemed to face were psychological ones, not ones of
material constraint. Yet, this book, by foregrounding the psychological alone,
does not let us see as clearly as we might the day-to-day struggles and
challenges that young people face. Block's utopian vision of education without constraint occludes the lifeworld of young people today—a lifeworld
made up of a volatile range of popular cultural texts, unpredictable associations, and a host of social and economic pressures. A recent *Time* magazine
cover story, "A Week in the Life of a High School: What It's *Really* Like
Since Columbine" (1999), highlighted the fact that to most of us, educators

included, young people's lives remain a mystery. One wonders how helpful Block's approach is here for understanding school life as well as the broad social context within which schools are imbricated.

Devine addresses many of these problems head-on in *Maximum Security*, an exploration of school violence and how it manifests itself throughout the physical infrastructure of school buildings, in their corridors, bathrooms, and entrances. Devine heads up a large tutoring program that works with "at-risk" students in New York City. *Maximum Security* is a look at the students' lives and the violence which surrounds them. This book provides a context for understanding the program and the varied issues its tutors, counselors, and administrators face daily.

Devine's thesis is intriguing. He notes that, in many respects, the extremely violent schools he works in are "anti-panopticons." Explicitly reacting to the idea that school is increasingly a totalizing mechanism of state surveillance, Devine argues that teachers have lost sight of, and control over, their students. They are increasingly left on their own, without any mature guidance or caring surveillance:

> The supervision of the minutiae of human behavior and the hierarchical surveillance, which Foucault associates with bourgeois society, humanism, and the modern era, have been breaking down drastically for some decades now . . . these controls over student behavior have all but disappeared—paradoxically so, given the plethora of "school safety officers" and security officers that jam the lobbies and corridors. (1996, p. 10)

Contra Block, Devine does not assume that one can "get outside" of disciplining structures. They are everywhere—in the home, in school, in courts, in the very narratives through which we live our lives. Devine is not committed to critiquing the idea of discipline itself. He seems more interested in forging progressive schooling environments and committed teacher-student relationships—"a new panopticon"—to help students lead more fulfilling lives (p. 220). He seems well aware that the other option is often violence, both on the streets and from the police.

Schools, however, are increasingly not serving this traditional function of engaging the whole student. As Devine notes, teachers have relegated much of their traditional authority to security guards. These guards are everywhere. They typically greet students in the morning, run them through metal detectors, and then shadow them all day, making schools de facto police stations, with their own particular languages and cultures. Terms like "scan days, access cards, holding pens, [and] corridor sweeps" now abound throughout such institutions (1996, p. 95). There is an increasingly visible discourse of "security" in schools today, entirely and noticeably separate from the discourses of "education" and "learning." As we noted, this has become even more pronounced since Columbine.

Like Block, Devine is worried that teachers are now engaged only with students' minds, narrowly defined. This stance is reinforced by directives from organizations like the United Federation of Teachers, which expressly forbids teachers from touching students when attempting to break up fights:

> This commonsensical policy [of avoiding any contact with students] also has the effect of decentering and fragmenting students' identities by establishing a sharp boundary between their bodies and the intellectual, spiritual, and cognitive "side" of their subjectivities. By managing student bodies as separate entities, the school renders them more visible, more real. (Devine, 1996, p. 84)

Schools now separate students into discrete bodies and minds. In direct response, students have lost the guidance of their more experienced elders, who are no longer able to engage them as full human beings, but only as fragmented objects. Teachers today can only engage heads without bodies, limiting the function of teaching as a holistic vocation.

Devine notes that teachers should cherish, rather than attempt to defer, their in loco parentis role. Though informed by the poststructuralist work of Foucault and thus radically different from Block's vision of humanism, Devine calls for an "interaction with the 'whole' student." This means,

> Dealing with schoolwide discipline at the moment an offense occurs, communicating firmly but in a consistent way what is or is not acceptable etiquette, correcting students on the spot, enforcing rules jointly with other teachers, teaching and modeling social skills, challenging adolescent beliefs and attitudes [and] allowing students the space to "open up." (1996, p. 131)

Indeed, Devine believes that schools should teach knowledge and values as well as general comportment, such as "etiquette." He thinks that teachers should engage their students with more than book-knowledge alone. They should engage the whole person, as they should be responsible for the whole person. They have something of value to offer and this should be acknowledged and, again, cherished as part of an important vocation.

Devine here seems the polar opposite of Block, who appears to think that any influence from elders is a form of violent coercion. While Devine sees interaction and, often, disagreement with students as a part of honest communication, engagement, and mutual growth, Block sees only coercive control. Block offers this particularly illuminating example:

My daughter may read the story of Cinderella as a metaphor for the decline of western civilization, but it is only my function to discover how she makes what she will of that story. I can correct her if I have the will, but then I have denied her play and creativity, given her an object with which she may not play, and I have myself become an object set in opposition and thereby threatening to her. (1997, p. 70)

Again, Block sees little possibility for challenging dialogue with young people, as such dialogue would imply a hierarchical exercise of power—the power of denial. Block sees any "panopticon," any form of social control, as inherently oppressive. In contrast, Devine acknowledges that one cannot get outside of disciplining practices. The more important question here is how one can forge better models of knowledge and guidance. Left to their own devices, he notes, students are vulnerable to the mercy of a world that (at best) does not care about them and (at worst) sees them as a threat that needs to be policed with force. Teachers should strive to guide, watch over, and protect young people as they work to realize themselves as full human beings in this often hostile world. His argument that teachers should be responsible for "the whole person" challenges those both on the left and those on the right.

This book offers a unique vision, one deeply rooted in long-term, action-oriented research. Devine cares for the participants and tutors that people his research design and program, and this ethic echoes throughout the text. He is to be commended for this effort, and critical pedagogues could learn much from him. Unlike Giroux, he is very clear about what "youth" he is dealing with and the particular problems they face, including extreme alienation. While Giroux assumes students to be well disciplined, willing to work, and only lacking a teacher willing to present a more relevant curriculum, Devine details the efforts of his tutors to search for wandering students in the corridors of the school. His is grounded and situated work.

Devine also does not paper over very real questions of power, as Block does. While Block refuses to look past his utopian, psychologistic model, Devine is in touch with the material realities that young people face—including the ravages of a racist, capitalist society that does not give young people of color the privilege of "running free." In sum, Devine's action-oriented research pushes him to address the material and discursive realities of young people in a way foreign to both Block and Giroux and his work benefits from it. We find his work extraordinarily useful.

However, there is a key elision here—one that seems all-the-more glaring in our post-Columbine moment. While Devine valorizes small-scale interactions between teachers and students, he does not seriously question what values get reproduced in this dialogue. Nor does he consider whether these values might work against the student's other cultural locations. Indeed, he implies there is a dichotomy between "legitimate authority" (i.e., school authority) and "street culture" (i.e., student culture). In doing so, he valorizes what teachers bring to the process of learning, often at the expense of young people. In key example, there is barely a mention of popular youth culture in *Maximum Security*. Indeed, during one of the rare moments when Devine does talk about popular culture (rap music, in particular), he stresses how young people respond negatively to its violence. While he calls for an honest dialogue between teachers and students, these binary oppositions can serve to reinscribe a hegemonic division between them. Such hierarchies—teacher knowledge/student knowledge, educational culture/popular culture—are simply untenable post Columbine. In fact, these are the kind of macro-structural cultural dynamics on which Devine is weakest, and which are best addressed with the critical tools Giroux so deftly wields. While Devine asks us to address these questions in situated contexts, his analysis seems to suffer from a Frankfurt-school marginalization of youth culture, media, and technology. The role of these cultural forms, now more than ever, need to be central for all of us.

As we noted at the outset, violence is a problem most people seem most comfortable to deal with from a distance, within the framework of overarching theoretical paradigms. In this regard, much contemporary critical scholarship simply misses the mark. While the left often constructs young people as victims of oppressive forces who lack all agency, the right sees them as irredeemably violent, symbolizing a social disease best eliminated through force. Devine's success is to put us in the middle of this violence, among young people who commit horrible acts with resolve and agency, in inferior schools that speak to the ravages of capitalism and racism. Devine asks us to address these questions in particular, embodied contexts. He does not prefigure what we might find, nor does he simplify the problems. We are invited to engage rigorously with the "complexities, conflicts, and disorder of everyday life" in rigorous and challenging ways (1996, p. 65).

Meeting young people where they are at, where they live, so to speak, seems the most viable response to school violence today. This is not a comfortable position. Young people, as Columbine demonstrated and as Devine argues, are capable of horrific acts of violence. Our inclinations, quite naturally, might be to stay as far away as possible from this kind of trouble, to guard ourselves with theory that silences the "complexities, conflicts, and disorder of everyday life" (1996, p. 65). Yet this seems an abdication of our responsibility as adults and as educators. Theory should be more helpful—and *can* be more helpful as Devine shows us in his uses of Foucault. Yet theory should also point us in new directions. We think a more rigorous look at Foucault's work, especially around discipline and governmentality, would allow us to see the school as merely one node in a much larger complex involving young people and violence, one which needs serious attention.

Specifically, the "everyday" to which Devine draws our attention needs clearer interrogation, especially vis-à-vis popular culture.

Concluding Thoughts

What we have tried to do in this essay is to extend the current discussion of schooling in the marginal field of cultural studies of education to address the urgent topic of youth violence. By drawing on the provocative Foucauldian reading of contemporary cultural institutions, sites of the elaboration of discipline and the panoptic regulation of bodies, we point to the value of this approach in the debate over the link between school knowledge, the project of social control and regulation, the disciplining of the body, and governing *tout court*. We specifically looked at attempts to conceptualize and explore the pedagogical dimensions of the youth/violence couplet by three exemplars of cultural studies in education, Giroux, Block, Devine. As we have seen, the first two authors, Giroux and Block, use neo-Gramscian and humanist perspectives to understand these dynamics, pointing to the corrupting logic of mass culture and the inadequacy of the current pedagogical and curriculum practices of teachers themselves. The third author, Devine, takes us to the terrain of the Frankfurt school in his lament for the end of the auratic status of the teacher as she/he loses the child to the security guard and the surveillance systems. Devine also sought to enhance his more developed Frankfurt-school approach to youth and education with a partial and selective Foucauldian analysis of disciplinary power.

Yet, as Foucault extended his examination of power to the broader field of governmentality, we need to extend Devine's already useful work here as well. We believe that cultural studies scholars of adolescent and youth education need more systematically to examine the expressions of symbolic and practical violence in schooling and their inauguration onto the bodies and souls of their youthful subjects. We need to look more closely at the nexus of media and popular culture—not merely to denounce them as Giroux does—and the disciplining of knowledge and the bodies and minds of school youth. And we need, further, to move beyond current methodological strategies in education that hermetically seal off the symbolic meaning systems of popular texts from the experiential world of everyday practices through which young people live, move and have their being. We, urge, too, that educators reevaluate the pedagogically pragmatic dimension of this opposition—the banishment of the texts of popular culture from the formal curriculum and the organization of knowledge in schooling. We seek a model of pedagogical practice and a related reflexive research strategy that will fully explore the youth/popular culture nexus in terms of the coarticulation of texts and young people's lives. This nexus constitutes a microphysics of power in which students, knowledges, and experiences exceed the simplistic, one-dimensional scenarios that have been charted for them in the present school curriculum.

These concerns inaugurate, for us, a striking new theme in critical educational scholarship—that is that aesthetic practices now underwrite the fiber of everyday modern life. As Arjun Appadurai (1996) usefully pointed out in *Modernity at Large*, aesthetic practices are no longer to be simply understood as the practices exclusive to the artist, a maverick citizen creating images about the past, present and the future of human existence. But, aesthetics are linked to the work of the imagination of ordinary people and connected even more earnestly to the work of capitalism and its reorganization on a global scale. Contrary to much contemporary thinking, aesthetic practices are at the epicenter of lived experience and commodified and institutional processes of modern societies. These practices of performing and shaping self and community are now broadly diffused through out society. These practices provide the language of cultural translation and revivification of identities. And, they cultivate, provoke and register the turbulent rearticulation of difference and multiplicity in our age—a notion at the center of several recent ethnographies of young people and popular culture, in the United States (Dimitriadis, 2001), Canada (Kelly, 2001), and South Africa (Dolby, 2001).

Indeed, as this work demonstrates, school culture has been overtaken by media culture, broadly defined to include music, film, video games, and the Internet. All of these have provided young people with models for self-fashioning more disparate, and now more compelling, than the ones offered in traditional schools and traditional curricula. As such, the coherence often assumed inherent in schools and school curricula has been replaced by an everyday reality suffused with multiple, overlapping, and contradictory influences. School life has fragmented into disparate orbits as unpredictable processes of self-fashioning have superceded any and all fixed narratives of pedagogy among teachers and policy makers alike.

Columbine, for us, represents a crescendo of these influences and forces, which offers a challenge for educators and thinkers to extend their frame of reference. Following Foucault and his notion of "governmentality," we need to extend our frame of reference to look at the ways in which schools are one particular node in a much larger elaboration of affect and sensibility working across different sites. These sites work both individually and in concert, in ways that are durable yet contingent and open to rearticulation (McCarthy & Dimitriadis, 2000). However, if the intensified disciplining of bodies, ideas, and modes of self-fashioning in the wake of Columbine tells us anything, it is that educators and policy makers are ignoring these challenges.

In closing, we want to note that, while all three of the scholars we have examined treat school violence quite differently, all are united in writing against the contemporary backdrop of a vicious *realpolitik* that has banished critical reflection from education as it has banished reflection and critique from culture and the public sphere. All three seem acutely self-conscious of their political marginality. Their vulnerability to the functional and positivist reality of education makes these works on school violence both alluring and intriguing. Their passionate and even utopian tones reveal the tension and fear that scholars now feel about the future and the fact that our work may be irrelevant to the challenges of our time and the forces we face. There seems the ever present danger that the sincerest efforts of these scholars may be crushed by the brutal realities of the world in which young people live and go to school, the precarious situations that threaten their social, psychological, and physical well-being—the ultimate lesson of Columbine.

REFERENCES

Appadurai, A. (1996). *Modernity at large: The cultural dimensions of globalization.* Minneapolis, MN: University of Minnesota Press.

Block, A. (1997). *I'm only bleeding: Education as the practice of violence against children.* New York: Peter Lang.

Devine, J. (1996). *Maximum security: The culture of violence in inner-city schools.* Chicago: University of Chicago Press.

Dimitriadis, G. (2001). *Performing identity/performing culture: Hip hop as text, pedagogy, and lived practice.* New York: Peter Lang.

Dolby, N. (2001). *Constructing racial selves.* Albany: SUNY Press.

Foucault, M. (1980). *Power/knowledge: Selected interviews and other writings 1972–1977.* New York: Pantheon.

Foucault, M. (1979). *Discipline and punish: The birth of the prison.* New York: Vintage.

Fraser, N. (1997). *Justice interruptus: Critical reflections on the postsocialist condition.* London: Routledge.

Gibbs, N., & Roche, T. (1999, December 20). The Columbine tapes. *Time,* p. 42.

Giroux, H. (1994). *Disturbing pleasures.* New York: Routledge.

Giroux, H. (1996). *Fugitive cultures: Race, violence, and youth.* New York: Routledge.

Giroux, H. (1999). Rethinking cultural politics and radical pedagogy in the work of Antonio Gramsci, *Educational Theory, 49*(1), 1–20.

Jenkins, J. (1999, May 4). Testimony before U.S. Senate Commerce Committee, Washington D.C., http://media-in-transition.mit.edu/articles/dc.html

Kellner, D. (1995). *Media culture: Cultural studies, identity and politics between the modern and postmodern.* London: Routledge.

Kelly, J. (2001). *Borrowed identities.* Unpublished doctoral dissertation. University of Alberta: Edmonton, Canada.

McCarthy, C., & Dimitriadis, G. (2000). Governmentality and the sociology of education: Media, educational policy, and the politics of resentment. *British Journal of Sociology of Education*, *21*(2), 169–186.

Morris, M. (1996). Banality in cultural studies. In J. Storey (Ed.), *What is cultural studies?* (pp. 147–167). London: Arnold.

Samsung Camera equips Secaucus High School with state-of-the-art video surveillance. (1999, November 19). *PR Newswire*, http://www.prnewswire.com

A week in the life of a high school: What it's *really* like since Columbine. pp. 67–115. (1999, October 25). *Time*.

Film's for Bibliography, "Creating a New Panopticon"

Clark, L. (Director). (1995). *Kids*. [Film].

Dickerson, E. (Director). (1992). *Juice*. [Film].

Hunter, T. (Director). (1987). *River's Edge*. [Film].

Singleton, J. (Director). (1991). *Boyz N the Hood*. [Film].

Part III

Technologies of the Self

Chapter 11

Doing Good by Running Well

Breast Cancer, the Race for the Cure, and New Technologies of Ethical Citizenship

Samantha J. King

The past decade in the United States has witnessed a proliferation of discourses and practices of volunteerism and philanthropy. In the postwelfare reform era politicians frequently appeal to volunteerism as a morally and economically viable solution to newly created gaps in the social safety net. The mass media offers a constant flow of stories recounting the generosity of individual Americans ranging from "ordinary" people striving to "make a difference in their communities," to the newest generation of billionaire philanthropists such as Ted Turner and Bill Gates. Increasing numbers of commodities are sold to the public through their articulation to social causes. Corporate-sponsored employee volunteerism programs are now commonplace. Ribbons of every color imaginable are worn to mark awareness of a myriad of social issues ranging from breast cancer to gun ownership.[1] And Americans walk, run, swim, and bike to raise money for any number of different charitable causes.

Of all the philanthropic causes that occupy the public imagination at this time, breast cancer has emerged as one of the most prominent, prompting a 1997 *New York Times Magazine* cover story to declare the disease "This Year's Hot Charity" (Belkin, 1997). It has attained this status in part because breast cancer foundations, nonprofit organizations, and fundraising events have multiplied since the mid-1980s (King, 2000; Klawiter, 1999). In addition, breast cancer is a—if not *the*—favorite charitable cause for corporations seeking to attract female consumers (Davidson, 1997; Goldman, 1997). Moreover, as activism around breast cancer has increased and intensified, the disease has become a major focus of federal and state health policy (Altman, 1996; Batt, 1994; Cartwright, 1998; Solomon, 1992; Stabiner, 1997), the content of which has at times encouraged and facilitated philanthropic approaches to fighting the disease (King, 2000).[2]

This essay takes as its focus one of the most visible symbols of breast cancer philanthropy in the United States: the Susan G. Komen Breast Cancer Foundation's network of 5K runs, the Race for the Cure. The Race's tremendous popularity and ability to draw participants has made it the nation's largest 5K series (with participation increasing tenfold to nearly 600,000 between 1988 and 1998, and reaching 1.3 million by 2001), and the National Race for the Cure held in Washington D.C. each June is now the biggest 5K run in the world.[3] The appeal of the Race is also apparent in its capacity to attract high-profile corporate sponsors, as well as the support and attendance of politicians and celebrities at events across the United States.[4] While the Race is celebrated for its success in raising money for breast cancer research, screening, and education (the series raised $54 million in 1999), it is also promoted and popularly understood as an authentic, mass-participation, grassroots social movement designed to bring about change. In this way, the Race for the Cure represents a potent site through which to examine relations between and among generosity, citizenship, consumption, and political action in the contemporary United States.[5]

In the pages that follow, I draw on field notes taken and interviews conducted at the Tenth Anniversary National Race for the Cure in Washington, D.C. in June 1999, Komen Foundation publicity materials and annual reports, and mass media coverage of the Race for the Cure and other physical activity-based fundraising events ("thons"). I examine not so much why the Race has gained such appeal, but how this appeal is constituted, deployed, and understood in these venues. Although my analysis is concerned with the popularity of the Race, it does not proceed from the assumption that the Race for the Cure simply attracts the participation of fully-formed subjects and citizens. Rather, it argues that as a fundraising venture, a marketing enterprise, a practice and site of consumption, a physical activity, a collective experience, a mass movement, and a pedagogical tool, the Race for the Cure is a technology of power, or a set of practices and discourses, that has constitutive effects (Foucault, 1979, 1980). Drawing on the work of Michel Foucault (1991) and contemporary theorists of governmentality such as Barbara Cruikshank (1999) and Nikolas Rose (1999), I conceptualize the Race as a mechanism of governance that helps to shape identities (for instance, "the breast cancer survivor"), cultivate political subjects (for instance, "the volunteer citizen"), and produce knowledges and truths about breast cancer and how it might best be responded to. Thus, through the course of my investigations, I explore the productive functions and effects of the Race and examine their articulation to broader questions about the character of contemporary American culture and citizenship.

By analyzing the Race in a broader context, my aim is to highlight the ways in which government, or the conduct of conduct, has in the past two decades become centrally concerned with the production of civically active, self-responsible citizens. While citizenship responsibilities in this configuration are almost always enacted as forms of—or through—consumption, the ideal citizen is not, to quote Nikolas Rose, "the isolated and selfish atom of the free market" (Rose, 1999, p.166). Instead, in the contemporary organization of political responsibility, subjects are addressed and understood as individuals who are responsible for themselves and for others in their "community." Ideally, however, responsibility is not to be demonstrated by the paying of taxes to support social welfare programs, or by the expression of dissent and the making of political demands on behalf of one's community, but through participation in practices of volunteerism and philanthropy. In the words of former President Bill Clinton, Americans must be taught that "to be a good citizen, in addition to going to work and going to school and paying your taxes and obeying the law, you have to be involved in community service" (Hall & Nichols, 1997, p. A12). As I move through my analysis, I pay particular attention the inclusions and exclusions that this new ideal of citizenship performs.

The first part of the essay offers a thick description of the Tenth Anniversary National Race for the Cure and examines the cultural practices, political logics, and social identities that were produced, performed and circulated during this event. Building on Lauren Berlant's (1997) account of the privatization of contemporary American citizenship and the concomitant demonization of collective political agitation, I argue that events such as the Race for the Cure exemplify—and help shape—an emergent form of ideal citizenship. They do so by developing and deploying a remolded view of the United States as a nation whose survival depends on publicly celebrated, personal acts of generosity mediated through—and within—consumer culture.[6] In this configuration, the ideal citizen—corporate or individual—demonstrates commitment to the nation-state by embracing bourgeois, humanistic values such as the need to perform organized, charitable works. Although my argument is indebted to Berlant's insights on the privatization of citizenship and the hegemony of familial life as the "utopian context for citizen aspiration" in the present, it also seeks to extend her analysis (Berlant, 1997, p. 3). It does so by pointing to the capacity of mass participation, charitable events such as the Race for the Cure—organized as they are through individualizing, therapeutic discourse; corporate values; and the displacement of dissent—to offer large groups of people the feeling that can and do make a difference in shaping the organization, direction, aspirations, and ideals of the nation-state in which they live.

The second part of the essay explores the particular significance of physical activity and fitness in these emergent forms of ideal citizenship. Situating the rapid growth of physical activity based-fundraising events in the past two decades in the context of the fitness boom and the ascendance of neoliberal notions of subjectivity, I argue that the popular appeal and cultural significance of these events lie less in their ability to raise money, and more in their capacity to solidify the contemporary articulation of physical health to moral and civic fitness.[7]

THE NATIONAL RACE FOR THE CURE

Celebrating Survivors

On June 6, 1999, I traveled to Washington D.C. to attend the Tenth Anniversary National Race for the Cure. Already the world's largest 5K event, the 1999 Race registered 65,000 runners and broke its own record for participation (52,000) set the previous year. Women with breast cancer and their colleagues, friends, and families traveled from all over the United States to take part, along with thousands of local residents from Maryland, Virginia, and the District itself. Many participants entered as members of sororities and fraternities or as employees running on corporate, government, diplomatic community, and voluntary sector teams.

While the Race itself took runners through the streets of the capital, the rally sight was located on the grounds of the Washington Monument, around which a huge area of grass and footpaths had been cordoned off. Immediately alongside the Monument stood a 150 foot-tall, bright pink, looped ribbon—the now-ubiquitous representation of breast cancer charity and awareness in the United States. The rally stage was situated immediately in front of these monuments; its backdrop consisted of three enormous black and white panels adorned with the names of the Race's numerous corporate sponsors (see fig. 11.1).[8]

The day's events began at 6:30 A.M. with the Sunrise Survivor Celebration. Thousands of participants lined up and filed slowly into the survivors' tent—its entrance marked by a metal archway festooned with bright pink balloons—to help themselves to a "survivors' breakfast" laid on by various corporate sponsors. The breakfast was followed, at 7:30 A.M., by the 10-Star Salute to Survivors' Parade (a feature that is common to Race for the Cure events across the country) and the Pre-Race Rally.

Led by Komen Foundation founder Nancy Brinker, thousands of breast cancer survivors (all sporting bright pink visors and t-shirts to distinguish themselves from other participants) marched down from the tent towards the main stage. Clapping and dancing to the words and music of Gloria Gaynor's "I will survive," they moved along a pathway lined on either side by a cheering crowd of thousands, and the Washington Mall was transformed into an immense sea of pink and white. As the music grew louder and the clapping

Fig. 11.1.   The stage backdrop.

more vigorous, this group of predominantly white, predominantly middle-aged, predominantly middle-class women took their place on the stage, their arms outstretched in the air, waving in time with the music (see fig. 11.2).

Priscilla Mack, cochair of the race, introduced the survivors to the crowd: "I am very proud to be surrounded by a sea of faith. Each survivor has to dig down deep and fight for her life. We applaud you and we stand behind you." Mack then proceeded to ask women who had survived breast cancer for 30 years or more to wave their hands and "be recognized." A handful of women raised their hands. As she counted down through the years until she reached one, the hands increased in number.

Standing close to the stage, I couldn't help but recall Audre Lorde's (1980) well-known entry in the *Cancer Journals* when she points to "socially sanctioned prosthesis" as "another way of keeping women with breast cancer silent and separate from each other" (p. 16). Lorde then asks, "What would happen if an army of one-breasted women descended upon Congress and demanded that the use of carcinogenic, fat-stored hormones in beef-feed be outlawed?" (p. 16). Here was an army of post-mastectomy/lumpectomy women, assembled in the nation's capital, but surely not in a way that Lorde imagined.

This was an intensely moving moment, both for the survivors on the stage and the crowds on the mall, many of whom wore signs on their backs with the names of loved ones who had survived or died from breast cancer. For some women on the stage it was the first time that they had publicly

FIG. 11.2.   Celebrating survivors.

declared their identity as breast cancer survivors (one of my interviewees told
me that it had taken her 2 years to pluck up the courage to attend the Race
as a survivor). For others, the Race marked the first time that they went
hairless in public. Moreover, these women were far from silent and stood as
a powerful symbol of the sheer number of people affected by the disease, as
well as the possibility of triumph over illness. Proud, vibrant, hopeful, and
passionate, clad in brightly colored athletic apparel, and participating in vigorous physical activity to raise money for a worthy cause—these survivors
seemed far removed from the alienated women with cancer of whom Lorde
wrote so eloquently. Their self-presentation also contrasted starkly with the
weak, pale, bedridden, cancer victim that had in prior decades stood as the
dominant embodiment of the disease.

But, as commentators on the AIDS epidemic have argued, the deployment of positive images of disease raises complex political questions. While
AIDS activists recognized early on the importance of challenging the hegemony of pessimistic, often hateful, images of people with AIDS and the
pervasive rhetoric of the "AIDS victim," it was also the case that overly bright
and hopeful configurations of the disease and of survivorship had the capacity
to both undermine demands that the syndrome be taken seriously *and* dissi-
pate the rage of activists that was so crucial to sustaining the AIDS movement. Likewise, the highly orchestrated survivor celebrations that are so central
to the mission and appeal of the Race for the Cure, highlight the individual

strength, courage and perseverance of women with breast cancer and offer an important source of hope and (albeit temporary) community, but they leave little room for the politically-targeted anger that Lorde envisioned. The resulting rhetoric is so upbeat and so optimistic that it is possible to deduce from these events that breast cancer is a fully curable disease from which people no longer die.

At 8.30 A.M. the race began. Led by Al and Tipper Gore (the Honorary Race Chairs) and numerous members of Congress, 65,000 wheelchair racers, runners, and walkers lined up on Constitution Avenue and moved slowly forward as they waited for their turn to cross the starting line. Many participants carried official placards emblazoned with the name of their team ("Bristol Myers Squibb," "AT&T," "Italy," "Myanamar," and "Bangladesh"). These names were called out by the master of ceremonies—to enthusiastic cheers from participants and spectators—as each team crossed the line. Their route took them along Constitution Avenue, around the U.S. Capitol, on to Pennsylvania Avenue, and across the finish line at Federal Triangle. All along the way the sidewalks were packed with hundreds of cheering onlookers, volunteers, and stewards. As participants finished the race by crossing under yet another giant metal archway festooned with pink balloons, they were given bottles of Deer Park spring water and all breast cancer survivors received a special medal donated by Bristol Myers Squibb Oncology.

Back on the grounds of the Monument, sponsoring corporations set up tables from which to distribute "free stuff, including, J. C. Penney water bottles, National Football League key chains, and Ford Motor Company bandanas. Large numbers of people crowded around the stands with their hands in the air, waiting to grab whatever goods were thrown their way. Participants could also spend time in the Mosaic Women's Wellness Tent in which an array of hospitals, cancer clinics, health insurers, alternative treatment centers, pharmaceutical companies, and cancer support groups and charities had tables with information advertising their products and services.

Cures, Corporations, and Consumer-Citizens

During the Pre- and Post-Race Rallies, the crowd heard various speeches from local celebrities, corporate CEOs (pharmaceutical companies that sell cancer products were particularly prominent), Komen Foundation members, and Al and Tipper Gore. We were also introduced to Secretary of State Madeleine Albright and numerous members of Congress, both Republicans and Democrats.

The Pre-Race Rally opened with a mass recital of the Pledge of Allegiance and the words of local radio host Randy Martin who proclaimed, "Today is about celebrating survivors and finding a cure for breast cancer.

And together we can do it!" Although in media coverage and in Komen Foundation press releases, the Race was framed as an opportunity to stress the importance of early detection—via mammograms—in the fight against breast cancer, the day's events focused predominantly on celebrating survivors and reiterating the importance of cure-oriented science underwritten by corporate support and good people with big hearts.[9] Nancy Brinker's hope-filled words were typical:

> Today is a defining moment in the breast cancer movement, because we are making progress. Twenty years ago, when my sister Susan Komen asked me to do something to cure this disease, we couldn't even imagine a day like today. Sixty-five thousand people turning out in our nation's capital to once again race, run, walk, and pray for the cure. It is coming! It is coming!

In a similar vein, a representative from Bristol Myers Squibb Oncology (BMSO) emphasized BMSO's commitment to the cause and its faith in scientific research as the key to finding a cure: "We have come together to form a team to Race for the Cure. Bristol Myers Squibb continues to believe that by working as a team to raise awareness and fund research, a cure for this disease can and will be found." Corporations thus emerged as exemplary citizens, upon whose philanthropic sensibilities the race to find a cure depends. Executive cochair of the race, Priscilla Mack, made this explicit when she declared, "With sponsors like these, we will find a cure!" Similarly, the Volunteer Coordinator for the Komen Foundation told the cheering crowd, "When you think volunteerism, you think reach out and touch someone and I just love that model. That model is the corporate logo of AT&T and they're a national leader in volunteerism."

Faith in the power of positive thinking, the promotion of research into finding a cure for cancer (above research focused on prevention), and the belief that large infusions of money into research can conquer anything have been remarkably durable features of the various manifestations of the alliance against cancer during the twentieth century (Patterson, 1987). The Komen Foundation's emphasis on finding a cure certainly articulates the Race to the national prestige bound up with the fight against cancer in a way that a focus on prevention—and all that it connotes—does not. That is, the search for a "magic bullet" (a specific treatment that will root out and destroy cancerous cells for good) channels research questions and public attention toward individual pathology or deviation from a biological norm and away from social conditions, environmental factors, and other "external" variables that might serve to threaten the nation's image of itself.[10] Economic factors are also relevant here: first, prevention does not promise profits to pharmaceutical companies and the medical industry in the way that early detection, treatments and cures do (although with the recent approval of Tamoxifen as a preventative drug for women at high-risk for breast cancer, this may change); second, the simplifying rhetoric and prestige bound up with the search for a magic bullet (whether intentionally deployed or not) helps maintain public interest in high stakes research and sustain giving to organizations such as the Komen Foundation.

Reconfiguring the "March on Washington"

Perhaps the most interesting speech of the day came from Rey Evans, a founding member of the National Race for the Cure. Evans began her address by misquoting Martin Luther King's most famous words. She said:

> About thirty years ago, the Reverend Martin Luther King stood on this hallowed ground and echoed the phrase "I have a dream." "I have a dream," he said, *"for girls and boys of all colors and shapes and sizes to walk together."* I'm here today . . . to share with you and tell you that Gretchen Poston and Susan Komen had a dream too. That dream is realized today by your presence, by your support, and by your enthusiasm. (italics added)[11]

Evans' misquote reveals as much about the incorporation of the image and legacy of Martin Luther King in the 1990s as it does about the Race for the Cure. Yet the Race for the Cure and the Civil Rights March of 1963 are related. As she transforms the content of King's speech from a concern with violent racism, injustice, and deep-seated inequalities into a multiculturally-informed concern with body shape, size, and image, Evans demonstrates how we rewrite and recreate the past in order to forge a more palatable present. Her words indicate, that is, how mass participation events such as the Race for the Cure might be implicated in the rewriting of history and the reconfiguration of what it means to act collectively and publicly in the present.

Lauren Berlant (1997) has argued that press reports of the thirtieth anniversary of Martin Luther King's March on Washington sanitized an event that in 1963 created panic and threats of racist counterviolence. In retrospect the event was transformed into a "beautifully choreographed mass rationality, an auteurist production of the eloquent, rhetorically masterful, and then martyred King" (p. 187). Thus, the sanitization of the King speech and march can be read as a symptom of nostalgia for a time when protest was apparently more reasonable and orderly. In the present moment, conflict and dissent are typically portrayed by the mainstream media as passions that are dangerous and destabilizing. By focusing on the most disorderly performances of resistance, the media casts public activism (on both the left and the right) as naïve, ridiculous, shallow, and juvenile. Protest has become, to paraphrase Berlant, doubly humiliated, both silly and dangerous. It subtracts personhood from activists, making their gestures of citizenship seem proof that their very claims are illegitimate. In contrast, personal witnessing about trauma or injury—a defining feature of the Race for the Cure if we think back to the survivor celebration—has become highly valued political testimony. What we learn from the rewriting of King's march and the Race for the Cure is that the only legitimate way Americans can claim both rights and mass sympathy is to demonstrate not panic, anger, or demand, but ethical serenity, patriotism, and proper deference (Berlant, 1997).

Indeed, anger and dissent of any kind were stark in their absence at the National Race for the Cure. There were no questions asked about—nor even any mention of—persistently high rates of breast cancer in the United States and worldwide. Although the participation of thousands of survivors should be indicative of these rates, their presence was celebrated as evidence of the promise of individual struggle against the disease rather than of a social/medical crisis that kills 40,000 women, in the United States alone, each year. Survivors, in other words, stood as symbols of hope for the future, rather than of urgency in the present. Differences of age, race, and class in mortality rates—for example, the fact that although breast cancer mortality rates dropped slightly among all women in the 1990s, rates among African American women continue to rise—were also ignored or subsumed under the banner of the "survivor." Moreover, no demands for action—beyond calls for continued participation in the Race for the Cure—were made of the various representatives of the cancer industries or the state, nor indeed of participants in the Race.

It could be argued, of course, that the Race for the Cure is designed to raise money (over $2 million, in this instance) and celebrate survivorship, not to provide a platform for the expression of dissent as Audre Lorde had envisioned. It could also be argued that there is a place in the United States for—indeed the United States *needs*—such celebratory and harmonious public gatherings. But to do so would be to ignore the implication of the Race in a broader war of position over what constitutes "the problem of breast cancer" in the present moment and over what kinds of actions and identities are legitimate or effective in bringing about social change. It would be to ignore, in other words, how the Race is implicated in the legitimation of particular forms of publicity and participation and the marginalization and closing down of others.

In order to explore these issues further, I want to turn to the pairing of the giant pink ribbon with the Washington Monument as a symbol through which to think about the articulation of breast cancer philanthropy to proper citizenship in the present moment.

THE RIBBON AND THE MONUMENT, OR,
THE POLITICS OF INNOCENCE

Although the Washington Mall is the site of a particularly circumscribed narrative of citizenship and nationalism with its white monuments and great man statues, it is also a primary location for national protest. In this context, the Mall is most usefully understood as an index of American history: the celebrations and demonstrations that take place in its shadow are events that both reflect and reproduce particular periods and versions of the nation's history (Sturken, 1997).[12] Thus, the placing of the ribbon alongside the Monument—a place of tribute to the nation's founder, an emblem of freedom and justice, and the most symbolic national locale of the United States— immediately establishes the Race in particular, and breast cancer fundraising more generally, as sites through which contemporary versions of America and American citizenship are produced and enacted.

The ribbon and the monument, side by side, represent an alliance between the nation-state, the nonprofit sector, and the corporate world (for whom the pink ribbon has become a staple of cause-related marketing). The ribbon: pink, round, feminine, and innocent, a national advertisement for grassroots and corporate activism and the "aware" philanthropist as ideal citizen. The monument: an emblem of the strong, yet compassionate and accommodating nation-state—a state that is at its best when collaborating with the private sector. Together they form a quintessential representation and pedagogical tool for the postwelfare reform era, in which well-intentioned, charitable consumer-citizens must share the burden of governing and the fulfillment of their needs with the state, the market, and the nonprofit sector.

One irony of these national symbols is that they permit and encourage national identification and inclusion at the same time that they deny the unequal material conditions and violence of everyday life under capitalism. In other words, the ribbon-wearing version of citizenship cannot accommodate recognition of other socioeconomic or environmental conditions that shape the history and experience of breast cancer in the United States and beyond. In addition to denying material conditions, the ribbon, the Komen Foundation, and the Race for the Cure symbolize and help produce a form of ideal citizenship that gains virtue and elicits identification and support precisely because of its innocence (and, perhaps, banality). Drawing on Barbara Christian's (1999) formulation, innocence is invoked here in a double sense to mean both prepolitical (as in the innocence of childhood) and a refusal to know. Christian argued that to be innocent or to refuse to know is to be unethical. Yet, I would add, it is precisely a refusal to know that has itself been taken up as an ethical practice in the government of the self in the latter part of the twentieth century.

It is not so much that we live in an era marked by a refusal to know anything, but rather that there has been a shift in the appropriate *focus* for knowing. That is, in the age of intimate citizenship (Berlant's term), in which politics via mass anger and disruption is dismissed as silly, futile, and even dangerous, an ethic of self-government has emerged that asks people to turn their critical selves inward, to question and work upon their psychic health and their self-esteem. Individual fulfillment and an ethical life are to be achieved through these styles of self-management, as well as through the work that individuals do in their communities. However, being an active, virtuous, and "community-minded" citizen does not mean starting with a view of the United States as a space of struggle violently divided along lines of difference. Instead, the preferred ideal is to work upon one's self and one's community based upon a vision of America as a classless, colorblind, ungendered nation whose survival depends on personal acts of volunteerism, charity, and unpaid service to one's fellow citizens. This is most definitely *not* an ideal, however, that incorporates the informal networks of support and care around which poor, urban and rural communities are often organized and on which they frequently depend, *as* volunteerism. So despite the exclusions performed by the logic of citizenship-through-volunteerism, it is precisely the well-intentionedness and apparent harmlessness of this logic that makes it so hard to contest.

Notwithstanding the absence of dissent that characterizes the Race for the Cure, the popularity of this event does depend on its offering large groups of people the feeling that they *can* make a difference. As one of my interviewees, a 51-year-old Army officer and breast cancer survivor explained:

> It gives people a way to actively show their support to find a cure. When a person just donates money through the mail, they are unable to "touch" the results of their contribution. With the race, the supporters can be right there with the survivors who represent the positive aspects of their support through contributions. They can see the result of the research and new drugs—mothers, grandmothers, and daughters who are still alive to share memories with their families.

The growth of the Race for the Cure has also coincided with a considerable increase in federal dollars for breast cancer research and a concomitant explosion in media coverage of a range of topics related to the disease. Thus, whatever radical critics might think of the kinds of change that have been won, or the way the money has been spent, participants in the Race for the Cure can see the tangible effects of their participation and their impact on the state.

The irony of the turn to volunteerism and philanthropy in the wake of Clinton's declaration that the era of big government is at an end, is, in the case of breast cancer at least, that it is precisely a profusion of breast cancer-directed charity that has helped to bring the state further into the funding and regulation of the breast cancer industry.[13] While this might appear as yet another example of the paradoxical nature of the workings of neoliberalism—and I think it is—the Komen Foundation and the Race for the Cure can also be read as quintessential modes and effects of neoliberal governmentality (if we accept that such paradoxes are inherent to its workings) (Burchell, Gordon, & Miller, 1991). While the Komen Foundation refuses to hold the state responsible for guaranteeing certain rights and needs to its citizens in the form of universal health care, for example, it is committed to the state as a crucial vehicle in the "elusive search for a cure" and for creating and maintaining the conditions in which free enterprise (individual and corporate) and the market for breast cancer can flourish.

AMERICAN FITNESS

The contemporary association of moral worth with both participation in volunteerism and self-responsibility for one's health and bodily maintenance converges in and is exemplified by the proliferation of physical activity-based fundraising events, or "thons," in the past 15 years. It is now virtually unheard of for a participatory sports event not to be linked to a charitable cause. Almost all of the major health charities organize national networks of exercise-based events—including walkathons, marathons, bikeathons, danceathons, aerobathons, and hopathons—and many smaller organizations, both health-related and otherwise, do the same.

The historical roots of exercise-based fundraising events in the United States are entangled with the struggle to forge international cooperation in the post-World War II era and with issues of "third world" development. During the 1950s, in response to high rates of poverty and malnutrition throughout the world, but especially in developing countries, the Food and Agricultural Organization of the United Nations launched the International Freedom from Hunger Campaign.[14] As part of this operation, member nations were asked to form National Committees of the Freedom from Hunger Campaign. In Western Europe, these Committees launched the "Walk for Development" as a strategy to raise money and public awareness of poverty and malnutrition. Eventually the idea for the walks spread to Canada, and in 1961 President John F. Kennedy's call for the development of youth leadership led to the establishment of an American affiliate—the American Freedom from Hunger Foundation (AFFHF) (M. Seltzer, personal communication, October 1999).

The AFFHF's mission was to encourage volunteerism and educate the American public about issues surrounding hunger. The AFFHF staged its first Walk for Development in 1968, and within a year 100 walks had raised over $800,000 and involved more than half a million people in 16 states across the United States. Between 1969 and 1970, 400 walks raised a further half million dollars and gained front-page attention in the *New York Times* and *Reader's Digest*. The Walks for Development had three main purposes: to raise funds for international development, to educate the public about the causes and effects of poverty and malnutrition, and to develop youth leadership (young people from junior high school through to college organized the walks). According to former AFFHF officer Michael Seltzer, Hunger Hikes and Walks for Development were in many ways different from the thons of today. Operating under a donor choice format, the money raised often went to controversial causes such as National Welfare Rights and the America Indian Movement, and their public education often included radical critiques of structural inequality, racism, and colonialism. In addition, these walks were the means through which many youth became connected to the anti-Vietnam war movement (M. Seltzer, personal communication, October 1999).

Seltzer claims that the professionalization and marketization of fundraising events was the driving force in the gradual dissolution of Hunger Hikes and Walks for Development (personal communication, October 1999). The March of Dimes was the first to copy the idea when in 1970 it launched its first walkathons (in San Antonio, TX and Columbus, OH), now known as WalkAmerica. Although walkathons became increasingly common through the 1970s, it was not until the mid-1980s that other exercise-based events proliferated.[15]

In order to understand the conditions that made the proliferation and cultural valence of thons possible, it is also necessary to consider the emergence, in the early 1980s, of what became known as the "fitness boom"—the turn to physical activity on the part of millions of previously sedentary middle- and upper-class Americans and the appearance of numerous new fitness-related products on the United States market. The beginning of the boom coincided, of course, with the ascendance of Reaganism and the engineering of a national fantasy by which the effects of economic and social conditions (poverty and welfare "dependency") were blamed on individual inadequacies or failings and the breakdown of the family. As scholars of this era have suggested, the "national preoccupation with the body" (Alan Ingham's term), the rise of lifestyle politics, and the fitness boom can be understood both as ways to circumvent anxieties about the crisis of the "welfare state" and the family *and* as appeals to and celebrations of individualism and free will that were so central to the logic of Reaganism (Cole & Hribar, 1995; Howell, 1991; Ingham, 1985; Jeffords, 1994).

As individuals were asked to take responsibility for their well-being and improve the quality of their lives, the film industry bombarded the American public with images promoting the hard and disciplined body, the marketing strategies of apparel companies like Nike and Reebok captured national attention, the figure of Rambo became an icon of national self-esteem, TV fitness gurus "stepped" into our living rooms, and the consumer market became flooded with a multitude of health and fitness products and services (Howell, 1991; Jeffords, 1994). In sum, the ethos of self-betterment and quality-of-life through consumption became the normative code of conduct—and therefore that by which bodies were judged, celebrated, or condemned—for everyday life in America (Cole & Hribar, 1995).

Whereas in prior decades, fitness had been associated with militarism, anticommunism, crises of masculinity, and competitive sport, in the 1980s, the body became at once a status symbol and an emblem of one's purchasing power, moral worth, and personal discipline. This relationship was induced not simply by the marketing and consumption of fitness products, but was a strategy of neoliberal governmentality. Individuals were encouraged and rewarded for adopting—or penalized for failing to adopt—strategies for biological self-betterment, by networks of government that sought to reduce health costs and encourage self-responsibility by educating the public against bodily neglect or abuse and by promoting the body as a locus of pleasure, self-expression, and personal fulfillment (Featherstone, 1991; Howell, 1991; Ingham 1985).

The consumer imperatives and moral codes associated with the fitness boom find clear expression in the discourses and practices of healthy individualism bound up with the Race for the Cure. Yet it would be a misleading to suggest that the technologies of the self encouraged and reflected by the thon in the present moment are no different than those that emerged during the Reagan era. Instead, the thon was promoted and understood in the 1990s through the post-Reaganite popular discourse which claims that people "need to find fulfillment by giving to others" and that "just being rich doesn't quite cut it anymore." The thon has come of age, in other words, at a time when the mass media devotes considerable attention to the giving practices of the very wealthy and the "average American." In these narratives (which tend not to extend their critique to questions of corporate tax breaks, deep-seated inequalities of income, or other girdles of global capitalism), massive accumulation of wealth accompanied by what is perceived as inadequate giving is condemned as crass and greedy, and the national character and spirit of America is judged on the grounds of the giving practices of its middle-class and wealthy citizens. At the same time, to exercise solely for one's own pleasure or health, or for purely aesthetic ends, is framed as narcissistic.

In an article for *Runner's World*, for instance, Lisa Hamm-Greenawalt (1999), a competitive runner, described how she had entered her first Race for the Cure because she "wanted to try and run a strong 5K race" in order to launch her racing season. But, as Hamm-Greenawalt took her place at the starting line, it "finally dawned on" her than "this race meant a lot more than PR" (p. 28). Her mother had died of breast cancer 6 years previously and she describes the anger she felt at herself for not wearing a sign "In memory of mom," for not finding sponsors to raise money, and for not "doing more" for the cause (p. 28). Hamm-Greenawalt frames her experience as a parable about self-absorption, enlightenment, and redemption: she concludes the piece with a promise to "bring a different attitude to the event" in the following year by recruiting participants. Moreover, she declares, "Instead of focusing on PRs (personal records), I'll use the Race for the Cure to focus on joining my sisters to combat this cancer that has robbed us of too much, this killer that puts our own lives in danger" (p. 28). A *Fitness Runner* article on the Race for the Cure and thons in general comes to a similar conclusion: "You get to feel good about yourself the whole time because you're not only (selfishly) running to get fit but you're (altruistically) helping others—you just can't beat that deal" (Hagman, 1999, p. 22).

In contrast to the elitist charity galas of the upper classes, thons are represented in media discourse as "athletic grass-roots events" that are accessible and affordable (Williams, 1995, p. 32). Patricia Cesar, vice president of Cesar & Washburn, a management and development consulting firm for foundations and nonprofit organizations, describes them as follows:

> The walks also open up your ranks of supporters of your organization. It's a way to get everyone involved: celebrities, adults, children, families. Besides, people are tired of the $500-a-plate rubber chicken dinners, and these marathon events have inspired a whole new way of giving. (Williams, 1995, p. 32)

In a similar vein, Marty Liquori, the national chairman of the Leukemia Society's marathon training program (which raised $38 million in 1998), told the *New York Times* that "it also gives those who can't make a financial contribution an opportunity to make a contribution of their time" (quoted in Williams, p. 32). The piece omits to note, however, that most of these events charge an entrance fee—which in the case of the Race for the Cure stood at $25 in 1999 (p. 32).

In an interview with the *Chicago Tribune*, Nancy Brinker, founder of the Komen Foundation, discussed her reasons for using a running race to raise money and awareness:

> Sports events were becoming very big in the early 80s. People were focusing on fitness, and I felt that there was so much fear associated with even discussing this disease that we had to create an environment that was fun, that was uplifting, that was empowering. (Libman, 1996, p. xiii–3)

Brinker's idea was to "make people feel a sense of community and be able to share their fears and whatever they were feeling" (p. xiii–3). When only 700 people turned out for the first race in Dallas in 1983, several people tried to convince Brinker that the event did not have growth potential and that she should continue with the more traditional events that were raising money. "But," Brinker said, "they weren't reaching the masses of people and they weren't providing education or helping to build a grass-roots organization so we could have a real political impact some day and get some money for research" (p. xiii–3). In popular discourse, then, thons are portrayed as technologies of democracy and empowerment, as vital tools in grassroots efforts to improve American society.

Moreover, as venues for charitable action, thons are portrayed as personal and humanizing, in contrast to what are implied to be more alienating, impersonal forms of giving. Many charities, for example, offer the opportunity for participants to express or forge personal connections to people with disease. As part of the Leukemia Foundation's Team in Training program, runners are paired with one or more leukemia patients and wear wristbands bearing their names during the race. As *Fitness Runner* put it, "You're not just running for research and education. You're running for somebody. . . . Many participants get to know their Honored Patient, and more than one has said that gets them across the finish line" (Hagman, 1999, p. 22). Similarly, in the Race for the Cure, participants wear pink signs on their backs with the names of either breast cancer survivors or loved ones lost to breast cancer. Because of the physical nature of the thon, moreover, participation is understood to be more proactive, or activist, than "simply" donating money. "The days of sitting back writing a check and sending it to a post office box or going door to door with a canister are bygone," said Dwayne Howell, president of the Leukemia Society of America (Williams, 1995, p. 32). The citizenship value of any charitable act is therefore increased when this act entails publicly performed physical exertion, while armchair philanthropy, or what might also be understood as anonymous or private giving, is rendered less valid.

Conclusion

As a practice that both elicits and shapes the physical, moral, and civic capacities of its participants, the Race for the Cure is an ideal technology for the production of proper American citizens. Given that the success of any particular thon is measured by its capacity to gain individual physical commitment from its participants, who in turn must secure individual promises to donate money, it is not surprising that the thon emerged as a new site for mass public participation in the 1980s—a decade that has witnessed the production of a constant flow of techniques, tools, and strategies designed to elicit self-responsibility and responsibility to others mediated not through the state, or through political agitation, but through the "freedom" of personal philanthropy and volunteerism.

In the specific case of the Race for the Cure, we can see how the therapeutic discourse of survivorship together with acts of personal and corporate giving come to be mobilized and deployed as forms of collective, political action, even as dissent or criticism of dominant socio-economic relations is marginalised. Further, as the belief that America's survival depends on publicly celebrated, personal acts of generosity mediated through—and within—consumer culture has attained hegemonic status, it becomes ever more difficult to think critically about such events and their place in U.S. culture. This is partly because the dominant brands of civic participation and belonging currently on offer appear entirely innocent, but it is also because they have been mobilized to appear less remote and divisive and more natural and authentic than those brands of citizenship against which they are defined. In this context, the challenge is to make visible the politics of philanthropy and volunteerism and to agitate against the narrow version of citizenship and American life on which their valence rests.[16]

NOTES

1. At a Midwestern university, shortly after the shootings at Columbine High School, members of the College Republicans handed out light blue ribbons to signify "awareness" that "guns don't kill people, people kill people."

2. Examples of such policy include the creation of the Breast Cancer Research stamp in 1998 (the first stamp in U.S. history to be sold at a higher price than that of a regular stamp in order to raise money), and the introduction of a tax check-off for breast cancer research on federal income tax returns.

3. Seven hundred women took part in the first Race held in Dallas, Texas in October 1983. By 1999, the Race was the nation's largest 5K series, with races in 99 cities across the United States. Between 1997 and 1998 alone, participation grew 44%. Significantly, the second largest 5K event in the U.S. is the Revlon Run/Walk which also raises money for breast (and ovarian) cancer (Kulman, 1997).

4. The 1999 Komen Race for the Cure series was "presented nationally" by J. C. Penney and "sponsored nationally" by American Airlines, Ford Motor Company, Johnson & Johnson, the National Football League, New Balance Athletic Shoes, Pier 1 Imports, and Tropicana Pure Premium orange juice.

5. For an analysis that compares the Race for the Cure to other collective responses to the breast cancer epidemic, see Klawiter (1999).

6. My project is not meant to be critical or dismissive of volunteerism and philanthropy per se and recognizes that nonprofits and foundations are central components of the American health and welfare systems. Rather, my concern is with the ways in which certain technologies of volunteerism and philanthropy get taken up and deployed and how they enable or constrain particular forms of social belonging or action.

7. My approach to these issues is indebted to the work of Michel Foucault (1979, 1980, 1991) and writers who have taken up his work to theorize questions of freedom, neoliberalism, and citizenship (Barry, Osborne & Rose, 1996; Cruikshank, 1999; Gordon, 1991; Rose, 1999).

8. Race sponsors included: Bristol Myers Squibb Oncology, Freddie Mac, Safeway, Konica, Schering-Plough, Washington Area Ford Dealers, Motorola, Genentech Biooncology, Chevy Chase Bank, Microsoft, The Fitness Company, Papa John's Pizza, Meridian Moving and Storage, Prudential, Monsanto, Mosaic Foundation, Nestle, Fluor Corporation, Les Halles Brasserie, the *Washington Post*, Soft Rock 97.1, *Washingtonian* magazine, *Families* magazine, *Metro* magazine, *Latina Style* magazine, *Shape (Jump)* magazine, Next Generation Network, WTOP 107.7FM Top News Nonstop, NBC television (D.C.), Eli Lilly, Fresh Fields Whole Foods Market, Nordstrom, SalomonSmithBarney, Kodak, Target, Amgen, ABB, CNG, First Union, Capital One, The Ann Hand Collection, El Paso Energy, Gateway Computers, Greenberg Traurig—Attorneys at Law, Marmot Foundation, Zeneca Pharmaceuticals, Fannie Mae Foundation, Open MRI, BlueCross BlueShield, NFL, Proctor and Gamble, Merck, Hecht's, Union Pacific Corporation, International Paper, Pfizer, Deer Park Spring Water, Romano's Macaroni Grill, Tanaka Memorial Foundation, and Precision Marketing Inc.

9. The focus on finding a cure for breast cancer, rather than on prevention, has been subject to critique from numerous breast cancer activists (see Batt, 1994; Brady, 1991; Solomon, 1992). Many of these critics also express doubt about the usefulness of mammograms in the fight against cancer and point out, among other things, that mammograms are not preventive but detective technologies and that the emphasis on mammograms as preventive is deceptive, and even dangerous (some scientists/activists argue that too many mammograms can actually cause cancer). Mammograms, they argue, are beneficial mainly to older women who have less dense breast tissue, and to the manufacturers of machines and X-ray films, many of whom are major sponsors of the Komen Foundation (for example, General Electric and Kodak).

10. For evidence of the silence of the Komen Foundation on the relationship between environmental factors and breast cancer incidence, see their website (www.komen.org); Nancy Brinker's book (1995), *The Race is One Step at a Time*; and the Foundation's triannual newsletter Frontline (recent issues are available on their website). The Komen Foundation's primary agenda is to encourage women to undertake early detection (via mammography, self-exam, and regular check-ups) and, more recently, risk evaluation.

11. Evans was presumably referring to the part of King's speech that went as follows: "I have a dream that one day, down in Alabama, with its vicious racists, with its governor having his lips dripping with the words of interposition and nullification; one day right down in Alabama little black boys and black girls will be able to join hands with little white boys and white girls as sisters and brothers." Gretchen Poston was White House Social Secretary in the Carter administration. She was also one of the founders (along with Marilyn Quayle and *Washington Post* fashion editor Nina Hyde) of the National Race for the Cure. Poston died in 1992 after a second bout with breast cancer.

12. Marita Sturken (1997) makes a similar point regarding the Vietnam War Memorial and the displays of the AIDS Quilt on the Washington Mall.

13. It is important to note here that debates about funding for breast cancer research, screening, and education do not map neatly or directly onto debates about "big government" or balanced budgets. Since the launch of the War on Cancer in 1971, a vast majority of politicians from across the political spectrum have consistently supported high levels of state spending on cancer research. Moreover, such spending has generally found favor with the American public. Although the consensus in favor of big spending on cancer has remained remarkably strong over the past thirty years, under current political conditions, almost any initiative that involves federal expenditures must address the now equally strong consensus against "big government" and "big spending." This is increasingly true even of those initiatives—such as cancer research—that have traditionally escaped designation as "wasteful government programs." Thus, as I have argued elsewhere (King, 2000), federal policy on breast cancer that requires increased public spending and which is not part of a public-private partnership, must be couched in the language of "government for good" in order to disarticulate such spending from that which is understood to be wasteful. On the other hand, federal breast cancer policy designed to incite personal generosity in the American public—such as that which created a fundraising stamp for breast cancer research—is justified and celebrated for its recognition that voluntary, philanthropic solutions to America's problems are inherently preferable to those that require state intervention, management, or financing.

14. This history of the Freedom from Hunger marches and the rise of the thon is indebted to Michael Seltzer, a researcher in the Nonprofit Management Program at New School University, New York. Seltzer worked as East Coast Field Director of the Freedom from Hunger Foundation between 1969 and 1972 and was generous in sharing with me his understanding of this history.

15. Examples of prominent 'thons' include the American Cancer Society's Relay for Life (est. 1985) and Making Strides Against Breast Cancer (est. 1993); the American Heart Association's Jump Rope for Heart (est. 1979) and Hoops for Heart (est. 1992–1993); the American Lung Association's Big Ride Across America (est. 1998); the Leukemia Society of America's Team in Training (est. 1988); Palotta Teamworks (a for-profit special events company); Tanqueray American AIDSRides (est. 1993); the Avon 3-Day (a 3-day walk for breast cancer held in major U.S. cities) (est. 1998); and the March of Dimes' WalkAmerica (est. 1970).

16. My sincere thanks go to all the participants in the "Foucault Reading Group" for their commentaries on this and other essays over the past two years. I am also grateful to Sonya Michel for her extensive critique of earlier versions of this chapter.

REFERENCES

Altman, R. (1996). *Waking up/fighting back: The politics of breast cancer.* Boston: Little, Brown.

Barry, A., Osborne, T., & Rose, N. (Eds.). (1996). *Foucault and political reason: Liberalism, neo-liberalism and rationalities of government.* Chicago: University of Chicago Press.

Batt, S. (1994). *Patient no more: The politics of breast cancer.* Charlottetown, Canada: gynergy books.

Belkin, L. (1996, December 23). How breast cancer became this year's hot charity. *The New York Times Magazine,* pp. 40–46, 52, 55–56.

Berlant, L. (1997). *The Queen of America goes to Washington City: Essays on sex and citizenship.* Durham, NC: Duke University Press.

Brady, J. (Ed.). (1991). *1 in 3: Women with cancer confront an epidemic.* San Francisco: Cleis Press.

Burchell, G., Gordon, C., & Miller, P. (Eds.) (1991). *The Foucault effect: Studies in governmentality.* Chicago: University of Chicago Press.

Carter, D. (1997, August 5). Running and swimming and cycling for their lives. *Denver Post,* p. 195.

Cartwright, L. (1998). Community and the public body in breast cancer media activism. *Cultural Studies, 12*(2), 117–138.

Christian, B. (1999). The crime of innocence. In D. Batstone & E. Mendieta (Eds.), *The good citizen* (pp. 51–64). New York: Routledge.

Cole, C., & Hribar, A. (1995). Celebrity Feminism: *Nike Style.* Post-Fordism, transcendence, and consumer power. *Sociology of Sport Journal, 12,* 347–369.

Cruikshank, B. (1999). *The will to empower: Democratic citizens and other subjects.* Ithaca, NY: Cornell University Press.

Davidson, J. (1997, May). Cancer sells. *Working Woman,* pp. 36–39.

Featherstone, M. (1991). *Consumer culture and postmodernism.* Newbury Park, CA: Sage.

Foucault, M. (1979). *Discipline and punish: The birth of the prison.* New York: Vintage.

Foucault, M. (1980). *The history of sexuality. Vol. 1: An introduction.* New York: Vintage.

Foucault, M. (1991). Governmentality. In G. Burchell, C. Gordon, & P. Miller (Eds.), *The Foucault effect. Studies in governmentality* (pp. 87–104). Chicago: University of Chicago Press.

Goldman, D. (1997, November 3). Illness as metaphor. *Adweek,* p. 70.

Gordon, C. (1991). Governmental rationality: An introduction. In G. Burchell, C. Gordon, & P. Miller (Eds.), *The Foucault effect. Studies in governmentality* (pp. 1–52). Chicago: University of Chicago Press.

Hagman, B. (1999, Fall). A higher purpose. *Fitness Runner,* pp. 16–17, 20, 22.

Hall, M. & Nichols, B. (1997, April 25) Clinton: Citizenship means giving. *USA Today,* p. A12.

Hamm-Greenawalt, L. (1999, May). Cause and effect. *Runner's World*, p. 28.

Howell, J. (1991). "A revolution in motion": Advertising and the politics of nostalgia. *Sociology of Sport Journal, 8*, 258–271.

Ingham, A. (1985). From public issue to personal trouble: Well-being and the fiscal crisis of the state. *Sociology of Sport Journal, 2*, 43–55.

Jeffords, S. (1994). *Hard bodies: Hollywood masculinity in the Reagan era*. New Brunswick, NJ: Rutgers University Press.

King, S. (2000). *Civic fitness: Breast cancer, philanthropy, and new technologies of ethical citizenship*. Unpublished doctoral dissertation, University of Illinois at Urbana-Champaign.

Klawiter, M. (1999). Racing for the cure, walking women, and toxic touring: Mapping cultures of action within the Bay Area terrain of breast cancer. *Social Problems, 46*(1), 104–126.

Komen Foundation. (1997). *Our biggest commitment* (Annual report). Dallas, TX: Susan G. Komen Breast Cancer Foundation.

Kulman, L. (1997, June 9). Stumbling toward the finish line. *U.S. News and World Report*, p. 13.

Libman, N. (1996, May 26). Leading the way. *Chicago Tribune*, p. xiii–3.

Loose, C. (1999, June 6). Race raises money, awareness and questions. *Washington Post*, pp. C–1, C–4.

Lorde, A. (1980). *The cancer journals*. San Francisco: Spinster's Ink.

Rose, N. (1999). *Powers of freedom: Reframing political thought*. Cambridge, UK: Cambridge University Press.

Patterson, J. (1987). *The dread disease*. Cambridge, MA: Harvard University Press.

Solomon, A. (1992). The politics of breast cancer. *Camera Obscura, 29*, 157–177.

Stabiner, K. (1997). *To dance with the devil: The new war on breast cancer*. New York: Delacorte Press.

Sturken, M. (1997). *Tangled memories: The Vietnam War, the AIDS epidemic, and the politics of remembering*. Berkeley, CA: University of California Press.

Williams, L. (1995, May 7). New charity strategy: Get up and go. *New York Times*, p. 1–32.

Yúdice, G. (1995). The vicissitudes of civil society. *Social Text, 45*(14)4, 1–25.

Chapter 12

God Games and Governmentality

Civilization II and Hypermediated Knowledge

Shawn Miklaucic

In this chapter, I take up computer games as a key site of cultural production. Specifically, I shall examine a genre of strategic computer simulations, often referred to as "god games", that has gained popularity in recent years. Computer and video entertainment sales were estimated at $9.4 billion in 2001 ($6 billion coming from software), up over 40% from $6.6 billion in 2000 (NPD, 2002). While recent media coverage has often represented computer gaming as consisting almost solely of violent first-person shooter games like *Quake* and *Doom* (titles made infamous by the Columbine shootings), these games actually make up a relatively small percentage of sales. In 2001, only one of the top twenty selling games was a first-person shooter, while twelve were god games of the sort this chapter examines (Walker, 2002).

God games include the Maxis corporation's incredibly popular line of Sim games, such as *SimCity*, *SimLife*, and more recently, *The Sims*, along with historical strategy simulations such as *Age of Empires*, *Caesar*, and *Civilization*. Such games range in subject matter from urban planning, economics, biology and ancient empires to human history and civilization itself. First, I provide an introduction to "god games," using *SimCity 3000* and *The Sims* as representative examples. Next, I discuss two concepts, *hypermediation* and *governmentality*, which I believe are central to understanding how these games function. Finally, I apply these concepts to the historical simulation *Civilization II*. This analysis draws on Tony Bennett's application of Foucault in *The Birth of the Museum* (1995). Relying on Foucault's notion of governmental rationality, or governmentality, I argue that god games such as *Civilization II* seem, at first glance, to model an outmoded form of state centered political rationality that has been replaced by less centralized, more diffuse forms of governmentality. However, I shall argue that *Civilization II* (and other games within this genre) contains a contradictory tension between its content, which is State-centered, and its form, which can be seen as a model of and tool for governmental rationality.

In more general terms, I hope that my analysis will show the importance and relevance of computer games to the study of popular culture. Popular representations of computer and video games have tended narrowly to define the medium by focusing almost solely on violent, arcade style shoot-'em-ups, where the player navigates complex virtual spaces and fires weapons at virtual enemies. This type of computer game, referred to as a "first-person shooter," is typified by titles such as *Doom, Quake, Unreal,* and *Half-Life* (see fig. 12.1). By focusing on strategic simulation games, I hope to show the variety and complexity in mass-market computer entertainment software, and provide one possible model for their analysis.

On another level, I examine the ways in which god games can be seen as examples of totalizing thought, with an eye towards several questions regarding current thinking on the concept of totality. Is the postmodern critique of totalizing thought valid, or can certain forms of totalization be beneficial and, as Jameson (1991) would argue, necessary? I believe the popularity of god games stems from what I would call a "will to totalization." Just as Jameson (1992) reads conspiracy narratives as an unconscious attempt to make sense of the vastly complex webs of social relations we inhabit, I believe

FIG. 12.1.   Graphs and screen shot from *Civilization II.*

these games are another example of the popular desire for sense-making at the macroscopic level. And while narrative itself tends to privilege the individual as an agent, I believe simulations provide certain aesthetic tools with which larger scale "narratives" of human relations can be wrought.

SIMULATING CULTURE

In the early 1990s, Maxis released *SimCity*, a game that would ultimately define a large segment of the gaming industry. The popularity of this and other similar games that followed was enormous and widespread. A later Maxis game, *SimLife*, models Darwinian evolution, allowing players to manipulate populations of plants and animals as they interact, crossbreed, and evolve over generations, and has been used in schools to interactively teach evolution. *SimCity* was not really so much a game as an interactive toy. There was no winning or losing, per se, nor did one play against an opponent. Instead, the game casts the player in the role of "SimMayor" of a fledgling city. The goal of the simulation is to manage an urban environment and allow it to flourish. *SimCity* has gone through several sequels and releases, and in 1999 was the top-selling computer game. A piece in *Time* detailed its appeal and influence:

> This week in Washington seventh- and eighth-graders from across the country will compete in the finals of the annual future-cities contest, judged by a panel of engineers. The contest's software of choice? Sim City, of course. "They should introduce this game to all classrooms," says Hayes Lord, a New York City planner.
>
> Lord's boss, Rudy Giuliani, would no doubt agree. He was in his first term when he found his son Andrew, then 7, playing Sim City. Andrew had placed police stations on every street corner. The crime rate was zero. Giuliani Sr. watched, fascinated, and began making suggestions on taxation, zoning, and so forth. Finally, Andrew wheeled around. "Dad," he told the mayor of New York, "this is *my* city." (Taylor, 1999)

One begins *SimCity* with the map of an empty, undeveloped and unpopulated landscape. By zoning sections of the map for different uses (residential, commercial, industrial), building initial infrastructures (roads, power plants), and then turning the simulation "on," a player begins to see tiny signs of movement and growth—residential zones begin sprouting houses, factories pop up in industrial areas, and tiny "sims" begin moving about the streets. The city develops based on various decisions the player makes—raising and lowering taxes, building various public services and works such as water lines, power grids, police stations, museums, parks, schools, and public transportation. The appeal of the game comes from the immersive quality of the interaction between the player and the ever-changing city. If taxes are too high, industries and commerce begin to stagnate, but if they are too low, the public coffers dry up. The player has no direct control over the population of sims, but influences them indirectly through controlling the shape and processes of the environment they inhabit. As populations grow, problems constantly arise, and gameplay becomes a constant juggling act of dealing with the next problem—new developments need power and water; rising crime rates require more police; the sims are unhappy because of pollution and trash piling up around them; jobs are available but the transportation is lacking and housing scarce.

One important approach to such simulations consists of critiquing the ways in which the simulation alters or fails to represent certain aspects of what it simulates. For instance, Julian Bleeker (Turkle, 1995) takes up the issue of race, which in earlier versions of the game is nonexistent as a category in relation to the city's population. He points to this key erasure of race as a category in the game, despite its presence on the margins of the text, and reads in the game a "systematic denial of racial conflict as a factor in urban life. SimCity 2000 associates riots with high heat, high crime, and high unemployment, 'all desperate allusions to life in the inner city ghetto. But race is not mentioned'" (in Turkle 1995, p. 73). Similarly, one can look at the *Time* example of Mayor Guliani and his son and realize that the solution to crime in the world of *SimCity* is largely one to be solved by more police. More complex explanations are often elided in favor of easily representable cures.

My analysis here, however, will focus on how simulation games subscribe to the Foucauldian logic of governmental rationality as it applies to the disciplining and differentiation of populations. Looking at *SimCity* through Bennett's application of Foucault's work to museums yields several useful insights. Foucault's work documents what can be called new modes of discipline and surveillance of populations. Governmentality is central to understanding museums and, I would argue, simulations like *SimCity*. The goal of the game is remarkably similar to the goals of governance that Bennett describes: to reduce ungovernable, undifferentiated peoples to a controllable, differentiated, demographically, and statistically defined *population* (Bennett, 1995, p. 62). The exhibitionary complex of the modern museum, in Bennett's words, seeks "not to map the social body in order to know the populace by rendering it visible to power," but rather, "through the provision of object lessons in power—the power to command and arrange things and bodies for public display . . . to allow people, and *en masse* rather than individually, to know rather than be known, to become the subjects rather than the objects of knowledge" (p. 63).

SimCity, The Sims, Civilization and other god games both subscribe to this logic and alter it in significant ways. In one sense, they constitute cultural technologies that aim to construct populations. There are, for all intents and purposes, no individual sims in *SimCity*. The game models not groups of individuals, but populations in relation to a given environment. This population is not really "controlled" in a direct sense. It cannot be commanded to build homes, or pay taxes, or use parks and hospitals directly. But by manipulating an environment of museums, parks, schools, and so on, the player turns these iconic representations of state apparati into instrumentalized tools of governance that affect how the population of sims "behaves." The game represents a series of metaphorical interfaces with a dynamic system, each part and process influencing all the others. The game models, in this sense, the disciplinary and surveillance functions that Foucault and Bennett locate in modern governmental forms.

Bennett isolates three key questions concerning this form of governmental rationality as it functions in the museum: how it uses culture as an instrument to shape behavior, how it regulates the conduct of its population of visitors, and how it constructs and configures this population as both subjects and objects of knowledge. These three questions can also be applied to god games. First, it is important to see the structures and cultural items of these games not as static objects but as iconically reified processes: a museum in *SimCity* is not a collection of art but a process through which the population is made "happier." Happiness itself is simply a quantifiably descriptive state measuring how the population is producing wealth and interacting (or not interacting) with other structures.

Bennett's second question raises an issue that I shall take up more fully in my discussion of *Civilization II*: how do we regulate the conduct of these populations? In the obvious and direct sense, this is exactly the point of the game. But on another level, given that the sims are not "really" a population of people but rather a simulation of certain population effects, how can we understand how such games actually work to regulate human behavior? My answer will be that we must understand these games always on two levels, one at the level of what is simulated, and the other at the level of how players interact with the software itself. This dichotomy is analogous to one in Bennett's work: his analysis is not limited to a textual reading of the works of art in the museum, but instead attempts to explain the kinds of knowledge that the space of the museum and the movements of populations through it produce. Similarly, I would argue, a theory of computer games must always function both at the level of the meaning of the simulation itself and at the level of how the player interacts with the game.

The third question addresses the intrinsic narratives and processes that structure computer simulations. While game designers often invoke the open-endedness of such games as *SimCity*, claiming that each player can approach it in entirely different ways and with different styles and objectives, such games necessarily involve metanarratives concerning human nature, economics, social interaction, technological progress, and so forth. Again, I shall take this issue up in more detail later, but it is important to note the dual nature of "man" as both subject and object of power and knowledge. The player of *SimCity* does well based on her understanding of how the population of sims functions as an object of management. Simultaneously, however, the narratives of growth and human advancement that structure such games produce a certain essentialized view of humans as subjects, as well as producing effects in the player him- or herself that shape subjectivity. Thus, god games both define human populations as the objects of manipulation, surveillance, and control and define their players as subjects who can autonomously control and shape their environments.

Having sketched out some relevant applications of Bennett's use of Foucault for understanding strategic simulation games, I now move to a more detailed consideration of the game, *Civilization II (CivII)*. First, I shall describe the game's content and objectives. Next, I will consider how the formal interface qualities of the simulation subscribe to a logic of hypermediation. Finally, I will read the game in terms of Foucault's work, showing the different ways governmental rationality functions on different levels of the game.

GAMEPLAY AND THE STATE IN *CIVILIZATION II*

There is no single driving force behind the urge toward civilization, no one goal toward which every culture strives. There is, instead, a web of forces and objectives that impel and beckon, shaping cultures as they grow. In *Civilization II*, there are four basic impulses that seem to be of the greatest importance to the health and flexibility of your fledgling society... Exploration, Economics, Knowledge, and Conquest.

—Manual for *Sid Meier's Civilization II*

CivII is a strategy game that allows a player to manage a civilization from its infancy in the prehistoric past through to a futuristic colonization of another planet. It is a game of sweeping movement: military expansion, technological growth, and economic maturation are modeled from their first manifestations in the settlement of the player's first city through to the macro-management of economic trade, scientific research, and the military-industrial complex of a futuristic society with millions of citizens.

In 4000 B.C., you begin with a single unit on a map, representing a "settler." The borders of the map are darkened, so that what you can see represents the horizons of your known world. Your options as a player deal mainly at this point with exploration, settlement, and the beginnings of social production. Once you build a city, its population and production begin to grow and it is able to produce more units. These units can be other settlers, who can in turn settle other cities, which also, in turn, can produce more settlers. Or, you can produce military units, at this point limited to groups of "warriors" (although by game's end cruise missiles, Aegis cruisers, and hydrogen bombs exist as potentials in your arsenal). Or, you may produce physical improvements to your city itself, which affect the welfare of its inhabitants: granaries, temples, and barracks are possibilities early on; universities, water plants, and nuclear power plants are possibilities later on.

Your imperatives, as the quote from the player's manual above suggests, are several. You must build militarily, for even if you plan never to assault your soon-to-be-discovered neighbor civilizations, rest assured they will take the first opportunity to attack you. You must generate knowledge, or more accurately, you must obtain the predetermined knowledges that the game provides for, either through research within your own civilization, or through trade or theft from others. Knowledge here is synonymous with technology: with a few exceptions, advances in knowledge equate with advances in practical know-how (such as "The Wheel" or "Pottery"), although often they are organizational (one can expend resources on pursuing "Monotheism," "Philosophy," or later on, "The Corporation") (see fig. 12.1).

Knowledge here is also synonymous with instrumentality: it only exists insofar as it is useful toward some end. You must generate enough food, water, and other resources (including cultural productions) to keep your people "happy," or they will rise in revolt. And you must explore the world to keep on top of what other civilizations are doing and to allow for the expansion of your own civilization, for expand you must.

Early gameplay deals mostly with military build-up and exploration. Your goal is to make sure you are strong enough to resist attack, and (if you choose) well-equipped enough to carry out expansionist campaigns against other civilizations. Middle gameplay adds a strong element of economics to the equation: once your civilization has "invented" concepts of writing, money, trade, and transportation technologies (seafaring, for example), then the dynamic of the game shifts toward economic matters. You build roads, set up trade routes, and generally begin to manage a wide-scale economic system that feeds resources into greater and greater increases in technology (mainly militaristic) and allows your civilization to pursue what are called "Wonders":

A Wonder of the World is a dramatic, awe-inspiring accomplishment. It is typically a great achievement of engineering, science, or the arts, representing a milestone in the history of humankind. . . . Wonders are the extraordinary monuments of a civilization, bringing everlasting glory and other benefits to their owners. (Manual, *Civilization II*, 1996)

As with most aspects of the game, a certain amount of "glory" is nice, but it is the "other benefits" that integrate Wonders into the game-system, providing specific and measurable means toward the end of better manipulating your civilization's project as a whole.

As with other simulation games, the "end" toward which players play is sometimes difficult to define. This is not exactly a game per se—certain aspects have been built in to allow you to "win," but these criteria are fluid and achievable through very different means. One avenue involves being the first to successfully colonize another planet. Each civilization, as it enters into a simulation of our present epoch, begins to develop space technology. The game's logic, built on the necessity of expansion, demands that once the planet has been explored and populated, fresh lands for exploration and conquest be found. The "space race" that ensues demands large portions of each civilization's resources, and the first to successfully land a colonizing expedition on Alpha Centauri "wins."

The other goal involves a more traditional route in gaming terms: total annihilation of all other civilizations. By funneling resources to military technology and production rather than space exploration, you can gain a military edge over other civilizations and simply wage war. Each successful campaign brings in the increased resource production of conquered cities, which increases your ability to manufacture weaponry, which in turn makes it easier to wage the next war. This method of "winning" is not really that far divorced from the other, and is often an integral part of it: one can make the space race much less suspenseful by wiping out the one or two civilizations that represent the greatest challenge, and then, using their pillaged resources, pursue great conquests in space without fear of competition.

THE LOGIC OF HYPERMEDIACY

What I have provided above is a synopsis of the content of *CivII*, but for those unfamiliar with such games, the form and logistics by which this content is expressed need elaboration. God games can be differentiated from other genres such as the first-person shooter by what J. David Bolter and Richard Grusin call "hypermediacy," which refers to the formal qualities of the interface. Bolter and Grusin (1999) assert that new interactive media forms subscribe to a representational logic they call "remediation," and that this logic is generated by the productive opposition of two elements: hypermediacy and immediacy.

Immediacy refers to the claims of direct referentiality and simulation that suffuse much of the discourse around virtual reality. Computer simulations are increasingly evaluated by criteria of immediacy—a first-person shooter or virtual reality application is judged by a concept of verisimilitude and analogy to our experience of our own senses. Thus, first-person shooters subscribe to the logic of immediacy. Players see, over the barrel of a gun, the spaces that open up before them, and they move through these spaces (fig. 12.2).[1]

Hypermediacy refers to the interface logic that has dominated Macintosh and Windows applications since their move away from textual-command interfaces (Bolter & Grusin, 1999, p. 32). Windows, scroll bars, buttons, menus, and tables typify the representational mode of hypermediacy. Metaphorical models (the paint brush, the trash can, the button) are employed to give a familiarity and ease of use in manipulating information technology. Figure 12.3 shows the hypermediation of my computer desktop, which holds to a logic not of direct representational realism, but rather of iconography and metaphor. The key element of hypermediacy for present purposes is its reflexivity. Bolter and Grusin write:

> Unlike a perspective painting or three-dimensional computer graphic, this windowed interface does not attempt to unify the space around

Fig. 12.2.   Scence from *Quake III: Arena*.

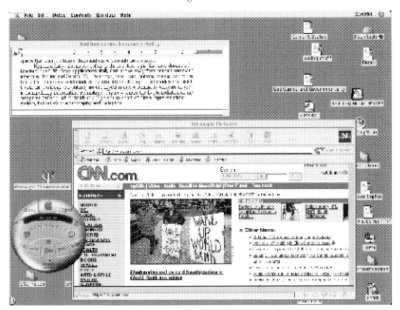

FIG. 12.3. The hypermediated desktop.

any one point of view. . . .The multiplicity of windows and the heterogeneity of their contents mean that the user is repeatedly brought back into contact with the interface, which she learns to read. . . . She oscillates between manipulating the windows and examining their contents. (p. 33)

Hypermediacy is thus an artifact of the interplay between interface and application, form and content, frame and canvas. It serves not to make the interface transparent, but instead to make the interface easier and more "intuitive." It aims, therefore, for increased efficiency and ease in the government and manipulation of heterogeneous forms and modes of information. As I shall argue later, hypermediacy can be understood as a tool of governmental rationality, a means of managing knowledge.

GOVERNMENTALITY

Many have defined governmental rationality in simple terms as "the conduct of conduct" (Gordon, 1991; Rose, 1999). According to Foucault and his interpreters, the government of a particular state or territory was understood in medieval and preindustrial times through a set of practices aimed at the exercise of power over that territory. In this model of the State, power flows from the central, hierarchized form of State that has at its head a sovereign in whose hands power rests. This sovereign, typified by Machiavelli's prince, wields power as a "means of securing the acceptance and respect of his subjects" (Foucault, 1991, p. 87). In this vision all activity is interpreted through its relation to the state: Practices radiate outward from a central seat of power, whether a single sovereign ruler or a bureaucratic ensemble of institutions.

Against this State-centered model of understanding government, Foucault, Colin Gordon, Nikolas Rose, and others argue that practices are not tools of government but rather constitute the state and government itself (Berry et al., 1996). Gordon summarizes Foucault's position as follows:

> The state has no such inherent propensities; more generally, the state has no essence. The nature of the institution of the state is, Foucault thinks, a function of changes in practices of government, rather than the converse. Political theory attends too much to institutions, and too little to practices. (1991, p. 4)

Governmentality, then, constitutes a way of understanding governing not as the intrinsic function of the state but as practices that are diffuse and heterogeneous. Government is a practice, then, not just of politicians and princes, but of everyone.

In recent contexts, governmental rationality has been intricately interwoven with the doctrines of neoliberalism. Two examples of such neoliberal doctrines are the de-governmentalization and privatization of education and the increasing marketization of health care. In each case, the theory of governmentality allows us to read these "deregulations" not as the diminishment of government, but rather its dispersion and transformation into different forms.

Central to governmentality is the process of policing, taken from the German *Polizeiwissenschaft*, or the "science of police." Policing entails the constant classification and codification of endless aspects of life. It employs statistics, demography, policy, training, and surveillance to produce a certain kind of self-governing subjectivity. As with neoliberalism, there seems to be a central circularity in the theory of policing: government's aim becomes the development of individuals such that these individuals will in turn develop the aims of government (Gordon, 1991, p. 10).

To take up a game like *CivII* in terms of governmentality is to ask not just how that content of the game configures political history, but how the form of the game enacts governmental power for those who play it. As I suggested earlier, reading computer games in this mode is akin to Bennett's reading of museums in *The Birth of the Museum* (1995). Bennett takes up museums at three levels: the way in which they function as instruments for the propagation of a given social structure, the ways in which museums are designed physically to govern a population of subjects entering them, and the construction of humanity and individual subjects as both subjects and objects of history (pp. 6–7). Bennett reads not just the exhibits in a museum but the museum itself, as instrument, structure, and institutional apparatus. I want to argue here for a similar approach to computer games in general, and to demonstrate this in relation to *CivII*.

GOD GAMES AS GOVERNMENTALITY

I read *Civilization II* as a product of and model for the contradictory impulse at the heart of neoliberalism and governmentality. Rose sees the shift from the welfare state to neoliberalism as a shift in subjectivity. The subject of the former governmental form was "subject to a kind of individualizing moral normativity . . . embraced within, and governed through, a nexus of collective solidarities and dependencies" (Rose, 1999, p. 40). Neoliberalism seeks instead to degovernmentalize the State and to destatize practices of government, to detach the substantive authority of expertise from the apparati of political rule, relocating experts within a market governed by rationalities of competition, accountability, and consumer demand. It seeks to govern not through "society," but through the deregulated choices of individual citizens, now construed as subjects of choices and aspirations to self-actualization and self-fulfillment (p. 41). *Civilization II* functions ostensibly to present a State-centered model of government. But its form and structure serve the ends of governmentality by working through the latter logic of marketization and the production of subjectivity based on policing, surveillance, and accountability.

In Bolter and Grusin's (1999) terms, this game relies heavily on the logic of hypermediacy. Citizens are represented iconically. Demographic data on populations is given, and menus and charts gauge levels of wealth, contentment, technological sophistication, and resources. The player is cast as the sovereign power in this model, much as in the State-centered theories of government. But the game contains no actual visual representation of the player as ruler. There is no representational avatar with which to identify, no gun barrel over which to look that gives the player a sense of embodiment within the context of the game. The most overt representation of the ruler functions through conspicuous absence—a "throne room" function allows one to call up the image of a ruler's hall and throne: as the player's civilization progresses, this room becomes more elaborate (fig. 12.4). But the room is never occupied, other than in the imagination of the player. Rather, it serves as a metaphorical gauge, although it is "immediate" in terms of Bolter and Grusin's twin logics of remediation.

FIG. 12.4. *CivII* Throne Room.

This image captures the productive contradiction that helps us under-stand the game's relationship to governmental reason. In one sense, *Civiliza-tion II* is based on a fundamentally State-centered model of government. This is not a neoliberal model of rule. The player comes to understand government as intrinsically centralized, hierarchical, and embedded in State form. Man-agement of one's civilization is an intricate process of vigilant surveillance and executive decree. The interrelated systems that together model a given na-tion-state must constantly be monitored and maintained—if the public cof-fers are running low, resources must be generated; if a neighboring state is building militarily, defensive actions must be taken.

While the game's simulated civilizations hold true in this sense to the doctrine of state-centered government, on another level, I believe that a dif-ferent reading of the game shows it to be commensurable with the precepts of governmentality. Gordon writes of the change from the State-centered theory: "The principles of government are no longer part of and subordinate to the divine, cosmo-theological order of the world. The principles of state are immanent, precisely, in the state itself" (1991, pp. 8–9). Similarly, the underlying structuralist architecture of the game's computer code itself is a form of immanent logic that cannot be transcended. Government, simplified to various forms of political structure such as theocracy, communism, fascism, democracy, and so forth, becomes in *Civilization II* a manageable commodity of the player. Thus, governmental reason as a form of immanence allows one form of governmental rule, the game itself, to subsume and structure every other form of government. The game's logic is ultimately one not of the State, but rather of the government of the individual.

By constituting an overarching simplification of certain metonymic properties of state and society (military, infrastructure, economy, etc.) into a symbolic currency of exchange, the game allows for an internalization of these processes on the part of the player. Exploration, Economics, Knowledge, and Conquest become interrelated logics that are sutured together at the site of the individual hinted at by the vacant throne room. The model of State-centered rule is replaced, as Foucault says, by a triangular model of "sovereignty-discipline-government" (1991, p. 102). There is not a sovereign separate from the state that s/he rules, but rather an integrated system of policing and security based on a structuralist political economy of signs.

As such, *Civilization II* subscribes to the policing theory model of governmental reason that Gordon elaborates, wherein "the mercantilist economic policy of striving to maximize the quantity of bullion in the sovereign's treasury [at the same time] emphasizes that the real basis of the state's wealth and power lies in its population, in the strength and productivity of all and each" (1991, p. 10). Thus, an underlying logic of growth pervades: population booms always bring on attendant problems (pollution, infrastructural needs, etc.), but these problems are far outweighed by the very power generated by the gain in population. The amount of labor required to maintain a population is always less than that population's output, if managed well. Also, Gordon's use of the phrase "all and each" invokes the interplay of totalization and individualization, here functioning as a reduction of "all" to statistical models of populations that are governed by a singular, individualized player/ruler. The game thus serves as a figure of governmentality in its reduction of social interaction, political rule and population management into the singularized site of the subjectivity of the player. The player acts as the subject of political rule, deciding between commodified political models—whether the government chosen is democracy or communism, this choice is ultimately made by player fiat. Simultaneously, though, the player is object of the system of governmentality itself, practicing, interiorizing and naturalizing governmental rationality.

This dual positioning of the player explains the necessity of hypermediacy as a representational logic. Immediacy seeks to reify the individual's experience as the measure of realism—virtual reality attempts to efface knowledge of its interface entirely. But hypermediacy is a dual representational mode in which the viewer is made aware of *and* a part of the interface. The role of the player in *Civilization II* is not to sit in the seat of government, but rather to disperse his or her subjectivity over the whole of the simulation, managing its various parts. The game works through a logic not of hierarchy but of immanence: a player-ruler's orders are not given, transmitted by a chain of command, and implemented, but are instead defined precisely by the player's individual activities as they draw together and coordinate various game systems. The player thus becomes not a sovereign ruler, but the embodiment of policing itself.

What I am arguing here is that hypermediacy promises, unlike immediacy, a built-in reflexivity that purports to give us control over the interface and, by extension, over information itself. Hypermediacy is the aesthetic version of instrumental science's "view from nowhere": the player is not iconically present in the game, nor is a stable and situated perspective available. The rhetoric of interactivity feeds off hypermediacy's illusory handing over of the controls of perception, claiming that control over the interface somehow gives us control over the information it mediates. But games such as this *do* have particular logics of rule within which the player works and over which the player ultimately has no control.

On another level, such computer games subscribe to a logic of neoliberalism in ways we need to consider. *Civilization II* is not a State- or school-sanctioned textbook but a narrative that the marketplace shapes, produces, and puts up for voluntary consumption. The State-centered content of the game is belied by the neoliberal conditions of its distribution and use, since the game consumer believes both that she is freely choosing what game to play in an open marketplace and also that, if she chooses a game like *Civ II*, she has control over the interface and gameplay as well. The game narrowly configures political forms in quantifiable and specific ways: "choosing" communism as a form of government is always to choose a more oppressive form of rule that will necessarily make populations discontented and more likely to revolt. Choosing democracy as a form means making populations more content, but this contentment is achieved not through actual participatory government but rather through the act of selecting democracy as a nominal governmental form.

MODES OF REFLEXIVITY

In applying hypermediation and governmentality as conceptual tools to *Civilization II*, my purpose is to problematize the form of reflexivity present in such games. These concepts share a dual, reflexive structure to some extent. In what follows, I want to lay out several levels and forms of reflexivity as it applies to god games, hypermediation, and governmentality, as a way to link together several key elements for understanding games like *CivII*.

First, as I have suggested, god games rely heavily at the level of form upon reflexivity as an interface mode. Hypermediated interfaces make us

aware of both content and our formal framing of that content through ma-
nipulable controls. As Steven Johnson argues in *Interface Culture* (1997), new
computer media create contexts that facilitate multiple forms of reflexive
interaction and commentary. New media, according to Johnson, provide the
tools for solving the problem of older media such as television: they comment
reflexively on the content of these media as a form of content itself. Television, and before it radio, were dominated in the past by narratively defined
content: sitcoms, dramas, comedies, and so forth. More recently, though, a
survey of cable television channels shows an increasingly reflexive form of
"content": we see not only films, but Roger Ebert telling us about films; not
just movie and TV stars in shows, but E Entertainment's 24/7 metacommentary
on these star's lives; not just music videos that give visual narrative content to
music, but pop-up videos and Beavis and Butthead's commentary as critical
mediated windows onto these videos; not just political events, but media
coverage that reflexively explains these events, and media coverage about the
media coverage. Hypermediation is a formal mode perfectly suited to this
kind of reflexive mediation: content is overtly windowed and framed by controls, charts, menus and other interfaces. Reflexivity itself becomes a new
form of content. However, we must remain critical of such forms of reflexivity
in that they often provide only nominal and/or illusory forms of self-aware-
ness and self-criticism. Reflexivity does not necessarily imply *critical* self-
reflexivity; MTV can be called reflexive, but is hardly engaged in critically
empowering self-reflexive critique.

Similarly, governmentality studies suggest that political rationality has
shifted from a state/subject model to one in which the state's function of
disciplining subjects is carried out reflexively by the individualized subjects
upon themselves. Reflexivity is both the tool by which individuals constitute
themselves as good political subjects and a means to reconfigure our understanding of diverse peoples into differentiated populations. Interactivity and
reflexivity stand in, in this model, for forms of autonomy. Whether we select
communism or democracy in *CivII*, high tax rates or lower ones in *SimCity*,
or Coke or Pepsi at our local convenience store, we define ourselves as active
subjects through the reflexive understanding of ourselves as choosing subjects.
Citizenship becomes consumerism, and the reflexive processes by which we
mold simulated civilizations or simcities reflects this process.

Another aspect of how reflexivity relates to agency in the context of
computer games is raised by Janet Murray (1997), who defines *agency* against
simple *activity*. The computer buzz-word *interactivity* denotes the extent to
which we perform activities as part of an application's process. Murray defines
agency against interactivity as a more specific involvement that entails not
mere activity but control over direction:

[I]n a tabletop game of chance, players may be kept very busy spin-
ning dials, moving game pieces, and exchanging money, but they

may not have any true agency. The players' actions have effect, but the actions are not chosen and the effects are not related to the players' intentions. (p. 128)

She compares such games to chess, which has relatively few actions as part of the game, but which permits a much greater degree of agency over interactivity.

Murray describes the immersive enjoyment that computer simulations provide on a very basic level: we click on the icon for a file, and to our delight a file opens (1997, p. 126). She counterposes this delight to our normal involvement with narrative interactions: when we read a story, or even play an interactive fiction, there is an extent to which the necessity of a certain movement from beginning to end leaves little room for agency. This may be one reason for the success of simulations like *SimCity* and *SimLife*: such programs have a minimum of overt narrativity to impinge on the user's freedom to make constant and substantive decisions on how interaction will unfold. In this sense, reflexivity produces certain effects that simulate agency: we have no significant control over how a film or novel's plot will end (although we can certainly impose differing meanings to some extent), but when playing *CivII*, we sense that our actions have immediate and significant effects on the course of the game. In this sense, such games mirror the kind of spatial and architectural concerns that Bennett takes up in relation to museums, or that Morris applies to the structure of shopping malls. Virtual game spaces and reflexive interfaces invite certain modes of interaction without commanding them, making questions of autonomy and agency much more complex.

Finally, I would argue that reflexivity is a key element in the processes of totalization and individualization that lie at the heart of governmentality as it applies to god games and new media more generally. Colin Gordon argues that Foucault's lectures on governmentality characterize modern Western government in terms of the dual impulses to totalize and to individualize (1991, p. 3). Governmentality thus functions through totalization of social groups into demographically constituted populations, while dispersing power through the constitution of individualized, self-policing subjects. These dual processes of totalization and individualization also characterize the function of governmentality in god games. *CivII* attempts, at the level of content, to totalize social relations and history for its player, while simultaneously individualizing that player as a subject and object of governmentality. The process of totalization in governmentality, however, needs to be separated from the Marxist understanding of the term. The transformation of societies into more easily administered populations is a reductive process in which experiential knowledge is shunned in favor of quantification. The Marxist concept of the totality suggests a utopian desire to conceptualize the whole of social relations without reduction. I would suggest that, like the conspiracy films that Jameson calls the "poor person's cognitive mapping" (1988, p. 356), popular computer simulation games serve a similar function in providing a (poor) site for the fulfillment of this desire. The postmodern disdain of totalization stems, I believe, from the confusion of reductive and totalitarian forms of totalization, such as Foucault's, with more utopic, imaginative, and sustaining understandings of totalization from the Marxist tradition from Lukács through Sartre and Althusser (Jay, 1984). I leave for another time a fuller consideration of this issue, but for now it is sufficient to note that hypermediated games lend themselves both to totalizing and self-reflexively individualizing thought, and it is important in analyzing them to keep these dual processes foregrounded.

NOTE

1. See Gunkel (2000) for an examination of the relationship between computer simulations and historical logics of representation, offering a deconstructive critique that extricates the concept of "simulation" from the dualism of truth/illusion in which it is often located.

REFERENCES

Barry, A., Osborne, T., & Rose, N. (1996). *Foucault and political reason: Liberalism, neo-liberalism and rationalities of government.* Chicago: University of Chicago Press.

Bennett, T. (1979). *Formalism and Marxism.* London: Methuen.

Bennett, T. (1995). *The birth of the museum: History, theory, politics.* London: Routledge.

Bolter, J. D., & Grusin, R. (1999). *Remediation: Understanding new media.* Cambridge, MA: MIT Press.

Foucault, M. (1991). Governmentality. In G. Burchell, C. Gordon, & P. Miller (Eds.), *The Foucault effect: Studies in governmentality* (pp. 119–50). Chicago: University of Chicago Press.

Gordon, C. (1991). Governmental rationality: An introduction. In G. Burchell, C. Gordon, & P. Miller (Eds.), *The Foucault effect: Studies in Governmentality.* Chicago: University of Chicago Press.

Gunkel, P. (2000). Rethinking virtual reality: Simulation and the deconstruction of the image. *Critical Studies in Mass Communication, 17*(1), 45–62.

Jameson, F. (1988). Cognitive mapping. In C. Nelson & L. Grossberg (Eds.), *Marxism and the interpretation of culture* (pp. 347–60). Urbana, Il.: University of Illinois Press.

Jameson, F. (1991). *Postmodernism, or, the cultural logic of late capitalism.* Durham: Duke University Press.

Jameson, F. (1992). *The geopolitical aesthetic: Cinema and space in the world system.* Bloomington, IN: Indiana University Press.

Jay, M. (1984). *Marxism and totality: The adventures of a concept from Lukács to Habermas.* Berkeley: University of California Press.

Johnson, S. (1997). *Interface culture: How new technology transforms the way we create and communicate.* New York: HarperCollins.

Murray, J. H. (1997). *Hamlet on the holodeck: The future of narrative in cyberspace.* Cambridge, MA: Massachusetts Institute of Technology Press.

NPD Data. (Feb, 2002). "2001 U.S. Interactive Entertainment Sales Shatter Industry Record." Retrieved August 15, 2002 from http://www.pcvsconsole.com/news/news.php?nid=1159&filter=4

Rose, N. (1999). *Powers of freedom: Reframing political thought.* London: Cambridge University Press.

Taylor, C. (1999, March 1). Technology: Playing god. *Time 153*(8): 52–53.

Turkle, S. (1995). *Life on the screen: Identity in the age of the internet.* New York: Simon & Schuster.

Walker, Trey. (Feb, 2002). "2001 game sales break records." Retrieved August 15, 2002 from http://gamespot.com/gamespot/stories/news/0, 10870,2846252,00.html

Chapter 13

Subjectivity as Identity

Gender Through the Lens of Foucault

Lisa King

> But, then, what is philosophy today—philosophical activity, I mean—if it is
> not the critical work that thought brings to bear on itself? In what does it
> consist, if not in the endeavor to know how and to what extent it might be
> possible to think differently, instead of legitimating what is already known?
>
> —Michel Foucault, *The Use of Pleasure*

Many feminists have turned to Foucault's notions of disciplinarity and normalizing power in order to articulate the historical contingency of our current
gender identities, and to identify the specific social practices through which
such identities are produced.[1] Nancy Fraser's analyses of social institutions
(1989), for instance, even though critical of his lack of normativity, are much
indebted to Foucault's notion of power as normalizing and disciplinary; Sandra
Bartky (1990) offers a Foucauldian, phenomenological analysis of the beauty
industry and its effects on the production of feminine gender identity; Judith
Butler (1990, 1993) draws heavily on Foucault's notion of power as productive in order to reveal the contingency of what she terms the "heterosexual
matrix," the confluence of gender and sexuality in a way that excludes and
thereby oppresses women and sexual minorities; and there are, of course,
many others. All of this work is important for thinking about feminist politics
and the formation of gender identity, and I consider my argument here to be
an extension of it. However, none of this work has, to my mind, adequately
explored Foucault's notion of the will to knowledge and his suggestions in the
later works for a new practice of the self. By focusing on these notions here,
I seek to articulate a more complex analysis of gender identity formation than
has been offered to date.

Butler's work on materialization and identification offers the most complex accounts of gender formation in contemporary culture of those feminists working with a Foucauldian paradigm, but even she, I would argue, does not address processes of individuation through the desire for the truth of one's self. While she convincingly articulates the abjectifying effects of normalizing power, her focus on the cultural symbolic takes her away from embodied practices, which is where I think Foucault is particularly insightful and interesting. Butler describes the linguistic matrixes through which subjects become such, but she does not specify the actual identificatory practices through which subjectivation takes place. My goal in this essay is to specify these practices by examining a particular case of seeking the truth of oneself, because it seems to me that without this piece of the normalizing puzzle, we misunderstand the operations of identity production.

In order to explore this aspect of Foucault's analysis, I consider the case of David Reimer, the now famous boy who lost his penis in a botched circumcision, was then raised as a girl, and subsequently underwent sex reassignment surgery as an adult to become male again. His story has been taken as definitive proof of the biological basis of gender identity, a conclusion I want to trouble by considering the case through Foucault's lens of normalizing power. The problem is not one of nature versus nurture, as it has been taken up in multiple public discourses; it is, rather, the assumption that specific gendered practices are presumed to arise from a core identity, that gender identity itself is the underlying force that gives rise to and makes sense of particular gendered practices. Reimer's experience reveals, then, the conflation of subjectivity with identity in the modern era.

THE PUBLIC SPECTACLE

Reimer's life became the focus of much media attention this past spring and summer: he appeared with hidden face on talk shows and nightly news programs, his case has appeared in various print media from *Newsweek* to the *New York Times,* and he finally agreed to grant in-depth interviews to a *Rolling Stone* reporter, John Colapinto, fully identifying himself and the principle players in his tragic story. Colapinto's book, *As Nature Made Him: The Boy Who Was Raised As a Girl* (2000), arose out of this series of interviews and provides a detailed account of Reimer's experiences from childhood female to adult male. Why all the attention? Why is our culture so fascinated with this person's life? Colapinto's framing of Reimer's life provides, I think, a clue: his is a case that encapsulates the nature/nurture debates about the basis of gender identity that have been on going for the past few decades. Gender has become a problem in our culture, and Reimer's experience gives us a way into the problem. John Money, the psychologist who worked with the Reimers from the time that David (then Bruce) was 19-months-old until she (as Brenda) terminated contact with him at age 12, used the case as proof that gender identity is socially constructed, presenting Brenda (as she had become when her parents elected the sex-reassignment surgery) as a perfectly happy, well-adjusted girl. Colapinto, on the other hand, reveals that the experiment failed dismally, as Brenda refused her girlhood from the beginning, which he considers proof that gender is biologically based and cannot be changed at the whim of others. I want to step back from this debate and question its conditions of possibility. It seems to me that Reimer's experience reveals neither that gender is natural nor that it's socially constructed. Rather, it reveals the normalizing power of gender identity itself: that particular practices that have been coded as feminine or masculine must be rooted in a preexistent identity, a sense of self that "matches" one's biology.

FROM BRUCE TO BRENDA TO DAVID

Janet Reimer gave birth to twin boys on August 22, 1965; she and her husband, Ron, named them Bruce and Brian. When at 7 months the twins began to suffer from problems, their pediatrician recommended circumcision to fix the problem. The surgery was scheduled for April 27, 1966. Bruce went first—and last, because of the horrible error that ensued: Bruce's penis was burned by the cauterizing instrument used for the procedure and, over the next few days, it turned black and fell off. A potentially reconstructed penis would not have passed for the "real thing," since such procedures were rudimentary at the time. After the accident, the Reimers were at a loss, depressed, and housebound, until they saw a television show on which psychiatrist and sex researcher John Money described the great successes he had with sex-reassignment surgery. They wrote to him, explaining their situation. Money eventually persuaded the Reimers to have Bruce undergo surgery to become a girl at the age of 22 months. The child was renamed Brenda. Janet and Ron were instructed on how to properly raise their daughter, and Brenda underwent yearly sessions with Money to determine her adjustment to her new persona. Brenda did not adjust well to her new self, and when her parents told her of her past at age 14, she decided to start living as boy, choosing the name David in reference to the Goliath of her past that she was about to slay. She underwent sex reassignment surgery once again, including a double mastectomy and reconstructed penis and scrotum, in the fall of 1980 and summer of 1981, respectively. He has been David ever since.

One of the more interesting aspects of Brenda/David's case is the way it has been taken up as a way of settling the nature versus nurture debate about gender identity. In its use on both sides of the divide, the case becomes a clear-cut example of Foucault's notion of confessional culture. Money, the

Reimers themselves, and Colapinto all use the mechanisms of surveillance and confession in order to figure out who Brenda/David "really" is. S/he must discuss in detail her/his various experiences and desires so that her/his true self can be revealed. In the early years, these confessions took the form of Brenda's attempts to please her parents by desiring the proper girl-like activities and making yearly visits to Money, where he probed the details of her likes and dislikes, her behaviors and misbehaviors. In recent years, these confessions took the form of David's extended interviews on various talk shows and with Colapinto himself, in which he revealed the minute details of his experiences as a child and an adult, trying to make sense of himself within gender norms that did not fit. These mechanisms constitute the search for the truth of Brenda/David through the normalizing power of gender identity.

To see the normalizing aspect of these mechanisms, consider the criteria used by both Money (and therefore, Janet and Ron) and Colapinto to determine the success of Bruce's transformation into Brenda. Across the board, the ideal was feminine *behavior*: did Brenda act like a girl, and did she *want* to? If so, it was presumed that she thought of herself as such; if not, it was presumed that she thought of herself as a boy, which would mean that her identity was fixed by biology rather than upbringing. Colapinto's main evidence that Brenda's reassignment surgery did not "take" was her consistently boyish behavior. Examples abound. Janet became worried when Brenda was put in her first dress, because she tried to tear it off. Janet thought, "Oh my God, she knows she's a boy and she doesn't want girls' clothing. She doesn't want to be a girl" (Colapinto, 2000, p. 56). Brenda also wanted to shave like her dad. Brian relates that, though he always thought of Brenda as his sister, "She never, ever acted the part. . . . When I say there was nothing feminine about Brenda, I mean there was *nothing* feminine. She walked like a guy. Sat with her legs apart. She talked about guy things, didn't give a crap about cleaning house, getting married, wearing makeup. We both wanted to play with guys, build forts and have snowball fights and play army" (p. 57). Brenda's reaction to being in the Girl Scouts was one of boredom: "I remember making daisy chains and thinking, If this is the most exciting thing in Girl Scouts, forget it. I kept thinking of the fun stuff my brother was doing in Cubs." About dolls as gifts: "What can you *do* with a doll? You *look* at it. You *dress* it. You *undress* it. Comb its hair. It's boring! With a car, you can drive it somewhere, *go* places. I wanted cars" (p. 58). Her grandparents noticed that she fought with boys and was more boisterous than her brother. Her teachers noticed that she was not interested in stereotypically feminine activities, and, horror of horrors, she refused to urinate sitting down. Colapinto presents all of these instances of Brenda's behavior as evidence that her "treatment"—the sex reassignment surgery—was not working, because it was not resulting in a feminine gender identity.

Money, too, based his psychological treatment on the assumption that being a female means being feminine. Indeed, it was on his direction that the Reimers tried to train Brenda to be a girl, and to do so by getting her to behave in feminine ways: "They furnished her with dolls to play with; they tried to teach her to be neat and tidy; they tried, whenever possible, to reinforce her identity as a girl" (Colapinto, 2000, p. 56). In his publications on the case, Money referred to Brenda's supposed stereotypically gendered behavior as evidence for the success of the sex-reassignment surgery. Colapinto gives the following summary of Money's account of the case from his book *Man & Woman, Boy & Girl*:

> By any measure, the account portrayed the experiment as an unqualified success. In comparison with her twin brother, Brenda provided what Money variously described as an "extraordinary" and a "remarkable" contrast. Brian's interest in "cars and gas pumps and tools" was compared with Brenda's avid interest in "dolls, a doll house and a doll carriage"; Brenda's cleanliness was characterized as wholly different from Brians' total disregard for such matters; Brenda's interest in kitchen work was placed alongside Brian's disdain for it. Money did describe Brenda as always the "dominant twin," though he gave the impression that this was changing over time. By age three, he reported, her dominance over Brian had become "that of a mother hen." All in all, the twins embodied an almost miraculous division of taste, temperament, and behavior along gender lines and seemed the "ultimate test" that boys and girls are made, not born. (as quoted in Colapinto, 2000, p. 69)

At an address to the Nebraska Symposium on Motivation, Money showed slides of the twins to make his point:

> Money also showed a shot of Brenda alone, taken by Money himself. The child is seated awkwardly on the patterned upholstery of his office sofa. She wears a floral dress and running shoes, her bare left knee lifted self-protectively against the lens, her left hand deliberately obscuring her face. "In the last illustration," Money told his audience, "you have a pretty persuasive example of feminine body talk." (Colapinto, p. 71)

Femaleness as femininity, itself defined as submissiveness.

At his yearly sessions with Brenda, Money also asked her a series of questions aimed at determining her identification of herself as a girl, questions which focused in part on her desire to do feminine things. He asked her if she fought, whether she liked to play with girls, whether she liked to play house, who was the boss in her relationship with her brother, and so forth. Colapinto remarks that she seemed to have learned to give the answers that Money was looking for, but she occasionally slipped up. She knew she was supposed to do girl-like things, but was also clear that she didn't much like to. In one session, when Brenda was 6, Money asked if she fought or ran away when boys started to fight her: "Brenda at first blurted out, 'Fight back,' but then immediately reversed herself. 'No,' she said. 'I just run away.' " Sensing she was just trying to please him, he asked the same question differently (Do you use your hands to fight people?), and "Brenda promptly contradicted her earlier avowals with the exclamation that she hit hard—'with my *fist*' " (Colapinto, 2000, p. 82). In sessions with Brian, it becomes clear that Brian is more interested in playing with dolls than Brenda is, that she parrots him in describing how one does so (no one seemed particularly concerned that Brian was "really" a girl, even though he was the more gentle, neat and "feminine" of the two). Clearly, she really had no interest in such games, and only reported that she did in order to make Money (and her parents?) happy.

Colapinto reports all of these incidents as evidence that Brenda was *really* a little boy who had been unjustly trapped in a girl's body. But perhaps the problem lies elswhere: perhaps the problem is precisely that we associate a particular set of behaviors with a particular kind of body, and when the behavior doesn't fit the body, we think something's wrong and needs to be fixed. Perhaps, in other words, the problem is that of normalizing power: rather than a *refusal* to allow Brenda/David to be who s/he truly was, the problem was/is an *insistence* that she have a "true" self at all. The narrative provides a clear example of how normalizing power operates through microlevel practices of surveillance and discipline. Brenda/David's story is a sustained example of the attempt to enforce a particular conception of appropriate gendered behavior by inscribing those norms on the body, both literally, through Bruce/Brenda's sex-reassignment surgery itself, and through the various feminine behaviors everyone around her wanted Brenda to willingly engage in. Her struggle also reveals the confession as a main mechanism of this form of power, as her parents and doctors constantly compelled her to proclaim her desires, hoping they would reveal her feminine sense of self, fearing they would reveal the "opposite," a male one. And it is clearly through these confessional moments that Brenda learns both what is expected of her and that she fails to meet those expectations; otherwise she would never have learned to try to fake it to please those around her. Not only did she outright lie to Money in some of their sessions, when her parents were obviously going through a difficult time (Janet became an alcoholic; Ron took to working too much and had an affair), she tried to become the girl they always wanted her to be: she started wearing makeup and "feminine" clothes, and she tried to clean up around the house and help with cooking and the like.

The force of gender norms appears throughout the book, from the Reimers' decision to have Bruce transformed into Brenda, to Money's and others' assumption that one cannot live *between* the poles of male and female, to Brenda's numerous difficulties growing up, to Brenda's choice to become David, to Colapinto's redemption narrative of the journey from loss to recovery of self. The Reimers, for example, decided to transform Bruce into Brenda because of the shame and embarassment they felt having a son with no penis: "they felt like prisoners in their house. They could not even go out together to see a movie . . . since they were afraid to hire a babysitter who might gossip about the tragedy" (Colapinto, p. 17). They were also worried, of course, about the humiliations that Bruce would suffer as he grew, having to endure taunting from peers when it came time for peeing contests and dating (p. 52). The head of Neurology and Psychiatry at a clinic in Winnipeg predicted that Bruce "will be unable to live a normal sexual life from the time of adolescence: that he will be unable to consummate marriage or have normal heterosexual relations, in that he will have to recognize that he is incomplete, physically defective, and that he must live apart" (p. 16). Money shared this conclusion: at one session during which he was trying to convince Brenda to undergo the last stage of genital reconstruction surgery to become biologically female, he told her that "she could not be a person unless she had" a gender identity (p. 139). Such concerns and assumptions emerge only within a binary system of gender norms rooted in the biological; only within such a schema is a penisless boy or a tomboy girl not fully a person.

Consider, too, the numerous problems Brenda faced growing up. What really made her life hell was not the specific belief that she was really a boy underneath it all but the general feeling that she did not "fit in." Her teachers, her peers, her parents, her brother, her grandparents all knew that she did not conform to stereotypically gendered behavior. Her kindergarten teacher, for instance, noticed that "there was a rough-and-tumble rowdiness, an assertive, pressing dominance, and a complete lack of any demonstrable feminine interests that were unique to Brenda" (Colapinto, p. 61). Her peers mocked her mercilessly from the first day of class. Because her behavior was "guy-like," she didn't fit in. Not fitting in led to behavior problems in the classroom, which led to performance difficulties as well. The school threatened not to pass her to first grade, but Money intervened and the school followed his recommendation to pass her. In first grade, she fared no better. She responded to her isolation from her peers by refusing to participate in any school activities. Only once she found a group of tomboys and misfits did she have a peer group at all.

Through all of these experiences, Brenda developed the sense of herself as an outsider because of her inability to be the kind of girl everyone—her peers, teachers, parents, and doctors—expected her to be: "'You know generally what a girl is like," David says, "and you know generally what a guy is like. And everyone is telling you that you're a girl. But you say to yourself, I don't *feel* like a girl. I liked to do guy stuff. It didn't match. So you figure, Well there's something *wrong* here. If I'm supposed to be like this girl over here, but I'm acting like this guy, I guess I gotta be an *it*" (Colapinto, p. 62). Brenda's notion of herself as an "it" is a clear example of Foucault's claim that power is productive rather than (or perhaps as well as) repressive: her self-understanding emerges only out of her positioning in relation to a rigid code of gender norms that is continually enforced by those around her, and which she has made her own. It is not that she's really a boy and only if her true self were allowed to flourish, everything would be fine. Rather, she learns that she is neither girl nor boy and *comes to be* an "it" through her continual experience of not meeting expectations, of falling short of the norm, of disappointing and exasperating those around her; she *comes to be* abnormal, pathological. Her realization that she is an "it" makes clear the search for an underlying identity that gives rise to and makes sense of our behaviors and desires. Her difficulty is not simply with her behavior, *that* she "liked to do guy stuff," but with what this behavior says about *who* she is: if not girl or boy, then it. She has learned to police her own behaviors and desires for clues about who she really is.

Brenda becomes in relation to gender what Foucault claims about sexuality. She is:

> a personage, a past, a case history, and a childhood, in addition to being a type of life, a life form, and a morphology, with an indiscreet anatomy and a possibly mysterious physiology. Nothing that went into [her] total composition was unaffected by his sex. . . . It was everywhere present in [her]: at the root of [her] actions because it was their insidious and indefinitely active principle; written immodestly on [her] face and body because it was a secret that always gave itself away. It was consubstantial with [her], less as a habitual sin than as a singular nature. (Foucault, 1990a, p. 43)

It is with recourse to her past that everyone, including Brenda herself, makes sense of who she is. All of her behavior comes to be seen as emanating from a true maleness that surgery and socialization could not repress. Each minute detail of her experience—her tomboyishness, the way she sat with her legs apart, her dislike of dolls and cooking, her confused sense of self—becomes evidence of the tragedy s/he endured. That belief leads her to want to "fix" her behavior by being reassigned as a boy: his desires and practices then match up with the right body; now he fits in.

The framing of Reimer's experience as a tragic fall from normalcy and a surgical redemption, together with his subsequent public discussions about his life, embody one of Foucault's central insights about the production of individuals through social categories such as sexuality and gender: in our culture, one of the most fundamental pleasures that subtends even what we take to be the primary pleasures of sex is precisely the desire to know the truth of ourselves.

> We have . . . invented a different kind of pleasure: pleasure in the truth of pleasure, the pleasure of knowing that truth, of discovering and exposing it, the fascination of seeing it and telling it, of captivating and capturing others by it, of confiding it in secret, of luring it out in the open—the specific pleasure of the true discourse on pleasure. (Foucault, 1990a, p. 71)

This pleasure of a discovered self-knowledge gives Reimer's story its narrative impulse.[2] Not only is s/he driven by the desire to know who s/he is, we readers are, too. We all want to know who David "really" is, just as we want to know ourselves. It is precisely the pleasure we take from this knowledge that drives the enforcement of gender norms generally and Brenda's hell in particular. The problem here is not the desire for truth per se, but the particular form it takes as the search for a deep self. Socially defined norms are taken as givens which each of us must embody. Brenda's quest for the truth of herself through these norms perpetuates the very terms of her life in hell.

Subsequently, David's life makes explicit processes of surveillance and normalization that operate in everyday life largely unseen. We tend not to notice them because we take them for granted as the tools for self-discovery, and because there are a plethora of categories for various kinds of deviants; David stands out only because of his past. Brenda is surely not the only girl to have resisted feminizing practices; it is only her past boyhood that separates her from other such girls. Without the knowledge of her past, she would instead be categorized as a dyke or tomboy (as Money constantly assured her mother she was), as boys who are not properly masculine are labeled fags. And, as Foucault notes, the categories themselves are broader than simply "normal" and "abnormal"; there are heterosexual women and men, as well as lesbians, gays, bisexuals, the transgendered, transsexuals, cross-dressers, drag queens and kings, and so on. In any case, one must fit into one of these multiple categories, one must have a gender identity of some sort, to count as a subject. As Judith Butler puts it in explicating Foucault, "The category of 'sex' thus established a principle of intelligibility for human beings, which is to say that no human being can be taken to be human, can be recognized as human, unless that human being is fully and coherently marked by sex and thereby becomes intelligible . . . to qualify as legitimately human, one must be coherently sexed" (Butler, 1996, p. 67).

This insistence that subjectivity be grounded in identity is precisely the problem that is normalizing power. The mechanisms that produce an internal

self are also the mechanisms of surveillance and discipline; the constant search
for the truth of ourselves is thus the product of and the vehicle for coercive
and oppressive practices. That is why the repressive hypothesis is misguided:
it assumes that the self is presocial, that it is given and self-defined, and that
power acts as an external force upon it, so that freedom can be gained by
simply throwing off that force. But if power actually produces rather than acts
on individuals, the task of freedom is much more complex. It cannot be a
matter of embracing and seeking recognition for various social identities, for
the identities themselves are part of the problem. While securing rights for
marginalized groups is important, it can be at best a first step. Hence Foucault's
distinction between liberation and practices of freedom (Foucault, 1988b).
His second two volumes of *The History of Sexuality*, *The Use of Pleasure* and
The Care of the Self, begin to offer ways of thinking about this notion of a
practice of freedom in relation to identity. By returning to Reimer again, I
hope to show the possibilities for unintended, liberatory practices in the
midst of normalizing power. First, though, I would like to spend some time
explicating the notion of practices of the self.

PRACTICES OF THE SELF

In *The Use of Pleasure* and *The Care of the Self*, Foucault's analysis of sexuality
shifts from a concern with power relations per se to a concern with the
formation of the desiring subject itself through power relations. This shift in
emphasis emerges through Foucault's genealogy of the modern, desiring subject that seeks the truth of itself in its sex/uality, whose rise he locates between the classical Greeks and the Romans. Not only does his analysis reveal
the contingency of the modern subject described in volume 1, but it reveals
possible forms of self-relation other than the modern version of self-monitoring
in relation to strict codes of sexual conduct and identity. By drawing a distinction between the moral codes and the forms of subjectivation that constitute ethics, Foucault is able to identify the very different ways that similar
codes of behavior have been taken up in different historical epochs, suggesting that it is not simply norms that matter in ethical behavior, but how
individual subjects relate to those norms. Thus the codes that we generally
take to define the domain of the ethical must themselves be understood in
light of the structuring elements of individual ethical formation through which
they are taken up. It is in this sphere of the "how" that Foucault is able to
identify alternative forms of ethical relation.

   Foucault's genealogy reveals that there has been a quite remarkable continuity in ethical codes related to sex since the time of the classical Greece.
This discovery flies in the face of common assumptions about differences
between classical Greek culture and our own, such as the assumption of a

tremendous change in attitudes toward and practices of homosexuality. These codes of behavior dictate how one is supposed to act toward oneself and particularly others, which acts are acceptable and which are not and in what circumstances, and they include examples such as incest taboos and the domination of men over women, but also concerns about masturbation, homosexual relations, marital fidelity, and sexual abstinence (Foucault, 1990b, pp. 14–20). The codes themselves, he argues, have remained remarkably similar.

Lest we think that sexual ethics itself has not changed, however, Foucault identifies other elements of the ethical landscape that structure in a fundamental way the very being of the ethical subject. These elements help constitute radically different kinds of sexually ethical beings from one historical epoch to another, even though their respective moral codes remain quite similar. He identifies four such structuring elements:

1. the "*determination of the ethical substance*; that is, the way in which the individual has to constitute this or that part of himself as the prime material of his moral conduct" (Foucault, 1990b, p. 26),
2. The "*mode of subjection*; that is, . . . the way in which the individual establishes his relation to the rule and recognizes himself as obliged to put it into practice" (p. 27),
3. The "forms of *elaboration*, of *ethical work* that one performs on oneself . . . to attempt to transform oneself into the ethical subject of one's behavior" (p. 27), and
4. the "*telos* of the ethical subject: an action is not only moral in itself, in its singularity; it is also moral in its circumstantial integration and by virtue of the place it occupies in a pattern of conduct" (pp. 27–28).

It is not simply a particular set of actions that is relevant here, but "a mode of being characteristic of the ethical subject"; not simply a moral code but the way the ethical subject takes up or embodies that code.

Let us consider the ancient Greeks' conception of the ethical subject in some detail. The most fundamental structuring element in the Greek ethical schema was the goal of self-mastery through moderation. One does not attempt to discover a true, deep self by examining every minute desire for its hidden meaning; rather, desires are to be known in order to be mastered, and sexual desires have no more primacy than the desires for, say, eating and drinking. The ethical goal is to create oneself and one's life as a work of art, with mastery of the desires as an important element in that work. The ethical code of conduct was thus not normalizing in Foucault's sense:

The moral reflection of the Greeks on sexual behavior did not seek to justify interdictions, but to stylize freedom . . . it should be noted

that for the most part their reflection was not concerned with analyzing the different pathological effects of sexual activity; nor did
they seek to organize this behavior as a domain in which normal
behavior might be distinguished from abnormal and pathological
practices . . . . The main objective of this reflection was to define the
use of pleasures—which conditions were favorable, which practice
was recommended, which rarefaction was necessary—in terms of a
certain way of caring for one's body. (Foucault, 1990b, p. 97)

It is precisely because the goal was to practice pleasure freely that the ethical
codes allowed room for considerable variation. Not only were factors like age,
social status and sex relevant to the manner in which one acted, but also the
regulations themselves were fairly broadly defined. There were thus no desires
that were considered in and of themselves unethical and to be avoided, as
there came to be under the Christian code. Rather, desires were to be mastered as an indication of the individual's capacity to master himself and others
as a political ruler.

This conception of sexual ethics requires a certain kind of self-knowledge
on the part of the sexual subject, but again, this self-knowledge operates quite
differently than it does under a system of normalizing power:

One could not form oneself as an ethical subject in the use of pleasures without forming oneself at the same time as a subject of
knowledge. . . . But it is important to note that this relation to truth
never took the form of a decipherment of the self by the self, never
that of a hermeneutics of desire. It was the factor constituting the
mode of being of the moderate subject; it was not equivalent to an
obligation for the subject to speak truthfully concerning himself; it
never opened up the soul as a domain of potential knowledge where
barely discernible traces of desire needed to be read and interpreted.
The relation to truth was a structural, instrumental, and ontological
condition for establishing the individual as a moderate subject leading a life of moderation; it was not an epistemological condition
enabling the individual to recognize himself in his singularity as a
desiring subject. (Foucault, 1990b, pp. 86, 89)

This role that knowledge of self played for the Greeks reveals that the search
for self-knowledge can take different forms. Foucault's concerns about the
will to truth in *The History of Sexuality* can thus be read not as a problem with
the search for self-knowledge itself but with the particular form that this
search takes in the context of normalizing power; it's not the search for the
truth of oneself per se that's the problem per se, but what that truth is taken
to be and how it operates in a broader system of normalizing power. For the

Greeks, it was ultimately about the moderation of desires, so that the truth of oneself was tied up in social relations; the question was *how* rather than simply *that* one is. Within the Greek schema, desires themselves are not bad, wrong, or unnatural; they are a site for work on the self, to be sure, but only because one wants to be in control of them rather than controlled by them. The kind of difficulties that Brenda/David Reimer faced, based on the idea that Brenda has the *wrong* desires for her body, simply wouldn't exist in the Greek world. The same can be said for homosexual desire generally, as such desires are coded as unnatural in our culture. In modern society, the worry in both cases is *whether* one has particular desires or not, rather than *how* one enacts those desires. Such a judgment about the nature of desire emerges only in a regime of normalization, in which desires are read as the sign of inner natures, some of which are normal and some abnormal.

Foucault's analysis of Greek sexual ethics places ethical subjectivity already within the realm of the political, for who we are is conditioned by particular social norms and specific mechanisms for relating to those norms, which we are incited to take on ourselves. Foucault's genealogy reveals the limits of our current conceptions of sexual ethics so that we might think and be differently, that we might find a way beyond our entrapment within the identity categories to which we cling as the truth of ourselves.

Foucault seems to be suggesting a shift in the mode of being of the ethical subject, from one that is concerned with discovering the truth about itself to one concerned with forming responsible ethical relations. With such a shift would emerge a different set of framing discourses about the ethical self. Exactly what these discourses would be remains necessarily unclear, for they may emerge only through as yet uncreated changes in ethical practices. But it does seem clear that this shift necessitates different practices around the truth of ourselves than those which operate within normalizing power. A sexual ethics that does not revolve around identities would have a different set of concerns than those faced by the Reimers, for example. We would not need to worry that our practices "match up" with our bodies, or that our practices fit an internal sense of ourselves as male or female, gay or straight. Our guiding norms would not seek to normalize individuals but to facilitate the kinds of relation through which we might create new ways of being with each other. Rather than trying to fix a penisless boy to fit into categories that cannot contain him, the goal might be to recreate familial and community relations to create a space for such a child as normal. The truth of oneself thus becomes not a stopping point but a starting point. As David Reimer himself points out, having become male again has not ended his quest for a meaningful life; it has given him the chance to begin creating such a life with others (Colapinto, 2000, p. 271).

One of the questions that arises is how this shift might happen. How, given the force and prevalence of normalizing, truth-telling discourses might new ways of understanding ourselves and of relating to others emerge. It seems to me that Reimer's experience can offer some suggestions here as well. In particular, I wonder if confessional practices, at the same time that they are firmly rooted in the normalizing practices of our day, might potentially open a space for reconfiguring some of our gendered and gendering practices. It may well be that Reimer's narrative could have implications for gender identity formation that exceed his own intentions in making his story public. His story has, for example, been taken up by transsexual activists who seek to stop the kinds of surgical practices imposed on Bruce/Brenda, since they are a common and accepted method of "fixing" those born with ambiguous genitals. Those who have been thus altered often suffer physically and psychologically for years afterward, as they confront unexplained and painful surgeries, hormone therapies, and general confusion and shame about who they are. Many such individuals have begun telling their own stories of pain and shame in order to draw attention to what they take to be an unjust imposition of social norms on their bodies. Part of what they seek is the autonomy to make their own decisions about gendering/sexing their bodies. They advocate waiting to perform any genital surgeries until the individual is him/herself able to understand what the surgeries are about and the effects they will have on their bodies.

While such confessional practices may seem to merely repeat the liberal norms of autonomy and self-determination of our culture, it seems to me that there is a radical potential in them. Were these activists able to alter medical procedures on infants' genitals, new, ambiguous gender categories may be created that would alter the existing gender binary in our culture. Without that binary, the justification for imposing gendered categories on those who don't fit would no longer have any force. Cultural space would need to be made for these individuals, which could in turn alter a host of other microlevel gendering behaviors. In short, it's possible (though by no means necessary) that the very gender system itself would be radically reconfigured.

These possibilities point to the promise in Foucault's shift to ethical subjectivity (and there are plenty of other ways to envision it) as a link between the ethical and the political. The ethical work he turns to has the potential to transform the conditions under which we are formed and form ourselves as subjects, to recast the practices through which we currently constitute subjectivity itself. As such, the kind of ethical work that he suggests we engage in *is* politics, for it is through this work that the largely invisible, silent discourses that form our subjectivity/subjection might be altered.[3]

Notes

1. For an overview of feminist scholarship on Foucault, see Irene Diamond and Lee Quinby (1988), Ramazanoglu (1993), and Hekman (1996).

2. Reimer's gender redemption resembles a gay coming-out story, tinged with similar attempts to overcome what was once shame (he acknowledges that it will be difficult to tell his son that he grew up wearing dresses) to a place of self-acceptance. I by no means want to downplay the importance of such stories; they can indeed help to open a social space in which "the abnormal" may be seen as normal, which is certainly a positive move. But I do want to point to the problems that such stories raise precisely because of the nature of the supposed redemption: in embracing categories of sexual identity as the truth of the self, they ultimately perpetuate the very norms they're meant to trouble.

3. I am indebted to Ted Bailey, Jill Conway, Stephanie Foote, Samantha King, Marie Leger, Cameron McCarthy, Shawn Miclaucic, Jeremy Packer, and especially Jack Bratich for providing insightful comments on previous drafts. I am also grateful to anonymous reviewers for SUNY press for useful criticism. The essay's faults are, as always, my own.

REFERENCES

Bartky, S. (1990). *Femininity and domination: Studies in the phenomenology of oppression.* New York: Routledge.

Butler, J. (1990). *Gender trouble: Feminism and the subversion of identity.* New York: Routledge.

Butler, J. (1993). *Bodies that matter: On the discursive limits of "sex."* New York: Routledge.

Butler, J. (1996). Sexual inversions. In S. Hekman (Ed.), *Feminist interpretations of Michel Foucault* (pp. 59–75). University Park: Pennsylvania University Press.

Colapinto, J. (2000). *As nature made him: The boy who was raised as a girl.* New York: HarperCollins.

Diamond, I., & Quinby, L. (Eds.) (1988). *Feminism and Foucault: Reflections on resistance.* Boston: Northeastern University Press.

Foucault, M. (1988a). *The care of the self: The history of sexuality, Vol. 3* (R. Hurley, Trans.). New York: Vintage. (Original work published 1984)

Foucault, M. (1988b). The ethic of care for the self as a practice of freedom: An interview with Michel Foucault on January 20, 1984. (J. D. Gauthier, S. J., Trans.). In J. Bernauer & D. Rasmussen (Eds.), *The final Foucault* (pp. 1–20). Cambridge: MIT Press.

Foucault, M. (1990a). *The history of sexuality: An introduction* (R. Hurley, Trans.). New York: Vintage. (Original work published 1976.)

Foucault, M. (1990b). *The use of pleasure: The history of sexuality, Vol. 2* (R. Hurley, Trans.). New York: Vintage. (Original work published 1984)

Fraser, N. (1989). Foucault on modern power: Empirical insights and normative Confusions. In *Unruly practices: Power, discourse and gender in contemporary social theory* (pp. 17–34). Minneapolis, MN: University of Minnesota Press.

Hekman, S. (1996). *Feminist interpretations of Michel Foucault.* University Park, MD: Pennsylvania State University Press.

Ramazanoglu, C. (Ed.). (1993). *Up against Foucault: Explorations of some tensions between Foucault and feminism.* New York: Routledge.

Contributors

Tony Bennett is Professor of Sociology at the Open University in the United Kingdom. His current interests focus on questions of culture and governance with special reference to museums, cultural diversity policies, and the history and theory of cultural policy. His publications include *The Birth of the Museum: History, Theory, Politics*; *Culture: A Reformer's Science*; *Accounting for Tastes: Australian Everyday Cultures* (with Michael Emmison and John Frow), and *Culture in Australia: Policies, Publics, Programs* (coedited with David Carter).

Jack Z. Bratich is Assistant Professor of Communication at the University of New Hampshire. He is the editor of *Interfacings: A Journal of Contemporary Media Studies*. His dissertation, "Grassy Knoll-Edges: Conspiracy Theories and Political Rationality in the 1990s" is being reworked into book form. His new project analyzes the relationships between U.S. culture, communications, and secrecy.

Mary K. Coffey is an Assistant Professor and Faculty Fellow in the Museum Studies Program at New York University. She has published widely on Mexican art, cultural policy, and popular citizenship. She is currently completing a book on Mexican muralism and the development of a national cultural infrastructure after the Revolution of 1910.

Greg Dimitriadis is an Assistant Professor in the Department of Educational Leadership and Policy at the University at Buffalo, State University of New York. He teaches in the sociology of education concentration. He is the author of *Performing Identity/Performing Culture: Hip Hop as Text, Pedagogy and Lived Practice*, and *Reading and Teaching the Postcolonial: From Baldwin to Basquiat and Beyond* (coauthored with Cameron McCarthy).

Lawrence Grossberg is the Morris Davis Professor of Communication Studies and Cultural Studies at the University of North Carolina at Chapel Hill. He is the international coeditor of the journal *Cultural Studies*. He is currently completing work on two books: *The Heart of Cultural Studies*, and *The War Against Children and the Third American Revolution*.

James Hay is an Associate Professor in the Department of Speech Communication, the Graduate Program in Cultural Studies, the Unit for Criticism and Interpretive Theory, and the Unit for Cinema Studies at the University of Illinois—Urbana-Champaign. His publications include *Popular Film Culture in Fascist Italy* and *The Audience and Its Landscape*.

Lisa King is an Assistant Professor of Philosophy & Women's Studies at the University of North Colorado. Her research interests include feminist theory, political theory, and identity politics.

Samantha King is an Assistant Professor of Physical Education at the University of Arizona, where she teaches and researches the cultural politics of sport, leisure, and health. She has published articles in *Social Text*, the *Journal of Sport and Social Issues*, and the *Sociology of Sport Journal*.

Cameron McCarthy is Research Professor and University scholar at the University of Illinois's Institute of Communications Research. His previous works include *The Uses of Culture*; *Race, Identity and Representation in Education*, and *Reading and Teaching the Postcolonial*.

Shawn Miklaucic is a doctoral student in the Institute of Communications Research at the University of Illinois, Urbana-Champaign. His areas of interest include cultural studies, the cultural effects of new media technologies, and contemporary fiction. His dissertation examines the strategic computer game genre from a critical cultural studies perspective.

Toby Miller is Professor of Cultural Studies and Cultural Policy in the Department of Cinema Studies, Tisch School of the Arts, New York University. He has authored and edited numerous books on film, television, sport and cultural theory including *Technologies of Truth: Cultural Citizenship and the Popular Media Sportsex* and *Global Hollywood* (with Nitin Govil, John McMurria, and Richard Maxwell). He is presently the editor of *Television and New Media*.

Jeremy Packer is Assistant Professor of Media Studies at Pennsylvania State University where he teaches cultural studies, communications history, and media studies. He has published essays on media, CB radio, transportation technologies, safety, and the work of Michel Foucault. He is currently writing a cultural history of safety and mobility in the postwar United States.

Carrie A. Rentschler is finishing her Ph.D. at the Institute of Communications Research at the University of Illinois at Urbana-Champaign. Her dissertation examines the U.S. crime victim movement's media activism and its role in news media coverage of crime and its victims. Over the past 9 years, Carrie has also been a women's and girl's self-defense and antiviolence educator.

Jonathan Sterne is an Assistant Professor in the Department of Communication at the University of Pittsburgh and a codirector of *Bad Subjects: Political Education for Everyday Life* <http://eserver.org/bs>. He has written widely on sound, technology, communication, and cultural studies. His book, *The Audible Past*, is forthcoming from Duke University Press.

Index of Names

Index of Subjects

Conduct, 69, 73
  and safety, 150
  civic, 215
  ethical, 6
  everyday, 60
  normative code of, 309
  of conduct, 4, 6, 11, 19, 31, 34, 38,
    56, 61, 72, 73, 112, 297, 326
  of cultural practices, 51
  of thought, 85
  on conduct, 39
  upon conduct, 35
  regulation of, 15
  sexual, 346
Consciousness:
  culture as, 127
  national historical, 213
  phenomenological, 67
  politics of, 107, 108, 119, 120, 121,
    122
  safety, 151, 247
Consent, 69, 81, 91n9, 92n9
  and dissent, 86
  and popular culture, 281
  and subjectification, 86
  as attachment, 77, 86
  as desire, 92n14
  to authority, 82, 84, 86, 92n12
Conspiracy narratives, 84, 318
  and disruptive possibilities, 88
  and regime of truth, 81, 92n11
Conspiracy theories, 10, 13, 69, 77, 78,
    79, 82, 85
  and conspiricism, 80, 93–94n20
  and seduction, 87
Crime:
  and *Accuracy in Campus Crime Reporting
    Act*, 267n18
  and assaults on men, 260
  and *Campustown 2000*, 256
  and computer games, 319
  and Crime Prevention Through
    Environmental Design (CPTED),
    244, 245, 247, 248, 249, 250, 251,
    252, 257
  and prevention, 258
  and property crimes, 244, 263

  and reporting, 260–261
  and University reporting of, 261
  and urban sprawl, 189
  and victims of aggravated assaults,
    260
  of opportunity, 244
Cultural bureaucrat, 120
Cultural Marxism, 108
Cultural materialism, 169
Cultural policy studies, 6, 13, 102–103,
    104, 105, 106, 107, 110, 111, 112,
    113, 114, 116, 117, 119, 122, 123
  and Ideological State Apparatus, 115
  and humanism/antihumanism, 126
  and the public sphere, 125
  and representational democracy, 129n8
Cultural technician, 120, 122
Cultural technology, 108, 171, 196,
    201n8, 201–202n11, 202n19
Cultural (the), 44, 50, 52, 54, 57, 58, 59
Culture:
  definitions of, 5–10, 12, 14, 15, 17,
    19, 29, 31, 48, 50–52, 60
  and cultural logic, 210, 274
  and commodification, 16
  and Marxist forms of, 13
  and patrimony, 213, 222, 223
  and rights, 209, 233
  and National culture, 208, 209, 213,
    216, 217, 230, 233
Culture and Society, 49, 201n8
Culture: A Reformer's Science, 126

Daily Illini, 243, 256, 257, 266, 267
Dees, Morris, 95n29
Différance, 51
Discipline-blockade, 144, 147
Discipline-mechanism, 144, 147
Disciplined mobility, 139, 142, 144,
    151, 157
Disciplined mobilization, 142, 143
  societies of, 141
  and Lawrence Grossberg, 142–144
Discourse, 28
Discursive practices, 53, 54
  and the "cultural turn," 50
  and technologies of government, 211

Truth or Dare, 256, 260, 261
Turner, Ted, 295

UNESCO, 208–209, 221, 236n9
 and *Cultural Rights as Human Rights*, 209
United Kingdom, 7, 30, 105
United Nations, 37, 307
United States of America, 7, 14, 23, 36, 42, 78, 92n11, 104, 105, 113, 117, 125, 127, 138, 143, 151, 158, 165, 167, 172, 183, 185, 188, 196, 199–200n1, 203n19, 215, 224, 225, 275, 283, 290, 296, 298, 304, 305, 306, 307–308, 312n3
 See also Reaganism; William J. Clinton; and George W. Bush
University of Illinois, 15, 129n9, 237n19, 243, 244, 245, 246, 248, 249, 251, 253, 254, 256, 258, 260, 263
 and Cultural Studies, 5
Urbanism:
 New Suburbanism, 190
 New Urbanism, 14, 185, 187, 188, 190, 191, 192, 195
 New Urbanist communitarianism, 195
The U.S. Department of Housing and Urban Development, 188

Violence:
 acquaintance rape, 263
 aggressive sexual masculinity, 260
 and athletic teams, 260
 and environmental security, 245
 gendered, 244, 261
 school violence, 278
 sexual assault, 244, 256, 260
 sexual harassment, 244, 259
 sexual violence, 244, 246, 252, 256, 260, 264
 violence against women, 244, 246, 259, 261, 262, 263
 youth and violence, 277, 278
 youth violence, 273, 280
Volunteerism, 9, 16, 17, 295, 297
 and American Freedom from Hunger Foundation, 307
 and corporate sponsors, 295, 302
 and ideal citizenship, 297, 304–305, 306
 and neoliberalism, 307, 314n13
 and philanthropy, 295

Warren Commission Report, 79
Washington Mall, 296, 305, 314n12
Whistlestop program, 248
WILL-TV, 251, 252, 267n16
Welfare, 16, 40, 142, 165, 188, 199n1, 209, 216, 224, 225, 230, 234, 276, 297, 308, 312n6, 328
World Bank, 34
World Health Organization, 38
World Trade Organization, 38

Zapatistas, 232